The Optimum SAILBOAT

Racing the Cruiser and Cruising the Racer

RONALD FLORENCE

Illustrated by David Johnson

1817

HARPER & ROW, PUBLISHERS, New York

Cambridge   Philadelphia   San Francisco   London   Mexico City   São Paulo   Singapore   Sydney

Also by Ronald Florence

Fritz
Mary's Daughters
Zeppelin
The Gypsy Man

Designer: C. Linda Dingler

Library of Congress Cataloging-in-Publication Data
Florence, Ronald.
  The optimum sailboat.

  Includes index.
  1. Sailboats. I. Title.
VM351.F55   1986   623.8′223   85-45474
ISBN 0-06-015498-5

CONTENTS

For the crews of *Scare*, *Agnes*, and *Ringer*

FOREWORD

Spend enough time on and around boats, and with boat owners, and you begin to realize how closely owners identify with their boats. To the non-sailor, they are all "boats," or if they are big enough, "yachts." But to the owner, the personalities are sharply articulated: in the crude idiom of the 1960s, "You are what you sail."

A confirmed cruiser will walk past a lean racer, with its towering rig, sloped transom, low freeboard, and parade of technology on the rig and deck. "I do my racing at the office," he declares as he glances at the meager galley and the unenclosed head. The racer in the next slip looks at a salty passage-maker, with baggy-wrinkle on the rigging and a self-steerer on the transom, and wonders if the boat can move in anything shy of a hurricane. "What's the fun of sailing a dog like that?" he thinks. Much of the literature on boats and sailing seems to validate the split. How often do you see an article on winch placement or sail shape controls in the cruising magazines? What do books about equipping a racing boat tell you about wiring or icebox insulation?

In truth, of course, the lines are not so sharply drawn. There are few cruising men who will not reach for the mainsheet, tweak in the genoa, and concentrate on their steering when another boat of comparable size sails into view. And what racer doesn't care about the comforts of his boat, or has truly never taken a sail for the sheer enjoyment of the boat and the water? But try to tell a confirmed cruiser that he could learn a lot about rigging and equipping his own boat from sailing on a round-the-buoys racer and you get a blank look of disbelief. Tell a racer that his boat would race better and faster with different safety gear and his response is astonishment. Sailors may share opinions about anyone who doesn't sail, but among boats and boat owners, sailing is an insular world.

The view from my study takes in three boatyards, a sailmaker, a rigger, several yacht brokers, dozens of moorings, and a constant floating traffic of everything from day sailers to solo passage-makers to grand prix racers. My lunchtime hangout is next door to one of the boatyards; the usual customers are the men who work in the yards and boat owners who have stopped off after a sail or a visit to their boats. Over the past thirteen years I have owned, worked on, crewed, raced, cruised, and just messed with boats from a 6-foot pram to 60-foot ocean racers. I have developed strong opinions about boats in those years, and anyone who elects to write essays on boats and boat ownership owes it to his readers to declare himself.

My first prejudice is that I believe that a boat should be

equipped for the *actual* use it will see. Fantasies and dreams are an important part of yachting, and there is much to learn from both grand prix racers and passage-making boats. But few of us ever enter grand prix events, and even fewer set off on offshore voyages. The reality of sailing for most of us is closer to home—a club race around the buoys, a weekend across the sound or the channel, a day sail with friends, an occasional one- or two-week cruise, an overnight or distance race in semiprotected waters. This book is primarily about boats and gear that are used for that kind of sailing, and about rigging and equipping boats for the kind of sailing that most of us do most of the time.

My second prejudice is performance under sail. I believe any boat, racer or cruiser, is a better boat if it can be made to sail well—fast, close to the wind, in a wide range of conditions, and with a helm and sail controls that make sailing comfortable and exciting for the owner and his crew. In the broader sense of "performance," I expect gear on boats to *function*, to effectively accomplish the job it is supposed to do. In my prowls of boatyards and yacht clubs, I see boats that are "fully equipped," their decks and cabins loaded with every item on a surveyor's or boat buyer's checklist. But watch the owner and his crew try to grind in a genoa with the tiny sheet winches! Watch the helmsman try to ease the awkwardly rigged traveler! Watch the struggle to get inappropriate ground tackle set or reset in an anchorage! To equip a boat well, with effective and appropriate gear, requires more than a perusal of the catalogs with their facile recommendations: "suitable for boats from 30 to 40 feet." The goal of these chapters is to invite an owner to ask questions about his own boat,

how it is used and how it performs, and then to look at a range of solutions to the challenge of rigging and equipping a boat for fast, comfortable sailing.

David Johnson, who did the illustrations for this book, and I have sailed, raced, and worked together on boats for eight years. Our close collaboration and his remarkable ability to capture both the details of complex gear and the "feel" of sailing and working on a boat have meant that in many instances a drawing or series of drawings could take the place of pages of prose.

Many other fine sailors and marine professionals have offered advice, anecdotes, and information that has found its way into this book. I would like to record a special thanks for their time and wisdom to Tom Anderson, John Atkin, Bob Barton, John Brewer, Frank Casey, Bill Chantland, Erik Christensen, Chris Cross, Dave Crawford, Joan and Art Ellis, Grove Ely, K. G. Gregory, Peter Harken, Rod Johnstone, Bruce Kirby, Charley Lance, Dave Levett, Oliver Moore, Tom Presti, Skip Raymond, Mike Whitehead, Peter Worcester, and the patient staffs and employees of the many boatyards, chandleries, sail lofts, marinas, yacht clubs, and hardware stores that I have prowled. The errors and judgments that remain, in spite of their good counsel, are my own.

R. F.

Five Mile River, Connecticut

THE OPTIMUM SAILBOAT

1

ORIGINAL SINS: BOATS and OWNERS

Listen closely to a boat owner talking about his boat: the form of address is personal, almost intimate; the boat is *she* or *her*, rarely it; the tone is frequently close to either infatuation or fury, terms of affection intermingled with cries of betrayal, language of praise punctuated with complaints of how much has been squandered on her.*

Boats inspire strong passions. Publicly we defend boats that in private we might curse; we tenaciously hold on to a boat that has failed us or chase after beauties that deep down we know are wrong, that can only lead to wrack and ruin. Bankers may call a boat the second largest investment an owner ever makes, but our words aren't the language of investment, of coldhearted calculations of returns and earnings; they are the language of a commitment, a relationship as demanding and as bound up with image and ego as a love affair or a marriage.

The statistics on boat ownership aren't very different from those on marriage. The average "relationship" between owner and boat lasts something on the order of three and a half years; for every relationship that goes to seven years or twenty years, there is another that falls apart after a season or two. Some of these "marriages" weren't meant to be. The choice of a boat can be a careful and deliberate process, but often passions and prejudices temper the most thoughtful analyses. Long winter hours may have been spent on brochures and evaluations, balancing the comments of one reviewer or owner against the criticisms of another; day after day may have been devoted to wandering the marinas and boat shows, studying and compar-

* The language of yachting and sailing hasn't really caught up with the times. Although there are many women yacht owners and certainly many, many experienced and talented women sailors, to avoid the awkwardness of expressions like *foredeckperson*, I have adhered to traditional terms and gender references, including the female gender for boats.

ing, compiling lists of pros and cons. Yet in the end, it is often the sweep of the sheer line, the salty look of the double ends, or the macho appeal of a towering rig or a sloping transom that proves irresistible. A man with neither the time nor the money falls for a sleek but fading beauty, a wooden sloop of incomparable grace that covers hidden surprises, a lady he is hard pressed to keep in the style she demands. A man picturing himself on the high seas, alone against the elements, next landfall the Marquesas, buys himself a heavy double-ended cruiser with baggy-wrinkle on the short rig, a massive self-steerer on the transom, and satellite navigation equipment installed over the chart table—and finds that the most distant island he ever cruises to is Catalina.

And whether it was a marriage of convenience, with every detail planned in advance, or a sudden infatuation that left no time for careful thought, the years of boat ownership often bring those inevitable discoveries that she isn't exactly what she seemed. The "world cruiser" designed for the trade winds turns out to be so underrigged in the prevailing light winds of the owner's usual sailing area that he ends up motoring more than sailing. The club racer, infatuated by the sleek reverse transom and towering rig of a new IOR semiproduction design, does well in his first race, with a high-powered crew from a well-known loft aboard; it is only two or three races later that he discovers that the boat is unmanageable with fewer than eight regular crew. The only way he can get a regular crew with the talents that the boat demands is to keep ordering new sails and hope that the sailmaker will reward his purchases with regular assignments of hot-shot kids from the loft.

Sometimes a boat is chosen for secret reasons, reasons that the buyer scarcely admits to himself. An underrigged boat was selected for a light-air area because a wife insisted that she didn't want a tippy boat; a telephone pole of a rig was chosen to avoid a babystay or runners (because they look as if they would be a terrible inconvenience), or because the salesman or some magazine article praised the safety and reliability of the oversized rigging; a boat with shoddy workmanship and little promise of speed was chosen because the galley offered three burners and an oven, or because there were quarter berths, V-berths, pilot berths, *and* settees. A boat that is a dog under sail, crowded below, uncomfortable on deck, and impossible to maintain without a full-time "BN" * is chosen because the reputation and workmanship of the builder, the beauty and integrity of the joinery, the solidity and heft of the fiberglass layup, the luxury of teak decks, the gleam of bronze and chrome and stainless steel, proved irresistible.

And then, for love, fidelity, infatuation, or fear of diminishing the resale value, an owner lives with the boat he has chosen or inherited, puts up with discomforts, inconveniences, sometimes with dangerous equipment and rigging, flawed designs, structural weaknesses. Sins are overlooked, forgiven, or assumed to be the price of sailing. Another boat owner, a sailmaker, a yard foreman, a rigger, or a crew member may notice the inelegant and inefficient rigging or cumbersome layout or ineffective stove, but rarely will they say anything. Why? Because just as ladies and gentlemen know not to criticize a spouse or a child, sailors know not to criticize a boat unless they want to lose a friend.

There are owners who through thick and thin, for better and for worse, will hold on to a boat that others would have

---

* "BN" is the abbreviation for a vulgar term which has unfortunately squeezed out all competitors, such as "marine domestic," in common usage.

consigned to the market or the junk heap long ago. These are the boats that don't see the water until midseason, the boats that are still being painted or scraped or scoured for some mysterious deck leak while everyone else is out racing and weekending. Indeed, there are boat owners whose true love isn't sailing but "messing about with boats," for whom the hours of spring commissioning, the days with sander or polisher or varnish brush, are more rewarding than the summer of doldrums. These are the boat owners who cannot resist one more improvement, one more gadget or addition or refinement, the owners who customize and personalize their boats until there is a dedicated shelf for every gadget and a special rigging trick for every sail.

There are other boat owners who find this kind of fidelity imcomprehensible; for them, trading up is the most rewarding part of boat ownership, the "rush" of anticipation and planning and purchasing and outfitting is as exciting and fulfilling as the hours at the helm. As soon as everything has been done for her and the relationship has run its course, the boat is sold or traded—often with a tender word and good memories, just as often with a sense of bitterness and betrayal because she was never as quick as you hoped, or as comfortable.

Whether faithful or fickle, almost every owner learns that the victories or surcease that a boat promises can be tempered by hours or weeks of infinite annoyance with a problem that resists all efforts at repair, by boatyard bills that each year retain their ability to shock, by petty irritations that seem to have been designed into the hull and rig under some perverse notion that perfection would be an affront to Allah. And while every boat provides days and moments that an owner never forgets—a fast passage, a screaming run with the spinnaker on edge and a rooster tail of water shooting up behind the transom, ghosting along on a flat night when you could hardly feel or see a breeze, a cozy meal in a sublime anchorage, or those quiet moments at the helm when the feeling of incomparable serenity can put the problems of the world at bay— too often bad memories linger too; the anger at a perennially balky engine, the struggles to reef the main when you always seemed to have one hand less than you needed, the perpetual battle of trying to get the genoa sheeted flat enough when the winches were too small, the crick in your neck after a long hard reach because you had to brace yourself at a poorly engineered helm or had to cock your head at an impossible angle to see the compass.

Whether it is the magic of the sea, the cost of the toys, or the romantic power of those inescapable images of billowing spinnakers and serene cruisers at anchor in remote coves, boats are the fuel of dreams. The helm of a boat can transform a workaday soul into a voyager of distant seas or a world-class competitor. With your hands on the wheel and your eyes on the luff of the genoa, you can be sailing the trade winds or the Transpac; the club race around the buoys can be as demanding and as consuming as the SORC, the cruise to Nantucket as much a respite as the vaguely planned escape to distant isles. When you cross the finish line to take the gun in a race, or settle down to a drink in the cockpit after a satisfying sail and a neat job of anchoring in a cove, the world is changed. For those few special moments the club race actually feels like the Admiral's Cup, and the cruise across the sound to a weekend anchorage feels like the approach to the Marquesas.

Alas, for most boat owners the line between fantasy and reality is a fuzzy one. Few of us have enough time, or money, or willing crew, to change the fantasies into reality—if we really even want to. Work and family and community and a thousand other obligations matter too much. The family that will sail as far as Nantucket draws the line there. The crew that can be recruited to go around the buoys on Saturday isn't available for a week at Block Island or a month in Florida. But anyone with a checkbook or a line of credit at the local bank can buy the magical dream machine. And so, far more world cruisers are sold than world cruises made, and there are far more grand prix racers than grand prix racing entries. The difference tells much about boat owners, their dreams, their sense of themselves on the water. As long as the boat still does its job, can still be sailed effectively and efficiently, offers the comforts and performance and convenience for the weekends in Puget Sound or club races in Tampa Bay or day sails in Buzzards Bay that are the real stuff of sailing for most of us, there is no harm in a boat fulfilling a dream too.

Few boats are built free of original sin. Sometimes there are grave sins: structural weaknesses; decks that tin-can under your weight; hulls so flexible that if the backstay is tightened the companionway won't slide shut; keels bolted on without the internal support of floor timbers so that the first encounter with an unyielding bottom shoves the aft end of the keel up through the hull; pumps, steering gear, heads, stoves, and engines installed carelessly, with disregard for safety or convenience in servicing and maintenance. Fortunately, real structural flaws are rare. But annoyingly slipshod design and construction is not so rare: leaky hull-deck joints, improperly bedded fittings, undersized hardware and fastenings, unfair or inconvenient rigging leads. Well-built boats sometimes come through with equipment designed for boat-show appeal, like

the "three burners and an oven" that is supposed to lure a balky wife into being a supporter of the purchase of the Dreamboat 37. Three and an oven you get, but in a cheap, poorly built alcohol stove that can't boil a pot of water by the end of a weekend cruise, and which despite your best efforts at maintenance manages to corrode from coppertone to rust-tone by the end of a single season. Or there is a bilge pump that might clear an inconvenient puddle but will never keep up with even a small leak. Or an ice chest with shelves and double opening doors, and so little insulation that a portable cooler is essential as a backup.

At the boat show the seven berths look terrific; throw pillows, a vase of flowers, and brightly colored place mats on the table give that homey touch that dealers know will turn a keel kicker into a check signer. It's not until the gear is loaded on at commissioning time that the owner realizes that there's no place for the sails except the berths, that the quarter berth that is used to store the genoas is the only berth that is usable in a seaway, that the under-seat lockers that looked so commodious are nearly inaccessible and guarantee instant mildew on anything stored there, that the enclosed head is claustrophobic, that only the toilet paper and towels get really wet in the shower.

Manufacturers produce what they think will sell. A wheel and midboom traveler over the companionway, the brochure and the salesman tell you, "keeps the cockpit open, leaves room for people." But for a shorthanded crew, the midboom traveler and wheel also keeps the mainsheet far from the helmsman, so that when a puff comes, the helmsman can't ease the mainsheet to control the weather helm. Many boats are sold with short rigs and extra-heavy rigging. "Overrigged for safety," says the advertising copy, which also calls attention to the "small, easy-to-manage sails." The salesman points to the massive backstay—a ⅜-inch 1 x 19 cable on a 12,500-pound, short-rigged boat—as if it were assurance against every kind of disaster. In fact, all that oversized stay has added is extra weight and windage, carried up high where it hurts. The boat isn't safer; it's less stable. (Don't think "the builder wouldn't have paid for oversized wire if the boat didn't need it!" The additional cost is insignificant when the builder can charge more for "oversized rigging.") The sin is then compounded when the owner decides to install an accessory such as a backstay adjuster. "How big is your backstay?" asks the chandler, who supplies a backstay adjuster that matches the clevis pin size. The two-sizes-too-large backstay adjuster adds more weight and more expense.

Another salesman talks up the seaworthiness of the short rig with the "small, easy-to-handle sails." Those "seaworthy" easy-to-handle sails might be great for reaching in steady 25-knot trade winds, but for the prevailing light air of most North American sailing areas, the short rig is a disaster. To get the boat moving in anything under a fresh breeze requires genoas with huge overlaps, which are hardly easy to handle.

Some boats are designed from the rig down, with bulkheads and other interior features designed around the requirements for chain plate positions or tie-rods from the chain plates to the keel or floor timbers. But because so many boats are sold at boat shows, where the interior arrangements receive greater scrutiny than the rigging and deck gear, the priorities are sometimes reversed. To accommodate an enclosed head or a full-length berth in the main cabin some boats fasten chain plates for the lower shrouds to the housetop, with no connections to a structural bulkhead or to tie-rods to the keel. The reason—to keep the interior "open"—will probably seem less significant in the owner's mind when he notices the housetop flexing as the boat pounds through a seaway.

For every oversized item like rigging, there may be three undersized items. Winches on production boats are frequently sized for "cruising," which usually means short-handed or family sailing. The irony is that a racing boat with a crew of strong grinders can get by with smaller winches, or at least winches with faster gear ratios. Less-experienced crew, and especially family crews, need all the help they can get to sheet in big sails. And that help comes from big, powerful winches. Control lines, from the mainsheet to the cunningham and the outhaul, are often rigged with inadequate purchases that take two hands and a mighty heave to adjust. Blocks are frequently selected because they were part of an OEM (Original Equipment Manufacturer) package deal or because someone thought the block "looked big enough." The result is turning blocks pressed to the limit, small sheaves turning heavily loaded lines or cables 180 degrees, acute leads on blocks that aren't built to take severe loads, travelers loaded to the point where they won't roll easily. The rigging isn't necessarily unsafe—the traveler probably won't break in ordinary conditions. It's just so inconvenient and inefficient that it doesn't get adjusted when it needs adjustment. What it means for the boat owner is that sailing isn't the pleasure it might be.

The sins aren't all the builders'. Many yachtsmen buy equipment from discount chandlers and electronics suppliers, whose catalogs and salesmen offer a wealth of advice. However well intended, the advice isn't always as useful as a yacht owner might desire. The generic vang that the catalog labels "suitable for a 30-footer"—typically a 4:1 tackle with snap shackles on both ends—is underpowered, inconvenient to set up and use, and impossible to release in a broaching situation. The prepackaged anchor line ("for boats 28 to 34 feet") is too short and oversized. "That's strong enough for a hurricane!" the man at the counter assures you, but what he doesn't explain is that the oversized anchor line requires a bigger anchor to hold the same load because it doesn't stretch to absorb surge loads that a properly sized line would take in stride. And that if you try to let out adequate scope when you really need it, the 150-foot anchor line is at its bitter end when you need another 100 feet.

One of the well-known marine discount electronics dealers used to pull his "good customers" aside to offer them illegal linear amplifiers as a cure for VHF radios that weren't "getting out." The same outfit sold one kind of coaxial cable: a cheap grade of RG8X with a low-density shield. Chances are those radios that weren't "getting out" had no problem that couldn't be cured by replacing the lousy co-ax that was supplied with the radio. The same outfit also sold old AM antennas as "high gain" loran antennas. A "high gain" antenna is exactly what most lorans don't need, and there are owners sailing right now with poorly functioning lorans that need nothing more than the right antenna and a sound installation.

What is a boat owner to do? Some learn to live with the sins of their boats, struggling along with reefing gear that requires five minutes and four people to reef the main, or a stove that takes most of a weekend to boil water. Some owners think that the pains and anxieties and indignities are a part of sailing, that every boat suffers those moments that lead to screaming on deck or the unwelcome question, "Is this really supposed to be fun?" Many owners haven't spent enough time on other boats to realize how exciting it can be to sail on a really well-rigged and well-equipped boat. There are even owners who take a perverse pride in the flaws and foibles of their boats, like a stand-up comic quipping one-liners at the expense of his wife. You can hear them bragging about a boat that won't sail in under 10 knots of breeze, or that has a weather helm so severe in anything over 10 knots that it can only be sailed with a brake on the wheel, or that has an engine that routinely fails to start or spews slippery pink hydraulic fluid on the cabin sole. Those who are truly addicted to yacht masochism should read no further in this book.

A few boat owners are wealthy enough to entrust their boats to riggers, yards, and sailmakers with a blanket authorization: "Do whatever she needs!" But most of us can't afford to be so cavalier, and the carte blanche approach doesn't always produce the best solutions in any case. A rigger may have a fixation about doing vangs or spinnaker poles a certain way that doesn't really fit your style of sailing. A sailmaker may fit you with an excellent inventory that is inappropriate for your needs. And the superb craftsmen and mechanics in the yard are often people who don't themselves spend time on boats; if they do, it may not be a boat like yours; their sense of your needs may not be the same as your own.

There are a few boats so badly designed, so poorly engineered, or so cheaply built that no amount of love can bring them around. There are boats with keels positioned incorrectly so that they do have a constant weather helm. There are boats with cockpit layouts that make it virtually impossible for even a talented crew to sail the boat well, and that make every maneuver so difficult for a cruising couple that they can only get off the boat angry after each attempt. There are manufacturers who produce boats and equipment so shoddy that only the miracles of advertising can explain the sale of even a single item. But those are rare examples.

Fortunately, most of the sins of boats are venial, not mortal. Most owners have chosen well, and most boats can serve their owners well if they aren't asked to do the impossible. A heavy double-ended cruiser can't be made into much of a round-the-buoys racer, and it's difficult to make a comfortable long-distance cruiser out of an ultra-lean racer without piling on so much gear that the performance of the boat is severely degraded. But there are few boats that cannot be made faster, safer, easier to sail, and more comfortable. Usually the real problem isn't the boat or the equipment; it's putting it all together—setting up the deck layout, rig, sail inventory, electronics, galley, and mechanical installations; making the thousand choices that distinguish one boat from another; dealing with the boatyards, riggers, sailmakers, electricians, and other high priests of the sailing world—in a phrase, transforming that elusive infatuation into a faithful partner in the magic relationship of owner and boat.

2

WHAT WILL SHE DO, REALLY?

What makes a boat owner choose a boat? A weekend cruiser tells you why he chose a heavy, full-keeled, short-rigged ketch: "She's safe, sea-kindly . . . good directional stability. . . . You know that rig will stay up. . . . If there's a problem it can be fixed in any port. . . . She stays on her feet in a breeze. . . . She tracks well, handles a self-steerer like a charm. . . ."

The language sounds suspiciously like magazine articles about passage-making; and every reason makes perfect sense for a passage-making vessel. But how does the same boat handle in the average conditions of a weekend cruise, or an annual two-week cruise to Nantucket? How well does the full-keel ketch sail upwind in light air? What happens when you try to spin a boat with "directional stability" in the short radius required for docking in many marinas? How safe is the boat in a sudden squall off a lee shore? How much of the time will the owner have to motor instead of sailing? And how much room for family and fun is there in a boat with deep bilges, narrow side decks, and a small, deep cockpit?

Or the determined club racer "upgrades" to a fresh-off-the-board production model of a recent SORC class champion, complete with a towering three-spreader rig; upper and lower runners; hydraulics on the backstay, vang, mainsheet, baby-stay, and flattening reef; all-Kevlar running rigging; a low-windage three-halyard masthead; and a complete inventory of the latest in composite construction Kevlar and Mylar sails. The boat is fast and amazingly responsive when they go out for the initial tune-up with the sailmaker aboard. But what happens when the same boat goes out with the usual pickup crew, or when the club racer decides to take a weekend overnight with family as crew? Who is going to trim the runner in during a tack before the mast crumbles? Who is going to adjust the hydraulics while the owner is single-handing at the helm?

PERFORMANCE

Ask questions about a boat owner's choice, and the answers you get invariably turn to performance. Owners love to talk about the performance of their boats, weaving memories, observations, and fantasies into a marvelous gossamer of language:

"She's got a real turn of speed . . ."

"She's a dog in light air, but once she gets into the breeze . . ."

"With a ballast ratio like that you better believe she's stiff . . ."

"Once she heels over and gets that waterline into it . . ."

Subjective characterizations are great for beer chats around the clubhouse, and an owner's description is perhaps the only way to convey the elusive "feel" that is part of every boat, but a boat that inspires one owner to rapturous talk of a "turn of speed" might inspire another owner to shop for a leash for the boat or to document the name as *Fido*.

Fortunately there are measurements and nondimensional ratios * that serve as useful and generally accurate indexes to the potential performance and characteristics of a boat. Some owners will complain that numbers cannot capture the "feel" of a boat, but nondimensional ratios, in particular, provide the means to compare boats—and to explain why the Fine-

* Nondimensional ratios, such as displacement/length, sail area/displacement, beam/length, and ballast/displacement, are numbers with no units attached. Within limits, they apply to boats of any size, so that design features of boats with differing displacements, lengths, and rigs can be compared.

nose 30s always seem to be able to outpoint you in the club race, why you have to shift down to a #2 or #3 genoa when the flatbottom 37s are still carrying their heavy #1 genoas, and why you always have to motor in the typical morning breezes while the Flyweight 28s ghost right along.

MEASUREMENTS

A naval architect or a performance analysis program will use a full set of hull measurements to predict the speed of a boat in different wind strengths and conditions. But even with the limited information available on a PHRF rating certificate or a builder's brochure—the length, displacement, beam, draft, and rig dimensions—it is possible to determine a great deal about the handling and speed characteristics of the boat.

Length

When a non-sailor asks how big a boat is, he means the overall length (LOA). Advertisers and boat show participants too like to speak of a "30-footer" or a "40-footer," as in a builder's claim that he has finally produced a 30-footer with the interior of a 40-footer. But to a naval architect, and to a boat owner, the more important dimension is waterline length (LWL). Waterline length is not only a basic determinant of the speed potential of the boat but also a good indicator of interior volume and size. A 40-foot-long boat with a 28-foot LWL and long, graceful overhangs has far less usable space inside than a powerful 40-foot LOA boat with a 35-foot waterline.

Unfortunately, the measurement of LWL is frequently exaggerated in published information about boats. Sometimes a rudder that is not properly part of the "sailing length" of the boat will be included in what is labeled as waterline length; other times it will be excluded.

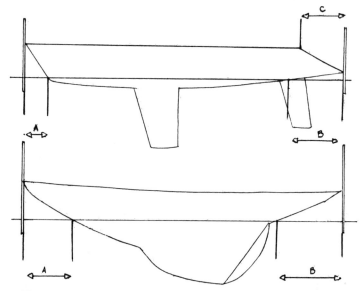

If you want to check the published figure, it isn't difficult to measure the waterline length. First measure the LOA from the stem to the aft edge of the transom. On a boat with a reverse transom you will need to separately measure the distance from the edge of the transom (marked with a vertical level) to the aft edge of the deck to get the LOA. Then, on a calm day, from a dinghy or a low dock, measure from the forward edge of the waterline to a vertical level at the stem, and from the aft edge of the waterline to a vertical at the edge of the transom. Subtract the two overhangs from the LOA and you have the LWL.

The form of the ends of the boat, especially the stern, can lengthen the effective sailing length as the boat heels or as the speed increases. Most rating rules try to go beyond waterline length by approximating a "sailing length" from girths and other measurements, which enterprising naval architects then try to exploit to reduce the rating of a boat. Because the measure of sailing length is not standardized, and because naval architects and boat owners routinely exaggerate the extent to which the sailing length of a boat increases with heeling or at speed, most nondimensional ratios are based on LWL (actual waterline length) or DWL (design waterline length) as the primary indication of the speed potential and size of a boat.

Beam

The beam of a boat indicates far more than the width of slip the boat will require. Naval architects and rating rule makers use a number of beam measurements—at the deck, the waterline, and at points in between—to estimate drag, stability, and wetted surface. Beam is also an important index to interior volume: beamy hull shapes, with their generous interior volumes, are one of the genuine benefits of the influence of the IOR and MORC rules. The brochure beam measurement is usually taken at the deck or at the maximum beam point on boats with tumblehome. In some very light boats an enormous deck beam is combined with a very narrow waterline beam; the beam on deck enables crew ballast to be used advantageously, since a crew member sitting 5 feet out from the centerline of the boat has 25 percent more righting leverage than a crew member sitting 4 feet out from the centerline.

The beam/length ratio is a useful index to sail-carrying ability, especially in lighter boats. A beamy boat will offer greater resistance to heeling but also increased drag and form resistance when heeled. In general, beamy boats want to be sailed upright; a narrower hull form may favor being sailed at a generous angle of heel.

Beam is one measurement where there can be too much of a good thing. The beam that provides initial stability to a boat can provide the same stability when the boat is inverted, so that in extreme conditions—seas and wind severe enough to lead to knockdowns or boats rolling over—a beamy boat can have the uncomfortable disadvantage of becoming temporarily stable with its cabin sole as an overhead and the rig serving as a keel. If you have ever tried to right a wide dinghy when it has "turned turtle," you can understand the enormous stability that beam gives to a boat.

Displacement

More than any other single figure, displacement* determines the characteristics of a boat. The relationship between displacement and length is a good indication of high-speed sailing resistance and the ultimate speed potential of a boat. The relationship between sail area and displacement is a good indication of the acceleration and offwind speed potential of

---

* Displacement is the volume of water displaced by the boat, which in net tonnage figures (as on a documentation certificate) is derived from the cubic measure of the water displaced by the boat. For measurement purposes the displacement is effectively the weight of the boat, usually expressed in pounds. To convert pounds to cubic feet, divide by 64 (a cubic foot of salt water weighs 64 pounds; a cubic foot of fresh water weighs 62.2 pounds; for purposes of standardization, the 64-pound figure is usually used). To convert displacement in pounds to long tons, divide by 2240.

the boat. And the cost per pound is a good indication of the quality of the construction.

Published displacements from a manufacturer's brochure or specification sheet are good for a start, although boat builders tend to exaggerate in whichever direction suits their pitch. With production boats that emphasize racing, the published displacement is likely to be optimistically light, often by the 10 percent or so that separates the naval architect's planned displacement from the weight that the builder was able to achieve. With heavy cruisers, the builders will frequently exaggerate the other way, to emphasize the solidity of the construction.

If the designer of a boat is secretive, you can pick up the displacement figure from an IOR certificate; the displacements calculated under the IOR rule are usually close to 90 percent of the actual displacement. It is also useful to go beyond the published figures by adding up or approximating the actual sailing displacement of your boat, which will usually be hundreds or even thousands of pounds more than the published displacement. Most owners sail with hundreds of pounds of gear on the boat, which is not included in those estimated figures. The brochure might say that the displacement of the boat is 13,420 pounds, which is the calculated displacement of the carefully hand-built prototype. The production versions of the same hull, built to less stringent standards, may come in at closer to 14,500 pounds. Add the excess gear that the average boat owner manages to stash away in lockers and lazarettes, usually with the casual observation that "a few pounds here and a few pounds there" won't hurt anything, and the displacement of the boat rapidly creeps up to 16,000 pounds or more. When the increased figures are factored into calculations of sail area/displacement or displacement/length, the addition of a "few pounds here and there" makes significant changes in the ratios that describe the potential performance of the boat.*

The distribution of the weight is also important. For every boat there is a frequency of pitch gyration that can, in certain sea conditions, become resonant with the frequency of the waves, producing a violent pitching motion that is not only uncomfortable but slow. If the weight is concentrated close to the center of gravity of the boat—by using a lightweight hull and rig, keeping heavy gear out of the ends of the boat, and selecting a keel that concentrates ballast inside the boat or high in the keel section—the boat will be less likely to reach that resonant frequency in a seaway. If a boat is pitching violently, it is possible to steady the motion by changing the distribution of weight—moving crew, heavy equipment, or gear. (Of course, equipment cannot be moved when you are racing.)

Sail Area

Sail area is horsepower: the more sail area, the greater the speed potential of the boat. The old saw about "already sailing at hull speed so more sail won't add anything" simply isn't true. The wind is rarely steady, and what constitutes enough sail for the puffs is rarely enough for the lulls. A boat carrying a spinnaker in a strong breeze will go faster than a boat not carrying a spinnaker, if the periodic losses of control and broaches are not so frequent or severe as to cancel the advan-

tage of the spinnaker. There are overcanvased boats, boats that are built for light-air areas or boats with rigs so tall that it is difficult to achieve sufficient stiffness to carry the normal canvas in anything over 10 knots of breeze. But far more often today, boats are undercanvased for the prevailing conditions in North American waters.

The simple rig measurements will give you a mainsail area and a foretriangle area,* but all sail area isn't equal. Taller sails are generally more effective than short sails, both because of wind gradient (the winds are generally stronger aloft) and because high aspect † sails are generally more aerodynamically efficient. With mainsails, however, much of a tall, high-aspect sail may be inefficient on the wind or on a close reach because of the disturbance of a thick mast; and a high-aspect sail is harder to adjust and depower (by changing the shape) than a lower-aspect sail. The sails of a sloop rig are generally more efficient than the sails of a divided rig.

The usual figure given for sail area is the combination of mainsail and foretriangle. Since most sailing is done in light to moderate air, often with an overlapping genoa as the headsail, it is useful to compare the sail areas of boats with a typical (150-percent overlap) genoa instead of the simple foretriangle measurements, especially when comparing boats with different rigs. Because the foretriangle is a larger proportion of the total sail area on a boat with a masthead rig, the comparison of 150-percent genoa plus mainsail areas will show more sail

---

* If you suspect that your boat is overweight, you can often get the designer to calculate the actual weight from freeboard measurements taken with the boat in sailing trim.

* Rig dimensions and measurements: I = height of foretriangle, J = base of mast to the stem of the boat, P = mainsail hoist, E = mainsail foot. The foretriangle = $(I \times J)/2$. The mainsail area = $(P \times E)/2$. The mizzen area for a divided rig can be calculated in the same manner as the mainsail area.

† The aspect ratio of a sail can be approximated by dividing the hoist by the length of the foot.

area for a masthead rig than a fractional rig, even though the boats may have comparable sail areas when foretriangle and main alone are compared.

Rig Types   The advertisements for new boats make extraordinary claims about the ease of setting or trimming sails in one rig or another. One manufacturer points out the "user-friendliness" of the masthead rig, and another points out that the fractional rig has "small, easy-to-manage" headsails. Both claims are valid.

The headsails on a fractional rig are smaller and easier to handle, and if the main can be reshaped to power up and power down the sail plan, it is frequently possible to sail a fractional rig with fewer headsail changes. But if the headsails on the fractional rig are smaller, the main is larger, and handling the mainsail of a large fractional rig can be tricky for shorthanded cruising. Three hundred or more square feet of mainsail is a handful to furl, may require complex or slow-to-handle mainsheet and traveler gear, and because it constitutes so much of the total sail area of the boat, requires attention and skill to trim properly. If the rig has been designed with swept-back spreaders to achieve headstay tension, rather than runners, the main is probably less controllable (in terms of powering and depowering the shape), and the great promise of no headsail changes may be compromised. To point well, boats with aft-swept spreaders instead of runners must either carry extreme tension on the upper shrouds or cut the genoas flat. The extreme tension can heavily load the rigging, chain plates, and hull, and the flat genoas will not be as versatile as a fuller sail.

With a masthead rig, the headsails are heavier, bigger, and tougher to handle, but the sail plan is generally easier to trim, because much of the driving power comes from the headsails and there are few possibilities for grossly mistrimming a headsail. Many newer boats combine the advantages of masthead and fractional rigs by using masthead rigs with relatively small high-aspect foretriangles, or 7/8 or 15/16 fractional rigs.

In the hands of a good designer, either rig can be an all-around performer. Generally, the strong sailing points of fractional rigs are headsail reaching and sailing off the wind in a breeze. Masthead rigs are frequently better off the wind in light air. On the wind, both can be very fast. The fractional rig, because of its smaller headsails, may be quicker to maneuver through a tack, but the larger headsail of the masthead rig provides better acceleration out of the tack.

Rig Details   For boats that are used primarily or exclusively offshore, in reaching or running conditions, sheeting angles for the genoas and spreader lengths are not major concerns. For boats that are used for coastal cruising or racing, the ability to sheet a genoa close can make the difference between pointing and not pointing, which is important not only to the racer but to any cruiser who would rather sail than motor to windward, and who knows that he needs a tacking angle of less than 90 degrees if he is to make any real progress to windward. Chain plates fastened to the sides of the hull, or long single spreader rigs, make it difficult to sheet the genoa close enough for efficient sailing to weather.

Although the rigging on a double- or triple-spreader rig is more complex than a simple single-spreader rig, and more difficult to tune, the multiple spreaders provide increased support to the mast panels. The advantage to the boat owner is that a lighter section can be used, which reduces weight aloft and windage. The multiple-spreader rig also permits shorter spreaders and a narrower sheeting base, which in turn allows the chain plates to come in from the sides of the hull to a position closer to the sides of the house.

Inboard chain plates have other advantages besides close sheeting of the genoa. Frequently, a bulkhead or tie-rods to the keel or floor timbers are a stronger point for mounting chain plates than the outside of the hull, especially on a fiberglass hull. Indeed, if the chain plates are mounted to the hull, the boat will generally need a bulkhead across the hull at the chain plates to resist the crushing loads of the chain plates. And with the chain plates inboard, the side decks can be open for people, sail bags, Windsurfers, or folding sails.

Freeboard

The freeboard of a boat, which designers often do their best in inventive hull decoration to enhance or conceal, can range from what seems hardly more than a Windsurfer profile with a cabin to slab sides that reveal their height only when you try to climb up on deck from the club launch. Low freeboard means less room below, unless there is a house. High freeboard can mean standing room below with a flush or blister deck.

But freeboard is windage, and it affects the performance of the boat under sail or power as well as the behavior of a boat when anchored or when docking in a breeze. A high slab side catches the wind and leads to skittish behavior at the anchor and uncontrolled sailing when your intention is controlled powering. A boat with high freeboard will put heavier loads on moorings and anchors and will misbehave in raft-ups. The

other side of the coin is that a boat with low freeboard is wet to sail, especially to windward. Your foul-weather gear will get a workout, and the bedding of deck fittings and the integrity of the hull-deck joint will be tested.

NONDIMENSIONAL RATIOS

Armed with the displacement, waterline length, beam, and sail plan dimensions, you have the basic information to evaluate the potential performance and characteristics of a boat. The next step is to combine these figures into ratios that enable the comparison of boats with differing dimensions. Comparing a boat that displaces 14,000 pounds with another that displaces 10,000 will tell you which one will be easier to stop when it coasts toward the dock with a broken engine, but it won't necessarily tell you which one will accelerate faster in light air or surf first in a breeze. To make those comparisons it is necessary to reduce the raw dimensions to ratios, which with a few corrections will work over a range of lengths and weights.

Displacement/Length

The ratio of displacement to length is an effective shorthand index to the high-speed sailing potential of a boat.* The usual formula is:

* Because displacement is a measure of volume and length a linear measurement, they cannot be put directly into a ratio. The usual formula converts displacement from pounds back into long tons and divides by the cube of the length (multiplied by 100 to yield a result in a manageable range). The lowest figures for ballasted sailboats are usually around 50, and the highest figure for a boat that will sail, as opposed to motor sailers that carry canvas for steadying, is around 350.

$$\text{Disp/LWL} = \frac{(\text{displacement}/2240)}{(.01 \times \text{LWL})^3}$$

Or you can use the table to approximate your disp/LWL ratio. Naval architects frequently use DWL (design waterline length) instead of LWL, both as a convention and because they are often talking about designs that have not been built and cannot be measured for actual waterline length.

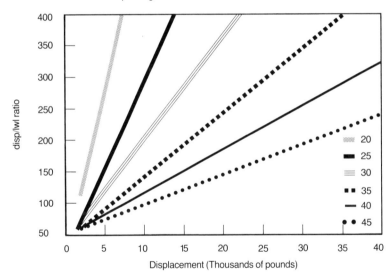

Displacement/Length
Use line corresponding to LWL in feet

A low figure, below 150, characterizes an ultra-light-displacement boat (ULDB). Boats with low displacement/length figures can surf or even plane in a breeze, and they frequently

exceed the $1.35 \times \sqrt{\text{LWL}}$ speed which is commonly thought of as the maximum potential speed of a displacement hull. High displacement/length figures, above 300, characterize boats that by contemporary standards are heavy: the additional weight may allow comfortable and even luxurious accommodations, but a boat with a displacement/length ratio in that range will do more motoring than racing.

Some owners, usually those with boats having high displacement/length ratios, deny the validity of the formula in characterizing boats, arguing that their boat is designed so that the waterline lengthens as the boat heels, or that some other characteristic of their boat makes it an exception. There may be some minor effect of long overhangs when a boat heels, but the reality is that boats that are light for their length have the potential to sail faster than those that are heavy for their length. Or to reverse the terms, for a given displacement, say 15,000 pounds, a boat that is 33 feet on the waterline can sail substantially faster than a boat that is 27 feet on the waterline—if there is enough wind and sail area to drive it to the higher hull speed.

The closer a boat gets to the extremes of high or low displacement/length ratios, the less likely it is that the boat will be versatile. The heavy "world cruiser" type does not sail well in any but steady trade winds, and it rarely makes a good all-around boat for family cruising or occasional racing in most sailing areas. At the same time, the margins of weight are so critical in an ultra-light-displacement racer that even a few extra pounds of cruising gear can destroy the performance potential of the boat. Within the extremes, in the displacement/length range of 150 to 275, there is a great deal of room for the compromises that make successful racer/cruisers.

Racing a heavy boat, such as the successful Ted Hood–designed *Robins*, generally requires more people and bigger sails than a lighter boat and usually relies on tactics that favor fewer tacks, more power reaching, and the ability to slog it out to windward in a breeze. The heavy boat will usually have a large foretriangle, and big headsails which require frequent sail changes. The lighter boat, whether fractional or a masthead rig with a big main, relies on quickness, fast tacks, acceleration, and surfing off the wind. Sails are changed less frequently as the boat is "powered up" or "depowered" by changing the shape and trim of the sails. The two styles of sailing require different techniques of helmsmanship, sail trimming, and sail handling. In light air, the heavier boat will be slower to accelerate, but the tall sail plan and the momentum of the boat will keep it going through light patches. The lighter boat is quick to accelerate in even a zephyr of breeze; it is equally quick to decelerate when the breeze dies.

For cruising, the light-displacement boat has the advantage of smaller sails and lighter equipment, which are easier for family crews to handle. Light boats are fast enough for exhilarating sailing and long runs in a day, and they are usually easy to maneuver in an anchorage or around a dock. The facilities belowdecks will undoubtedly be more spartan, with canvas storage or bins instead of drawers and lockers, but there is no reason that a light-displacement-boat cannot have an efficient stove, a decent head, and comfortable berths—the basics of a good cruiser.

The heavier boat may be slower and may make less distance in a day, but it will frequently offer a gentler motion in a seaway, with a steadier helm that will be less responsive but easier to steer for long hours, and is better suited for self-steering gear. In an anchorage or marina the heavy boat is harder to maneuver and requires heavier ground tackle, but it will often ride better at anchor, with less skittish dancing as the breeze shifts. Down below, the heavier boat may not offer the spaciousness of a lighter boat, but the weight allows the luxury of crafted joinery, fitted storage drawers, and lockers.

Sail Area / Displacement

The ratio of sail area to displacement, the marine equivalent of the horsepower-per-pound figure given for automobiles, characterizes the acceleration and offwind potential of a boat. Boats with high SA/disp ratios generally accelerate easily and have the sail power to get moving when others are slatting around. A boat with a very high SA/disp ratio (such as some ULDBs or boats that have been optimized for light air with super-tall rigs) may be tender, or may need to reef down early to maintain optimum sailing angles. The formula is:

$$\text{SA/disp} = \frac{\text{sail area}}{(\text{displacement}/64)^{2/3}}$$

The sail area is the mainsail plus foretriangle, in square feet; the displacement is in pounds. If your calculator doesn't handle fractional exponents, you can approximate the SA/disp ratio for the boat from the table below. Even if you have calculated your own ratio, take a look at the table to see what happens to the ratio as you add 1000 or 2000 pounds of extra gear to a boat. The slope of the lines is steep, and the addition of extra weight drops the ratio dramatically.

Although boats with high SA/disp ratios often do well in

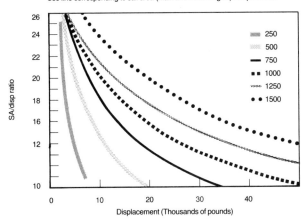

Sail Area/Displacement

Use line corresponding to sail area (Main and Foretriangles) in square feet

Legend:
- 250
- 500
- 750
- 1000
- 1250
- 1500

Y-axis: SA/disp ratio
X-axis: Displacement (Thousands of pounds)

wetted surface constitutes the principal drag until boat speed begins to approach the square root of the waterline length, at which point wave-making and form drag will be greater than the drag of wetted surface. The greater the ratio of sail area to wetted hull surface, the more easily the boat is able to overcome that drag. Unfortunately, the ratio of sail area to the wetted surface of the hull is not as easily calculated as SA/disp or disp/LWL.

In general, the ratio of sail area in square feet to wetted surface of the hull in square feet will be somewhere between 2:1 and 3:1. The higher the ratio, the better the light-air performance.

light air, the ratio itself is not a measure of light-air ability. Rather, it is a measure of the ability to accelerate when a puff hits the sails and to come up to speed quickly after a tack or jibe or in a seaway, where the boat encounters sudden changes in apparent wind velocity as it sails down a wave or up the back of the next wave. A boat with a low SA/disp ratio may do well in light air, but the sailing technique will be different. The boat with a lot of sail for its displacement can afford to make more frequent and more radical moves; the boat with less sail for its displacement will nurture the wind it has, coaxing every last inch from the puff, trying to keep moving at all costs.

Sail Area / Wetted Surface

To get a boat moving in light air, the pull of the sails must overcome the friction of the hull against the water; indeed,

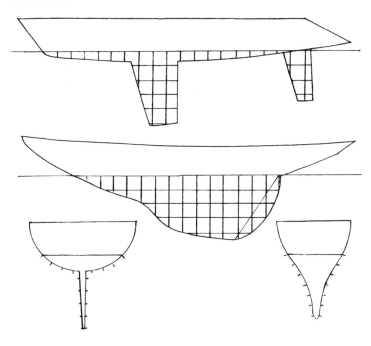

There is no easy way to construct a table for wetted surface, and without the lines of the boat there is no simple formula to approximate the ratio. But a close look at the profile of the boat, its sail plan, and, if available, the lines of the hull can at least characterize the boat.

There are two ways to approximate the wetted surface. One is to count squares on the profile drawings (multiply the hull squares by 2.5 to approximate the wetted surface of the whole hull). The other is to study the lines of the hull and try to measure or at least compare the underwater sections. If you count the tick marks on the end views of the drawings on page 17, you can see that the wide, flat hull shape has a greater wetted surface (for a given hull volume) than the slack-bilge hull shape more common in heavy-displacement hulls.

It is frequently considerations of wetted surface that determine many of the yacht designer's decisions about the shape of the keel and rudder, as well as the underwater form of the hull. A wide, flat hull shape gives the boat substantial stability and sail-carrying ability, but to maintain a relatively low wetted surface the designer will probably use an efficient fin keel. The designer of the heavy full-keel boat, with the substantial wetted surface of that keel area, cannot afford the wetted surface of rounded bilge sections, so his hull has slack sections (a straight line is the shortest distance from the waterline to the bottom of the keel). The keel and rudder designs required by considerations of wetted surface in turn will determine the steering characteristics, and the windward and offwind ability of a boat.

The reason some heavy boats do well in light-air racing is that an increase of displacement has less effect on wetted surface than it has on sail-carrying ability. The light boat with its wide, flat hull frequently has almost as much wetted surface as the heavier boat of the same rating, yet most rating rules allow a heavy boat to have substantially more sail area for a given rating than a light boat of comparable rating. With less sail area and the same wetted surface, the light boat can be at a disadvantage.

Prismatic Coefficient

This formidable-sounding term describes a relatively simple concept. Essentially, the prismatic coefficient is the ratio between the volume a hull would have if the entire underwater form had the shape of the fullest section, and the actual volume. Thus a boat with full ends has a higher prismatic coefficient than a boat with fine ends. It is difficult to calculate the prismatic coefficient without the full lines of a boat, but it is not difficult to compare the lines of two boats, or the underwater shapes of two boats as they sit in their cradles, to determine which one has the fuller ends (higher prismatic coefficient).

The range is generally from about 0.5 to 0.7. Heavier-displacement boats (boats with relatively high disp/LWL ratios) will generally have lower prismatic coefficients; boats that are capable of reaching high speed/length ratios (boats with low disp/LWL ratios) will generally have fuller ends and higher prismatic coefficients. If the relationship of prismatic coefficient to speed sounds reversed, compare a typical planing hull (say a Flying Dutchman) to a long displacement hull like a 12-meter.

Although the variation in prismatic coefficient is much narrower for conventional-hulled sailing boats, it is worth comparing the shapes of hulls and analyzing the speed ranges that will be expected of them. In general, boats with higher prismatic coefficients (fuller ends) are at their best in heavy air; boats with lower prismatic coefficients favor lighter air.

HULL SHAPE

A boat with fine sections forward will generally have greater windward ability, but at a price: a man on the bow changing a headsail dramatically affects the trim of the boat. During a sail change, some small boats with fine forward sections look like a U-boat in a World War II movie after the command to "Dive." Off the wind a boat with a very fine entry may lack buoyancy in the bow and require drastic weight trims to keep it on its lines. Some fine-bowed IOR designs require that the entire crew crowd against the pushpit on a breezy spinnaker run.

Broad, undistorted aft sections can give the boat a smooth run for high-speed sailing off the wind. But broad aft sections that sit in the water in light air create excess wetted surface. The trick is to keep the broad stern up out of the water in light air, and on racing boats it is usually accomplished with human ballast—crew who sit forward and to leeward in light air to keep the stern out of the water. IOR boats that have been distorted to fool the rule (by making the boat measure shorter than it really is) and some boats with very fine aft sections can misbehave off the wind in a breeze, with motions that range from skittish steering to gut-in-the-throat death rolls.

The shape of the bilges* can have a great influence on the

---

* Although "bilge" is usually used to refer to the area of the boat where water from unknown sources, oil dripping from the engine, and lost objects seem to accumulate, in naval architecture it properly refers to the section of

performance and handling characteristics of a boat. The slack bilges of a heavy-displacement hull provide relatively little form resistance to heeling; the flat bottom of a dinghy-like hull will provide considerable stiffness as the boat heels. At the same time, the displacement hull maintains a relatively symmetrical underwater shape when the boat heels, which results in relatively little directional instability in the form of weather or lee helm. And since the lines of the boat are relatively straight, there is little added wetted surface from heeling, so the boat can be sailed at moderate angles of heel without excessive drag. On the other hand, the flat dinghy-shaped hull will present drastically increased resistance and a radically asymmetrical waterline plane when sailed at high angles of heel; the increased weather helm and resistance will make the boat slow and hard to handle.

KEELS AND RUDDERS

Traditionalists cite all kinds of arguments in favor of full keels of the world-cruiser type. There are some lovely boats with full keels, boats that are close-winded and well behaved on the wind and off. But naval architecture has come a long way in the past decades, and for a contemporary boat used in most coastal sailing areas a full keel has many disadvantages in comparison with a fin keel and separated rudder.

Full keels are supposedly more rugged in a grounding. If you periodically put your boat up on coral reefs, there may be

---

the underwater shape where the hull turns in toward the centerline and the keel. A boat with slack bilges has a gentle turn or slope to the hull shape; a boat with firm bilges has a sharp turn, or hard chines.

an advantage to a full keel. But if your usual grounding experience is a bump-bump in sand or mud, the fin keel, with its short footprint and easy turning ability, may allow you to shift weight to one rail, or to the bow, and quickly get off.

Another supposed advantage is that a full-keel boat can be careened to paint the bottom. Careened? A few owners may have the facilities and time to careen their boat for bottom work, but the argument is usually made by owners with visions of themselves on some undiscovered South Pacific island, surrounded by willing natives, the women performing beckoning dances while the men help to careen the boat and paint the bottom. The image is appealing, but most boat owners have to make do with a Travelift.

Finally there is the argument about what full-keel advocates call "tracking ability," an argument which seems to forget that the corollary of tracking ability is "lack of maneuverability." A full-keel boat may require less attention to the helm, but it is also less responsive to the helm, less able to turn quickly, harder to maneuver around docks and moorings. It is true that some fin-keel boats can be naughty off the wind in a breeze, either because they have fine sections at the ends or because they have inadequate rudders; on a long passage, a fin-keel boat will require more attention to the helm and will require more effort from a self-steering apparatus; and there are boats with no skegs and balanced spade rudders which can be skittish under power, requiring constant attention to the helm if they are not to motor in circles. But those are questions of execution, not general characteristics of a fin keel.

If you are considering a full keel it is important to remember the trade-offs: the heavy full-keel boat is often a dog in light air; its ultimate speed potential is generally so low that for most owners exciting off-wind sailing will be confined to fantasies or magazine stories of mid-ocean gales; and many full-keel boats are so inefficient sailing to windward that in a real blow they are incapable of beating off a lee shore—an ability which for most boat owners ought to rank ahead of careening, protection from grounding on a coral reef, and tracking ability.

There is more to the question of keel shape than the question of full versus fin keel. Fin-keel sections can range from long, shallow keels, designed for sailing areas like the Chesapeake where a depth of more than 5 feet can severely limit cruising, to deep super-critical sections that are unexcelled for windward ability but can severely curtail mooring, docking, and cruising. It is common for a high-performance 35-foot boat to have a draft of 7 or more feet, of which 6 feet is the keel foil. Between the extremes of the racer's deep fin keel and a full keel, there are a range of "cutaway" designs and designs that incorporate a skeg in front of the rudder. While less maneuverable than the spade rudder, and with greater wetted surface, the modified fin keel and skeg rudder designs do preserve the "directional control" of a full keel, which for the

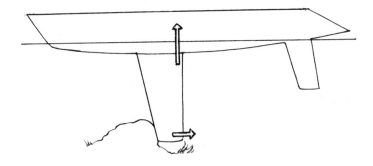

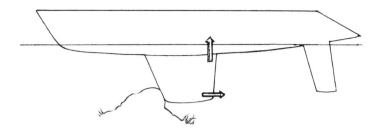

long-distance cruiser who is spending many days under self-steerer is a definite advantage.

The chief disadvantage of deep, thin keel sections, besides cruising or mooring inconvenience, is that the leverage of the keel, if you meet up with a rock that has drifted off its charted position, can cause considerable damage to the hull.

The shorter (fore and aft) and deeper the keel section, the greater the leverage of an impact. Unless a boat with a deep fin keel is built with strong floor timbers to absorb and distribute the shock of an impact, the risk of damage from hitting a rock or other object is considerable. Walk around a boatyard in the winter and you will see dozens of boats with cracks and separations between the fin keel and the hull, usually at the point where the forward edge of the keel joins the hull. And if a boat has been in a hard grounding, it is not uncommon to have cracking or structural damage where the aft edge of the keel meets the hull. The solution to either problem is strong floor timbers or an internal grid which will distribute the load of the fin keel. For a boat that lacks floor timbers, it is possible to fabricate wood, fiberglass, or metal floors in place, but it is a complex boatyard job.

The keel is not the only critical underwater shape. A big rudder makes a boat maneuverable, gives you a weapon to fight an imminent broach, and in some instances can provide lift to windward. The big rudder also adds wetted surface and drag, especially if the helm is misbalanced so that the boat is frequently sailed with the helm over. And with rudder sections, as with keel sections, the longer and thinner the section, the more efficient it is as a foil.

Not too many years ago, the use of NACA sections for the shapes of keel and rudder sections was considered a breakthrough, as naval architects realized that the considerable research on airfoil shapes that had been spent on airplane development could, with certain qualifications, be applied to racing and cruising yachts. Compare the planform of a modern fin keel with the wing shape of a contemporary fighter plane and you can see how far the development has come. Designers now, especially in Europe, are going a step further, to elliptical planforms with radically curved trailing edges on keels and especially on rudders, in an effort to achieve the same amount of lift with less wetted surface.

And after the success of *Australia II* many naval architects have begun to experiment with permutations of the winged keel for cruising and racing boats. The winged keel offers tremendous advantages in a heavy meter boat; it remains to be seen whether comparable advantages can be obtained in cruising boats and racing boats designed to the common handicap rules.

STIFFNESS

Naval architects, working off a full set of lines, are able to calculate measurements of the stiffness of a boat: righting moment, transverse metacentric height, and Dellenbaugh

Angle. The boat owner is interested in more direct questions: How much sail will she carry in a breeze? How much will she heel? How soon will I have to reef or change headsails?

To the racer, "stiff" may mean the ability to carry a heavy #1 genoa and a full main with 24 knots of apparent wind over the deck. To the day sailor, "stiff" may mean a boat that isn't too "tippy" in an average afternoon sea breeze. Unfortunately, there are no standard measures of stiffness that a boat owner can calculate without performing an inclining test or timing the period of roll of the boat. And the simple calculations that may tell you something about the ultimate stiffness of a boat—the ability to resist rolling over—often don't tell much about the ability to resist the heeling moment of the wind on the sails.

Ballast/Displacement Ratio   The ballast/displacement ratio of a boat is so easy to calculate that boat owners are quick to compare them as an indication of stiffness. Alone, the ratio doesn't tell you much. There are stiff boats with a 35-percent ballast-to-displacement ratio, and tender boats with a 60-percent ratio. If you were to compare two boats of similar hull form, rig, and displacement, and if the ballast were in the same place in each boat, then a difference in ballast/displacement ratio would represent a difference in stability. In general, the beam, the hull form, the placement of the ballast, and the configuration and size of the rig are all as important or more important in determining the stiffness of the boat than the ratio of ballast to displacement.

Beam/Length Ratio   Wide beam, especially with firm bilge sections, makes a boat stiff by increasing the immersed vol-ume as the boat heels. Thus the beam/LWL ratio is a useful measure of stiffness: boats with higher beam/LWL ratios are usually stiffer. Beamy boats also make more effective use of human ballast on the rail. It is useful to examine the midsection of the boat from the designer's lines if they are available. Very slack or round lines will have less form stability as the boat heels than will firm lines. At the same time, the firm lines make for increased wetted surface and potential imbalance of the helm when the boat heels.

Ballast Position   Ballast carried deep is more effective in righting the boat than ballast carried high in the bilges, for the same reason that a person sitting on the rail of a beamy boat is more effective ballast than a person sitting on the rail of a narrow boat. The righting moment of ballast is a product of the weight and the distance from the center of gravity of the boat. Thus a boat with ballast placed low in a deep keel can have a lower ballast/displacement ratio but still be much stiffer than a shoal-draft boat that is carrying more ballast, but in the bilges or in a stub keel. Boats that are not designed to a rule that effectively penalizes stability, like the IOR rule, may have their ballast more efficiently placed, for example low in a deep keel rather than high in the bilges.

Movable ballast, such as water ballast, which can be shifted from one side of the boat to the other, can make a boat extremely stiff. Although movable ballast is illegal for IOR, MORC, PHRF, or MHS racing, it is used for some "no-holds-barred" offshore racing, and as the systems are refined, it may find its way into cruising designs.

Although owners often brag about the stiffness of their boats, the terms they use sometimes reveal that what they are really bragging about is the reduced size of their sail plans. A boat with a short rig can carry its 150-percent #1 genoa in more breeze than a similar boat with a taller rig, but the boat doesn't necessarily have the ability to carry more sail than the tall-rigged boat. And while many boat owners seem to equate stiffness with manhood, depending upon the prevailing winds of a given sailing area, extreme stiffness may not be desirable in a boat, especially if the stiffness comes at a sacrifice of light-air sailing ability.

MOTION

Motion is one of those elusive concepts that sometimes escape description in numbers. The usual generalization—that heavy boats have one kind of motion and light boats another—is not always true. What is true is that the distribution of weight on a boat will affect its motion in a seaway, and that different hull forms have distinctly different motions and directional reactions to heeling, to rolling, and to the push and pull of quartering, beam, head, and following seas.

A heavy full-keeled displacement cruiser can have a gentle motion in a seaway because the displacement and easy lines * tend to damp the violence of the sea. At the other extreme, a

---

* "Easy" refers to neither the difficulty of drawing the lines nor the morality of the boat. Easy lines are fair lines without abrupt turns, like the sweep of the counter in a long-ended cruiser. The opposite of easy lines are the abrupt cuts, bumps, shelves, and steps that are sometimes put into the lines of a boat in an effort to shave a rating under one measurement rule or another. The arguments about whether easy lines make a boat go through the water better or not will probably go on forever. It is unlikely that anyone will make a greater contribution to the debate than the crewman on *Mariner*, the twelve-meter yacht that Britton Chance designed with decidedly *uneasy* flatbacked steps at the end of the waterline. "Even a turd is tapered," he said.

flat-bottomed, light-displacement racer may have a rapid choppy motion that can be exhausting on a long passage. A boat with most of its weight concentrated in the middle will have a more violent motion in a seaway, rising and falling with each wave, but it will usually be much faster than a boat with weight in the ends. Most racers, and increasingly many cruisers, are becoming sensitive to the distribution of weight in their boats. Heavy gear in a lazarette, or full water tanks under a forward V-berth, will change the motion of a boat in a seaway and will decidedly slow the boat in those conditions.

Sailing downwind, a long-keeled boat will resist yawing in a quartering sea and will require less energy and attention to steer than the flat-bottomed, short-keel boat. But remember that these observations apply to sailing in a seaway for long passages. The motion that a sailor making a passage would find intolerable is the other side of the "responsiveness" or "quickness" that a sailor going around the buoys or sailing across the sound for a weekend may find exhilarating.

COMFORT

Heavy-displacement passage-makers, despite their weight, generally are not roomy on board. There are deep bilges for the canned goods that the magazine articles are forever telling you to store without their labels, but there is very little hull volume for sitting, stretching, or lounging. Advocates of the heavy-displacement boat argue that on a long passage the "cozy" space is comfortable, that in a seaway you don't get thrown around as far, that the deep bilge forms a sump for bilge water which then doesn't get into the bottom of every locker. But for weekend or holiday cruising, with children or guests, there is no substitute for the room—to stretch out, sleep, play, read, or whatever—that a beamy contemporary racer-cruiser hull can provide. The beam and relatively full bilge sections of a contemporary racer-cruiser provide a huge interior volume, much of which is usable space rather than storage nooks and crannies. True, there is little space for cans in the bilge, and unless the bilge is carefully designed and maintained, substantial water taken through a hatch will find its way into lockers. But for most coastal cruisers those are small prices to pay for the comfort of being able to stretch out in privacy, with enough interior volume for children or guests on a rainy day.

On deck, too, the modern racer-cruiser has evolved a long way from the small cockpit and narrow side decks of the traditional cruiser. The traditional cruiser was designed before decent foul-weather gear was available; the small, deep cockpit was designed for protection rather than easy access to deck gear. The narrow hull and relatively wide chain-plate base of the traditional cruiser leaves side decks that are difficult to negotiate, especially with a sail bag in hand. The house, coamings, and sail-handling hardware usually take up so much of the deck that there is little space for stretching out, lounging around with a drink, spreading out appetizers, or whatever else people like to do at an anchorage. That kind of deck space may not be missed in a long passage at sea, but it can be sorely missed when a family or a racing crew are drying out or resting at a mooring or at anchor. And it's not only at the mooring or anchorage that the room on deck is appreciated. The beam of modern boats allows room on deck to separate people, whether it is room to separate the genoa tailers and grinders from the helmsman, or room to separate sunbathers from conversation in the cockpit.

CHOICES AND CHANGES

Up to now, we have examined the numbers and lines on a boat as though the boat were fresh out of the box—the way the designer intended or drew the boat. But few boats are truly stock. Just pile aboard the usual cruising equipment, 500 or 600 pounds of gear, and all the numbers that the naval architect so carefully calculated are suddenly way off. On a typical hull with a 30-foot waterline, 600 additional pounds of displacement will make the boat sit ½ inch deeper in the water. That may not sound like much, but it will produce approximately 2.7 square feet of added wetted surface. A small dinghy has about 8 square feet of wetted surface, which means that in terms of wetted surface alone, the added displacement is the equivalent of towing one third of a dinghy! On a boat with a shorter waterline, an extremely beamy boat, or a boat with broad, flat sections aft, the effect of extra weight is even more pronounced.

Added displacement also significantly affects the sail area/displacement, sail area/wetted surface, and ballast/displacement ratios of a boat. A moderately light-displacement boat of 10,000 pounds with a sail area (main and foretriangle) of 630 square feet has a SA/disp ratio of 21.77. To maintain this ratio when the boat is 500 pounds "overweight" will require approximately 21 square feet of additional sail area, which would mean either lengthening the boom by 1 foot or making the

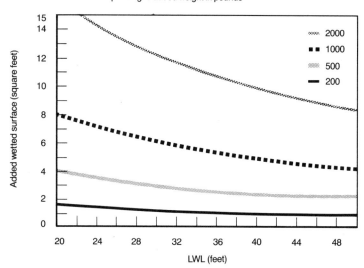

Increased Wetted Surface

Use line corresponding to added weight in pounds

Added wetted surface (square feet)

LWL (feet)

Legend:
- 2000
- 1000
- 500
- 200

mast 1½ feet taller. Increase the extra baggage to 1000 pounds and you will need 2 feet of extra boom or almost 3 feet of additional mast height.

Think the difference won't matter on a heavier cruising boat? If the base displacement of your boat is 14,000 pounds and the waterline is 30 feet, to make up for 1000 pounds of extra gear you will need almost 30 square feet of additional sail area: a boom 1½ feet longer or a mast over 2 feet taller.

What about the ballast/displacement ratio? The modest change in the ratio when 1000 pounds is added to a 14,000-pound boat may not seem significant, but remember that the additional weight is generally either high up in the boat or in the ends of the boat, which means that it contributes to insta-bility or pitching moment. Unless the weight consists of chain stored deep in the bilge (not in a chain locker in the bow), the weight does not contribute to the ballast part of the ballast/displacement ratio.

Weight alone is often the difference between the perfor-mance of the prototype raced by a factory team that does phenomenally well (and thus assures an initial low PHRF rat-ing for the type) and the production models that are later sailed by frustrated owners who have trouble sailing to the assigned rating. The hull and rig are the same, but the light- and heavy-air sailing potential of the stripped boat is so differ-ent from the production model that they are effectively differ-ent boats. Watch a factory team come aboard a boat before a race. The amount of gear that they can strip off, in the inter-est of lightness, is striking. And for cruisers who are interested in lively sailing or decent distance traveled each day, the same attitude can make a big difference in the sailing ability of the boat. Removing an unused barbecue, cans of extra food, or an electric pump for the inflatable makes a real difference!

Short Rig

Or look what happens when you decide to order a short rig because someone in the family didn't want a "tippy" boat, or because one of the cruising magazines suggested that a short rig is appropriate for passage-making. Or when a sailmaker persuades you to get a "low-maintenance, easy-to-trim" bat-tenless mainsail with no roach. The roach may total as much as 10 percent of the sail area of the mainsail, or 25 to 30 square feet of sail area on a 35-foot boat. The short rig will decrease the I and P measurements by 2 or even 3 feet, which will have a drastic effect on light-air performance. A boat that might have had an average SA/disp of 17.50 suddenly has a SA/disp of 16.00, which means that to go at all in light air the boat will need a huge drifter, and even that won't really make up for the lost sail area because the area of the drifter isn't as high up, and a huge overlap is less efficient than un-overlapped sail area. By contrast, a boat with a sufficiently tall rig can cruise with a 110 percent lapper in everything from 5 knots to 30 knots. Which is easier—to pull a few strings to change the shape of the mainsail or to change the headsail? Which sail is easier to hoist—the lapper or the genoa? Which is easier to tack?

Shoal Draft

Shoal draft is another choice that dramatically affects performance. For some cruising areas there is no choice, but whether it is a shoal keel boat or a centerboard boat, it usually means a heavier boat because extra ballast is necessary to maintain its ultimate stability. And even with the additional ballast the boat will probably be tender, because the internal ballast has less effect on the initial heeling moment of the boat. At 20 or 30 degrees of heel the boat may be as stiff as its normal-draft cousin, but modern designs don't sail as well at extreme angles of heel, and most families out for a day sail or a cruise find life more comfortable at 15 degrees of heel than at 25.

Windward ability is almost invariably proportional to the depth of the keel, and in ordering shoal draft you probably knew you were sacrificing some windward ability. But there are other consequences, too: the added weight required for ultimate stability with the shoal keel alters the disp/LWL and SA/disp, both for the worse; the boat sits lower in the water, increasing the wetted surface. In sum, the performance is degraded significantly on all points of sail. It may be worth the choice, but it is important to realize the nature of the compromise.

IMPROVING PERFORMANCE

Many boat owners have discovered that modifying a yacht for improved performance—while preserving familiar accommodations, deck layout, and "feel"—is a wiser investment than a new boat. Boats designed years ago frequently had keel shapes and keel depths that were less than optimum. Almost any boat with a scimitar-shaped keel section, or another unusual keel shape designed to get maximum weight into minimum draft, will discover that a deeper keel with a straightforward planform will improve performance by making the boat stiffer, more efficient to windward, and with less drag and wetted surface off the wind. Rudders too can be improved by modification or replacement. The cost of a new keel can range from a few hundred dollars for an added wood or lead shoe to increase depth up to $5000 or more for a new keel designed and poured from scratch. A modified rudder can be had for as little as $500, which may be a small price to pay for improved maneuverability, the ability to carry a spinnaker without broaching, or for a general reduction of wetted surface and improved performance to windward.

Rigs too can be changed. Boats built years ago were frequently underpowered for the typical light-air conditions of most North American sailing areas in the summer, and adding a few feet of rig can often make the difference between decent performance in light air and a boat that always needs a breeze. A penalty pole for the spinnaker or a longer boom is a cheaper modification, but the boat will not profit from the lightness, control, and efficiency that a new rig can provide. Even with no change in the rig dimensions, a new rig with shorter spreaders, a lighter section, internalized halyards, and improved running rigging and sail controls will make a tremendous improvement in the speed of the boat. The reduction of weight aloft will also reduce the pitching moment in slop or powerboat wakes, making the boat faster and more pleasant to sail in today's typical conditions.

CONSTRUCTION

Boats are built to varying standards, not only for reasons of cost but because it really doesn't make sense to equip a boat for conditions that it will never see. A super-heavy layup of the hull will indeed afford extra protection if a boat is stranded on a coral reef in breaking seas. But boats that sail in Lake Michigan or Long Island Sound or the Chesapeake aren't likely to get stranded on a coral reef, and the extra-heavy layup serves only to increase the weight of the boat and make it slower. Oversized rigging with Norseman terminals might make sense on an extended cruise in the tropics, when there is a possibility of rig breakdown or deterioration far from a rigger equipped to make new swaged terminals for wire or rod rigging. But most sailors in San Diego or Florida or Texas aren't likely to run into the problems of the solitary voyager in the tropics, and the oversized rigging isn't really safer for their

boats; it's only heavier, increasing the windage, the heeling moment, the cost of turnbuckles, backstay adjusters, and similar hardware, and making the rig that much heavier and bulkier for winter storage or for routine inspections and maintenance. All-bronze portlights are stronger than plastic portlights; they would be more likely to hold up in a North Atlantic storm. But the average coastal cruiser is never in a storm at sea, and while he may see a brief wild squall, or a day-long beat into a 35-knot breeze that builds up a good sea, a cracked portlight won't jeopardize his ship. What the bronze portlight adds to his boat is weight, maintenance, and cost. The trade-off may make sense for a yachtsman who derives much of his sailing pleasure from having and maintaining the finest of traditional fittings. But if it is the gleam of bronze that you like, the reason to insist on bronze portlights should be the enjoyment of the patina and the pride of ownership, not a questionable argument about the safety of the boat; and the choice should be made with an awareness of the price—in performance, maintenance, and cost—that the heavy fittings can exact.

Just as some details are needlessly specified for extra strength, there are many details that are overlooked. Production builders trying to get by with an inexpensive rig will install external halyards and external tangs, which are cheap, easy to fabricate and install, and which can be promoted as "clean, safe, accessible for repair." They are also bulky, high in windage, usually heavier, and in the case of halyards, likely to promote both wear and chafe, and despite the best efforts of owners and gadget makers, a nightly symphony which will quickly make you the least-liked boat in any anchorage. The alternatives—T-ball terminals for smaller boats and internal tangs for larger boats—are suitable not only for the racer but for the cruiser as well, presenting a cleaner rig with fewer protrusions to catch on the sails, and depending upon the installation of the tangs and the thickness or reinforcement of the spar in the way of the tangs, a potentially stronger rig in which the loads of the tang are distributed over a larger bearing surface.

There are some areas of boat equipment where no compromise is reasonable. Marginal layups, inadequate internal structures, hulls and decks that tin-can or flex in normal sailing usage, keel attachments supported only by an extra layer of fiberglass or roving on the bottom of the boat, undersized or marginal-quality standing and running rigging, blocks with small sheaves, inadequate winches, shoddy bedding and fastening of fittings, nonmarine through-hull fittings, brass plumbing fixtures, slap-dash zipcord wiring—any kind of shoddy construction and fitting practices—have no place on a boat. But between sound construction and overkill, there is room for many trade-offs. And so it's a good question to ask whether the cost and weight of bronze portlights, or oversized rigging, or extra-heavy hull laminations, or any number of other additions or specifications make sense on the boat. It may be wiser to buy the stock boat and if changed usage means that the construction should be upgraded to higher specifications, make the necessary changes.

AESTHETICS

There are conventions of aesthetics that can't be denied. The features that characterize the IOR hull (the reverse transom, wide beam, open deck, large rig) have come to characterize a look of "speed" for many boat owners, just as the features of the heavy-displacement cruiser (high freeboard, split rig, doubled-ended hull shape) have come to characterize the look of offshore passage-making for others. Yet both extremes, or even features of either extreme, can look absurd when a boat is mismatched to its use. The offshore cruiser outfitted with ratlines, wind vane, windmill, and solar cells looks as out of place on Long Island Sound as an open-transom IOR one-tonner in a club race on a small lake.

But aesthetics remain a question of personal style. What may seem silly, impractical, phony, or arrogant to one sailor may be an important fantasy or image to another. If you want to sail a boat built for offshore passages in the trade winds in an area like Long Island Sound, or if you want to refit a ULDB as a passage-maker, go ahead! Just be aware of the compromises that are inevitable in your choice and of the ultimate capabilities of your boat.

3

ON DECK

Some boats just seem to work. You may have been on one as crew in a race and noticed how people didn't get in one another's way during the most complex maneuvers, how frequently used controls lines were always at hand when they were needed, how setting the spinnaker or reefing the main didn't require jury-rigged systems and line-juggling tricks. Or you may have been in an anchorage when a well-rigged boat hoisted sail to leave, and noticed how smoothly every step seemed to go, how two people, or even one, could accomplish what on other boats would take far more hands.

Then there are the boats that have all the right equipment —big self-tailing winches, expensive hydraulics, the latest in go-fast gear or gadgetry—and nothing ever seems to work right. The winch grinders and tailers are on top of one another on every tack; hoisting or dropping sails always results in some kind of chaos; the helmsman is forever craning to see the luff of a sail or the instruments, or stretching to reach the traveler control line to ease the helm. The cruising counterpart is those boats on which picking up a mooring or dropping an anchor turns into a scene from a *Three Stooges* comedy as everyone scrambles from the cockpit to the mast to the foredeck in a melee of slatting sails, tangled lines, and frenzied shouting. From a distance it may seem funny, but on board the misunderstandings and shouting leave bruised souls and bad feelings at just the moment when everyone should be looking forward to the pleasures of a relaxing drink in the cockpit.

Whether on a racer or a cruiser, hapless deck layouts, gear, and rigging are a disaster. The crew that have been recruited for racing can laugh off snarls and confusions for only so long before they conclude that the boat is a "bummer" and drift off to other boats; after enough shouting, cruising companions will conclude that sailing really isn't the way to preserve friendships, or that a weekend in front of the TV will do more for family unity than another attempt at togetherness on the boat. On some cruising boats, sailing in conditions other than a beam reach in a steady 10-knot breeze is so complicated or unpleasant that the most common sail choice becomes the "iron genoa," usually with the excuse that the wind is too _____.*

FIXING WHAT AIN'T BROKE

It's not surprising that sailors who are shopping for a new boat pay more attention to the accommodations belowdecks than to layout and gear on the deck—even though it is on deck that they will spend most of their waking hours. At a boat show, the red carpet that leads below is often draped over some of the most important deck hardware. The salesman, his brochures laid out on the table next to a vase of flowers, eagerly shows you the hand-rubbed joinery, or the clever interior design that has somehow sandwiched six berths, an enclosed head, a galley, a semblance of a navigation station, and standing headroom into the cabin of a 26-foot boat. If you ask about the deck layout, the salesman points to the "first-rate hardware" and a list of features that all sound convincing, like

---

* Depending on the sailing area, the blank might be filled in with any of the following: *light, heavy, far forward, far aft, fluky, shifty, gusty, unsettled, frail.* Readers who have heard particularly inventive versions of the excuse are encouraged to submit them for inclusion in subsequent editions of this book.

the midboom traveler or the halyards led aft for "short-handed sailing" or "quick spinnaker hoists."

All too often the strengths and weaknesses of a deck layout aren't apparent until the boat is delivered and commissioned. And then it is with a rude shock that the owner discovers that the cockpit that seemed so spacious with a tiller at the boat show feels crowded with the pedestal steering option. It's not until the sails are bent on for "sea trials" that the skipper and crew discover that the genoa trimmer and the helmsman have to choreograph a *pas de deux* for every tack, or that the option of halyards led aft to the cockpit, which sounded so good in the broker's pitch, means that during a spinnaker hoist six members of a crew of seven are crowded into the front of the cockpit where there is scarcely space for two. It is not until the first shorthanded sail that the owner discovers that the midboom traveler option that was supposed to leave the cockpit "open for people" means that the mainsheet is so far forward that the helmsman cannot ease it to relieve a strong weather helm.

In time, as the problems are discovered, the owner and the regular crew develop compensating habits—tricks and jury-rigs—to get around the foul-ups in the rigging or layout. If the cockpit is too crowded during a spinnaker hoist, then control lines are pretrimmed or ignored, or spinnaker sets are delayed and done in exaggerated slow motion to minimize the problems. If the genoa trimmer is always eaxactly in the helmsman's line of vision, the genoa is trimmed less frequently, and less optimally.

If the mainsheet is difficult to ease, so that the boat threatens to round up with every puff, the problem is assigned elsewhere, usually by diagnosing the boat as having a chronic weather helm. The prescription? Install a wheel! Of course the wheel only masks the weather helm; the boat is still heeling too much, the rudder is still over, and the boat is still slow. And with a wheel in the middle of a cockpit that was designed for a tiller, the genoa sheet winches are positioned so that tacking the boat resembles the college stunt of stuffing students into a telephone booth. It might have been easier to change the mainsheet, but it's hard to believe that the designer and builder would have put an inadequate mainsheet rig on a $75,000 boat, especially if there was an obvious alternative that wouldn't cost much more. After all, they've built a lot of boats, haven't they?

They have indeed, and more often than not they have built them to meet marketing specifications, or what the builders, designers, and salesmen identify as the current "marketable" style. If most 35-footers offer a midboom traveler ("open cockpit") option, a boat that is going to compete in the marketplace in that size range will offer one too. If most 28-footers are offered with wheels (which let the salesmen make the pitch that "boats have tillers, yachts have wheels"), then a new boat in the same size and price range will have a wheel option, or even a standard wheel. And there are times when the marketing considerations can make mincemeat of a superb design. The naval architect may have drawn up a cockpit that works perfectly with a tiller, and that turns into a disaster of black-and-blue knees, tangled bodies, and spaghetti lines with a wheel.

Conventions too play a part in creating boats that are much less convenient or pleasurable to sail than they might be. It is a convention on wheel-steered boats to have a large compass mounted on the binnacle. Since most wheel-steered boats are steered from the leeward rail on the wind, the compass is almost useless to the helmsman, who must either crane his neck like a giraffe and then transpose the compass readings from a 45- or 90-degree lubber line, or ask someone else to watch the compass. On many club racers the upshot is that no one watches the compass on the windward legs, wind shifts are missed, the boat does poorly, and something like the genoa or the bottom paint or the foredeckman or "bad luck" gets the blame for the miserable performance.

Each foible of the rigging or layout—whether a backstay adjuster that cannot be reached without climbing over the helmsman or a genoa sheet winch that must be tailed and ground just so ("Only two turns, and never let the line go slack!") to avoid overrides—is addressed with rituals and procedures that in time seem absolutely natural to the boat owner. When that same owner happens to sail on a boat that is rigged simply, cleanly, and efficiently, the reaction can be sheer wonder: "You mean you don't have to set up the vang each time you sail off the wind? You can trim it on either jibe without climbing all over the boat? You can release it instantly, even with the boom under water? It doubles as a preventer?" That sense of wonder usually dissolves into something like "I'm not into that kind of sailing," or "Custom rigging is out of my league," or "If it ain't broke, don't fix it."

True, most inefficient and inconvenient rigging ain't broke. But if you sail for pleasure, there is little reason not to make sailing as pleasant as it can be. And no matter what kind of sailing you do, efficient and convenient deck layouts and rigging will make the sailing more fun. It doesn't take custom rigging or consultation with a naval architect. Most deck layouts and rigging designs can be improved without great expense, and most of the work that is required is simple enough to be done by the average boat owner with simple tools. If an owner has enough coordination to sail, he or she has enough coordination to do the work without scarring the pristine decks and spars of the boat.

AN IMAGINARY SAIL

One of the most valuable contributions you can make to your boat is to take a sail with a notepad or tape recorder in hand. You can do it with a boat in commission; sometimes it is almost as effective to do it in your imagination, aided perhaps by photographs or a sketch of the deck layout. What is important is to make this a typical sail, not the kind of sail you fantasize, the cruise you *might* take next year or the race you *might* enter, but the kind of sail that your boat most often does. If you usually go out for a day sail with family and friends who as often as not can't tell a dock line from a flattening reef tail, then imagine a day sail where you will do most of the string-pulling. If you usually race around the buoys or take long weekends with extended point-to-point sailing, do that. If you usually race with a few regulars and two or three pickup crew who may or may not have been on your boat before, make your observations with that crew in mind or on hand, remembering that it may be one of those newcomers who will be expected to set the preventer that even the regulars can never find, or to tail the genoa sheet that sometimes overrides when the lead comes from the #2 genoa on the inside track.

If you actually attempt this assessment during a race or a cruise, your crew or companions may decide to have you permanently committed to an institution for lunatic sailors. But there is nothing to keep you from observing, perhaps only a few maneuvers at a time, then going home to write notes to yourself that you can later assemble into a real assessment of the boat. What is important is to watch everything, even the simplest maneuver, from stowing gear when you first get aboard, to dropping dock lines or the mooring, to collecting gear and "putting the boat to bed" when you leave. Every boat has quirks—a special way that the tiller has to be tied up, a special place where the winch handles are stowed—and there may be nothing at all wrong with those quirks. But notice them and ask why it has to be done that way. In the course of your imaginary sail you may discover that there are easier, better, simpler, faster, more efficient, safer, or more aesthetic solutions. Or you may discover that you truly have the answer to a problem that has troubled many yachtsmen for a long time.

The Helm

The helm of almost any boat is comfortable on an easy reach, when the helmsman can stand behind the wheel or sit on the cockpit seat to hold the tiller. But try to catalog all the places you sit or stand when you're actually sailing. Picture where you are when the boat is sailing hard to windward. Or when you're trying to ghost along in light air. Where are you when you maneuver close to a dock under power?

If the boat is steered with a tiller, how do you keep yourself up on the rail or coaming when you're reaching hard or sailing to windward in a breeze? Are there foot braces? Do you loop an arm around the lifelines or the running backstay or a stanchion, or sit straddling a secondary winch? How comfortable are the lifelines? Does the front edge of the coaming dig into the bottom of your legs? Are there cleats or other gear that you have to carefully avoid? Do you ever need two hands for the tiller? How do you maintain your position on the rail when you have to give a mighty heave to forestall a broach?

Unless the wheel is very large, most wheel-steered boats are driven on the wind from the leeward rail, even in heavy air. Do you use your knee to hold the wheel when you have to push or pull the helm farther than your arm can reach? How do you brace yourself? Can you see other boats, the instruments, the masthead fly, the compass, and the headsail during a tack? How straight or bent is your back when you are driving? After a long stint at the helm, what do you rub first?

A Puff . . .

Imagine yourself sailing to windward in a moderate breeze. If you're racing, your crew is probably lined up on the windward rail; someone has perhaps suggested thinking about a sail change to the heavy #1. If you're cruising, imagine where everyone would usually be when the boat is heeling 20 degrees hard on the wind. Even as you're enjoying the breeze, someone may be suggesting that there is a little too much sail. A puff comes, the boat suddenly heels another 5 degrees, you feel a strong weather helm. You glance at the compass to see if the puff was a header . . .

Stop! Can you read the compass from your normal steering position? On most wheel-steered boats, a helmsman steering from leeward cannot see a pedestal-mounted compass without craning. If he can see, it is usually a lubber line that is 90 degrees off the course sailed. Do you mentally convert that figure into the course sailed? Or do you depend on another crew member to watch the compass? On tiller-steered boats, the compass or compasses are usually mounted on the cabin bulkhead, the side decks, the bridge deck, or the housetop. Is there a crew member in the way who has to be asked to move back so you can see the compass? Do lines dangling down from a housetop winch regularly obscure the compass? If a compass is easy to see, you will glance at it frequently; the check for a wind shift becomes an almost instinctive move. If not, you have lost a valuable instrument for sailing efficiently to windward.

The same is true of the other instruments. Most instruments are positioned for aesthetics and symmetry—a row of steam gauges across the bulkhead, on pods around the steering pedestal, or in a raised module over the companionway. Can you see the instruments in a quick glance from your normal steering position? Or are you forced to crane your neck, to ask someone else to glance at the knot meter, or to shout at someone in the companionway to get down so you can see the apparent wind indicator?

What happens on your boat when the sudden puff results in a strong weather helm? Do you ease the mainsheet? The traveler? Or do you feather until the puff passes because it is too inconvenient to ease the traveler or the mainsheet, or too difficult to trim back in after an ease?

When the puff subsides, can the mainsheet be retrimmed easily? Or does it take a mighty tug or perhaps a few temporary turns around a winch to get it back in? The mainsheet and traveler can be trimmed on any boat in a 10-knot breeze, but more and more boat owners are discovering that an unreefed mainsail and a small genoa are an effective combination in breezes from 15 to 25 knots. The traveler that rolled easily in 10 knots of breeze may require a kick, the steady pressure of a foot, or the efforts of two people to adjust it in 25 knots of breeze. If it is eased in a strong breeze, it may be almost impossible to bring it back to windward. And the mainsheet purchase that was adequate for 10 knots may require two hands or a temporary lead to a winch to trim in 25 knots of breeze.

Bearing Away . . .

What happens when you bear off to a broad reach? What does it take to get the boom properly vanged down? Can the vang be played readily—trimmed or eased—as the wind changes? What happens when you are reaching hard and need to dump the vang to keep the boat from broaching? If the vang is readily accessible and easy to operate, it makes sailing downwind more comfortable and safer. If the vang must be dug out of a locker and hooked up, or if someone must go foward or down to the rail to adjust the vang, it will not be used and you have lost a great deal of potential sailing comfort and efficiency.

What about a light-air run in a seaway with the boom bouncing around? Is a preventer permanently rigged or do you have to jury-rig a line from the boom to a block on the rail? When you jibe or come back on the wind, is there a course trim for the mainsheet that brings it in quickly, or do you have to contend with a massive tangle of spaghetti? What happens to the vang—does it have to be moved during a jibe?

Ready About . . .

A tack can be nothing more than throwing the helm down and letting self-tacking sails take care of themselves. Or it can involve grinders, tailers, a cast-off man, someone to adjust the position of the genoa lead blocks, one or two crewmen on the foredeck to get the genoa around the mast, along with crewmen tacking the traveler, easing off and retrimming the main, easing and retrimming the backstay, cunningham, jib halyard or jib cunningham, outhaul, and runners. Whether it is simple or complex, everyone has to start on one side of the boat and end up on the other—which on most boats is not a simple maneuver.

Try to picture your own boat during a tack. Where does whoever releases the old jib sheet stand? Does he or she have to follow the sheet as it runs out to prevent a hockle in a turning block? Where does the tailer stand? Who grinds the winch? Is there room for everyone, or is there constant juggling for position? Who watches the leech of the sail as it comes in toward the spreader tip? Who adjusts the traveler and/or mainsheet? Does anyone have to duck for the boom?

Would the boat be faster coming out of a tack if you could ease the backstay? Would it be easier to tack the genoa if you could ease the babystay? Would the boat respond well to a "powering up" of the sails by adjusting the leads, the halyards, or other controls?

On family-sailed boats, the tacking ritual usually involves the helmsman as tailer or to cast off the old jib sheet. Is it possible to do whatever is required while still steering the boat? Or does the helmsman have to resort to feet, knees, or other tricks to keep the boat on course while he or she reaches

forward to release or tail a sheet? Who grinds in the genoa on the boat? What kind of position can he or she assume over the winch? Is the grind a struggle in a breeze?

What happens when it is time to fine-tune a headsail, to ease the genoa a few inches or to tweak it in? How easy is it for someone to grind in an inch or two while keeping eyes on the spreader or the knot meter? On some boats the winches are so underpowered that it takes two people, a grinder and a tailer, to fine-tune a sail. On others the only comfortable trimming position requires a second person to watch the spreader tip or the knot meter while the sail is tweaked. Sometimes the genoa trimmer is directly in the line of vision of the helmsman, blocking his view of the jib luff and the oncoming seas.

Jibe Ho . . .

Especially with a spinnaker up, or with enough breeze to slam the mainsail over, jibes seem to cause more problems on boats than almost any other maneuver. The usual problem is overcrowding, or blocked views. The trimmer on the spinnaker sheet can't see the luff of the sail; the helmsman can't see exactly when the foredeck man has the new guy in the pole end; or the cockpit is so crowded with lines that the cockpit crew feel as if they are trying to escape from a bowl of Fettucine Alfredo.

On some boats, spinnaker jibes never seem to work. It may be a different screwup each time, but there is always something that goes wrong, and the foredeck man or some hapless guest who was given the task of tending the foreguy and topping lift is blamed afterward in a chorus of sarcasm or shouting. Some of those boats might indeed have a foredeck man who can't tell left from right, but just as often the boat is rigged so that only a crew of four-armed experts could jibe the boat without some kind of disaster. The lines may be so concentrated that there isn't room to do what needs to be done; the spinnaker pole may be so difficult to use that no one could ever jibe the spinnaker smoothly; or the mainsheet and vang may be so awkwardly rigged that just centering the boom is a bear of a job. Some boats have winches placed so awkwardly in the cockpit that sheets and guys have to be swapped from the primary to the secondary and back during or after a jibe. If the boat is set up for sailing by a steady, experienced crew that is adept at swapping lines and winches, this may be no problem. But for family sailing or club racing with pickup crews, adding the rituals of winch swapping to the other tasks of a spinnaker hoist or jibe is an invitation to disaster.

Reefing . . .

Most boats today are rigged for what is optimistically called "jiffy" reefing. Theoretically it is a simple maneuver: ease the sheet, lower the halyard, hook on the luff cringle, retension the halyard, pull on the leech reefing line, cleat it off, retrim the mainsheet! That's all it takes, right?

Can your normal crew put in a reef and have the boat back in trim in less than thirty seconds? Really? If you haven't actually timed the sequence, from the monent someone says "We better throw in a reef" to the moment when the reefed mainsail is sheeted in hard, then try it with a stopwatch and no practice sessions. Try listing the exact steps that take place. Are the reef lines left rigged or do they have to be rigged each time? If they are not left rigged, are there messengers on the sails, or do you have to either plan for a reef when the sail is hoisted or climb out on the boom to reeve the leech reefing line? Where is the halyard winch and how many hands does it take to ease the halyard and then to grind it back up again? How easy is it to pull the luff of the sail down? Are there handgrips on the luff? How easy is it to hook the luff cringle on the hook, or to rig a downhaul for the cringle? How easy is it to pull on the leech line? Does it need a winch, and if so is the lead easy and convenient? Is there a self-tailing winch? Is the winch powerful enough for one person to tail and grind the line? How is it locked off? Is the gear clean and unobtrusive when it is not in use, or are there lines hanging off the boom? Does the sail jump out of the track on the mast? Do the jacklines get tangled? How easy is it to shake a reef?

Most boats have the rudiments of reefing gear, but too often the gear is sited as something of an afterthought, with lock-offs, winches, or other gear placed so that it requires far more hands to reef than the simple list of steps would suggest. Even if you sail in an area where reefing is infrequent, or you have a boat with a very adjustable and responsive mainsail that can be flattened so that reefing is rarely required, if you cannot reef in thirty seconds with your normal sailing crew—whether a husband and wife or yourself and a non-sailing guest or seven regular racing heavies—you owe it to yourself to think through the rigging gear and make the changes that will convert reefing to a simple process.

Setting Sails

What about hoisting, changing, or dropping a sail? Watch an anchorage in the morning, or watch a race course just before the start, and you can see a showcase of struggles: reel winches loaded with wire that have to be ground up with the greatest of care lest the handle suddenly go flying; mast-mounted winches that require an exhausting vertical turning motion; halyards that lead from a deck-level exit box directly to a winch without an exposed vertical section of halyard that allows a good "jump" on the sail. There are 30-foot boats on which each sail has to be laboriously ground up, a foot at a time. And there are boats with the halyards led so awkwardly that an adjustment to the halyard tension is a major operation, so much so that when the jib is underhoisted, hanging off the headstay in scallops, it is ignored. There are boats laid out so that lowering the sails with a cruising crew seems to require more arms than are aboard; you see them—or hear them, a chorus of flapping sails and shouting—in the afternoon, when a sea breeze has suddenly built up. No wonder one sees so many boats motoring instead!

Watch the operation of sail hoisting and lowering on your boat. Can a person stand at the mast and "jump" the sail up, pulling full-arm lengths of halyard with each jump? Any other way of hoisting a sail on a boat over 30 feet is slow. Can another person tail the halyard easily, so that it doesn't have to be untangled in the midst of each hoist? Can the jib halyards be adjusted easily while you are sailing? Do the halyards slip or slacken while you are sailing? If you often sail short-handed, can you and your regular crew lower the sails without resorting to lashing the tiller or locking the wheel?

Is there any dangerous equipment involved in the halyard rig, such as reel winches or winches mounted on the mast? Reel winches seem to have been designed for accidents. You can be careful and cautious, never getting oil on the brake, making sure that there is never a handle in the winch when the sail is being lowered, and still, sooner or later a flyaway handle will catch someone in the jaw or the eye. And while the handle on a mast-mounted drum winch doesn't rotate if the line is eased, the cranking position is awkward; if a non-locking handle is used, or if the locking mechanism of the winch handle fails, the handle will sometimes fly loose while someone is grinding. The mast winch setup is simple and inexpensive for the builder, and it does keep the deck clear, but it is dangerous as well as inefficient. Fortunately, rerouting halyards is among the easiest modifications that can be made to a rig.

Control Lines

The most confirmed of laid-back, elbow-in-the-water, leeward-rail cruisers will still have sail shape controls on his boat. The cunningham, flattener, backstay, babystay, running backstays, jib cunningham, and genoa car controls of the racer may be left off, but it is rare that a boat will also omit an outhaul, a vang, and some provision for adjusting the lead positions of the headsail. And on club racers and performance-oriented cruising boats—any boat that does not let pass easily the challenge of another similarly sized boat sailing nearby—it is common to have at least a cunningham to adjust mainsail luff tension, an adjustable backstay, a cringle for a flattening reef in the mainsail, and perhaps a babystay or other mast-bend controls.

If the control lines on a boat are easy to use, they will be adjusted frequently; if not, the control probably shouldn't have been installed in the first place. Some sailors really don't care if the draft is too far aft in their mainsails; they don't need a cunningham. Far more sailors may pretend that they don't care, but watch them when a boat of similar size begins to sail by. Watch the tweaking of the mainsheet and the genoa sheet and the outhaul! If there were a functional cunningham, it would be tweaked too. The fact is that they do care, and would have the draft adjusted properly if it weren't so complicated to rig a cunningham and go up to the mast and pull the under-powered tackle, and then go aft to see the effect of the adjustment, only to realize that it was pulled too hard and now needs to be eased. They would ease the outhaul when the boat was off the wind if it didn't take two people, pulling with everything they have, to get the outhaul back out again. They would rig the flattener and use it as the sailmaker recommends, as a flexible extension of the outhaul, if it were simple to adjust the flattener instead of being a maneuver as complicated as a full-scale reef.

Go down the list of controls on your boat. How long does it take to adjust the outhaul, cunningham, or backstay? Can the person adjusting any of those controls see the sail that is most affected by the change in mast bend or luff or foot tension? Can the controls be "dumped" quickly and easily when you round a mark or bear away? Can the controls be adjusted easily from normal sailing positions? On a heavy-displacement 40-foot boat, normal sailing positions might have crew members anywhere on the boat; on a light-displacement 30-foot boat, where a single crew member going forward from the rail is going to affect the trim of the boat, the controls should lead aft and many might even be double-ended so that they can be adjusted from either rail.

Watch ordinary sailing maneuvers on your boat long

enough and carefully enough and you will probably discover weaknesses and mix-ups, jury-rigged or half-baked systems that you and your crew have grown to accept as normal or inevitable. Then just imagine what it would be like to sail with sail controls that are easy to use, with a vang that can be adjusted with one hand, a mainsheet that can be eased and trimmed easily in response to any change in wind, a backstay adjuster that can be played with puffs and lulls, halyard or reefing systems so clean and smooth that there is no hesitation about reefing or changing sails.

Identifying systems and controls that aren't all they could be is the hard part. Once you realize that a mainsheet system is giving you a case of advanced bursitis, or that the placement of the cockpit winches is contributing to the breakup of your crew or your marriage, the next step—changing deck layouts, mainsail, genoa, and spinnaker controls, and the configuration of the spars—is often a relatively simple project that a boat owner can do himself. And even if you decide to have the work done by a rigger or a yard, by knowing exactly what you want the improved system to do, you can avoid the problems that sometimes arise when you tell a rigger to "put in a new vang that will work better than this one" or ask a chandler or a discount dealer for "a cunningham for a 33-foot boat."

4

SELECTING
GEAR

How do you choose the right block, the right winch, or the right kind of fastener to mount a new fitting on your boat? At a chandlery, there are rows of blocks on the wall, from bullet blocks to 6-inch sheaves, from wooden-cheeked beauties to the latest hi-tech creations of aluminum, titanium, and precipitation-hardened stainless steel. You can spin blocks and listen to the ball or roller bearings, you can heft them and try to imagine their strength, you can remember the decks of other boats and the blocks that seemed to work just fine there, you can read through manufacturers' catalogs and see listings of strength ratings and recommendations—and still not be sure whether any of those blocks is the right one for the new vang on your boat.

If you shop at one of the marine discounters, the prices are usually inviting, but advice on the appropriate size or style for blocks, winches, line, or any other items is either not forthcoming or is to be taken with a grain of salt. The sales staff at most of the discounters, whether they are dealing over the phone or over the counter, usually derive their information and recommendations from manufacturers' catalogs. Ask "Is this block big enough for my boat?" and you are likely to get one of two responses—either a withering glare that tells you to step aside for the next customer, who knows what he wants, or a quick glance at a catalog and the pronouncement, "Rated at 4500 pounds . . . ought to be strong enough, right?" Forty-five hundred pounds sounds strong, but unless you know what the number is measuring, what the actual loads on your boat are, and whether the size, design, construction, and appearance, as well as the strength, of the block are appropriate to your boat, the selection is guesswork.

The alternative is to shop at a riggers' shop or a chandlery, where there may be a rigger who can make sound recommendations based on experience. He or she may have seen a block of a certain series fail or distort on a boat close to yours in size, or know that the swivel blocks in one series are substantially weaker than the other blocks in the same series. If the chandler or rigger is experienced and knowledgeable, his time and recommendations may very well be worth the high prices that most chandleries and boatyards charge for gear. And if you are going to rely on the advice, it is only right to pay the premium price. I know one hot-tempered rigger who came close to murdering a boat owner who came by with a catalog from a marine discounter to ask the rigger what size winches to order from the discounter. If they had asked me to testify, I would have called it justifiable homicide.

If you're shopping by mail, you can try to check the ratings of blocks and other gear in manufacturers' catalogs, where you will probably find recommendations for every size of boat. But if you try to compare strength ratings, or gear ratios, or any of the other numbers that are listed in the catalogs, to determine whether there is a reason to choose a Barient 28 or a Lewmar 48, a Harken 2.25 inch or a Schaefer series 5, you are left with a befuddling array of confusing numbers. Strength ratings come in more flavors than Baskin-Robbins ice cream: breaking strength, safe working load, ultimate tensile strength, maximum recommended working load, distortion load, 2 percent friction load, and a few designations that seem to have been only loosely translated from the Japanese or Swedish. The ratings themselves are sometimes in pounds, sometimes in kilograms.

Even experienced riggers are often guilty of taking shortcuts to sizing gear for a boat. If you order a backstay adjuster from a rigger, he might make some quick calculations based on displacement, rig dimensions, and righting moment to determine the actual working loads on your boat. More likely, the rigger will check the clevis pin size on your backstay and fit a backstay adjuster that matches the pin size. You look at the unit and wonder, perhaps out loud, "Do I really need one that big?" The answer: "The builder must have known what he was doing when he put that backstay on, right?"

Maybe. Chances are that somewhere in the design process a naval architect or spar designer sized the sections and rigging to the calculated load on the spars.* Then, depending upon the boat market or the availability of materials, all sorts of events could have changed that original recommendation. A marketing decision could have chosen "oversized" rigging as a selling point; a supplier could have offered an irresistible deal on 3/8-inch 1 x 19 cable, even suggesting himself that the slight extra cost could be more than recouped with an "overbuilt for offshore sailing" advertising campaign. Whatever the reasons, boats do not always start out with the right size rigging. And blindly using clevis pin sizes or other stock equipment to size subsequent rigging can lead to extra expense, extra weight, and cumbersome gear.

Some catalogs simplify their recommendations by describing a certain series of blocks as "suitable for boats up to 30 feet," which is roughly analogous to going into a clothing store and sizing the clothes by announcing that you are forty-five

* There is no black art of spar design. *Skene's Elements of Yacht Design* shows you how to calculate the shroud and panel loads for a mast, and while many of the examples in the book are based on square spruce spinnaker poles and manilla rope, the formulas—with a few corrections for contemporary materials and the stresses induced by mast-bending, high-speed sailing and modern low-stretch sail materials—are still valid.

years old! A forty-five-year-old man can be 7 feet tall or 5 feet tall, can weigh 100 pounds or 300 pounds. A 35-foot boat can have a huge main or a tiny main, can be heavy displacement or an ultra-light, can be stiff enough to carry a #1 genoa with 25 knots of air across the deck, or can be so tender that the #3 genoa and two reefs in the main is the only way to keep the boat standing up in 20 knots of air. Using the same blocks for both boats is as foolish as trying to fit the 5-foot man and the 7-foot man with the same suit jacket.

What then is a boat owner to do?

The surest way to size hardware is to calculate the actual loads on sheets, halyards, and other rigging and then to base the selection of hardware on the loads and an approximate safety factor. Many naval architects and hardware companies use sophisticated computer analysis programs to approximate the loads on various fittings. As an alternative, most of the hardware on a boat can be safely sized from two numbers which an owner can easily calculate from the sail dimensions of the boat: MaxGenoa, which approximates the maximum anticipated genoa clew load; and MaxMain, which approximates the maximum anticipated mainsheet load.*

MAXGENOA

A precise calculation of the maximum anticipated genoa loads on a boat requires measurement or calculation of the righting moment of the boat, the size and aspect ratio of the

---

* Don't look for MaxMain or MaxGenoa in handbooks of naval architecture or stress engineering. The terms were invented for this book, and the basic formulas for computing sail loads were reworked to come up with useful figures from the limited data available on a PHRF certificate or a builder's brochure.

foretriangle, and the anticipated wind strengths for various sails. A simplified formula which approximates the genoa clew load of a sail is:

$$\text{Clew Load} = \text{WS}^2 \times \text{SA} \times .00431$$

WS is wind speed in knots and SA is the area of the genoa in square feet.

What you need in order to select hardware is the *maximum* anticipated clew load (MaxGenoa), including an appropriate safety factor. Although it will have to be adjusted for extremely light, heavy, stiff, or tender boats, or boats with extremely high- or low-aspect ratios in the foretriangle, MaxGenoa can be approximated safely for most boats by a simple formula, where I is the height of the foretriangle in feet:

$$\text{MaxGenoa} = \text{I}^2$$

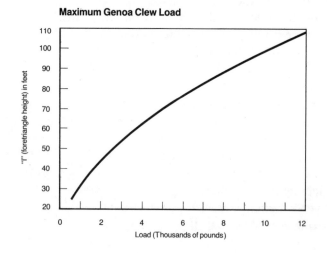

Maximum Genoa Clew Load

MaxGenoa is the safe maximum working load for the genoa clew in pounds. Thus for a boat with an *I* dimension of 40 feet, MaxGenoa is approximately 1600 pounds.

MaxGenoa, used with appropriate multipliers, is a good working figure for estimating sheet winch loads and for selecting genoa lead blocks, foot blocks, spinnaker sheet and guy blocks, backstay adjusters for masthead-rigged boats, and auxiliary spinnaker gear, such as foreguys, topping lifts, and sheet and guy shackles. For example, the safe working load for a genoa turning block on the boat above would be approximately 3200 pounds. because the 180-degree line-direction change of the genoa sheet through the turning block doubles the load on the block.

MAXMAIN

MaxMain cannot be derived as easily as MaxGenoa, because mainsheet loads are determined by sail area, the stiffness of the boat, the wind velocity, and the aspect ratio of the sail. For boats that are not extremely stiff or tender, the following formula will approximate a maximum anticipated mainsheet load, including a safety factor:

$$\text{MaxMain} = \frac{\text{E} \times \text{P}^2 \times 3.87}{\sqrt{\text{E}^2 + \text{P}^2}}$$

E is the mainsail foot length in feet, P is the mainsail hoist in feet, and MaxMain is the maximum anticipated mainsheet load in pounds, including a safety factor. Although the formula is tedious to calculate, it need be done only once, and the figure can then be used to select blocks, hardware, and lines for mainsheet, travelers, reefing gear, vang, cun-

Maximum (end-boom) Mainsheet Load

Mainsail foot	Maximum mainsheet load (pounds)	Mainsail hoist
—		
— 6	500	20 —
8	1000	30 —
— 10	1500	
12	2000	40 —
— 14	2500	
16	3000	50 —
— 18	3500	
	4000	
20		60 —
— 22	5000	
24	6000	70 —
— 26	7000	
28	8000	80 —
— 30		
		90 —

Use straightedge from mainsail foot to mainsail hoist to find maximum mainsheet load.

ningham, and flattener gear, and to select backstay adjuster hardware for a fractional rig.

SELECTING BLOCKS

Even if you know exactly how strong a block needs to be, the listings of block strength provided by manufacturers in their catalogs are usually more confusing than enlightening—

not because the manufacturers are trying to confuse the public, but because for reasons known only to themselves they have chosen different standards to rate their blocks. Schaefer rates their blocks by SWL, safe working load, theoretically the load at which the block will function safely and effectively. Nicro/Fico and Lewmar rate most of their blocks by breaking strength or distortion load, the loads at which the block fails. Merriman rates some hardware by breaking strength and some by safe working load, which they generally define as 40 percent of breaking strength. Harken gives both breaking strength and recommended maximum working loads for their smaller blocks; for their larger blocks they give maximum recommended working loads in terms of the point when friction exceeds a specified percentage of load. This is perhaps the most useful of the catalog ratings. In general, the recommendations in this book are based on maximum recommended working load, which corresponds roughly to safe working load, or approximately one half of breaking strength.

Even more confusing is the way blocks of similar size but varied configuration end up with the same rating in certain catalogs. It is a convenient scheme, but it often leads to misratings of blocks. The common feature of the blocks in a given series is generally the sheave, which is rarely the weak point. The usual breaking point of a block is in the swivel, or a failure in the shackle that hangs the block. A cheek block, which has no swivel, and which mounts the sheave and cheek to a strong plate, is usually much stronger than the block that ties the entire load to a swivel pin. A multi-sheave block which uses the same swivel and shackle as a single block is going to be no stronger than a single block, even though the load is distributed over two, three, or even four sheaves.

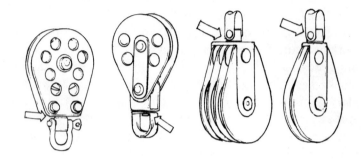

Even if the manufacturers had a common rating scheme, the actual loading of blocks on a boat is difficult to duplicate on a testing machine. A machine can tension a block to destruction and record the tension at the breaking point, but it is difficult to duplicate the usual causes of failure on a boat: shock loading and misuse. A shackle will break when it is led at an inappropriate angle. A sheave will seize because of inadequate cleaning or lubrication, crushing bearings, or breaking the sheave. A snatch block left half open will be bent into a pretzel. A block that "looked strong enough" will be destroyed by the tremendous shock loads as a hard-sailed boat falls off a wave, pumping the mast and filling and collapsing sails. Even a block that is strong enough for a particular use may be inappropriate in size, or may demand a maintenance schedule that a boat owner cannot or will not supply. A strongly built block with a small sheave may not break if used as a turning block, but the small radius will weaken line and create unnecessary friction. Racing boats with a full-time "BN" who will wash and lubricate blocks every week can use blocks that might be risky on a boat that realistically gets an occasional wash-down and a squirt of WD-40 when blocks begin to squeak.

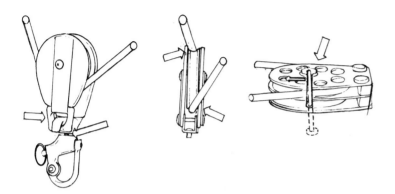

How then do you choose the right blocks for a boat? One naval architect has said that he only recommends blocks which in rated strength exceed twice the breaking strength of the largest line or wire used with the block. It seems like an easy formula, but since lines sizes are normally chosen for handling comfort rather than strength, it will often result in blocks that are much larger or heavier than they need to be.

It isn't difficult to select blocks or other hardware if you can estimate the working load on the line or lines leading to the block, and then allow for the percentage of a purchase that is borne by a given block. For example, in a compound purchase, such as the vang tackle shown on page 110, block A carries the full load of the vang. Blocks B and C and the snap shackle at the end of the wire tail carry only half of the vang

load, which is effectively split by block A. In a simple 4:1 purchase with a fiddle block on each end, the load on any part of the purchase is only one fourth of the total load, but the mounting shackle for each block carries the entire load, and the blocks should be selected for that load. If instead of a fiddle block, separately mounted single blocks are used at one end of the tackle, the mounting for each of the single blocks carries only half the load of the tackle.

In some instances, you need to allow for the angle at which a line enters and leaves a block.

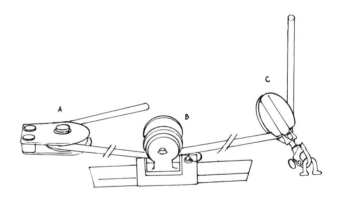

The load on the line leading from block A to the winch and on the line leading from block C to the clew of the sail, is the same; the three blocks only change the direction of the pull. The load on the mountings of block A is close to twice the load on the end of the genoa sheet; the load on block C, which turns a 90-degree angle, is 1.35 times the load on the line; the load on block B, which hardly changes the direction of the pull, is a fraction of the load on the line. In addition, any unfairness in the leads to or from a block greatly increases the loading on shackles and other block mountings. If a slightly unfair lead cannot be avoided, make certain that the block or other hardware is oversized.

Finally, blocks used with wire and hardware subjected to extreme shock loading, such as runners, babystays, blocks for low-stretch spinnaker sheets and guys, and blocks used for wire purchases in a backstay or vang, may require larger margins of safety. The ratings for blocks are based on the expectation that the sheave will turn freely. If it does not, as would be the case with a wire purchase around a sheave that is too small, the loads on the block increase dramatically.

For any use, large sheaves lower friction and reduce wear on the running rigging; for Kevlar lines or wire, large sheaves are essential. Sheave materials range from nylon, Delrin, and phenolic in the lighter blocks to machined aluminum, bronze, or stainless steel in heavier blocks and blocks intended for use with wire. There are different sheave shapes for different lines and wires, and mixing them usually leads to excessive wear on the running rigging. Wire should be used with a grooved or V-shaped sheave; Kevlar should be used on a flattened sheave, or at least a sheave with a generous radius.

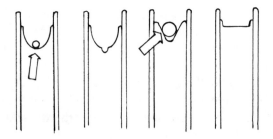

Wherever possible, sheave sizes should be matched to the potential friction loading of the angle turned. If you are using a snatch block for a spinnaker sheet that makes a 180-degree turn, a large-sheave snatch block would be a better choice than one of the small-sheave blocks. For a genoa lead block that turns the line no more than 30 degrees, a small-diameter sheave is not a problem, and may have the advantage of providing a low lead point.

Maintenance is also a consideration in the selection of blocks. Some blocks are designed for low maintenance. Many ball-bearing blocks require no more than a hose-down to clean out excessive salt or dirt from the bearing races. Other blocks are designed with close-tolerance bearings that are supposed to grind any intruding dirt to harmless size. But for any block, regular maintenance with a hose and with appropriate lubricants will prolong the life of the block and extend the effective working load. If you know that a block will be neglected—because it is high in the rigging and you aren't about to go up there with a can of WD-40, or just because hosing down and lubricating blocks isn't your style—it may be wise to select an oversized block or a block style that can tolerate neglect and abuse.

Custom Blocks

Sometimes you will have an idea for a clever bit of rigging and none of the blocks in a chandlery or a manufacturer's catalog will fit what you need. Fortunately, the marine industry is made up of mostly small companies, often staffed by sailors who understand an explanation and are willing to help. If you call one of the block manufacturers, you can usually find someone who can suggest an alternative solution or who will offer to adapt a block from stock, or even a block that you already own, for your special purpose. Several of the rigging ideas in this book work best with special blocks, and I have found that most manufacturers have been willing to make up or modify blocks at very modest charges.

WINCHES

The trick in selecting winches is to balance the competing needs for speed and power. It is easy to make a winch powerful: make the drum small and the handle long, or put a high gear ratio in the drive train between the handle and the drum, and it is possible to reach theoretical power ratios of 40:1, 60:1, or even 80:1. The trade-off, of course, is that a full turn of a 10-inch handle on a winch with a power ratio of 40:1 pulls in only 1.57 inches of line.*

Power versus Speed

The trend among winch manufacturers has been to ever higher power ratios, but the theoretical power ratios listed in the manufacturers' catalogs do not take into account the efficiency of the winch. Depending upon the kind of bearings used in the drive train, the effectiveness of the lubrication used, and the slippage of the line on the drum, the actual efficiency of a winch will vary from as low as 50 percent to as high as 85 percent. In theory, a winch with a 40:1 power ratio will produce 2000 pounds of output (pull) if 50 pounds of input

are applied to the handle; if the mechanical efficiency of the winch is 50 percent, it will yield only 1000 pounds of output with an input of 50 pounds.

Winches with roller, needle, or ball bearings throughout the drive train come out at the high end of efficiency. Winches with minimal bearings, and especially winches which are serviced infrequently, come out at the low end. The advantage of a winch with high efficiency is that it can provide the same power as a less efficient winch with a substantial gain in speed.† For a halyard or a control line, the speed may not be important, but for sheet winches that are used to grind in the genoa, speed is the difference between spinning the boat around the way you want and agonizingly slow tacks.

The usual assumption is that the larger the boat, the higher the power ratios needed, but a close examination of two winches may hold some surprises. Winches A and B both have 4-inch drums. Winch A has higher gear ratios and thus higher power ratios:

		high gear	low gear
Winch A			
	gear ratio	3.4:1	9.5:1
	power ratio	17:1	48:1
	line pulled/turn	3.7 in.	1.3 in.
Winch B			
	gear ratio	2.5:1	7.4:1
	power ratio	12.8:1	37.7:1
	line pulled/turn	5.0 in.	1.7 in.

---

* Power Ratio = Gear Ratio × Handle Length / Drum Radius. The tables published by the winch manufacturers are usually based on 10-inch handles, which yield the highest power ratios, 25 percent higher than an 8-inch handle. The shorter handle, of course, can be turned faster, and with an acceptable power ratio will make for fast grinding. In some cases an overpowered winch with a short handle is a good idea—for example, when the winch must be mounted close to lifelines or to another winch.

† The line pulled in with each turn of the winch handle = π × drum diameter / gear ratio. The higher the gear ratio, the less line pulled by each turn of the handle. If the winch is more efficient, the same output power can be achieved with a lower power ratio (bigger drum or lower gear ratio), which means that each turn of the winch handle will pull in more line.

If the handles of the winches are cranked at the same speed, winch B, with the lower gear and power ratios, is faster by approximately 30 percent; that is, 30 percent more line is pulled in with each turn of the handle.

The speed at which the handle can be cranked, of course, depends on the handle load, which in turn depends upon the output needed from the winch. If the maximum clew load on the genoa is 1300 pounds, and if winch A in our comparison has an efficiency of 60 percent and winch B has an efficiency of 85 percent, the loads on the handles would be as follows:

		Handle Load (pounds)	
		high gear	low gear
Winch A	(60% efficiency)	127.5	45.1
Winch B	(85% efficiency)	119.5	40.6

The figures are close. And since 50 pounds is the load that a fairly efficient grinder can put on a winch handle, both winches are powerful enough to grind in the sail. Both winches will probably be turned at roughly the same speed in each gear; if anything, winch B will be turned slightly faster, because the handle loads are less. Even if they are turned at the same speed, winch B, with its lower power ratios and higher efficiency, will pull in almost 30 percent more line with each turn of the handle than winch A. In short, the boat equipped with winch B for its primary winches will be able to tack faster.

Efficiency

Manufacturers generally don't publish efficiency ratios for their winches, but a careful inspection of the guts of a winch can tell you a lot. High-efficiency winches have bearings—needle, roller, or ball bearings—on all rotating parts, not only the bearing cage on the drum but also roller or ball bearings on the gear shafts. The high-efficiency winch may also be heavier, because of the weight of bearings and metal bearing races, and perhaps more difficult to service, since there are that many more crevices and bearings that have to be cleaned out and relubricated. But efficiency will explain why a Barient 28, with a top power ratio of 37.7:1, is suitable as a genoa sheet winch on a larger boat than a Barient 27, which has a top power ratio of 45.7:1.

Size

A winch with a drum diameter of 2.5 inches, even if it were strong enough, powerful enough, and efficient enough to grind in the genoa in our example above, would not be a good genoa sheet winch for a boat that size. With a sail of 340 square feet (or over 500 square feet in the case of the #1 genoas) and genoa loads of 1300 pounds, the boat will probably use genoa sheets of at least 7/16-inch line, and probably 1/2-inch or even 9/16-inch. To prevent slippage of a 1/2 inch line would require five or more turns around a 2.5-inch drum, which would make for inefficient tailing and a good chance for an override on every tack. A boat that size needs a drum of at least 3.5 inches, and perhaps larger, to allow speedy tailing with minimal turns on the winch.

How big should a winch be? The obvious answer is that it should be big enough and fast enough to do its job efficiently. If it is a struggle for your normal crew to grind in the last few inches of genoa sheet, the winches aren't powerful enough. If the luff tension of the genoa cannot be adjusted readily, the halyard winches aren't powerful enough. In some cases the winch may be powerful enough but geared wrong, so that it is too slow in one gear and not powerful enough in another. The problem is most critical with genoa sheet winches, which can be excruciatingly slow if too much of the grinding requires the highest and slowest gear ratios; or with secondaries, which are often less expensive winches with a great spread in gear ratios between the gears: the fast speed is not powerful enough to trim the spinnaker except in very light air, and the powerful speed is so slow that it is impossible to trim fast enough to avoid a collapse. A winch with a big spread of gear ratios may be fine for a halyard, since there is little premium on speed of the final adjustment, but for work with sheets, a more efficient winch with closer gear ratios will be better.

For large winches, one solution is three speeds, with a direct-drive speed that is used at the beginning of a tack or perhaps in light air for the spinnaker sheets, then a middle gear and finally a very low gear. A three-speed winch that can be left in gears 1 and 2 instead of automatically shifting up to gears 2 and 3 may be more useful for spinnaker sheet work, especially in light air.

Selecting Winches

In general, the way to select a winch is not by the overall length of the boat and not from tables that offer a choice between "cruising" and "racing" winches. The critical factor for the power and size of sheet winches is the maximum genoa clew load (MaxGenoa).

A grand prix racer with a shallow cockpit and inboard winches that allow a grinder to get his arms over the winch might opt for the faster winches in any given range; a boat that has the winches outboard on the coamings, where the

PRIMARY WINCHES	
MaxGenoa (pounds)	Drum Diameter (inches)
under 800	2.5–2.75
800–1000	2.75–3.0
1000–1500	3.0–3.5
1500–2000	3.5–4.0
2000—2500	4.0–4.5
2500–3500	4.5–5.5
3500 +	5.5 + (and grinders)

full circle of grinding is inefficient and cumbersome, might need the more powerful (and slower) gearing offered by other winches within the range.

For secondary winches, drums one size smaller or the same size would be appropriate. It is sometimes wise to select similar-size drums but slightly different gearing in primary and secondary winches, or two-speed self-tailers for secondaries (especially if they are also used as runner winches) with three-speed primaries.

Halyard winches can generally be selected on the basis of the maximum hoist of the sail.

HALYARD WINCHES	
I or P dimension (feet)	Drum Diameter (inches)
under 28	2.0–2.5
28–32	2.5–2.75
33–37	2.5–3.0
38–45	2.75–3.250
46–50	3.0–3.5
51–57	3.25–4.0
58 +	4.0 +

In general, except for very large boats which require that the headsails and mainsail be cranked all the way up, the gear ratios in halyard winches are not critical, as long as the highest power ratio is adequate to adjust the luff tension of the sail. It is usually not necessary to be able to tension the genoa luff when the boat is hard on the wind in a breeze, when the loading sufficient to overcome the friction of the luff groove may be enough to rip the head off the sail. Unless you prefer to replace your sails after each race, it may be better to luff up for an instant or adjust the luff tension during a tack.

Self-Tailers

Self-tailing winches are popular now for almost every purpose on a boat. The various manufacturers have all produced self-tailers, and each has taken a different tack in developing a self-tailing mechanism. Barient uses spring-loaded jaws that adjust automatically to a wide range of line sizes, but which are hard on lines, especially on heavily loaded lines. Lewmar's self-tailing mechanism relies on jaws somewhat like a clam cleat. The mechanism is easier on the line than Barient's, but must be adjusted internally to a specific range of lines and will not automatically handle the wide range of lines that a Barient mechanism can accommodate.

Where should you use self-tailers? On a halyard or an afterguy, a self-tailing winch lets one person grind a sail up or a pole aft when it might have taken two people before. Self-tailing winches can make reefing or other control lines easy one-man jobs instead of tough two-man jobs. On a cruising boat, a self-tailing genoa sheet winch may let one person finish grinding in the genoa after a tack instead of having the helmsman lean over to lend a hand. Trimming a genoa, tweaking in an inch or two because the breeze has picked up or because the sheet has stretched, hoisting a spinnaker that fills before it is fully hoisted, or grinding out an override—all this can usually be done by one person on a self-tailing winch.

For some jobs, a self-tailer is less efficient or more cumbersome than a regular drum winch. Stripping the line off the winch during a tack is slower and less certain on a self-tailing winch, because the line sometimes catches on the self-tailer feeder; and it takes longer to switch from grinding in to easing out on a self-tailer, because the line has to be disengaged from the self-tailing mechanism before it can be eased. Thus many racing boats will use self-tailers for the secondary winches (especially if they are used with runners or barber haulers) but stick with regular drums on the primaries for speed in tacking; the same-size boat used for cruising might want self-tacking primaries to reduce the need for crew and might economize on the secondaries because they are used less.

There are self-tailing attachments, like the Lewmar clips for smaller winches and the Wincher for different sizes of winch up to 4-inch drums, but these gadgets, if somewhat helpful, are no substitute for a real self-tailing winch.

Materials and Construction

Finally, the materials used in the contruction of a winch can affect the efficiency. The internal parts of winches are generally bronze, although some winch makers save weight by using plastic parts for bearing cages and in the shifting mechanisms. The cheapest winches may have parts made of brass or plastic, and while these winches might suffice for very light duty, the materials used are so soft that stripped gears or bearing failures are common under even moderate loads.

Winch drums are usually available in aluminum and chromed bronze, and occasionally in natural-finish bronze, stainless steel, or titanium. The chief advantage of aluminum is its light weight. On a 35-foot boat the use of aluminum drums on the winches might save 40 or more pounds of weight on deck, which is significant. Years ago aluminum drums were used only for sheets, with stainless or chromed bronze drums used for wire halyards. Now it is common to rig boats so that only rope is on the drum of the halyard winches, either by using stoppers ahead of the winches, by setting up the halyards so that the splice is between the winch and the mast, or by using long tail splices with rope cover over the tail of the splice that is on the drum of the winch. Some racing boats even go to the extreme of allowing the wire halyards to score the aluminum drums, which are then replaced. In the case of a few of the larger sizes of winches, aluminum drums with stainless sleeves are available. Aluminum drums can also save money, as they are usually priced somewhere below bronze and substantially below stainless steel.

In addition to its softness, the primary disadvantage of aluminum is that its dark anodized finish raises the temperatures inside the winch in direct sunlight, which dries out the lubricants quickly. And repeated bangs with winch handles or prolonged exposure to sunlight will eventually chip or fade the finish. Bronze drums are usually chromium-plated, and while the appearance is fine for the first few years, the drum eventually will need replating, which frequently means reknurling as well, to preserve the non-slip surface. Stainless steel is available on only a few winches, sometimes only on special orders. It is lighter than bronze, though much heavier than aluminum, and it requires no replating or other servicing attention.

The ultimate drum material is titanium, which is lighter than aluminum, extremely strong, highly resistant to corrosion, nonmagnetic, and attractively hi-tech in appearance. Unfortunately, titanium is so expensive that it is used only for custom winches, and even on 12-meter yachts the titanium drums are saved for races, with cheaper aluminum or aluminum and stainless drums used for practice.

Dark aluminum winches should be serviced frequently, perhaps as often as monthly. On aggressively raced boats the winches may be serviced weekly, using light "gunks" concocted from sewing machine oil, Marvel Mystery Oil, and secret ingredients, instead of the heavier greases used for winches that are serviced less frequently. The lighter lubricants make for a more efficient winch but need to be replenished more frequently. Thus ease of disassembly and reassembly may be a criterion in the selection of a winch. Most of the major brands are easily stripped down for cleaning and lubrication, but in choosing a winch it may be a good idea to look for brands that can be stripped without the pawls and springs dropping out of the drum as soon as it is lifted off the winch.

Servicing Winches

If winches are serviced regularly, major strip-downs or overhauls are rarely necessary. All that is generally required is a large enough bucket to hold the drum and other parts, kerosene to clean all traces of the old lubricant off the winch parts, a toothbrush or other small brush to reach into crevices, and plenty of dry lint-free rags. If you have never stripped the winch before, it is a good idea to have the manufacturer's manual at hand, or to make a sketch as you are pulling out pawls, gears, and bearings. A routine servicing consists of nothing more than removing the drum, the shaft bearings, and the pawls; cleaning all traces of the old lubricant off all moving parts with kerosene; relubricating the gears, bearings, and inside of the drum with either a recommended winch lubricant (the winch manufacturers each produce lubricants, or Lubriplate "A" is acceptable) or with a lighter "gunk" made of grease and oil if the winch is serviced frequently; then reassembling the winch. Be sure to use only a light oil on the pawls, to replace any pawl springs that seem weak or bent, and to make absolutely certain that the pawl springs are put back the way they came out, and not reversed.

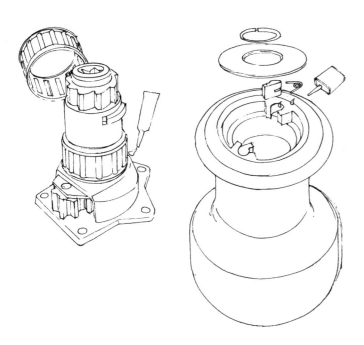

Watch out for worn or chipped gears, bearings seized to the inside of the drum or to the winch shaft, and broken or jammed pawls. A seized bearing (it usually happens on aluminum drums that have been left baking too long in the sun without lubrication) can usually be tapped free with a plastic or rawhide mallet. If the drum is corroded on the inside, it can be cleaned off with fine emery paper. It is a good idea to keep a kit of spare pawls and pawl springs, plus the ring clips or allen bolts that are used to hold the winch together, in the spares department on the boat.

SPARS AND RIGGING

On some contemporary racing boats, the demands for minimum weight and windage and optimum control of spar bend and headstay tension have led spar designers to what are euphemistically called "marginal" rigs. These rigs are designed to a safety factor of 100 percent or even less of the maximum anticipated working loads on the rig, instead of the 200-percent safety factor that is usually allowed on a rig. If the marginal rig is perfectly maintained, and if there are no slipups in the crew work—which means that tensions are eased off in heavy seaways, the runners and other midsection stabilizers are kept properly trimmed, and the loads on the spar are monitored constantly—the rig will stand up and do all that is expected of it, presenting the smallest possible windage and weight and allowing the crew to squeeze the absolute maximum out of each sail. But if a crew isn't quick enough getting the runner in after a tack, or if the helmsman gets into a downwind death roll bad enough to dip the spinnaker pole into the water, or if the slightest corrosion or other maintenance problem is ignored, there is a good chance that the rig will come tumbling down. And when it falls down, the boat owner stands to lose more than just the race.

The extremes go the other way too. Sailors with fantasies of sailing offshore sometimes select rigs so overscaled that they are severely penalizing the performance of their boats for normal sailing. There may be an argument for oversized rigging on a boat that is to be used for long voyages in the tropics, where the greater cross section of the shrouds will stand up longer to corrosion and where repair facilities are distant or unavailable. But for the coastal cruising and racing that most boat owners do, oversized rigging adds nothing but excess weight and windage aloft, reducing sail-carrying ability and generally degrading the performance of the boat. Removing 100 pounds from a spar 50 feet long is the equivalent, in terms of sail-carrying ability (overall stiffness), of adding 500 pounds of ballast 5 feet below the center of gravity of the boat! The saving in windage from smaller sections and lighter, cleaner rigging is comparably dramatic: the cross-sectional area of the spar and rigging of a boat is substantial enough that most boats actually sail under bare poles in a breeze. The wind resistance of the bulky external tangs, oversized rigging, external halyards and reef lines, and other unnecessary mast gear is drag that must be overcome by the available sail power on the boat.

To find out if your rigging is undersized or oversized, measure the diameter of the rigging. Use one of the V-shaped gauges made by the wire rope companies (which you can usually obtain free from a rigger or chandler), or use a caliper or a fine ruler and a square to make the measurements. It is also a good idea to measure the clevis pins of the rigging turnbuckles. The correspondence of clevis pins to rigging size

is almost standardized in the industry, but some boats, especially those with metric rigging or with custom rigs, may have odd matches.

In general, the maximum load on the backstay of a masthead-rigged boat will be approximately 1.75 times the maximum genoa clew load. An appropriate safety margin for a backstay is 300 percent, which means that the backstay should have a breaking strength of approximately 5¼ times the maximum anticipated maximum genoa clew load (MaxGenoa).* Thus if MaxGenoa is 2000 pounds, the maximum backstay load would be about 3500 pounds and the backstay should have a breaking strength of 10,500 pounds. A ⁹⁄₃₂ wire or −10 rod would be about right.

BREAKING STRENGTHS

| 1 × 19 Stainless Cable | | Rod Rigging | | Clevis Pin |
diameter (in.)	break str.	size	diameter (in.)	diameter (in.)
⅛	2100			¼
⁵⁄₃₂	3300	−3	.143	⁵⁄₁₆
³⁄₁₆	4700	−4	.172	⅜
⁷⁄₃₂	6300	−6	.198	⁷⁄₁₆
¼	8200	−8	.225	⁷⁄₁₆ or ½
⁹⁄₃₂	10300	−10	.250	½
⁵⁄₁₆	12500	−12	.281	⅝
⅜	17500	−17	.330	⅝
⁷⁄₁₆	22500	−22	.375	¾
½	30000	−30	.437	⅞

* Large masthead rigs, extremely stiff boats, or boats sailing in unusual conditions would probably adjust the multiplier upward. For a tender, light-displacement boat, the rigging sizes might go down a size.

If your boat is overrigged, you probably won't want to change the rigging to a smaller size unless you are planning extensive changes to the rig. But beware of chandlers and riggers who use rigging or clevis pin sizes to recommend hardware and gear for your boat, or as a shortcut to computing the actual loads on the rig. If the maximum anticipated backstay load on your boat is 3500 pounds, you don't need a backstay adjuster with a safe working load of 6500 pounds. A unit rated for a safe working load of 4000 pounds, which is smaller, cheaper, and lighter, will do the job just fine. On the other hand, too much can be made of ratings and safe working loads. There is also a factor of what we might call "easy" working load. A backstay adjuster, for example, might be perfectly safe at a working load of 3500 pounds, but so difficult to adjust that it doesn't get used.

The shrouds, headstay, and backstay will probably be made of either rod or 1 x 19 stainless cable. Rod rigging has many advantages over cable: it resists corrosion better, it has less stretch, it is aerodynamically cleaner, modern cold-headed terminals are stronger than swaged or user-applied (Norseman) terminals for wire cable, and rod rigging will soil sails less than cable. The disadvantages are cost, the relative scarcity of riggers who can make up new rigging, and the need to be careful to avoid bending or scoring the rigging during winter storage. But if you are adding or replacing any standing rigging, it makes sense to consider rod for the performance and maintenance advantages it offers.

At typical working loads, rod rigging stretches approximately 0.1 percent less than 1 x 19 cable. The difference may seem insignificant, but 0.1 percent of a 50-foot-long upper shroud is more than half an inch. Easing the uppers on your

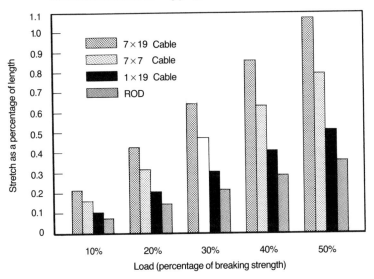

boat by that much—which is what happens when you are sailing hard on the wind with cable rigging—will have a considerable effect on the windward performance of the boat.

RUNNING RIGGING

On the boat, cut to length and tied to the clew of the genoa, snapped to the head of the spinnaker, or threaded through a purchase to trim the vang or control the mainsheet, it is called line. In the chandlery, it is nothing but rope, wound on spools, in a rainbow of colors and in enough varieties to confuse anyone. For all the colors and brands, there are really only a few kinds of line that are of interest to the boat owner. What is important is to match the characteristics of a line to its use.

Line Choices

Nylon Nylon line has two important characteristics: it is exceedingly strong for its size, and it is stretchy. Together they make nylon the ideal line for mooring, dock, and anchor lines, where the stretch is desirable to lessen the shock loads on ground tackle and cleats in a surging sea. Nylon line is available both twisted and braided; the braided line has less stretch, resists abrasion better, and has a softer "hand." For dock lines that are used regularly, it may be a better choice. Used in an anchor line, the braided nylon may not be stretchy enough and may require a larger anchor for a given size of line.

Polypropylene Polypropylene line is relatively weak for its size, deteriorates rapidly in sunlight, and is stretchy. Its virtue is that it floats, which makes it ideal for dinghy painters that may catch in a propeller. Its other use is in mainsheets for very small boats (like a Laser), where a wet line will be heavier, or in light spinnaker sheets, which if made of polypropylene will float when the air is so light that the sheet dips into the water.

Braided Dacron There are dozens of brands of braided Dacron, which in sizes over 3⁄16 inch is essentially two lines, one inside the other. Both manufacturers and magazine studies make claims that one brand is less stretchy or stronger than another, and certainly some brands are easier to splice than others. The line is generally available in two surface finishes: the filament or smooth finish is marginally stronger for a given size (because the filaments in the outer braid are continuous) but is slippery both for the hands and for winch drums; the spun or rough finish is slightly weaker for a given diameter of rope but easier to hold and gives a better grip on the surface of a winch. The inner core in both types is generally of smooth or filament braid. Braided Dacron is the workhorse of lines, used for halyard tails, mainsheets, control lines, and on many boats for genoa and spinnaker sheets and sometimes spinnaker guys. It is long-wearing, easy on the grip, relatively inexpensive, easy to splice, and substantially less stretchy than nylon or polypropylene. It is also available in a variety of colors, which facilitates color-coding lines.

Prestretched Dacron Of the many lines that are called prestretched Dacron, some are nothing more than ordinary Dacron braid that has literally been stretched, tightening the braiding, making the line somewhat harder to the touch and smaller in diameter, and removing a certain amount of stretch that would otherwise come out only after the line has been loaded for a while. Others, like the Marlow prestretched lines, are made without a core—in a solid braid for the smaller lines and in a laid construction for the larger lines. These constructions do reduce the stretch in the line; the trade-off is a hard feel to the line and lack of spliceability in the solid braids.

Straight-Filament-Core Dacron If the core of a Dacron line is made of straight filaments, instead of a braided line-within-a-line, the resulting line will have a higher Dacron-to-air ratio, which will result in better stretch characteristics. Two examples are Cup-Sheet, imported by Samson, and Sta-Set X, made by New England Braid. These lines provide the best stretch characteristics of all the Dacron lines, which makes them excellent for rope halyards, sheets, and guys, and those control lines which require minimal stretch. They are relatively difficult to splice and are much stiffer to the hand than the softer Dacron braids.

Kevlar Kevlar (Aramid) lines provide the best stretch characteristics of all lines. In the solid-Kevlar-core lines, the stretch is so low that when the line turns around a tight radius, the entire load is borne by the outer strands of the core. Thus the lines fatigue quickly on a small sheave or under chafe. The Kevlar/Dacron blends, which generally mix something like 65 percent Kevlar with 35 percent Dacron in the core, have somewhat better chafe resistance and are much softer, but at a sacrifice in stretch characteristics. The all-Kevlar lines provide the ultimate in no-stretch control for spinnaker guys and critical control lines. The Kevlar/Dacron blends are a good choice for spinnaker sheets and guys where a slight trade-off of stretch versus handling and durability is warranted. The blends are also good for genoa sheets (especially sheets used for the #3 or #4 genoa, which have a relatively long lead from the winch to the sail).

Kevlar/Dacron blends can be spliced with the same splice used for braided Dacron. The all-Kevlar lines require a relatively difficult splicing technique, and usually need leather chafe guards around any potential chafe area.

Spectra 900 A new high-density polyethylene, Spectra 900 from Allied Corporation, is now being made into lines which promise an even greater strength-to-size ratio than Kevlar. Like Kevlar lines, the newer Spectra 900 lines are often so strong that they are sized on the basis of handling rather than strength. Sheaves for Spectra 900 and any other very-low-stretch line need to be large and with a flattened groove that allows the line to flatten under load.

The other lines that are sometimes used on sailboats, like the laid Dacron that some traditionalists use instead of braided Dacron, or the hemp and manilla ropes that purists use, make sense only if nostalgia and appearance are more important than performance. A braided line will twist and hockle less than a laid line, and will generally have superior stretch and abrasion characteristics.

Sizing Line

Strength is rarely the problem in sizing line. For most jobs on a boat, relatively small lines, even lines as small as 5/32 inch, are strong enough to handle the loads generated. There are small Kevlar lines strong enough to handle the genoa loads on a good-size boat, if you and your crew want to tail heavily loaded genoa sheets of 3/16-inch Kevlar. As long as a line is strong enough, the important criteria are stretch, handling, and resistance to chafe.

The stretch in a line is not directly proportional to load. Under moderate loads, the stretch is minimal. Once the loading reaches 25 percent of breaking strength, the stretch increases rapidly. Thus a 7/16-inch Dacron genoa sheet is strong enough for a boat with a maximum genoa clew load of 3000 pounds, but the stretch in the ⁷⁄₁₆-inch line is so great that frequent trimming of the genoa sheet will be required just to compensate for the stretch in changing breezes. And the extreme loading of the line will eventually break down the fibers, wearing the line out before its time. Because stretch is a percentage of length, larger lines or low-stretch materials become more important as the length of loaded line increases.

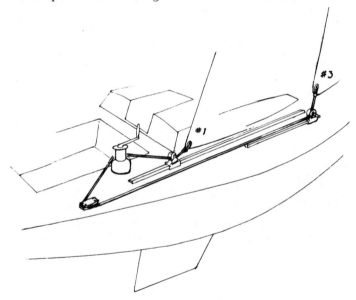

The length of loaded line on the #1 genoa is less than 3 feet from the clew, through the lead block, to the winch. On the #3 genoa, the line from the clew to the lead block, to the turning block, and back to the winch is all loaded—a distance of 18 feet, which means that under the same load, the line will stretch six times as much. And since it is the top range of the #3 genoa that usually provides the maximum clew loads,

if you are buying a single set of genoa sheets, the size and stretch characteristics of the line should be selected for that use.

In general, lines that are tailed or trimmed substantial distances—jib sheets, mainsheet, spinnaker sheets, and halyards—should be sized for an easy grip with the hand. Three-eighths inch is about the smallest line that is easily tailed. For loads great enough to require double-handled grinding on a winch, ½-inch or larger lines are easier and faster to tail. The only real limitations on line size for winched lines are the size of the winch drums and the weight of the line. If you use ½-inch genoa sheets on a winch with a drum that is under 3 inches in diameter, it will be impossible to get enough turns on the winch to keep the line from slipping. And in light air, the heavy ½-inch sheets will drag the sail down.

SHEET AND GUY SIZES

MaxGenoa	genoa sheet size		
	Dacron	*Kevlar/Dacron*	*Kevlar Guys*
under 600	⁵⁄₁₆ (8 mm)	⁵⁄₁₆	¼
500–1000	³⁄₈ (10 mm)	⁵⁄₁₆	¼
800–1700	⁷⁄₁₆ (11 mm)	³⁄₈	⁵⁄₁₆
1500–2200	½ (13 mm)	⁷⁄₁₆	³⁄₈
2000–2700	⁹⁄₁₆ (14 mm)	⁷⁄₁₆	⁷⁄₁₆
2500–3600	⅝ (16 mm)	½	½
3300–6000	¾ (18 mm)	⅝	⅝
5000 +	1 in. (25 mm)	¾	¾

In the smaller sizes, straight-filament-core Dacron line of comparable size could be substituted for the Kevlar/Dacron-core line. For sailing areas with heavier than average conditions, where the #3 genoa is used as often as the #1, a size larger might be advisable.

Spinnaker sheets and guys are not as heavily loaded as the genoa sheet, but the lengths of loaded line are longer, which makes stretch a more important consideration. In general, spinnaker guys would be the same size as genoa sheets. For low-stretch straight-filament-core or Kevlar/Dacron-core line, the guy can be one size smaller than the genoa sheet; with an all-Kevlar core, the line can be as much as two sizes smaller than the genoa sheet, assuming that the line has a fair lead and runs only through blocks with large sheaves that are adequate for Kevlar.

Spinnaker sheets, used with a separate guy, can be two sizes smaller than genoa sheets, or even smaller if one of the low-stretch materials is used.

Halyards

For minimum stretch and maximum resistance to wear and chafe, wire halyards with rope tails are generally used for main and genoa halyards, although weight-conscious racers experiment with all-Kevlar halyards to cut down on the weight aloft. For spinnaker halyards, and for the wing halyards on three-halyard rigs, low-stretch rope halyards (parallel-core Dacron is ideal) can often be used at a savings of weight. Some cruising boats use prestretched or Dacron braid for all-rope genoa or main halyards, citing the ease of handling and the lack of chafe from the soft line. You can usually recognize the boats from far away by the scalloped luffs of the genoas and the undertensioned main luffs that are a result of the stretch in the line. Some boat owners may not realize that poor pointing ability, or even weather helm, can be caused by a halyard that is too stretchy.

The usual choice for halyards is 7 x 19 stainless cable, but galvanized cable of the same size is softer to handle and less likely to chafe into meat hooks. For main and genoa halyards that do not turn over excessively small sheaves and do not lead over chafe cages (as in a triple-halyard masthead rig), stainless wire is fine. For the wing halyards in a triple-halyard rig, or for use on unavoidably small sheaves, galvanized halyards will wear longer. Galvanized halyards do require care, however, including frequent cleaning and lubrication with light oil. Marvel Mystery Oil and Lubriplate "A" is a good combination. And pay special attention to any Nicopress fittings on galvanized cable. Copper Nicopress fittings set up a spectacular galvanic sandwich on galvanized wire.

Halyard tails are usually scaled to the halyard wire. A tail twice the diameter of the wire is easiest to splice and generally makes for easy handling. Thus 3/16-inch wire halyards will have 3/8-inch tails. For all-rope halyards, the controlling factors are stretch, handling, and chafe. Small-diameter Kevlar halyards are strong enough and low enough stretch for most halyard purposes, but the internal chafe around the masthead sheaves will quickly wear out the line. A wire tail for the end of the

HALYARD SIZES

I or P dimension	Main	Headsail
under 28 feet	1/8 inch (3 mm)	5/32 inch
27–32	5/32 (4 mm)	5/32
32–37	5/32 (4 mm)	3/16
37–45	3/16 (5 mm)	3/16
45–50	3/16 (5 mm)	3/16 or 7/32
50–60	7/32 (6 mm)	1/4
60–75	1/4 (7 mm)	9/32
75–85	1/4 (7 mm)	5/16
85 +	9/32 (8 mm)	5/16 or 3/8

line is one solution, but the wire-to-rope splice is tricky with Kevlar. As an alternative, the halyard can be shortened frequently. Because an eye splice is time-consuming in Kevlar, a halyard that is shortened frequently might be terminated with a tied-on shackle rather than a splice. A fisherman's or anchor bend is probably the best knot, because it reduces the line strength much less than a bowline. A good alternative is the straight-filament-core Dacron lines like Sta-Set X or Cup-Sheet. The braided Dacron and prestretched halyards that are supplied on some production boats are too stretchy for anything other than the most casual sailing.

A good guide to sizing rope halyards is to make the halyard the size that the tail of a wire/rope halyard would be, or one size smaller if all-Kevlar line is used.

Control Lines

Control lines are usually sized for handling characteristics. An infrequently adjusted line, such as a flattening reef, might be no larger than the $5/32$-inch tail of a magic box. A traveler control line or a foreguy, which will be adjusted frequently, should be large enough to grip easily. Kevlar has the best stretch characteristics, but it is stiff and prone to chafe in stoppers, clam cleats, small sheaves, and cam cleats. Kevlar/Dacron blends or the prestretched or straight-filament Dacrons are a good compromise for low-stretch applications that require better handling and wear characteristics.

STOPPERS

Halyard stoppers or rope clutches allow one winch to serve several control lines. They work well, and if selected and in-stalled correctly can avoid the clutter, weight, and cost of multiple winches. The original stoppers were simple cams against a plate, and while they would hold a line, it required either retensioning of the line, a lever, or a mallet to release the stopper. The newer line clutches use secondary cams to permit the line to be tailed through the stopper or clutch while the cam is engaged; they also make it possible to release lines under load.

The simple cams are reliable but inconvenient. If a line is adjusted, you have to remember to re-engage the cam, and you are likely to end up easing out an inch or two of line in the process. If you are shorthanded or in a hurry (and when are you not in a hurry during a race or sail change?), releasing the loaded cam can prove trying.

The rope clutches also work well, but they have to be sized to the anticipated loads and the size of the line used. In general, the actual working load of a stopper (load it can hold without slipping) will be less than the rating assigned by the manufacturer, and depending upon the line used and whether or not the clutch is adjustable, you may find that with heavily loaded lines, like a genoa halyard, the clutch either slips or eats up halyards faster than you are willing to replace them. If the clutch or stopper is not mounted directly in line with the winch (remember to align the stopper with the incoming side of the winch drum), or if the line feeds up or down as it enters or exits the rope clutch, the holding strength may be sharply reduced.

Clam Cleats An alternative to stoppers for smaller boats, and for control lines on larger boats, is an ordinary clam cleat, preferably made of aluminum. The problem with clam cleats is that they are very difficult to release, requiring a hard crank on an already loaded line. There are quick-release clam cleats which flip forward at the release of a toggle; the action is very fast and might be suitable for boats used in closed-course racing. They also require protection for the deck where the unit swings forward (a hard plastic or wood pad is sufficient), and protection for the trip line, lest it get accidentally pulled. To keep lines from accidentally catching in a clam cleat, (1) use the clam cleats with built-in gates that can be swung up, (2) drill the clam cleat for a large cotter or ball-lock pin, or (3) keep a short length of heavy line nearby that can be jammed into the cleat to keep other lines out.

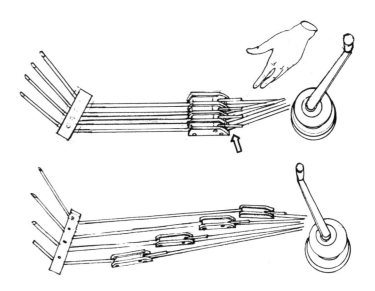

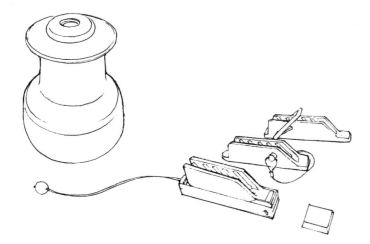

Stoppers are frequently used in banks of two or more, which can present problems in getting fair leads to turning blocks at the mast or on deck, and at the winch. Usually the problem is that the stopper is too close to the winch; one lead, say from the middle stopper of a bank of three, is fair and the others are foul. The cure is to move the stopper farther from the winch, or to use separate stoppers which can be mounted at staggered intervals on the deck. Separate stoppers have the advantage that you are less likely to trip or to try to set the wrong stopper when you are hoisting a genoa and dropping a spinnaker in one sequence.

Finally, with stoppers as with any deck hardware, watch for projections that can catch a line. Some stoppers have handles and releases that sit poised to catch lines, with results that can be comical to watch and disastrous to experience—for example, when a sharp tug on the spinnaker sheet catches the stopper and releases the spinnaker halyard, letting the spinnaker tumble into the water.

5

BEFORE YOU DRILL . . .

Few owners haven't had the need to mount a fitting on a boat, whether a simple accessory like a teak holder for pencils and dividers or new primary winches. Timid owners, contemplating the smooth gleam of the fiberglass, the rich finish of the teak joinery, or the resale value of a "virgin" boat, sometimes decide they would rather live without the shelf or the new winches. "How will I fill the holes where I am removing the old winch?" they wonder. "What about the hole on the boom where the old mainsheet block was riveted on?"

Others plunge in with drill and saber saw as though they were installing a fixture on the wall of the kitchen at home, merrily sawing and drilling away, filling imperfect holes with gobs of silicone bathtub sealant, screwing or bolting their shelves and other additions with a variety of brass, stainless steel, aluminum, or mystery-metal fastenings of no particular grade. Sometimes these quick and dirty jobs work just fine. More often, something goes wrong. Perhaps it is only an annoying leak or a fastening that won't stay tight; another gob of some miracle goop or a bigger screw might fix things up just fine. Usually, the problems caused by careless work on a boat don't show up immediately. Indeed things may look just fine until four or five years later, when the prospective buyer's surveyor finds that your deck is spongy because a tiny leak, caused by sloppy bedding of a deck fitting, has gone untraced long enough to rot the core of the deck.

DECK FITTINGS

Water doesn't need much of an opening to start a leak into the deck of a boat. Even a pinhole will do. And once water finds its way in, it will follow tiny channels that can never be traced, riding along the underside of a deck, following a sloppy joint, dribbling down the shaft of a fastener. If the water can ultimately find its way out, for example by dripping onto your face as you lie in a bunk, you might be annoyed and it might take you a while to track exactly where the leak started, but as long as no moisture remains inside the deck, the problems are minor.

The real trouble starts because much of the time the water doesn't find its way out, and because most boats have wood somewhere in the deck structure. Wooden-boat owners know that the plywood or laid decks of their boats can be trouble; they are usually alert to any flaws or cracks developing in a fiberglass covering or deck canvas. But just because a boat is built of fiberglass doesn't mean there is any less potential for trouble. The decks of most fiberglass boats are cored with balsa, or in some cases plywood, especially in high-load areas like the location of the primary winches or turning blocks. The balsa core provides tremendous strength and stiffness to the deck, but a wood core, like wood anywhere on a boat, can rot. A deck fitting, with multiple holes for the fastenings, can provide a perfect pathway for just enough fresh water to achieve that magic moisture level that will assure rotting, delamination, or deterioration of the core of a deck. The answer is care in drilling, bedding, and fastening fittings.

The first precaution to take in mounting any fastening is to make certain that you have drill bits of the correct size, and that the drill bits you use are sharp. The brad bits and Forstner bits that are sold for carpentry and cabinetmaking work well on fiberglass, taking a bite without skidding. If you use a regular twist drill instead, you will generally need to drill a pilot hole first, or at least a depression in the fiberglass so the bit of

your drill will not skid. A good tool for pilot holes is a Yankee push drill with a small bit.

With few exceptions, all deck fittings on a boat should be through-bolted, so the key measurement is the outside diameter of the bolt shaft. The drill bits should be chosen to match exactly, with enough clearance so that bolts don't need to be hammered or driven in, but with no excess clearance. For those few situations where a self-tapping screw is used for a very-light-duty fitting, the drill diameter should match the inside diameter of the threads. The easiest way to size the bit is to hold the bit and screw together against the light and see if the bottom of the thread matches the bit diameter. As a substitute, instead of a self-tapping screw that may crack or chip the fiberglass, you can use machine screws and holes tapped into the fiberglass for light fittings with loads taken in sheer. With wood screws, the pilot hole must be matched to both the threaded portion of the screw and the shaft; the best way to drill a pilot hole is to use a special countersink bit that is matched to the screw.

A moderate-speed electric drill is ideal, and if you are planning much work on the boat, the most useful drill is one of the cordless rechargeable models, like those made by Makita or Black & Decker. A ⅜-inch drill is generally large enough for the bits you will use, and is usually available in slow enough speeds to work well on fiberglass, aluminum, or even stainless steel. You will probably find that your work will standardize down to a few sizes of fastenings. If you are planning to do much drilling in stainless steel, or to use large-diameter hole saws to cut holes for vents, compasses, or instruments, you will need a heavy-duty ½-inch drill.

Small fittings and loads that are taken in sheer, such as a

deck lead block for a cunningham or outhaul, offer few problems. Make sure the holes that are drilled for fastenings are the right size, and that they are drilled true so that there is no misbalance of loads. Unless the fitting is countersunk for flat-head or oval-head machine screws, use pan-head machine screws in the smaller sizes (or round-heads if your local supplier does not have pan-head machine screws), and hex-head bolts in the larger sizes. Fastenings should match the fitting: bronze with bronze, stainless with stainless or chrome-plated fittings. For aluminum fittings, use Monel or stainless fastenings, and either a thin mica washer and sleeve or some kind of insulating paste, preferably zinc chromate paste—or in a pinch, silicone sealant or even bedding compound—to keep the dissimilar metals apart.

To secure the fitting on the underside of the deck, you can use either a lock washer and a nut, a Nylock nut that requires no lockwasher, or if the nut is exposed, either a cap (acorn) nut or a barrel nut. The cap and barrel nuts are attractive, especially for boats that use the underside of the deck as a headliner, but to use them the mounting screws must be cut to the exact length that will permit the fitting to be tightened. For barrel nuts the underside of the deck also must be drilled out to the outer diameter of the barrel shaft, and a larger washer used. If you are planning to use barrel nuts or cap nuts, buy or borrow a bolt cutter for the sizes of bolt you will be using. You can shorten a bolt by driving it through a nut, sawing it off with a hacksaw, then backing it out of the nut, but it is a time-consuming job. Whatever kind of nuts you use, it is a good idea to search out oversized washers for the fittings. They may not be needed for loads in sheer, but the large washer will prevent crushing of the deck when the fitting is bolted home.

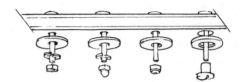

The silicone seal that is sold in most boatyards as an all-purpose gunk is not a good bedding compound. It is better to use a natural bedding compound or one of the polysulfide or polyurethane bedding compounds. Just make sure that if it is a fitting you will ever want to remove for maintenance or replacement, you do not use 3M 5200 or Sikaflex or any other adhesive caulk, and that if you are installing fittings with any plastic surfaces you do not use an incompatible bedding compound. (Some polysulfides will make short work of plastic instrument cases.) Natural bedding compound (sometimes sold as "boatyard bedding compound") is the easiest to clean up, especially if it is applied with an artist's palette knife. You can buy cheap palette knives at an art supply store for under $1.

Put the fastenings into the fitting, then apply the bedding compound around every fastening where it emerges from the fitting, and in a bead around the perimeter of the fitting. Apply generously enough so that when the fitting is bolted home, the compound squeezes out from underneath the edges of the fitting. If you are using a natural bedding compound, clean it up with turpentine. If you use a silicone seal, don't try to clean up the uncured sealant. Wait for it to set and then clean it off with a knife later.

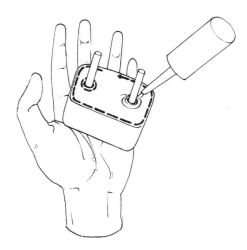

For any fitting, make certain that fastenings are the correct size. In some cases it may be possible to drill out a fitting to take a larger bolt (the amount of metal remaining around the hole on all sides should equal at least one half the diameter of the bolt). Never use a bolt that is too small, unless the play is taken up with a spacer, and never try to get away with fewer fastenings than there are mounting holes. If a pad eye is drilled for four bolts, use four.

Fittings that are heavily loaded, and especially any fitting with a load in tension, require more care in the installation. A heavily loaded fitting in tension—such as a pad eye for a staysail tack, a mast-base halyard block, a runner pad eye, or a spinnaker guy block—applies enough force to crush the core of the deck, even when the load is spread out with large backing plates or oversized washers on the underside of the deck.

And once there is deflection in the deck from the crushing of the core, leaks are almost certain, followed either by a failure of the deck (something like the afterguy block pulling out on a hard reach) or by a dull "thwump" under the mallet of the surveyor that signals a punky deck (read: a large reduction in the price you will get for the boat).

Even if a load is entirely in sheer, like a genoa turning block, the load can be heavy enough to move a block laterally on a deck, enlarging the mounting holes and admitting water. If you're lucky, a leak dripping in the face of someone asleep in the quarter berth tells you that something is wrong. Otherwise, the deck (or in a fiberglass boat, the core of the deck) quietly rots until the turning block suddenly gives way, flying off the deck like a sea-to-air missile. Anyone standing in the bight of the line will be lucky to get launched instead of crushed.

Both potential problems—crushing of a deck and lateral movement—can be controlled with the same solution. And if there are fittings on a boat that have been mounted without the proper precautions—such as stanchion bases, primary winches, or turning blocks that a manufacturer put on with a quick and dirty technique—they can be repaired if they are caught before there is damage to the deck.

Epoxy Spacers

The usual means to prevent crushing by a heavily loaded deck fitting is metal spacers, cut exactly to the depth of the deck and fitted over the mounting bolts in oversized holes. Spacers are talked about, and even specified, but rarely used. It is hard to find the right materials, and even harder to cut to the exact needed length without a cut-off saw, a tool that most boat owners don't own.

Even riggers who have access to that kind of tool are not likely to take the tool to the boat, and instead either guess or punt. Most boat owners will find it easier to make epoxy spacers instead.

To make an epoxy spacer, drill mounting holes through the upper fiberglass layer and the core, but not through the lower fiberglass layer (which in some cases may be the headliner) of the boat.* If you drill a pilot hole with a hand drill or a slow-turning electric drill, it should be possible to' feel the point of the bit meeting the second layer. Stop and use tape or a drill stop to set up your bits for the rest of the holes. You want the holes to be substantially larger than the fastenings, twice as big if possible (½-inch holes for ¼-inch fastenings). Square-tip bits (Forstner or brad) will do the best job.

Once the hole is bored, you can use a bent and sharpened rod on the drill to ream additional core material out of the sides of the mounting hole. Don't worry about the roughness of the edges of the core inside. The epoxy will soak into and bond with the core material.

Blow or vacuum all the debris out of the holes, mask the deck around the holes with plastic sheeting and tape, and mix the epoxy, which should be a high-grade viscous epoxy that will penetrate the core as much as possible. The West epoxies

are outstanding for the purpose, but others can be used as well. If the mixture is too thin, you can add one of the recommended thickening agents, such as microballoons or Cabosil. Follow the mixing instructions exactly;† then put the epoxy into a large plastic syringe, which is available from medical suppliers, hardware stores, or sometimes cooking supply stores. You don't need a needle; just cut the end of the syringe off to a size that will easily fit into the hole and still allow you to inject the epoxy into the hole. If it is a large, deep hole, it may be wise to fill it in two or three sessions, because of the excessive heat that the curing epoxy can create. In any case, it will probably be necessary to top off the epoxy once or twice to get the surface flush with the deck. You may be surprised at how much epoxy soaks into the core.

When the epoxy is fully cured, which usually means overnight, make sure the surface is level with the deck. If it is too high, grind, file, or sand it down to deck level. An automobile body file or a Surform plane is a good tool for this kind of filing. Then, using a very sharp bit, drill your mounting holes through the epoxy plugs. If you measured and drilled right the first time, the holes should be in the center of each plug. Use bedding compound and large washers and locknuts or lock washers to mount your fitting. If the load is in tension or

---

* If you are refitting a stanchion base or other fitting onto old holes that have worn out of round, probe to measure the thickness of the layers of deck and core, and drill the larger hole only to the top of the bottom layer of deck. When filling the hole with epoxy mixture later, you will need to plug the old hole in the headliner or the bottom lamination of the deck. You can try tape, but a temporary bung of the correct size, driven in from below, is more reliable at keeping epoxy off your upholstery and cabin sole.

† Both the temperature and the proportions are important with epoxies. With some of the polyester fillers, such as the Bondo materials that are popular for body work on automobiles and for repair of topside dings on boats, the mix of catalyst and filler can be fairly casual; if you use too much catalyst, or if the temperature is too high, you just have to work a little faster. With epoxies, straying with either the proportions or the temperature may lead to an unusable batch or to a hole filled with a sticky goop that refuses to cure. Use a measuring cup to get the proportions close to exactly 5:1 or 1:1 or whatever the particular epoxy demands. (The pumps that can be purchased for West system epoxies make the measuring easy; a single pump on part A yields the correct amount for mixture with a single pump on part B.)

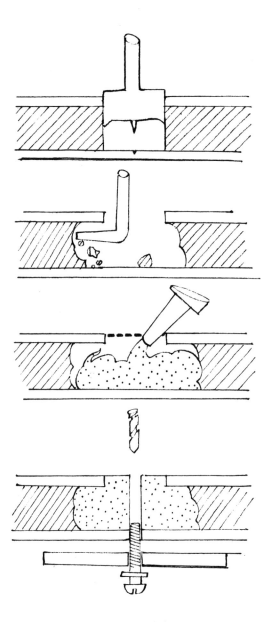

is a very large sheer load (such as a primary winch or a turning block), use a backing block or plate of aluminum, stainless steel, or wood.

Backing Blocks

Steel makes the most compact backing blocks, but it is difficult to cut and drill. Aluminum, even inside the boat, will need protection to avoid corrosion under stainless washers and/or nuts. Wood backing blocks are generally the easiest to fabricate and often look the best in the interior of the boat. A few minutes with a saber saw and sandpaper will fabricate a block of teak for a backing block for almost any fitting. For boats without headliners, the backing blocks can be varnished or oiled to provide a relief from the spartan appearance of fiberglass and stainless hardware.

For turning blocks or other heavily loaded fittings that may have a tendency to creep on a deck, epoxy can also be used under the fitting to increase the adhesion. Make certain the bottom of the fitting is clean of all grease and wax, and sand the deck to remove any traces of wax or gloss. A wipe with acetone or MEK (methyl ethyl ketone) will remove the last traces of wax and grease from both. Then put the fitting in place, trace around it, and mask the area completely. Spread the mating surfaces with epoxy, and bolt the fitting in place.

Once a fitting has been fastened this way, removal will require heating with a torch. As an alternative, use an adhesive like 3M 5200 as the bedding compound for the turning block. It will make the block close to impossible to remove, but it will reduce the chance of creep across the deck.

Old Holes

Unless you have been extremely careful in planning the deck layout of a boat, or have stolidly refused to make any changes to the boat, it is unusual not to have some leftover holes from fittings that are moved or removed from the deck. It is tempting to make every future change of hardware so that it covers the old holes, but replacing a cleat that was in the wrong place with a compass that is in the wrong place doesn't really solve any problems, and it is so easy to fill holes with no structural or aesthetic consequences that it makes sense to lay out the deck exactly as you want it and then just take care of the extra holes.

On a wood deck the hole should be bunged, and this is one case where epoxy would be appropriate to glue in the bung. The bung should be of the same wood as the deck, except, of course, in the case of plywood decks. On fiberglass boats it is tempting to fill holes with a dab or a gob of filler, but even for small screw holes in a deck, a gob of polyester filler (Bondo) will generally not do a good job, especially on a cored deck. A better solution is to block up the bottom of the hole temporarily with a well-fitted bung, or even with tape, and then fill the hole with epoxy (thickened with Cabosil or another thickener as needed), letting the epoxy soak into the core material and refilling as necessary until the surface is flush or close to flush. The top of the hole can then be resurfaced with gelcoat to match the surrounding deck, and after the bung is removed, the bottom (if it is the headliner) can be resurfaced. Applying gelcoat is not difficult, but matching gelcoat after even a year of sun exposure and polishing gelcoat to match a deck are not easy jobs. Many boat owners fill the holes themselves and have a good fiberglass man surface the gelcoat during the off season, especially on complex curved surfaces or non-skid surfaces.

INTERIOR FITTINGS

Fastenings to the inside of the hull are a little more complicated, since they generally cannot be through-bolted. The exceptions are fittings that are put in the bilge, such as a pad eye for a hold-down cable for a babystay, which can be bolted from the outside; the head of the bolt can then be buttered over with a filler compound. There should be a substantial block on the inside of the hull, preferably glassed to the hull with several layers of cloth. The bilge in the area of the block will have to be thoroughly cleaned of all grease, oil, and paint, which will generally mean strong solvents and heavy sanding to produce a surface that will bond to the glass and resin. Use epoxy or a strong adhesive caulk such as 3M 5200 under the pad eye and around the bolts to absorb the loads.

To mount a shelf, pipe berth, or electronics on the inside of the hull, a block should be glassed or epoxied in place, thick enough to take large wood screws or self-tapping screws. For a lightweight shelf or a plaque, an epoxy bond on an absolutely clean surface, or the bond of an adhesive sealant like 3M 5200, may suffice. But for any substantial load, such as a loran or a VHF radio, or a pipe berth, the mounting block will have to be glassed in place with several layers of cloth and resin. For the strongest bonds, epoxy rather than polyester should be used to glass the wood in place. Once the block is glassed into place, the whole mounting zone can be painted or covered with whatever ceiling material is used in the boat.

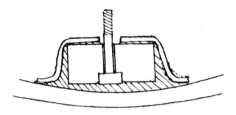

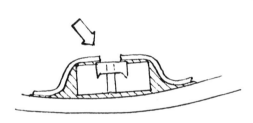

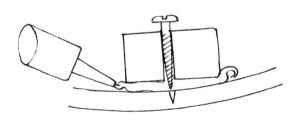

The screws used to mount a bracket or pipe berth should be carefully sized. If the hull is cored, the screws can go through the mounting block and through the inside layer of the hull. Otherwise, the screws should stop short of the hull. The alternatives to screws are captive nuts or bolts epoxied in place in the mounting block.

Bunging

The one skill that can make a big difference in the appearance of add-on interior fittings is bunging. A shelf with carefully bunged mounting screws looks finished; a shelf screwed on with exposed screws looks like an add-on. And when it is time to finish or refinish the wood, there is no agonizing question of whether the exposed screws should be removed (they should!) before you paint or varnish.

Bunging is simple if you use the right tools and take a little time. If you are going to be making a lot of holes, buy one of the special bits that will drill the pilot hole, the countersink for the head of the screw, and cut the hole for the bung in one operation; they are not expensive, and they make the operation quick and foolproof. If only a few holes are required, you can get by using twist drills of the appropriate sizes.

The depth of the hole for the bung should be at least one half the diameter of the bung. For the usual #8 or #10 wood screw, ⅜-inch bungs work well, and they are readily available from chandleries in a variety of woods. Half-inch bungs work well for a large #14 wood screw or a ¼-20 machine screw, and ¼-inch bungs are available for #4 and #6 screws. Too many different sizes of bungs in the same piece are not attractive.

Mix up the glue on a sheet of cardboard. If you are ever

planning to remove the fixture, it is not a good idea to use epoxy for bungs. Wood glue works just fine and will allow you to get the bung out relatively easily. Or varnish will work. Roll the bung in the glue, trying not to get too much glue on the bottom, then line up the grain of the bung and tap it in gently with a soft mallet. It should not be flush with the surface. You can wipe off any excess glue, but let the bung set until the glue is completely dry before you try to trim the top.

Trimming the top is where most goof-ups happen. Your chisel should be sharp. The larger the chisel the better, and if you have access to a slick, it will make the job that much easier. You can use a mallet to tap the end of the handle, but with a large enough chisel you will be able to push without a mallet. Begin by taking off a slice, *no more than half of the exposed length of the bung*. If you try to level the bung with the surface in one cut, nine times out of ten you will catch the grain so that a part of the bung is chipped below the surface. After the first cut, you can see how the grain of the bung runs, and by making progressive slices, you can get the bung down to the surface without gouging below. Finish off with sandpaper on a block, sanding with the grain.

A bung that has been glued in with wood glue or varnish can usually be removed easily. One trick is to cut the head off of a brass wood screw, put the shaft into a slow-speed drill, and drive it into the center of the bung. The bung will usually lift out or split so that it can be cleaned out without the need for redrilling for a larger bung.

For fittings that are too thin to take a bung, such as ceiling strips or thin plywood panels, or for fittings or panels that must be removed frequently, the neatest and strongest mountings are flat- or oval-head screws in finishing washers.

Spar Modifications

Most modern spars are made of aluminum extrusions. Fortunately aluminum is an easy material to work, and modifications to running rigging and wiring in a spar are generally easy for a boat owner to make. More substantial modifications, such as changes to the standing rigging or lightening of spars, should not be undertaken without the advice of an experienced rigger or naval architect. And even in minor work, there are certain precautions which will help ensure that your sailing days are not spoiled by a broken stick.

Precautions

First, spars (mast, booms, and spinnaker poles) are subject to a crazy mixture of tension and compression loads, especially in high-load areas like the gooseneck, the spreader attachment points, and the vang attachment points. If you are attaching fittings or exiting lines in any of those areas, make certain that you do not make too many holes or holes that are too large in a concentrated belt. For example, if you are installing exit boxes to bring out internal halyards, spread them from chest height to a point beyond your reach instead of concentrating them all at the same height. Too many holes in a single area are like the perforations in a magazine tear-out coupon, and failures of spars frequently occur on "the dotted line."

Second, cutouts made in an aluminum spar should always have rounded corners. Sharp corners invite cracking. If you notice cracks starting at the corners of a spar cutout that has been made for an exit box or other fitting, drill preventer holes to stop the spread of the crack.

Finally, aluminum will corrode in contact with stainless steel, bronze, or any other marine metal, even Monel. Bronze fasteners should never be used on aluminum, and stainless or Monel fittings and fasteners should be insulated from the aluminum with mica or nylon washers, with zinc chromate paste, or if nothing else is available, with silicone sealer. If the aluminum is left in direct contact with the stainless steel, the result is a bubbling mess that attacks paint finishes, freezes fasteners in place, and ultimately weakens the attachment of the fitting and the spar. Surprisingly, many spar builders do not take proper precautions to insulate aluminum from stainless fittings, so that after a year or two the paint begins to bubble and none of the fittings can be removed without the laborious chore of driving out stainless screws with impact drivers or screw removers, or in the worst cases, drilling out the old fittings. Spend one afternoon trying to drill out a stainless bolt, and you will be inclined to take the time to bed aluminum/stainless contacts properly to avoid frustration in the future.

Cutouts

Most of the modifications that are made to a spar involve cutting slots or holes for halyards or fittings, drilling and tapping or drilling and riveting to fasten fittings to the mast, and perhaps filling old holes where fittings or winches have been removed. None of the work is difficult.

The first step in cutting a slot or a hole in a spar is to measure carefully (experienced riggers measure at least twice before they start drilling or cutting). The measurements almost always involve offsets, allowances for thickness, or other calculations, and trying to "eyeball" it is usually an invitation

to disaster. Better to measure, write it down, then measure again. If both measurements are the same, walk away for a while, then come back and measure a third time, or get someone else to confirm your calculations. Then, if everything still comes out the same, go ahead!

It is almost always worth the trouble to build a simple jig to hold a spar for cutting or drilling. One end can rest on a sawhorse, but for the end you are working on, take a piece of scrap plywood, trace the outline of the spar on it, cut out a piece a little larger than the outline with a saber saw, and staple scrap carpet around the opening. Then clamp or fasten the jig to a workbench or a sawhorse. With the spar held snugly, it is easy to drill and saw without slipups.

Once the size and position of the slot or cutout has been measured and drawn on the boom or mast, use a center punch to mark the center of any holes you will be drilling. For a cutout, it is usually easiest to drill a hole at each corner, then saw between them with a saber saw.* Make the holes at the corners as large as possible, saw slowly, using plenty of lubricant with sharp bits and blades, and you should have no problems. For a really easy job, try lubricating your bits and blades with a metal cutting compound. It's hardly necessary for aluminum, but the minimum-size container is so large that if you ever buy cutting compound to use on stainless steel (where it is essential), you'll have enough left over to use on every kind of metal cutting. And the compounds do make the job much easier.

To smooth the cut and to make any little indentations that may be required, use a file or a small grinding wheel in a high-

---

* If you're fortunate enough to have a good router, you can buy metal cutting bits and use it as a power "nibbler" to make your cutouts.

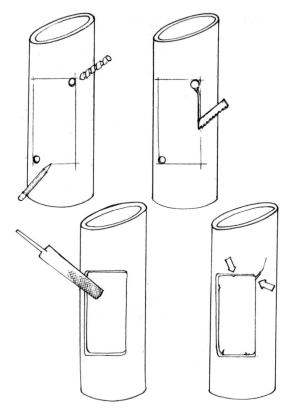

Fastenings

The most reliable fastenings for attaching a fitting to a spar are rivets or machine screws. Sheet-metal screws (self-tapping screws) may seem easier, but they leave sharp edges inside the mast and they are more difficult to use with a proper insulation to limit corrosion.

Pop Rivets An ordinary cheap pop-riveting tool will work for ⅛- and ⁵⁄₃₂-inch stainless or Monel pop rivets, but for ³⁄₁₆- or ¼-inch rivets you will need a heavy-duty tool, either pneumatic, hydraulic, or mechanical. You can often borrow or rent them from riggers or boatyards. Aluminum rivets are not strong enough for anything other than filling holes for cosmetic purposes.

Drive Rivets For fittings that are not in tension, and especially for fittings that need fastenings only for alignment, such as pad eyes installed internally with the tension taken by the entire inside surface of the spar, drive rivets are an easy alternative.

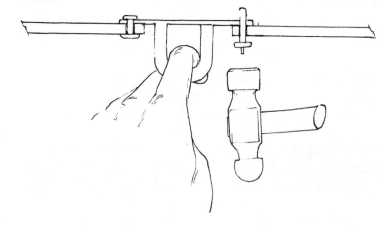

speed drill. Make sure that all edges are smooth and deburred, inside the mast as well as on the surface, and that there are no sharp corners on any cutouts. When everything fits and the mounting holes have been drilled and tapped, or just drilled if you are using rivets, it is a good idea to blow out the inside of the spar with compressed air, or even wash out the inside of the spar with a hose, to make sure all the metal grindings are removed.

Drive rivets are generally available only in aluminum. If the length is scaled correctly and if the hole is carefully drilled, they are easy to use. Just keep the fitting under tension and tap the drive pin until the rivet is fully spread inside. Drive rivets should never be used on fittings in tension or even sheer load where the load is taken directly by the fastening, or on fittings—such as internal tangs—which cannot be easily checked for corrosion.

Machine Screws If you are *ever* going to remove a fitting, it is a good idea to use tapped machine screws to fasten it to the spar. (You may find that far more fittings need removal and replacement than would be obvious. Any fitting that has a sheave can seize up, and it is a lot easier to free if you can remove it. Any fitting that covers a hole large enough to let you see inside the mast should be removable so you can use the hole for fishing for a halyard or checking a wire. When in doubt, use machine screws and make the fitting removable!) If you drill carefully, and in the right size (the correct drill sizes are written on the sides of taps), it is not difficult to tap holes. Any machine screw that is not through-bolted should be bedded in Loctite or a similar compound, or inserted with a lock washer at the head—although even with zinc chromate paste or silicone seal as an insulator, a slight degree of mast corrosion will probably form and guarantee that the screw does not drop out. If you're installing many fittings, it is a good idea to standardize on one size of screw, such as $^{10}/_{32}$ pan heads. Be sure to use zinc chromate paste, or at least a silicone sealant, on any stainless screws used on an aluminum spar.

To mount a bail on a boom, or at the base of a mast for a vang, it is possible to use tapped screws from each side of the spar, but a through-bolt is stronger and allows the bail to pivot. Often you will find that the available bails do not fit exactly. It is generally all right to bend a bail to fit, or to bend a long stainless bolt, if you do the bending carefully and slowly in a vise. You can also use threaded rod in place of a long bolt, with a nylock nut on each end.

There are also proprietary fittings available from Kenyon, Metalspar, and other spar makers which allow a vang to pivot to follow the boom, and which provide the double attachment points needed for compound-purchase vangs. Most can be mounted with tapped screws or large stainless pop rivets.

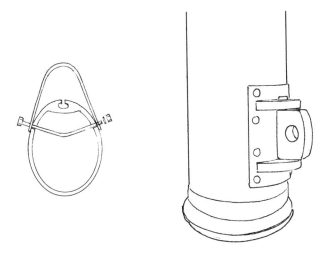

Filling Holes

It is not difficult to fill holes left in spars. If the spar is anodized or raw aluminum, use aluminum pop rivets in the extra holes. You can use set screws to "fill" threaded holes, but it is difficult to find aluminum setscrews, and a stainless-steel setscrew will set up a corrosive reaction in the surrounding aluminum. If the mast is to be painted, the small holes can be filled with a polyester body filler like Bondo or with epoxy filler. Larger threaded holes can be filled by using a setscrew driven in and filled over with body filler.

Many modifications to boats and spars are relatively easy and inexpensive, and can be done either by an owner who is used to working with hand and power tools or by a rigger with some guidance from the owner. The most important thing to remember is that there is no room for sloppy workmanship or jury-rigging on a boat. The sheave that binds "a little" will almost certainly seize up in a masthead; the rivet that didn't pop quite right will loosen; the screw driven in without silicone or zinc chromate paste as an insulator will corrode the aluminum and freeze itself in place; the slot that you "eyeballed" for position will not line up; and the inadequately backed-up block will ultimately break, probably in the midst of a jibe broach when the one thing you really don't need is for the babystay to come flying off! But if you're cautious, careful, and honest in the hardware that is added and the workmanship that is used, there is no reason to be afraid of modifications to a rig or to the layout of a boat.

SPLICES

There are, or should be, dozens of eye splices in the lines on your boat. Every line that leads to a becket on one of the blocks of a purchase, and every shackle on the end of a sheet, guy, rope halyard, or control line, should terminate in an eye splice for neatness and to maintain maximum strength in the line. A bowline, depending on the kind of line, will reduce the strength of the attachment to anywhere from 50 to 65 percent of the strength of the line; even a fisherman's or anchor bend, which probably retains the largest percentage of the line strength, comes in at around 80 percent. By comparison, a good eye splice should be as strong as the line.

A rigger will usually charge anywhere from $5 to $35 to make a splice in a line, take a week to get it done, and require that you drop it off and pick it up. If you are having a new spinnaker sheet made up, it is embarrassing, and probably unfair, to expect a rigger to install the shackle you bought at a discount store onto the line you got on sale, when he has rolls of line and bins of shackles right there in his store. The answer is to do your own splices. Most boat owners will readily splice laid line but seem daunted by the Chinese-finger-puzzle splices required by braided line. In fact, once the principle is clear, splicing braided line is easier and quicker than splicing laid line. And once you learn to do your own splices, it is possible to set up control lines, halyards, and other splices right on the boat, without worries about measurements and without repeated trips to a rigging shop. The average eye splice should take no more than five minutes once you have the hang of splicing.

The basic technique is simple to learn by watching, though it sounds complicated in a description. Essentially, a length of the core of the line is pulled out some distance back from the point of the eye splice, then the outer braid is unbraided, tapered, formed into the desired eye, and inserted into the core. When the core has been smoothed over the inserted outer braid, the tail of the core is then inserted under the outer cover in the opposite direction, and the bulked-up cover

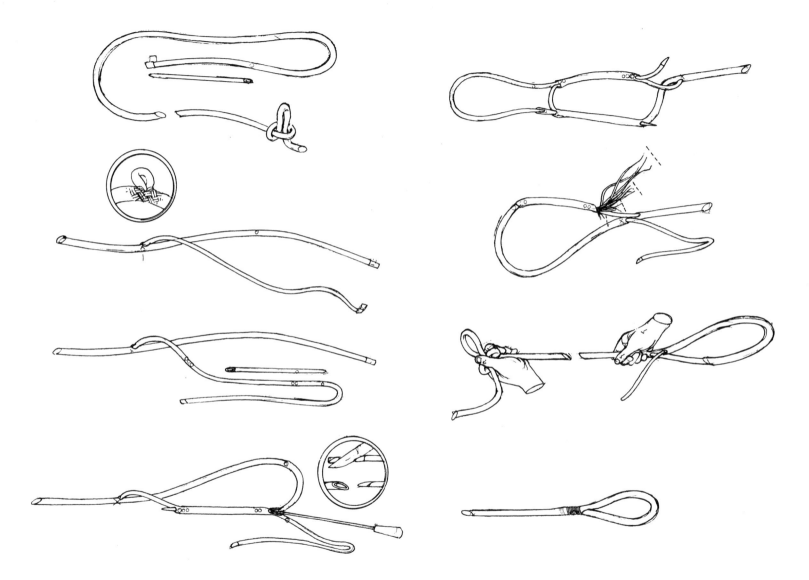

(which was pulled back to expose the long section of core) is "milked" over the exposed length of the splice.

There are some tricks to making the splice easier. You can buy sets of tapered fids to use in pushing the core and cover through. The fids are marked to show the length of the long and short measurements for the splice, which is a convenience, but trying to push the line through without the end coming out of the hollow end of the fid is always much easier in the drawings than in reality. The line companies suggest taping the tapered outer braid to the fid, but it doesn't always work anywhere near as easily as you expect. A simpler technique is to make a puller, which need be nothing more than a length of thin, stiff wire, doubled over. Instead of pushing the line through, you lead the puller from the outer end, hook the line into the doubled-over end, and pull it back. It rarely doesn't work the first time.

The second aspect of a splice that sometimes causes trouble is the milking. The first part of the splice goes easily, then the last part of the core refuses to bury itself and leaves an annoying patch of white exposed. To avoid the problem, take care to make a neat taper of the outer cover before it is inserted. The cover should be unbraided and combed out, then divided into three or four bundles that are cut off at appropriate intervals. Then spend a few seconds smoothing the taper before the line is inserted for the splice. If the line is old, so that the lubrication is worn off, it will be easier to milk down if liquid soap is used as a lubricant and if the line is held in tension by hooking the eye or shackle onto a strong point. Finally, if it really doesn't want to go and you are wearing out your best sailing gloves trying to get it down, try rolling the splice under your foot or even beating the line a bit to loosen it up. With patience, sailing gloves, and a hook on a post to keep tension in the line, it should be possible to milk down even very old line.

There are other splices besides the eye splice, and it is possible to join lines end for end and to back-splice a line to make a neat end. An easier termination for a line is a simple whipping, with or without a "butane back-splice" of the exposed end, done with either a torch or a rope cutter. If you are doing much work with lines, a rope cutter is a good investment. The flat blades made for soldering guns work fine, a little slower than the gadgets that are actually sold as rope cutters, but at a cost of about $1, they can't be beat for occasional work. An unwhipped heat-sealed line, or line dipped into the liquid gunks (Elmer's glue works as well as the special marine gunks at half the cost), is simply not as satisfactory as a properly whipped line.

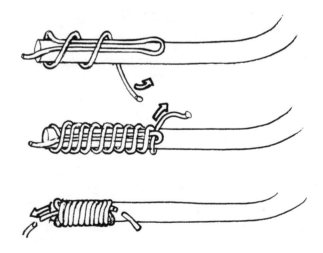

For a halyard or a reef line, it is a good trick to whip a Flemish eye into the end of the line. Webbing is available from riggers and sailmakers, and a short loop under the whipping, secured by the final stitching through the line of the whipping, makes it easy to attach a messenger for a reef line or halyard. As an alternative, you can use a simple messenger knot to tie in the messenger line: the knot is compact and reliable, and much stronger than the wads of tape that are usually used and that serve mostly to foul in masthead sheaves.

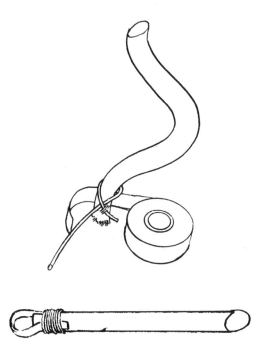

The splices for parallel-core lines (Kevlar and Dacron) and tail splices (wire to rope) are not impossible for an amateur, but they require patience, practice, and a modicum of tools. Most of the manufacturers of Kevlar line will gladly send you a sheet of instructions, but prepare for lots of practice and frustration, as the materials are generally unyielding and the unbraided core requires that the cover be milked down over what is essentially a sandwich of three layers. A tail splice is also possible for an amateur, and there are instructions available from the line makers. The tools you need are a bench with two vises, a propane torch and silver solder, a good Swedish fid, strong palm gloves, hands that won't mind a few cuts for a while, and infinite patience. After one or two tries and the time spent to patch up your cut and bloody fingers, you may conclude that riggers' charges for a tail splice are reasonable.

NICOPRESS FITTINGS

What an eye splice is to line, the Nicopress fitting is to wire. Every piece of wire used in running rigging, from halyards to the bridles for spinnaker poles and the wire links used in compound purchases or as tails for spinnaker guys and other high-chafe areas, needs to be terminated in a loop on the eye of a shackle, the becket of a block, or the pins of a spinnaker pole. Being able to apply these fittings yourself will save you many trips to a rigger and much frustration and anguish from mistranslated measurements.

In any rigging shop you can see coiled halyards that have been rejected because they were originally made to "owner's specifications" which turned out to be too short, too long, too small, or too heavy. The alternative is to have a rigger come out to your boat and measure, at $35 per hour, for a job that will take about five minutes from start to finish.

A Nicopress tool can usually be borrowed or rented from a rigger or sailmaker, or a club or group of sailors can buy a tool to handle the most common sizes of wire for under $100. There are also inexpensive tools that are a little slower to use, because they require a wrench to tighten instead of the long lever arms of a normal tool.

Here's how to do it. You will need a cable cutter that will cut the wire easily and cleanly, the proper size thimble, and the proper size Nicopress sleeve. Thimbles come in many sizes, and some chandleries will sell both large and small thimbles for ⅛-inch and ³⁄₁₆-inch wire. If there is no special need for compactness, use the largest size that fits your wire properly. It is possible to use no thimble where the wire goes around a large stud, such as the shank of a Presslock fitting.

To prepare a thimble, clip off the ears and file the surfaces smooth. This will enable you to pull the eye down tighter with no loss in strength. If you have to bend the thimble open to get it onto the eye of a shackle, open it carefully and make sure it is straight when you bend it back. Then lead the wire through the Nicopress sleeve, around the thimble, and back into the sleeve. Pull the wire until the sleeve is close to the end of the thimble. When the length is exactly correct, mark the tail of the wire one full diameter of the wire beyond the end of the Nicopress sleeve. Pull a length of wire through the thimble and sleeve to cut the wire at the mark.

Now, pull it all back into proper position, set the Nicopress

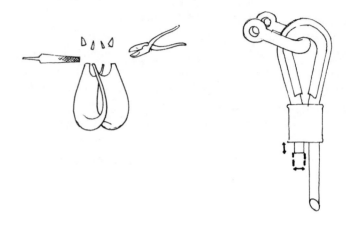

sleeve into the tool, and squeeze home. If it is one of the smaller sizes (¹⁄₁₆ or ³⁄₃₂), center the sleeve in the tool. If it is a larger size that requires multiple squeezes, try to space the crimps equally, and remember to reverse the tool for adjacent crimps so that the sleeve will come out straight. If any rough edge of squeezed-out material is left, it can be removed with a file. If you start away from the thimble, the eye may be squeezed too tight at the end of the thimble. It is better to start at the thimble end, making the first crimp far enough back so that the throat of the splice is not crushed.

To check if the crimp is good, make certain that the bitter end of the wire has not been sucked down into the sleeve; it should be even with the end. The proper number of crimps (three for ⅛-inch fittings, four for ³⁄₁₆-inch) should be spaced evenly. And make certain that you have not made the eye so tight that there are unfair loads on the thimble.

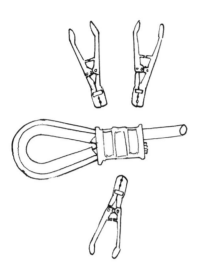

If the Nicopress is for a halyard, it is a good idea to put a parrel bead on the halyard above the shackle. The bead will keep the Nicopress sleeve from getting pulled into the mast-head sheaves, where it will either jam or score the sheave, and by using colored beads you will have a quick and easy color-coding of your halyards.

It is possible to use Nicopress fittings to terminate smaller sizes of 1 x 19 wire, such as the 1/16- or 3/32-inch wire that is sometimes used for boom topping lifts. Use a thimble large enough so the wire is not crushed or kinked when it is bent, and leave enough tail to apply two Nicopress sleeves, with the tool reversed for the second fitting so that the bending moments of the two fittings cancel one another.

The trick with any modification work on a deck or a spar is care. Marine materials are generally easy to work with, but precise measurements, a careful examination before you drill or saw, and planning before you start the project can avert the disasters of drilling into a spar and catching the drill bit on the outhaul tackle, dribbling the cuttings or epoxy from a mounting right through the deck onto the loran case, or measuring and installing a new halyard only to discover that the splice ends up inside the turning block, under load, whenever you use the heavy #1. Measure first. Measure again. It is even worth the bother of dummy rigs. Try cable clamps to hold a shackle on a halyard so that you can check the length. Or use tape. Remember to allow for stretch and mast bend in your measurements, and be certain that whenever you install a critical fitting on deck or on a spar, you measure with the boat fully rigged, so that you can make provision for the control lines and other gear that can get forgotten in the midst of a winter project.

6

THE WORKING PLATFORM

Whatever else it may be—a floating terrace for cocktail parties, a sun deck, a laboratory for tinkering with expensive toys, or a stage for fantasies of sailing off to never-never land—the deck of a boat is a working platform. It takes room for a person to grind a winch, tail a line, pump up hydraulics, or throw a helm; and there are optimum positions for efficient physical activity. Without sufficient room to throw his elbows, a man will tail a line half as fast as a tailer who can develop a rhythm of movement; a grinder who cannot stand or kneel over the winch will grind half as fast as a grinder who can put the full strength and speed of his shoulders and upper arms into the turn; a control line that requires a long reach or an awkward stance will be harder to pull and less likely to get trimmed.

At the same time, while efficiency may be the only criterion for deck layout on a grand prix racer—indeed, some designers would argue that making the deck comfortable will lessen the efficiency of crew who should be "on their toes"—on boats that are used for cruising or day sailing as well as racing, the deck must also be comfortable and clear for a drink in the anchorage, for a sunbath on the foredeck on a lazy reach, or for children to play on during a long passage. There are a few boats that have sacrificed the deck layout to the interior, expanding the volume belowdecks to the point where there are few if any options left in rigging the cockpit and deck that are begrudgingly left over by the vast house. They are the exception. Most decks can be improved with a little thought given to how the boat is really used, and what layout of winches, control lines, and helm makes the most sense.

THE HELM

Helms can be changed and improved, and it is surprising how many helms need modifications. The most common problems are wheels that are too small, tillers that are too short, and steering positions that make little or no provision for the comfort of the helmsman or his ability to see the sails, instruments, compass, and the other inputs he needs to sail well.

The size of a wheel or length of a tiller makes a tremendous difference in the control of a boat. A small wheel or short tiller is quick in its steering response, requiring only small movements to steer the boat. A larger wheel or longer tiller is more powerful, but requires larger movements for the same amount of steering. The larger wheel or longer tiller allows a finer touch, avoiding the oversteering that makes the wakes of some boats look like the meandering of a drunken sailor. A larger wheel also lets a helmsman sit farther outboard, improving visibility of the seas ahead of the boat. And with a long enough tiller, a well-balanced boat as large as 40 or 45 feet LOA (overall) can enjoy the quick steering response that only a tiller can provide.

In many cases, a small wheel has been installed to allow walk-around room in the cockpit, or the tiller is made short to allow room at the forward end of the cockpit. But if the wheel is too small or the tiller too short, the boat can be unmaneuverable in a breeze. The only cure if you find yourself frequently fighting the helm is to change it. Many boats will accommodate a larger wheel with little sacrifice. It is not difficult to substitute a longer tiller for a marginally short one, or to add a tiller extension. A tiller-steered boat can often be converted to a wheel, either with the owner-installed kits that both Edson and Yacht Specialties sell or by a boatyard. And some racing boats as large as 40 feet are even changing from wheel steering to tiller steering for the improved handling that a tiller offers in certain conditions.

The important consideration in making any modification to the helm is to think through what the change will do to the rest of the cockpit. If the sheet winches were well placed for a tiller, will they be as well placed with a wheel? Try to measure exactly where the helmsman will sit or stand when the helm is changed. If possible, have someone stand in the various positions where winch grinders or tailers would be during a tack or jibe or other common maneuver. If you add a tiller extension or a longer tiller, where exactly will you sit when sailing to windward? On top of the cleat for the genoa sheet? Straddling the secondary winch? And if a wheel is substituted for a tiller, or a larger wheel is substituted for a smaller one, what happens when a crew member tries to get aft of the helmsman, whether to adjust the backstay or to take a leak off the stern of the boat? With a tiller-steered boat, an adjustment to the genoa sheet usually doesn't block the helmsman's vision, because the helmsman sits to windward; on a wheel-steered boat the genoa sheet trimmer and the helmsman may block each other if the cockpit isn't carefully planned.

The actual work of a conversion to a wheel is more complicated than the brochures of the pedestal manufacturers would make it seem. In particular, the installation has to be accessible for maintenance, and the mountings of the quadrant on the shaft, the pulleys for the cable, and the pedestal itself must be solid, reliable, and without play. If you are ordering a wheel installation from a boatyard, make certain that you have discussed the details of the installation with them beforehand. How will they stiffen the cockpit sole where the pedestal will be mounted? Where will the cables lead? How are they mounting the quadrant on the rudder shaft? What is the access to the steering gear? Remember that the access should be adequate for maintenance *at sea*. Steering gear rarely breaks at the dock or mooring; it breaks in confused seas, with a good breeze blowing. The steering equipment made by the major manufacturers is reliable and effective, but the loads and demands on a rudder and steering gear are so great that a reliable emergency tiller is essential. On some boats the emergency tiller is reversed or needs strong auxiliary tackles to have enough power to steer the boat. Make sure it can all be fitted and actually function to steer the boat.

A longer tiller is not a complicated installation. Some of the wood-fabricating companies, such as H & L Woodworking, have a catalog of stock tillers that they produce for manufacturers, and it may very well be that a stock tiller will fit the head of your rudder shaft. Even a custom tiller is not as expensive as it would seem, and replacing a tiller with a longer tiller is often a chance to remedy the design defects that are inherent in stock tillers, most of which are too lightly built in the body and head, too heavy in the handle area, and without adequate provision for a tiller extension.

Tiller Extensions

Few tiller-steered boats are comfortable to steer hard on the wind or on a hard reach without a tiller extension. A properly sized tiller extension allows you to sit well out to windward, where you can see approaching seas and breeze. To preserve the feel and responsiveness of the tiller, the extension should be strong and free of play. For most boats, it should also be either adjustable or have some provision for different grips, so that it can be used comfortably by different helmsmen and in different breezes.

For a boat of under 6000 or 7000 pounds displacement, one of the small-boat tiller extensions is usually adequate. Nico/Fico, Forespar, and other companies produce them with a variety of grips and swivel mechanisms, and with a choice of screws, single bolts, or a quick-disconnect mounting. Although the quick-disconnect mounting may seem appealing, the ball-pin mechanisms have a lot of play and the large hole required for mounting the mechanism unnecessarily weakens the tiller. It is usually a better choice to use a conventional mounting and use a clip on the top of the tiller to hold the extension when it is not in use.

For larger boats, the tiller extension should be strong enough to take the loads of heavy reaching or broaching seas. The Forespar Ocean Racer and some of the other heavy-duty extensions work well. The custom-fabricated tiller extensions that Tillotson Pearson has made for the J-30 are even stronger. Whatever the choice, if the extension is mounted on a wooden tiller, the mounting hole should be carefully drilled and either bushed with a short length of metal tubing or soaked inside with epoxy. If the hole has not been bushed, after a year or two of heavy sailing it will probably be necessary to drill out the hole and make an epoxy bushing for the tiller extension mounting bolt.

Very large boats with tillers will probably require custom extensions and side handles that can be used when steering from inside the cockpit.

Adjustable tiller extensions are available with "twist-lock"

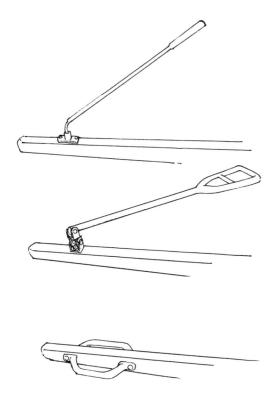

adjustments and with pin-lock adjustments that fix the length of the extension with a pin in a hole. Either can be reliable for a small boat, if they are kept repaired. But plastic pins can sheer off, springs can weaken, and compression locks can wear out. If you cannot find a repair kit, a call to the manufacturer will usually bring the necessary parts and some good advice. For a large boat, a tiller extension with a ladder grip is more reliable than any adjustment mechanism.

Footholds

Very few boats have a really comfortable position for the helmsman when the boat begins to heel. If the helmsman sits on the windward rail, which allows a view of the luff of the genoa, he is often forced to brace himself with a white-knuckled grip on a stanchion, a foot against the mainsheet block, or by straddling a winch. On most boats, it is easy to install foot blocks or rails that enable a helmsman to hold his position even when the boat heels or rolls.

Some typical locations for footholds are the sole of the cockpit, the edges of the seats, the traveler support beam, or in the case of boats with a crew well instead of cockpit seats, the sides of the cockpit. For the seats or the sole of the cockpit, a cleat can be bolted in place from underneath. Teak is the usual choice of wood, because most boats have teak external trim and because teak will survive outdoors with an oil finish or no finish. A varnished foothold will need frequent retouching. The cleats should be large enough to be through-bolted, and the edges should be rounded so that lines and foul-weather gear will not catch on them.

A foothold can also be mounted on a traveler bridge, but watch out for the lines, knees, and shins that will also find the foot brace. If a fixed mainsheet block is mounted on a block off the edge of the traveler beam, the block can be made large enough to serve as a foothold. Sometimes the cockpit will be wide enough to require two footholds, one for each side; they should be carefully streamlined to avoid snagging lines and shins.

Finally, for wide cockpits the best solution is a fabricated metal foot brace, which a heliarc welder can bend and weld

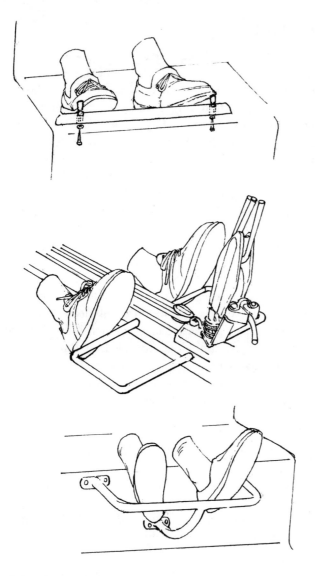

up out of tubing and stanchion braces. It should be bolted securely to the cockpit sides, which will probably require substantial backing blocks for stiffening and support.

For boats steered with wheels, it is difficult to place footholds that are useful. Two low-profile cleats on the cockpit sole sometimes work for reaching in strong breezes, enabling the helmsman to brace himself and keep from sliding down to leeward. The helmsman's seats that are often built behind the wheel are rarely useful in anything other than light breezes downwind. If the wheel is large enough to allow steering to windward from the weather rail, the same blocks used on tiller-steered boats will work. Otherwise, the most useful suggestion is to cover the lifelines with soft foam padding, either refrigeration tubing or the ready-fabricated lifeline paddings that are available.

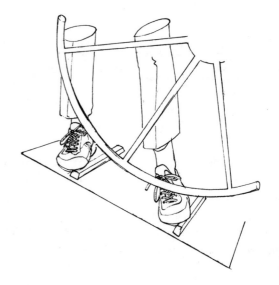

SITING WINCHES

Except on the smallest and lightest boats, winches provide the power for trimming sheets, hoisting and tensioning halyards, and sometimes the control lines. On a racing boat, the deck often seems like little more than a platform for winches: the cockpit is a well for the winch grinders and tailers, the selection of winches is a decision akin to the selection of firepower for a battleship, and the positioning of the winches is, after the location and configuration of the helm, the most important decision in the deck layout.

To operate a winch efficiently requires room—room for a tailer to pull line quickly, and room for a winch grinder to put him- or herself over the winch, with legs braced and with a full turning radius for the winch handle. If the room is compromised, so that the winch can only be cranked with one

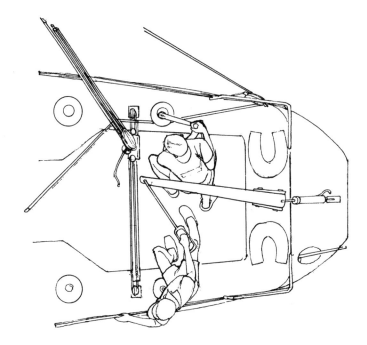

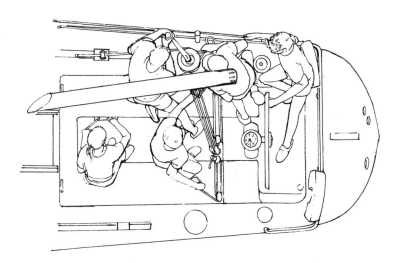

hand or a tailer cannot swing elbows wide enough to tail the line in long pulls, it will take a long time to sheet in the line, and it will probably require a very powerful and hence slow winch to sheet in the last few inches of a heavily loaded line.

A winch that is used only for control lines or to adjust the tension on a halyard can be positioned wherever it is convenient for the deck layout. If the halyard arrangement is efficient, with provision for someone to "jump" the sail up, the winch will be needed only for the last few feet of the hoist and to adjust the luff tension of the sail. For headsail sheet winches, on the other hand, real efficiency requires that the handle of a winch be at chest height for either a standing or a kneeling grinder; the grinder should be able to brace his or her feet so that the winch can be turned rapidly in each gear, and on boats of over 7000 pounds displacement, it should be possible to use a double-grip handle.

The requirement that a winch be situated with a full 10-inch turning radius for the handle, on a platform large enough and strong enough to mount the base, often determines much of the deck layout of production boats. Frequently builders will place sheet winches at the widest spot of cockpit coamings, not because that is the ideal spot, but because it is the only spot wide enough to mount the winch without an overhang of the base. If the wheel is close by, the result during a tack can be cockpit gridlock.

Winches and Lifelines The other common problem with winches, especially on production boats in the 26- to 34-foot overall range, is winches placed so close to the lifelines that the winch handle cannot make a complete revolution. Winches placed too far outboard are inefficient to use, because the winch grinder cannot get a decent stance over them. One solution to both the inefficiency and the lifeline problem is to move the winch inboard to a platform built onto the coaming. The platform can be fabricated of aluminum or stainless steel, but a built-up teak platform is often easier to make and presents fewer potential snag points for lines.

If the winch cannot be moved, the lower lifeline can either be tied down with shock cord, re-led from the adjoining stanchion or pushpit verticals to the deck and back, or omitted in the offending section.

Sometimes the best cure is to move the winch out of the coaming area. Moving secondary winches from cockpit coam-

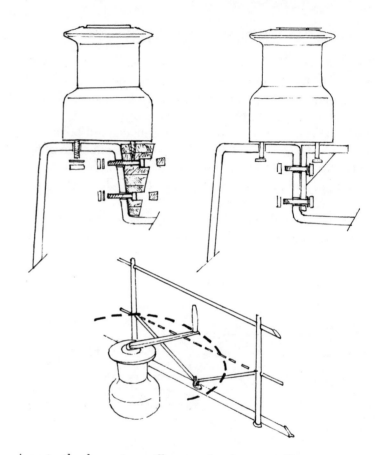

ings to the housetop will not only clear a traffic jam around the helm but will often provide an efficient working platform, because the housetop raises the winch to a comfortable working height. Halyard winches that are taken off the mast and put on deck are easy to adjust in almost any weather, compared to the task of holding a winch handle in a mast-mounted winch, tailing the halyard with one hand, and finding that there is no hand left to hang on to the boat. It is not difficult to move a winch, or to cosmetically fill the holes where the winch has been removed or moved.

Another alternative for hard-to-use winches is to replace them with control systems that don't need winches. On many boats of 30 to 35 feet, an awkward mainsheet winch can be replaced with a mainsheet system that needs no winch. Control lines that lead to winches (like outhauls, flatteners, cunninghams, vangs, or foreguys) can often be redesigned to need no winch, with the benefit that they can be controlled from positions other than the fixed location of the winch.

PURCHASE

No, this is not an exhortation to buy! Purchase refers not only to the mechanical advantage that can be given to a tackle or lever or other device but also to the position that a crew member can assume when pulling on a line or cranking on a winch. There is a vast difference between the efficiency of someone who can brace legs and pull on a line with two hands, or with a steady hand-over-hand pull, and a crew member who is wedged between a wheel and a cockpit coaming, barely able to swing one hand as he or she tails in a sheet. If the mainsheet is situated low in the cockpit, with space around it where a crew member can stand and pull steadily, it is no trick to tail in 30 or 40 feet of line from a multiple-purchase tackle.

Any exertion requires room to pull and a platform from which to pull. If the boat is heeling or pitching and the platform is precarious, then the crew member will have one hand free rather than two, and the efficiency drops to about one-fourth of what might be achieved if he or she could stand in a secure position and work with both hands. For example, picture a reefing rig that requires a crew member to stand at the mast, facing aft, to pull a leech reefing line coming forward on the outside of the boom: the sail is blowing or flapping at him, the boat is pitching and rolling. (Remember, it's breezy enough to reef, and until that reef line is trimmed, there is no mainsail to dampen the rolling!) If the winch that is used for reefing is also on the boom, the crewman must hold the handle in the winch, tail the line, keep himself from being slapped by the sail or the boom, and hope to quickly gather in the leech reef line. By contrast, picture a reefing rig in which the reef line is led aft to a winch on the housetop, where a person can stand securely in the cockpit, tailing the line with two hands until the last few feet are ground in on the winch.

The difference between those two reefing systems is the difference between efficient gear and marginal gear, between rigging a boat for comfortable sailing and rigging that will "get by." In general it is not difficult to modify systems on a boat, sometimes at little or no cost, to convert marginal systems into efficient ones. The same blocks that are used for an awkward outhaul can be incorporated into an efficient outhaul, sometimes with the addition of nothing more than a length of wire and a single block to double the purchase. The boom-end sheave that works for an inconvenient boom topping lift might work instead for a super-efficient flattening reef. And the winch that is difficult to use on the boom may work perfectly on the deck.

7

SAILS

ost boat owners give diligent lip service to the adage that the sails of the boat are its engine. Many of those same boat owners sail with sails that are three, five, or more years old, spend less money and less time each year on their sails than on the maintenance of their "iron genoas," and give less thought to the planning of their sail inventories than to the drink holders on deck.

THE REAL ENGINE

The analogy with an engine isn't really appropriate. Engines are rarely custom-built. If an engine is powerful enough for one 30-foot, 12,000-pound boat, it is powerful enough for another; the only constraint is whether the engine can be adapted to the available engine compartment, shaft, control placement, prop size, and pitch. By contrast, although it is possible to buy ready-made sails, which are produced for both OEM (original equipment manufacturer) package deals and by mail-order sailmakers whose principal appeal is price, it is rare that a "generic" sail can realize the performance potential of a boat. Two stock Ragmop 33s, sailing in different sailing areas, will probably need different sail inventories, even if both boats are used for the same balance of racing, cruising, and day sailing.

The effectiveness of an engine is usually obvious: if you hear coughing or the whirr of the starter motor instead of the familiar purr, if no amount of throttle will get you up to your usual rpms, if the exhaust discharge is black instead of white, or if you just can't get up to your usual six knots cruising speed, you know something is wrong. Except on the race course or under the gaze of an experienced sail trimmer, sails do not reveal their condition with such obvious signs. Many boat owners sail with five- or six-year-old sails that have been carefully folded and protected against chafe and tears, and which, because they have no patches, look "good as new." But watch a boat with old sails when it sails alongside a comparable boat with newer sails. The difference in performance can be remarkable, because the "good as new" sails have often lost their shape and effectiveness, and because the recent advances in sailmaking design and technology have made possible sails that are faster, more versatile, and in some instances tougher than the sails of even five years ago.

LOOKING AT SAILS

If you are ever invited on a powerboat for a day, take along a pair of binoculars and use the opportunity to study the sails of other boats. In most sailing areas, you will probably see fully half of the boats with mainsails and headsails that do not fit the boat. Light-air genoas are cut so that they are anywhere from 3 inches to a foot short of full hoist. Mainsails do not come up to the black band on the mast, or have a foot which, when fully stretched, is either short of the black band on the boom or cannot be fully stretched within the limits of the black band. You will see genoas that cannot be properly trimmed to the tracks on the deck of the boat, and which require lead points farther forward, farther aft, or farther inboard for effective use. Up close, you can see more subtle misfits: the tack fitting of the mainsail does not line up properly with the tack fitting on the gooseneck, so that there are always distortion lines around the tack; the luff reef points have not been offset by the same amount as the reef hooks,

so that the reefed sail is under tremendous unfair loads; the clew fitting of the mainsail does not match the type of outhaul fitting or car, and has to be lashed or otherwise jury-rigged.

Even when sails fit exactly, you can see sails of which no sailmaker should be proud: mainsails with a hard crease on the inside edge of the batten pockets; genoas that have the shape of one half of the back end of an elephant, no matter how hard the halyard is hoisted. Some sails, from a distance, look picture perfect. When you get close you realize that the smooth appearance of the sail has been achieved by building a sail with almost no shape in it. There are no wrinkles, but there is also no power in the sail. You see genoas with spreader patches that do not line up with the spreaders, and a patchwork of chafe patches on the foot of the sail that gives it roughly the appearance of an Appalachian bed quilt.

Sometimes the problems with sails stem from bad sailmaking: an inappropriate design, shoddy construction, or materials that are either deficient or mismatched to the probable use of the sail. Far more often, the disasters result because an owner has picked the wrong sailmaker for his purposes, or because he or she has not taken the time to plan and maintain an inventory of sails that are right for the real use that the boat sees. Most sailmakers are highly skilled craftsmen and superb sailors: they know how to build a good sail, they know how to make a sail fit a boat, and they know how to design and cut sails to fit the needs of different sailing areas, boats, and sailing styles. The problems arise because boat owners do not take the time to analyze their sails and sailing needs, and to cultivate an effective relationship with a sailmaker.

MEASURING FOR SAILS

Your boat is unique. Even if you have purchased a stock Muckaround 32 with a stock rig, made no changes to the deck layout, and added no new equipment, the boat is unique because no one else sails with exactly your style and use of the boat. And even among stock Muckaround 32s, there are frequently changes in deck layout and spar design that affect how the sails should be cut and built.

Midway through a production run, the builder may have switched from one spar company to another, which may mean a different placement of tack and clew fittings, a different offset of reefing hooks, even the use of different spar sections with different bending characteristics. Many boats are produced in several models, with an optional "tall rig" later becoming the standard rig. The sail plan for a shoal draft version of a boat may be the same as the sail plan for the standard keel, but the boat will probably be more tender and less weatherly with a shoal keel; sail changes will come at lower wind velocities, which in some sailing areas will mean different overlaps for the genoas. Later boats in a production series may have the deck tracks positioned closer inboard, or running farther forward or aft.

Once you begin modifying the stock rig and deck layout, your boat will probably have the ability to tune and position sails in ways that demand different cuts and fabrics. If you have an effective backstay adjuster and babystay or runners, so that you can control the bend of the mast, the boat will profit from a more powerful cut in the mainsail. If the jib leads can be brought further forward, aft, or inboard than the stock leads, you may be able to use sails that were unusable on the stock boat. If you have a flattening reef that can be adjusted

easily and quickly, the sailmaker can build a mainsail with a full lower section that would be uncontrollable on a boat with less versatile sail-shape controls. If you have tuned your rig with the mast tilted forward to minimize a weather helm, the genoa hoist on your boat may be less than the design sail plan.

The way to get sails that fit on your boat is to have the boat measured by the sailmaker or one of his staff. The process takes a good sailmaker less than half an hour, and in the course of looking at the boat, the sailmaker will also form a sense of what kind of sail-shape controls are available. On board the boat, the sailmaker can pump up the backstay and see exactly how much mast bend is possible. He or she can measure the maximum genoa hoist and get it right for your boat. He can sketch the genoa and main tack horns, the reef hook offsets, the outhaul carriage or shackle, the placement of deck tracks. A conscientious sailmaker will note the placement of primary winches and foot blocks, the position of the lifeline stanchions, the rake of the spar, and the position and rake of the spreaders. He might note that the runner tails are carefully wrapped around their tackles, indicating that they are almost never used. "The kind of mainsail we have been talking about will require regular use of the runners to limit the mast bend," he might say. "Are you sure you want to do that?" And if you realize that with your usual crew you really don't want to use the runners, and tell the sailmaker, he can design a mainsail that will not require as much fiddling with the sail-shape controls.

It may be impossible for a sailmaker to come to the boat and measure it. Sometimes that refusal could be reason to look for another sailmaker. In other cases, you might volunteer to take the measurements yourself. Nothing more than a steel tape and a ruler is necessary, but if you are doing measurements for a sailmaker, have him send you a measurement form so that you can be certain that you are talking about the same measurements. For example, if you are measuring genoa hoist from the bearing surface of the tack horn to the bearing surface of the genoa halyard snapshackle, does the sailmaker want the measurement with the Nico-press fitting of the genoa halyard all the way up to the masthead sheave? Or does he normally ease it a little to allow for stretch in the luff of the sail? A confusion of terminology can result in a sail that is an inch or two too long or too short on the luff: too long and you will need a genoa cunningham to properly tension the luff; too short and you have needlessly given away effective sail area aloft, where it does the most good.

Some measurements sound easy but are difficult to take. When the sailmaker asks how much mast bend you get, find out exactly how he wants you to measure the bend. "About six inches" is not a precise enough description of mast bend to get a mainsail that will fit right and work right. And once the sailmaker has designed the broadseaming and the luff curve of the sail, it can be difficult, time-consuming, and expensive to recut the sail to achieve a sail shape that will work with your mast. As tedious as it sounds, it may be necessary to go up the mast, tape a rule to the spar, and use binoculars to observe the intersection of a taut wire (from the masthead to the tack) with the rule. If you can tell the sailmaker that at maximum mast bend you have 6.5 inches at the lower spreaders, 8.0 inches at the midpoint of the mast, and 5.5 inches at the upper spreader, you have a much better chance of getting a main that truly fits your boat. If your sailmaker has measured your boat, be sure to keep him advised of any changes to the rig.

There are some details that cannot be measured. A sailmaker can approximate the position of spreader patches or lifeline patches, but when they are put on in the loft, more often than not they will be slightly off, too high or low, so that part of the patch is serving no use or part of the sail is not protected. The best way to get the patches right is either to put them on on the boat, or to build the sail without patches, hoist it on the boat and mark the sail with pencil where the patches go, then take it into the loft to have the patches put on. If the sailmaker will not come to the boat to get the patches right, you might offer to mark it yourself, or ask for precut patches of insignia cloth that you can put on the sail yourself.

There are even some sails for which the final cut of the sail is best left for after it has been hoisted. To build a maximum-size #3 genoa that will trim inside the chain plates, the leech has to be cut to just clear the front edges of the spreaders when the mast is bent to its maximum bend. The best way to get the shape of that leech exactly right is to build the sail with an unfinished leech, hoist it, bend the mast, and then finish the leech to an exact fit. It means a trip to the boat and back, but if you are paying a king's ransom for a custom built Kevlar/Mylar #3, it is not unreasonable to expect it to fit exactly.

SERVICE

Computer design programs have changed the sailmaking business. The design process that used to require hours on the loft floor and repeated experiments can now be handled, with far greater flexibility, on a computer terminal. The sail designer feeds in the rig measurements and factors such as displacement, righting moment, and hull flexibility, and the program will then design a sail, put it on a computer screen or plotter in three dimensions, and allow the sailmaker to view the shape of the sail from a variety of viewpoints while he twiddles the parameters until the sail looks right for the designed wind strength and the sailing characteristics of the boat. The computer program will then either produce the offsets to cut out the panels for the sail, or in some cases will cut the panels directly on a laser or hotknife cutter. Not only are many of the potential errors in designing the broadseams and the luff rounds of the sails eliminated, but successful sail designs can be duplicated without requiring full-size Mylar patterns for the panels.

The newest computer programs go a step further and actually model the loading on a sail in different wind strengths and points of sail. Thus the sail designer can choose cloth types and panel layouts that will optimize the effectiveness of different cloths for different jobs. Some of the "discoveries" of these computer programs can be applied generically, as in miter-cut cruising genoas with lighter cloth weight close to the luff, where the loading is less, and stronger cloth weights closer to the leech.

These programs do a terrific job, *if* they are fed the right information about the boat and about what the sail is supposed to do. It is up to you and your sailmaker to discuss exactly what you need in a new sail so that he can feed the right parameters to the program, and so that he can select the right materials for your intended use. If you tell your sailmaker that you need a "new #1," instead of explaining exactly what wind and water conditions you will need the sail for, what other sails it is meant to complement, and what kind of sailing you will do with the sail, you stand a very good chance of being sorely disappointed with the sail. And if your sailmaker has had no real sailing experience on a Wiggly 31, and doesn't realize how tender it is, or how squirrely it is off the wind, he may build the wrong sails. Most sailmakers, especially in the larger franchised lofts, have the ability to consult centralized databases on the characteristics of various designs. If the sailmaker has no specific experience on your boat, you may want to invite him for a sail before he builds a new $5000 mainsail.

Even with the best data fed in, the programs are not perfect. In the race to produce better sails, sailmakers are constantly refining their programs, using newer or different cloths, changing the panel and general shape parameters of their sails, and altering construction methods. In some cases, a racer may elect to be a guinea pig by ordering one of the first of the new Turbo-Mains or Screamer-Genoas. The decision could lead to a breakaway sail. It could also lead to a lot of time spent in fine tuning and recuts, which might never make a decent sail, or to a sail that is either ineffective or so delicate that it breaks down in normal sailing conditions. If you have not made clear arrangements about what happens if the sail does not perform, you may find that choosing the experimental sail can be a trial of your patience and pocketbook.

The ultimate test of a sail is how it fits, looks, and performs on your boat. Most boat owners can identify egregious mistakes, but new sails often demand different trimming and helming techniques, and there are times when a sail looks wrong because it has wrinkles that an owner doesn't expect but which the sailmaker *wanted*. For example, some all-purpose spinnakers are supposed to have puckers in the head when they are used for reaching. In a pamphlet or a phone call, a sailmaker can give you guidelines for the position of the genoa car and for setting halyard tension. On the boat, you may discover that the guidelines are not enough to get the sails looking and performing right. Mylar and Kevlar sails, for example, don't respond to halyard tension as a Dacron sail would, and many high-aspect #3 and #4 genoas profit from being trimmed well inboard, even barber hauling so that the sails look like the jibs on a highly tuned one-design. You might discover the right trim by experimentation, but often the tricks that are necessary to make sails look right are not easy to discover on your own.

If you cannot get a sail to look right or sail right, your sailmaker should make arrangements to come out on the boat for a sail check. Many boat owners assume that the service is available only to the owners of Maxis and racers who buy a complete inventory each year. In fact, many sailmakers are eager to come out on your boat, to look not only at the sails they have built for you but at the other sails in your inventory as well. You will probably get a pitch about what needs replacing, but in the meantime you will get some valuable advice about your sails, deck layout, and rig tune and the way you have been trimming your sails.

If this is the first sail you have bought for three years and it is obvious to the sailmaker that you won't buy another for three more years, don't expect the head of the loft to come on your boat for a height-of-the-season regatta. But if you are having trouble with a sail, if the leech of the main won't stand up in light air, if you can't get what looks like a decent twist into the sail, or if the sail just isn't performing as you expected, invite the sailmaker out for a sail. If it is a big boat, make sure you have enough crew along so that the sails can be changed as needed, and let the sailmaker spend his or her time looking around, checking leads and trim. Ask him or her to trim the sail until it is right, and make careful note of just what he does. And if he can't get it right, make certain he takes the sail back to the loft with him. If you have paid for a custom sail, designed to fit your boat and your needs, you should not be content until the sail is right.

HIGH TECH OR LOW?

The technology of the last decade has produced dramatic and significant changes in sail cloth and sail design. As recently as two or three years ago, the new sail fabrics were still experimental, and too delicate for all but the most aggressive racers. Mylar fabrics would delaminate or rip from the slightest chafe, Kevlar would come apart in astonishing rips from even a minor chafe of a spinnaker sheet across the leech of the mainsail, and the basic construction techniques for the new sails—primarily glue, strategic patches, and prayers—meant that only boat owners who were willing to consider sails seasonal purchases could equip themselves with the latest in technology.

What the intrepid early owners of those sails got—as long as they lasted—were sails that would hold their shapes through a wide range of wind velocities. The differences in the performance of boats equipped with the new sails were so dramatic that many clubs and one-design classes outlawed Mylar and/or Kevlar sails as an unfair advantage for the well-heeled racers. Today, the same advantages are available to a wide range of sailors.

With a woven Dacron sail, even a sail made from a cloth that has been finished with a hard resin coating to control or limit the stretch in the material, a sailmaker has to design his sails to *control* the stretch. No design or construction method can eliminate the bias stretch inherent in woven materials. As the wind strength increases, the loading on the sail increases exponentially, and the material stretches. If the shape was perfect at 5 knots, it will be too full at 18 knots; the fuller shape will contribute to heeling moment rather than forward drive for the boat. And while an adjustment of halyard tension and headstay sag can reposition the point of maximum camber in the sail, the shape is still a compromise. To give a sail a useful range, the sailmaker is forced to cut the sail flatter than he would prefer, so that it does not stretch into too full a shape at the high end of its usable range. For the most common range of wind in North American waters, from 3–4 knots up to 15–18 knots, when most boats are stiff enough to carry an overlapping genoa of perhaps 150 percent, the stretch inherent in woven Dacron means that for real efficiency under sail most boats need two or even three sails to cover the wind range.

With Mylar or Kevlar fabrics, it is possible to mold the shape into the sail. Within its designated wind range, a well-built Kevlar or Mylar sail will show very little change in shape, except from the fullness that is induced or removed through mast bend on a mainsail, or through adjustment of headstay sag (with the backstay adjuster on a masthead rig or the runners on a fractional rig). The newer fabrics are also substantially lighter than woven Dacron of comparable strength: in many cases a Kevlar or Mylar fabric will weigh half as much as woven Dacron of comparable strength, which is an advan-

tage not only in light air, where the lighter fabric is easier to fill to shape, but in general sail handling. And with lighter sails that hold their shape up into a much higher wind range, the once elusive dream of an "all-purpose" #1 genoa—a single sail light enough, strong enough, and with the ability to hold its shape from 2–3 knots up to 15 or more knots of breeze—can be realized for many boats.

With Dacron sails, it generally requires more sails to cover a given wind range, and the transition point between the sails is a sensitive question: put the heavy #1 up in a dying breeze and you lack power and end up changing again, or motoring. Put the light #1 up in too much breeze and it quickly stretches out of shape; keep it up too long and you risk destroying it, or making the stretch permanent. A flat Dacron #3 genoa may be fine in a breeze, but it will lack the power to drive the boat when the breeze momentarily drops. Often, boats with a flat Dacron #3 genoa will need a #2 genoa to cover the wind range from 15 or 20 knots up to the 25 knots or so where the #3 becomes effective.

With sails designed for heavier air, the advantages of modern sailcloth are even more pronounced. Because the loading of a sail increases exponentially as the wind velocity builds, it is only since the development of tough Kevlar and Mylar sailcloth that sailmakers have been able to build tall, powerful #3 genoas that are effective over a wide range of wind strengths. These sails are full enough to drive a boat well in breezes that extend down to the range of the #1 genoa, and because they hold their shape, they can be carried up to 25–35 knots of breeze, depending upon the stiffness of the boat and the flexibility of the mainsail controls. The power of these #3 genoas not only gives the boat the ability to drive through seas but often makes it possible to eliminate the #2 genoa from the sail inventory.*

For a mainsail, the advantages of the newer sailcloth are not so obvious. The tremendous strength-to-weight ratios of Kevlar and Mylar sailcloth do permit the use of much lighter mainsails, but these fabrics still remain susceptible to delamination and deterioration from chafe and flogging, and in a sail that is up in winds from 0 to 50 knots, and which must be flogged when it is hoisted, during reefing, and sometimes just to keep a boat on its feet, the newer fabrics can have a significantly shorter lifespan than woven Dacron. The shape-holding ability of the newer fabrics may also be less important in a mainsail, since a well-rigged main has a range of controls to bring the sail back to shape. The older a mainsail, the more tugging and tuning it will take to get it into an acceptable shape. The soft cloth will be a pleasure to furl on the boom, but it will require constant fine tuning to maintain an effective shape in the sail.

The chief disadvantages of modern sailcloth are potential fragility, inconvenience of folding and storage, and cost. Modern construction methods and designs have made the new sails substantially more durable than the earliest Kevlar and Mylar sails, but the fabrics do break down, and are more susceptible to chafe than traditional fabrics. Unlike the Dacron sail, which may hold together long after its shape has deterio-

rated, the modern fabrics hold their shape until the sailcloth itself breaks down. Stuffing these fabrics into a sail bag will drastically shorten their life expectancy, and while they are lighter than Dacron, the firmness of the cloth sometimes makes a crew wonder if they shouldn't have a sheet metal brake on deck to assist with the sail folding. Genoas should always be stored in a turtle, rather than a sail bag, and for maximum sail-changing convenience and optimum sail life, many boats opt for a full-length turtle which stores the sail flaked without folds from clew to tack.

CHOOSING SAILS

How do you choose an inventory? With the versatility of modern sail designs and sailcloth, it is possible to generalize, at least for sloop-rigged boats sailing in most North American coastal waters: most cruisers need a good all-purpose #1 genoa, a #3 genoa, and a soft, forgiving mainsail; the basic inventory for most racers is light and heavy #1 genoas, a powerful #3 genoa, an all-purpose ¾-ounce spinnaker and a versatile mainsail that can be shaped for maximum power. As boats get bigger, or the racing gets more aggressive, the inventory needs increase: depending on the sailing area, a racer may need a ½-ounce spinnaker and/or a 1.2- or 1.5-ounce reaching and "chicken" spinnaker. For racing with long offwind legs, an all-purpose staysail can add a critical ½ knot of speed under the spinnaker; the same sail can be tacked at the stem and used as a zero-air windseeker, which because it does not overlap the spreaders will not slat as much as a full-sized drifter or superlight genoa. For heavy air, a strong heavy-air jib or #4 genoa is a better addition to the inventory for most

---

* Even on boats that do not need a #2 genoa for upwind sailing, the sail is often useful for other purposes: as a blast reacher for heavy air reaching, especially if it has been built with a second clew ring higher up the leech; as a strong, versatile, easy-to-fold-and-store delivery or cruising sail on racing boats; or as a sail to have on deck and ready to hoist on long downwind legs when a sudden windshift or a spinnaker disaster means that you want a headsail up in a hurry.

boats than a postage-stamp-sized storm jib. The heavy-air jib is also a terrific sail for family or short-handed sailing in moderate air; responsive boats will often sail well in breezes as light as 12–15 knots with a full main and heavy-air or working jib, and the combination is easy to set and trim. Boats that venture offshore need storm sails: a storm jib and trysail.*

The real choices come in deciding exactly what you expect of each of these sails for *your* boat, and *your* sailing area. To know what kind of #1 genoa to build for your boat, a sailmaker needs answers to a lot of questions: What is the usual breeze in your sailing area? Are there patterns to the breeze, like a sea breeze that comes up every afternoon? What percentage of your sailing is spent in competition? Cruising? What kind of crew is usually available to change your sails? How do you feel about constant attention to sail-shape controls? Are you willing to sail with runners or a babystay all the time? Are you willing to replace sails every season or two, or do you expect sails to last for four, five, or more years?

If you generally sail shorthanded, you will want versatile sails that hold their shape through a wide wind range. If you are planning an extensive world cruise, and the sails must stay up day in and day out for months on end far from any available repair facilities, you are going to be more concerned with

longevity of the fabric than the shape of the sail. Indeed, in trade wind reaching and running, the fuller shape of "blown-out" sails may prove more effective.

And since there are invariably overlaps in range between sails, a sailmaker should know what other sails are in your inventory, and what you perceive as the weakness or gap in your inventory. Be cautious when you order sails to fill gaps, instead of shoring up the basic inventory. Often, a boat will start with an OEM package of a main and lapper, or with the sails that were on the boat when it was purchased. The genoa that came with the boat might be tired, with a shape that bears little resemblance to what it once was or what a good genoa should be. But the sail is not torn or stained, and it is light air where the boat seems to have the most trouble, so the owner buys a drifter, in the hope that it will fill the gap in his inventory. The drifter is fine in breezes of 1–5 knots but hopeless in anything more, and the owner is now in the situation of having to change sails every time the breeze builds over 5 knots. And when the genoa then reaches the end of its useful life, because the owner now has a drifter, he will probably not get a wide-range #1 but will buy a replacement for the old sail because "I've got the drifter for the real light stuff." A good all-purpose genoa might have been a better choice than the drifter.

If you sail in an area where the breeze frequently, or usually, builds from 10 knots at noon to 15 knots with an afternoon sea breeze, the most important sail in your inventory is going to be a #1 genoa strong enough and heavy enough to handle that range of breeze. If a sailmaker recommends two #1 genoas, one that is "good to 12–13 knots" and another that "comes into its own at 10–11 knots," it may seem that you

---

* The danger with storm sails is that they are almost never used, so that when the time comes to hoist them, no one knows how they should be trimmed. A gale is not a good time for experimentation of lead positions. If you have storm sails, make certain that they can be trimmed properly on your boat, and that the gear for trimming them includes no weak links like snatch blocks. Storm jibs and most heavy-air jibs built for boats with luff-groove devices on the headstay have lacing holes to use in place of the luff groove in storm conditions. It is a good idea to practice lacing a sail on before you have to do it on a pitching bow in 50 knots of breeze.

have perfect coverage of the range, but what you really have is a guarantee of a sail change every day. On a family day sail, the change will come just as everyone is comfortable. On a race, it will mean agonizing before the start ("Should we use the light or the heavy #1?"), a decision that is probably wrong as often as it is right, and then the anxiety that comes from having the wrong sail up for a short leg: "If we change, we'll get rolled by everyone in the fleet; if we don't change, that light #1 will end up confetti."

Inventories that must serve for racing and cruising present special problems. Modern sailcloths of Mylar, Kevlar, and Spectra 900 are strong, and if handled carefully can survive normal sailing conditions. But sails of Mylar and Kevlar cannot be stuffed into sail bags and cannot tolerate chafe. A cruising couple can turtle the heavy one on a large cruiser-racer, but it takes time and care. And using racing genoas for cruising, while it makes your boat quick in pick-up races, eats into the serviceable life of the sail as an effective racing sail.

One solution for boats that cruise and race is to design an inventory with one or two sails of Dacron. In an area of mainly light air, the light #1 might be Mylar or Mylar/Kevlar, and the heavy #1 could be a softer Dacron sail. The #3 could be Mylar/Kevlar and the #4 or heavy-weather jib could be Dacron. In general, the light #1 and #3 would be used only for racing. Although a heavy #1 is flatter and hence less effective in light air, it would probably be fine for cruising.

An alternative is to a buy or convert an old sail as a cruising/ delivery sail, which can be cut with a high clew for visibility and effectiveness as a reacher. Most racing boats will do fine for cruising with an inventory of three headsails: an all-purpose #1, which can double as a reacher, a heavy-weather jib,

and a ¾-ounce spinnaker. You can take one of the racing jibs along as a backup on the summer cruises, but it usually isn't necessary. In general, blown-out racing sails don't make good cruising sails. A Mylar light #1, when it is too tired for racing, is probably beginning to delaminate and come apart at the seams. Usually, a Dacron sail is more salvageable, and with some clever cutting can be made into a serviceable cruising and delivery sail.

MAINTENANCE

No matter what you do, sails wear out. You can take every possible precaution, getting the sails down before they are in too much wind, folding them carefully, washing them frequently, and after a while, either the fabric will begin to break down or the shape of the sail will bear scant resemblance to its out-of-the-bag form.

Aside from the normal precaution of folding sails instead of stuffing them, the most important sail maintenance is preventive maintenance, and the most important tool is a roll of tape. Spreaders, turnbuckles, stanchion tops, pulpits, lifeline connections, the vees between tangs and the mast, and every other sharp or abrasive edge that can get near a sail should be taped carefully. You usually don't need a wad of tape, but a quick turn will slip off or chafe through, and before you notice it, you will have a worn spot or a tear in a sail. The new elastic tapes which stick only to themselves (Navtec Rig Wrap is one brand) are neater than conventional sticky tapes, since they will stretch to shape and leave no residue when they are cut away. Vinyl tape, available in colors from most hardware stores, also works well. Whatever kind of tape you use, be generous and thorough in your taping. And if you have fittings that cannot be taped, such as deck cleats that often catch on sails, consider installing rod or shockcord guards.

The other common source of sail damage is tears from meat hooks in wire halyards. It is easy, if painful, to check for meat hooks by running your fingers up and down the wire of the halyard. The usual spots are the last few feet of halyard, which bear on the masthead sheave when the sail is fully hoisted, and the section of halyard that bears on the sheave when the halyards are stowed. If you find a meat hook, don't try cutting it away with wire cutters. You will never cut it close enough, and the stub will quickly work its way through your delicate sails. Instead, rub the back edge of a knife back and forth over the meat hook until it fatigues off. Generally it will break off flush and you can get more service out of the halyard. When more meat hooks appear, it is probably time to replace the halyard.

There isn't much other maintenance for modern sailcloths. Spinnakers profit from being washed to get out the salt, and soft Dacron sails are not hurt by a wash. For firm Dacron cloths and the laminated Mylar and Kevlar fabrics, in general the tumbling action of any wash beyond a hose-off on the lawn will do more harm than good. A sailmaker can give you advice on removing stains, such as the blood of your over-zealous crew, but most cleaning chemicals are bad for sails, and other than hosing off the salt, little cleaning is required for most sails. It is also not a good idea to hoist sails to dry them after a hosedown. The free "clothesline" is tempting, but flogging destroys a sail quickly. Use the lawn instead.

Other than an occasional hosedown and constant attendance to potential sail rippers on the boat, the most important maintenance is to monitor the sails for the indications of chafe or rips. A sailmaker will gladly check the sails for you over the winter, but you can check the sail yourself each time you fold it by looking at areas of potential chafe: especially the corners of the sail and any place where the sail rubs against rigging or fittings, such as runners, lifelines, the spar, spreaders, or pulpits.

PATCHES

Many boats carry a ditty bag of sail-repair tools, and if you are handy with a palm and sail needle, you can do major repairs on your sails. For quick repairs on Mylar and Kevlar sailcloth, you should try to carry a large square of what the sailmakers call "insignia cloth," the sticky-backed heavy cloth that they use for numbers and letters on sails. If you have a tear or worn spot in the sail, and you need to use the sail before it can be taken to the sailmaker for a proper repair, clean the torn or worn area until it is free of salt, grease, and dirt, and measure a patch of insignia cloth large enough to overlap the worn area on all sides. Cut it out, smooth the sail on a flat surface (foredeck hatches or companionway boards work well), peel the backing paper off the insignia cloth, and press the patch home. For a tear, do the same thing on the other side of the sail. Then cut another patch twice as large as the first patch and put it over the first, so that it overlaps on all sides. On a tear, build up the patch in two layers on both sides of the sail. For spinnakers, use rip-stop tape, which is sticky-backed nylon, for a temporary repair until the sail can be taken into the sailmaker.

TURTLES AND BAGS

In selecting sail bags and turtles, you should be guided by the same honesty that you need to select sails. A racing boat with a full crew can handle full-length turtles, which make hoisting and sail changes quicker. They also take space and technique to fill, and are unwieldy to store and move around belowdecks. They are particularly difficult to use if a sailmaker has made them too big or too small.

A turtle or sail bag should fit the sail the way it is *usually* folded. Too often, sailmakers either grab a bag or turtle that was made up during the slow season and which isn't quite right for your sail or boat, or they make a turtle that fits fine when the sail is carefully folded on the loft floor, and which is impossible to use quickly on the boat. Unless you normally take all your sails off the boat and fold them on the lawn or the clubhouse floor, you will need a larger bag or spend a lot of time cursing as you try to stuff the sail into the bag. An oversized bag or turtle is almost as bad.

8

MAINSAIL CONTROLS

The modern mainsail is a spectacular achievement of the sailmaker's art: a single sail that can be massaged and reshaped to work effectively on any point of sail from hard on the wind to a dead run, and in anything from drifting conditions to 40 or 50 knots of breeze. Even when the sail is small,* the trim of the mainsail controls the helm of the boat; the vang and mainsheet provide the panic button in hard reaching, and the size and shape of the main provide a quick control of sail area, balance, and angle of heel. The sail shape controls that are usually thought of as racing tools—like the cunningham, flattener, babystay, and runners—are being discovered by day sailors and cruisers who would rather "power up" or "power down" the mainsail as the wind and sea conditions change than switch headsails or reef.

MAINSHEET

The problem with most mainsheet rigs is that there is either not enough power, so that trimming or easing the sheet when the boat is hard on the wind becomes a slow two-hand or two-man job; or there is too much purchase in the mainsheet tackle, so that easing out or trimming in from a broad reach or a dead run involves so many coils of line that the cockpit begins to feel like a snakepit.

There is rarely a magic purchase ratio that will solve the problem. When a boat is off the wind, the pull on the mainsheet is easy to handle, even on a large boat, because the

---

* On some mid-1970s IOR designs, the mainsail accounts for as little as 36 percent of the foretriangle + mainsail area. By contrast, on some contemporary fractional rigs the mainsail constitutes 60 or more percent of the main + foretriangle area.

apparent wind velocity on a boat sailing off the wind is lower, and because the pull on the mainsheet controls the angle of attack of the sail rather than the tension of the leech. (The mainsheet is pulling the boom in and out, not down.) Once the boom end crosses the rail or, more properly, once the boom is over the traveler, the pull on the mainsheet is vertical, controlling the tension on the leech of the mainsail and requiring substantially higher tension.

The attachment point of the mainsheet block or blocks on the boom, and the angle that the mainsheet tackle makes with the boom, significantly affect the sheeting efficiency of the rig. Midboom sheeting requires a mainsheet only half as long, but it requires almost twice as much tension on the sheet to achieve the same leech tension on the sail as a mainsheet tackle that is positioned at the end of the boom. The fittings and attachments for midboom sheeting are subjected to double the load of an end-boom rig, and the load should normally be divided among blocks mounted separately on the boom rather than a double or fiddle block. The boom section used for midboom sheeting must be heavier and stiffer than a section used for end-boom sheeting on the same boat, to resist the bending moments of the leech load of the mainsail pulling against the midboom sheet. (If the boom bends downward in the middle, even a fraction of an inch, it will flatten the foot of the mainsail and ease the leech, usually just when you are trying to sheet the main hard to tighten the leech for pointing.) Thus end-boom sheeting is generally more efficient, although a place for the traveler has to be found in the cockpit —usually on the bridge deck, on a horse across the cockpit, or in the case of a well cockpit without seats, on the sole of the cockpit. The relationship between the helmsman, genoa

sheet winches, and traveler/mainsheet makes for the most difficult decisions of cockpit and deck layout, especially on cruising or cruising/racing boats with relatively small cockpits.

A mainsheet that does not lead vertically from the traveler to the boom is less efficient (because the nonvertical sheeting vector is wasted in trying to compress or stretch the boom). The nonvertical mainsheet will also put unfair loads on the traveler car and track.

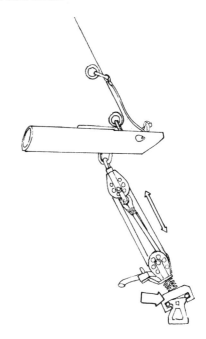

The obvious solution to a nonvertical mainsheet is to move either the attachment point on the boom or the traveler. If neither can be done, make certain that the traveler is designed for nonvertical loads (the Nicro/Fico and Ronstan X-track travelers or one of the Harken travelers will move freely with loads off the vertical), that it is sized at least a size larger than would be necessary for a fair lead, and that the mainsheet system is sufficiently powerful to compensate for the inefficiency of the lead angle.

Most production boats come with a variation of one of the mainsheet rigs illustrated here. Unfortunately, all three arrangements have problems.

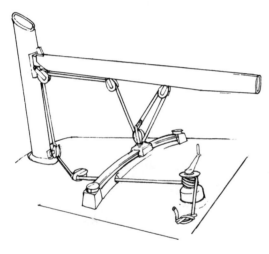

Using a winch for the mainsheet means that it is possible to use a small purchase, anywhere from the 1:1 direct lead of a 12-meter yacht to the 3:1 or 4:1 purchases (often on a mid-boom traveler) that are common on production boats. Until the boom reaches the rail, the line can be tailed in by hand, and the moderate purchase means there isn't too much line to tail in going from a run to a beat. On the wind, the winch

supplies the power to trim the mainsheet hard. It sounds like an ideal rig, but to tweak the mainsheet an inch or two means getting the handle and putting it into the winch; if the winch isn't self-tailing, the tail must be uncleated, trimmed, and recleated. To ease an inch, even if the winch is self-tailing, means uncleating and easing the line; in some cases a turn or two has to be taken off the winch to get the line to ease.

On a racing boat, where one man can be assigned full time to the mainsheet, the winch can be a fine rig. For a short-handed boat, such as the average family cruiser, a winch for the mainsheet is usually too far from the helmsman and involves too much work for it to be properly tended. As a result, steering, which could be made simple with control of the mainsheet, becomes a trying task. The owner complains of weather helm when the breeze fills in. And a boat that might steer easily with a tiller requires a wheel just to control the weather helm.

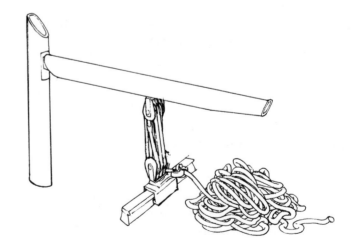

On smaller production boats, the usual mainsheet rig is a simple tackle, ranging from 4:1 for a 22- to 30-foot boat to 6:1 or even 7:1 for a 35- to 40-foot boat. The simple tackle allows a quick release or trim by the helmsman, but it generally has two disadvantages. First, the power of the mainsheet remains 4:1 or 6:1 for the entire play of the main, even when the sheet is eased for a run or broad reach. The length of line (about 139 feet for a boat with a 14-foot boom and a 7:1 tackle) is unwieldy, and the friction of seven turning sheaves and seven parts of a purchase rubbing against one another makes the effective power of the tackle less than the 7:1 ratio would indicate. And when the boat is hard on the wind, that 7:1 purchase that was so much more than needed off the wind is often not quite enough to get the main sheeted really hard in a flat-water pointing trim. It often takes two hands, or two people, to sheet the sail hard enough. Although a good cam cleat will hold the sheet once it is trimmed, most cam cleats under those conditions are difficult to release, so that tripping the line out of the cleat to ease an inch or two is inconvenient for a helmsman. Increasing the purchase by another part or two won't help. Even with good ball-bearing blocks, the friction of a 7:1 purchase makes it marginally more powerful than a 6:1. And each additional part to the purchase means that there are another 20 feet or so of line that have to be trimmed, and that threaten to lie in the cockpit like overcooked spaghetti.

Simple Tackles

On a boat under about 28 feet, where simplicity is a paramount concern, a straight tackle is usually the best rig. If the traveler is at or near the end of the boom, across the bridge deck or across the cockpit, the power required to trim the sheet can usually be handled by a 4:1 or 5:1 tackle. A few relatively simple additions can make the tackle more effective.

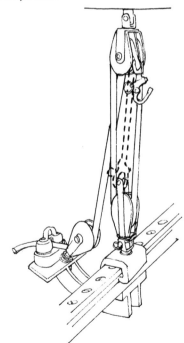

- First, if the last part of the tackle does not lead around a ratchet block, change the block. A ratchet block functions like a snubbing winch, greatly increasing your ability to hold a line that has been uncleated and making it possible to trim a line under greater load. Harken and Schaefer make excellent ratchet blocks in configurations and sizes that suit any boat.

- Second, the last part of the tackle can be terminated in a snap shackle (a lightweight fixed-eye shackle is ideal) instead of an eye splice or bowline. In light air or off the wind, the snap can be taken off, reducing the tackle by one part and making for that much less line to trim from a run to a beat.
- Third, if the cam cleat is taken off the traveler block and a swiveling deck block is substituted, the mainsheet lead will always come from the same spot, the mainsheet will be less likely to tangle when 60 or more feet of line are eased out off the wind, and trimming the mainsheet won't automatically move the traveler car. Either a teak block or an aluminum bracket can be fabricated to hold the swiveling block.

Winch Mainsheets

For large boats with mainsail areas over 350 or 400 square feet, there is really no choice except a winch with a tackle of between 2:1 and 4:1, or a combination of a tackle and a hydraulic or mechanical fine-tune. The two-winch rig, with a double-ended purchase and a winch on each side of the boat, has been popular for a long time with racers and does offer the advantage of putting a mainsheet trimmer up on the rail instead of in the middle of the cockpit. It would also permit a shorthanded cruiser to reach the mainsheet from the helm. The disadvantage is that every adjustment of the traveler requires the heavily loaded mainsheet to turn at least three blocks, and from time to time the mainsheet has to be adjusted from one side to the other to even up the two tails.

The alternatives are a single winch mounted horizontally or vertically on a traveler platform or the bridge deck, or a cabin-

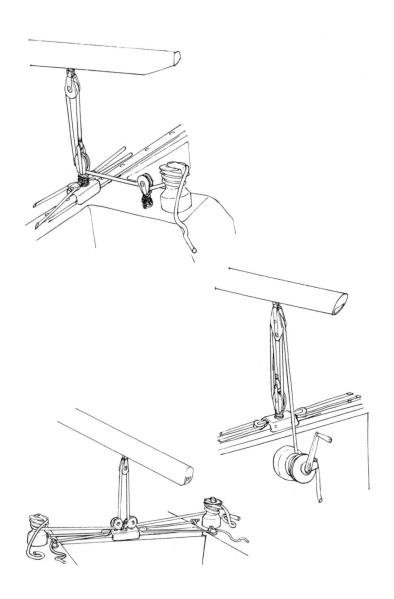

top winch. A self-tailing winch can make trimming easier, but it doesn't help much with easing. In general, the mainsheet will be a two-hand job unless an auxiliary mainsheet control ("fine-tune") is added to the system.

Compound Tackles

Finally, there are the great number of boats from about 28 to 45 feet or so for which a simple tackle, even a 6:1 or 7:1 tackle, is not always powerful enough and for which a winch with its weight, manpower requirements, and slowness is unacceptable. The solution here is to address the two mainsheet requirements—a long pull with a relatively light load and the short pull with a strong load—with two different solutions: in other words, a compound tackle. The main (coarse-tune) purchase is sufficient to trim the sail to the center of the boat. The secondary tackle makes it possible to fine-trim and ease the sail when the boat is hard on the wind.

The simplest compound rig uses a "head-knocker" mounted on the boom. The mainsheet on the traveler is the coarse trim; the pigtail dangling from the boom is the fine-tune. On the wind, when a puff or a lull or changing sea conditions call for more or less leech tension, the helmsman can reach up and tweak the fine-tune without losing concentration. With 5:1 on the main traveler and 3:1 on the fine-tune, the ultimate power is 15:1, which is sufficient for a moderate-aspect mainsail of 300 square feet. A smaller mainsail might use 3:1 on the main tackle for a total purchase of 9:1. If the leech tension of the mainsail is super-critical, as it is with many high-aspect-ratio sails, the fine-tune can be increased to 4:1 or even 6:1. The goal is to keep the coarse purchase as low as possible, just strong enough so the sail can be trimmed in typical conditions

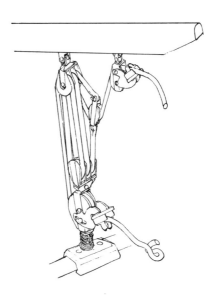

by typical crew.* If the block sizes are chosen carefully, it is possible to experiment with different ratios by swapping blocks back and forth. Ball-bearing blocks are essential, the line sizes should be small enough to avoid excess friction, and Monel or stainless rivets (or through-bolts) should be used to fasten the head-knocker to the boom.

An alternative is to put the fine-trim down on the traveler with the coarse-trim. The fine-tune can also be made double-ended and led to either side of the cockpit. Or the fine-tune tackle can be inside the boom and led back out through a pigtail at the end of the boom. The latter rig requires a large boom because the mainsheet fine-tune will be back with the

* On some racing boats, especially those used in round-the-buoys racing, a tackle system with a relatively low purchase ratio on the coarse-tune is used for speed on the starting line and in mark roundings. The mainsheet man on the boat will generally go through sailing gloves quickly.

sheaves for the reefs, flattener, outhaul, and possibly the boom topping lift. It is also possible to add a fine-tune tackle to a boat with a primary mainsheet led to a winch.

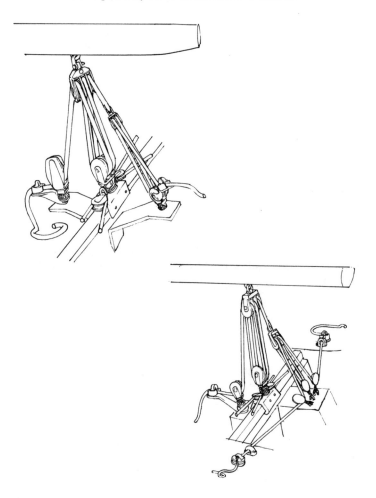

Finally, for grand prix racers and generous pocketbooks, the fine-tune can be hydraulic, usually done with the entire mainsheet lead rather than a single part because of the limited travel of the hydraulic cylinder. Navtec makes extra-long cylinders for use in mainsheet systems. Or a regular cylinder can sometimes be used with a 1:2 purchase that will trim 2 inches of mainsheet for every inch of movement of the hydraulic cylinder. Hydraulic panels are mounted on either side of the cockpit or in a central position, giving the specialist mainsail trimmer instant control of the mainsheet, and frequently the vang and flattener as well. The gear is expensive, complex, and heavy, but for the ultimate in fingertip control, especially for boats in the 40- to 50-foot range, it is incomparable.

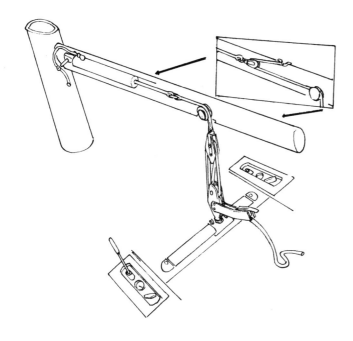

Sizing Mainsheet Blocks

The primary blocks in an end-boom mainsheet purchase, whether the upper and lower blocks of a simple 4:1 fiddle tackle or the coarse-trim blocks of a compound purchase, should have a safe working load equal to MaxMain.* If three single blocks, each mounted on a separate bail or eye, are used instead of a triple block, the blocks can carry a lower rating, since each block carries only a fraction of the total load (the load is not divided precisely in three because of the fric-

* See Chapter 4.

tion of the blocks), but it is not a good idea to downsize the blocks too much. Larger sheaves reduce friction and hang-ups when you are tailing long lengths of mainsheet, and strong shackles resist the breaking loads that are hard to avoid when a mainsheet rig is twisted unfairly.

For a midboom mainsheet rig, the blocks should have a safe working load at least equal to 1½ times MaxMain. And with a midboom mainsheet, it is even more important to distribute the loads of the attachment to the boom by using two or three separate blocks instead of a single fiddle or triple block.

Fine-tune blocks can usually be two or three sizes smaller than the main tackle of a compound tackle. The important limitation for the fine-tune is generally not the breaking strength, but the size of line that can be used.

In rigging any compound-tackle mainsheet system, make sure that the heavily loaded cleat on the coarse-trim can be released under load. A relatively easy-to-release cam cleat, such as the Harken cam cleat, is fine on a sail of up to 325 square feet or so. Beyond that, a sheet stopper that can be released under load, such as the Howard stopper mounted on the big Harken offset fiddle block, is a better rig. For any but the largest tackles used with a hydraulic fine-tune, it is usually possible to find a ratchet block that can be used in the coarse purchase which will enable a mainsheet trimmer to hold a heavy load while easing or trimming the line.

Sizing a Mainsheet

There are no special requirements for a mainsheet that cannot be met with Dacron braid. For most simple and compound-purchase systems, ⅜- or ⁷⁄₁₆-inch line is adequate for the main purchase and will present less friction in multiple-purchase systems than larger lines. Heavily loaded winch mainsheet systems may require larger line. The blocks should be sized up accordingly, to avoid both the chafe of large line in narrow sheaves and the friction of heavily loaded lines turning on small sheaves.

To calculate the length of mainsheet needed for a simple mainsheet tackle or the coarse-trim tackle in a compound mainsheet system, use the following formula for an end-boom system:

$$\text{Length} = \text{Purchase} \times \sqrt{2 \times (E-1)^2} + 10$$

Purchase is the mainsheet purchase ratio (e.g., 4:1) and E is the length of the boom. For a midboom mainsheet, use E/2 instead of $E-1$, and add whatever length is needed to reach the mainsheet winch to the 10 at the end of the formula.

VANGS

There are still boats sailing without vangs, their booms swooping and rolling from side to side and up and down with each wave, the top of the mainsail so twisted off that perhaps a third of the sail is driving the boat, the rest contributing to a sickening "death roll" that leaves everyone aboard dreading the prospect of a run or a broad reach. And there are perhaps as many more boats that have vangs that are so complex to set up and so difficult to tension or release that they are hardly ever used.

There are essentially three purposes for a vang:

- First, it controls the leech tension of the mainsail when the boom is beyond the end of the traveler. On some boats, a powerful vang is used instead of the mainsheet ("vang-sheeting") to control leech tension on the wind, with the mainsheet serving only to control the angle of attack of the sail.
- Second, some vangs can double as a preventer, holding the boom to leeward and preventing an accidental jibe in light air and sloppy seas.
- Third, a solid vang can take the place of the boom topping lift, holding the boom up while reefing or while the mainsail is not up.

The usual vang, often sold as a package with the boat or by discount houses, is a 4:1 self-contained tackle with a snap shackle on each end. The boom end is attached to a pad eye, a bail, or in some cases to a Dacron strap or stainless clips that fit into the bolt rope track; the other end is either attached to the rail, which means that it must be detached for a jibe and trimmed or eased every time the mainsheet is adjusted, or it is attached to a pad eye or bail at the base of the mast. If the tackle is mounted with the cam cleat block at the base of the mast or at the rail, it cannot be trimmed or eased except by a person standing at the base of the mast or at the leeward rail. The alternative, mounting the cam cleat block on the boom, increases the purchase to 5:1 but means that to release or trim the vang someone has to reach out precariously to leeward. When the tackle is heavily tensioned, which hard breezes require, it will be almost impossible to release in an emergency, such as a hard broach. All told, it is not a very effective rig for most boats.

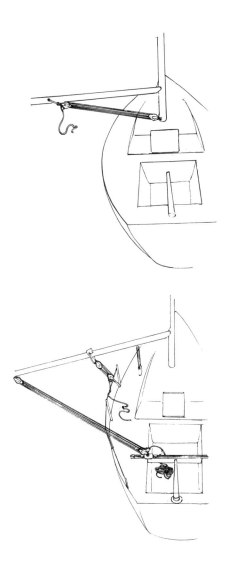

Since the total throw of a vang is on the order of 6 to 8 inches, the rigging requirements are much simpler than for a mainsheet. What is required, essentially, is sufficient power to trim the boom down in any conditions, along with a quick and easy release. With a powerful, easily adjusted vang, the main can be played aggressively on a reach, dumping the top of the sail when the boat is overpowered or about to broach, then trimming the sail back in when the puff subsides. If the vang can also be made to double as a preventer or a topping lift, so much the better.

A true vang attaches to the mast, so that the vang tension remains constant as the mainsheet is trimmed or eased. The tackle to the rail, which is really a vang/preventer, is simpler to install but much less useful, because it must be adjusted every time the mainsheet is adjusted and must be removed for a jibe, which is one moment when you really want a vang to hold the boom down.

The purchase power required for an effective vang is substantial, and the loads that can be generated by a vang, especially during a heavy-air jibe or when the mainsail suddenly empties and fills coming off a wave, are impressive. Because the trim to the base of the mast is at an angle, a good part of the pull is pushing the boom toward the mast rather than pulling it down; thus the power required for a vang is generally much higher than that required for a mainsheet.

The actual power required depends on the aspect ratio of the mainsail and the angle that the vang makes from the boom to the base of the mast. If the boom is low or the house is high, the vang requires much greater power. It is possible to build a vang powerful enough to function at low angles, but the mast, boom, and gooseneck must be strong enough to take the additional loads, which will put strong bending moments on both the mast and boom. An alternative for a low boom or a high house is to put the lead farther forward on the boom; a lead much farther forward than one third of the boom length will require a very stiff and strong boom. For any installation, the attachment points should be strong: through-bolted pad eyes or bails, or welded eyes. The safest installation for a bail is to use a bolt all the way through the mast or boom; it is usually safe to bend the bolt slightly, if necessary. Pad eyes can be placed inside the spar and riveted from the outside (see the drawing on page 72). It is also possible to have a rigger weld a bail, or ears for a gooseneck-type fitting, onto the spar.

Simple Vangs

For a small boat with a 3:1 or 4:1 mainsheet, a magic box or a simple 6:1 tackle makes a good vang. The tail should be led aft to a cam cleat so that the vang can be adjusted and released easily from the cockpit, or perhaps from the rails, depending on how hard the boat is usually sailed.

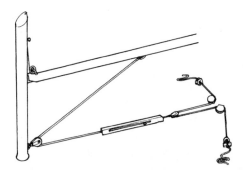

Compound Vangs

For a boat with a larger main, requiring a mainsheet purchase of 5:1 or more, an effective vang will require 8:1, 10:1, or 12:1 total purchase. A compound tackle, cascading one purchase into another, is an economical solution and works well because the total travel needed is not great. The compound tackle also offers a tail which can be used as a preventer whenever it is needed.

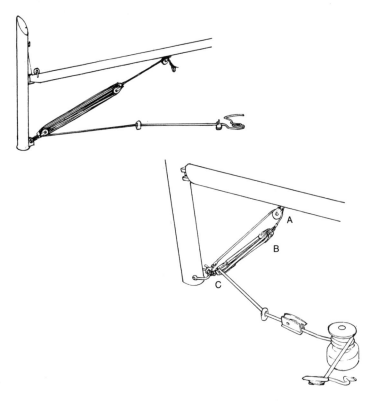

For light boats and boats that are raced hard in heavy conditions, a vang powerful enough to need no winch offers the quickest response. For heavy boats that are less likely to be involved in planing conditions, a tackle with fewer parts can be led to a spare winch, usually through a stopper. In any case, it is essential that the vang be powerful enough to get the boom down in any breeze, and that the release mechanism be reliable enough to dump the vang instantly in a broaching situation. A ratchet block in the vang tackle is a good idea for boats that do not use a winch with the tackle: the holding power of the ratchet makes it easier to dump the vang in an emergency and to retrim the vang in heavy air.

The loads on the upper (wire) block of a compound vang are considerable; the block should have a large sheave, a very strong shackle, and possibly roller bearings. If covered wire is

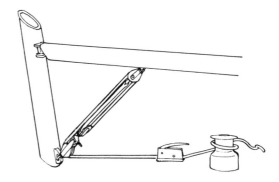

used, it should be nylon-covered tiller cable rather than lifeline material, which will chafe through the covering very quickly.

Big-Boat Vangs

Twelve-to-one is about the functional limit for a purchase system. For boats that require more power, generally boats with MaxMain figures of over 2200 pounds, the choices are either a purchase lead to a winch or a hydraulic vang. Blocks strong enough for a purchase system for a large boat are available, and many boat owners prefer the purchase/winch system because it can be released quickly in an emergency and because a winch and purchase gives some "feel" of the tension on the leech of the mainsail before the sail is vanged in too tight.

Hydraulic vangs offer incredible power, fingertip control, and the advantage of supporting the boom in the place of a topping lift. They have the drawbacks of expense, weight, plumbing that has to be snaked through the boat, the need

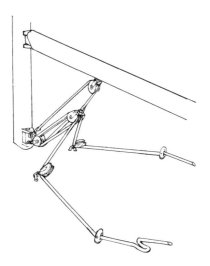

for a separate preventer, and the temptation to overtrim the vang, which sailmakers will tell you is one reason mainsails get replaced so often. Unless the vang is rigged with a special quick-release button, the hydraulic vang is also slower to release in an emergency broach situation.

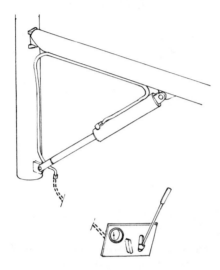

The trick in setting up a hydraulic vang is to position the panel so that the vang is easily released and trimmed, preferably with the trimmer able to watch the leech of the sail instead of the gauge on the hydraulic panel as he pumps down the vang. It is also important to keep the whole panel visible, so that the valve that is used to select between the backstay, vang, and other hydraulic functions isn't accidentally in the wrong position. Pumping hard on the backstay while you are watching the mainsail leech is a good way to turn the mast into a crossbow.

Solid Vangs

There are also nonhydraulic solid vangs, which are popular in several versions in Scandinavia, and which have been imported into this country by Merriman and by several Scandinavian boat builders. The EasyKick vangs are essentially a magic box inside a telescoping aluminum tube. It is a clever idea and it does away with the need for a topping lift, but the friction of the tubes and the internal tackle makes the system less powerful than the 6:1 or 8:1 ratio would suggest. The

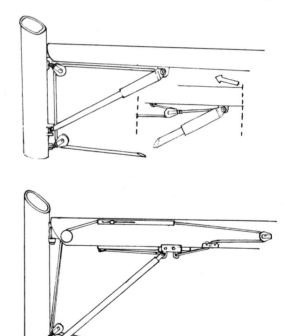

construction of the systems limits their use to boats with mainsails of under 250 square feet.

A solid vang can be custom built, using a traveler track and a magic box or a compact tackle. The vang itself should be a tube with appropriate end fittings, rather than rod (which would have to be unacceptably large and heavy to be stiff enough to support the boom). Both ends should swivel freely, giving the entire tube a universal action, and a strong traveler should be used for the boom end.

Lever Vangs

It is also possible to use a lever vang, which can generate tremendous power with minimal friction. The problem with most lever vangs, for cruiser-racers, is that the range of adjustment of the lever is so limited that if the boat has a flattening reef or regular reefs, one end of the lever vang needs to be disconnected, or perhaps fastened to a track, in order to allow the boom enough movement to put in the flattener.

Sizing Vang Gear

For vangs that lead at approximately a 45-degree angle from the boom, MaxMain is a good figure for the safe working load of the vang blocks and other gear. Line sizes for a tackle will rarely be a problem; ³⁄₈- or ⁷⁄₁₆-inch line is strong enough for any vang that does not lead to a winch. The wire in a compound vang should not be used at more than half of its breaking strength; thus if MaxMain is 1800 pounds, the wire for a compound vang should be ³⁄₁₆-inch 7 x 19 stainless cable with a breaking strength of approximately 3700 pounds. The secondary blocks in a compound tackle could be rated a notch lower, but the potential shock loads on a vang are enormous when the main suddenly jibes, or if the boom ends up in the water, so that an upgrading of the blocks and other gear is probably wise. If the angle between the vang and the boom is more acute than 45 degrees, the gear should be sized up accordingly.

The solid vang constructions will hold the boom up and replace the boom topping lift. The compound tackles will double as a preventer but require a separate topping lift. The tackles are cheaper, lighter, and generally simpler to install and maintain. Either system can provide enough power to hold the boom down. My inclination is to use tackles that don't require a winch for lighter boats, especially fractional rigs or boats with large mainsails that need instant "depowering" on a reach. On larger boats the winch and tackle is powerful and easy to release in an emergency. If hard reaching is not a problem and the idea of the vang supporting the boom is irresistible, hydraulics or a solid vang is the solution. Take your choice!

TRAVELERS

Most travelers work easily in light air, when they are pulled to windward to allow the boom to remain at or near the centerline as the mainsheet is eased to twist off the top of the sail. It's in heavier air, when the traveler has to be played to control the angle of attack of the mainsail without changing the leech tension, that most travelers cause trouble, usually because of excessive friction or inadequate control tackles. Sailing upwind in a breeze, a helmsman needs to be able to release the traveler instantly when a puff gives him more helm than he

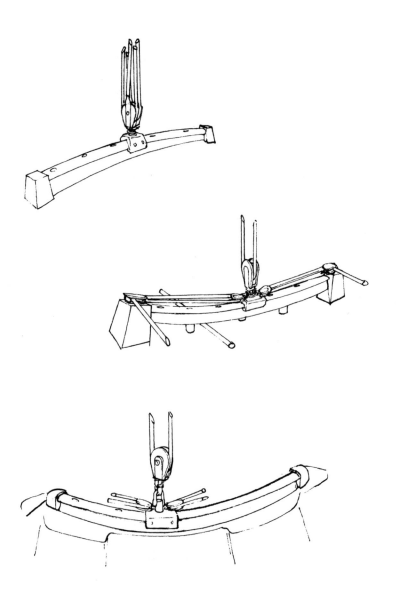

can handle. When the puff subsides, the control lines should be sufficient to pull the traveler back to its optimum position.

It is common now to carry a full mainsail and a #3 (95 to 105 percent) genoa in true winds of 20 to 25 or even 30 knots, which means that the full main (with perhaps only a flattening reef) is up in apparent winds of 30 to 35 knots. The loads imposed on the traveler in these conditions are high, and while the travelers on most boats won't break, they often won't roll easily either. The worst offenders are travelers that are not directly under the trim point, such as travelers across the transom that are led to the end of the boom. Another offender is midboom travelers that are bent to follow the camber of the housetop. To maintain a steady tension on the mainsheet, a traveler should either be curved up at the ends or should be bent in the same arc as that swung by the end of the boom. Except in the most refined grand prix racing, this kind of absolute leech control may not be necessary, but a traveler that is curved to parallel the cabin top is exactly wrong, because it increases the leech tension as it is eased.

Location

If the traveler on a boat does not roll freely, there are several solutions short of a new traveler. Changing a curved traveler bridge or moving the traveler from a housetop bridge to a position on the bridge deck or across the cockpit will almost certainly help. One of the best places for a traveler on many boats is across the cockpit, directly ahead of the helmsman. If the cockpit is wide open, without seats, the traveler can either be bolted to the cockpit sole, with adjustment leads up the sides of the cockpit, or can be built on a deck-level bridge. The traveler across the sole will probably not have enough movement to windward in light air, but it will keep the cockpit open for crew work; the deck-level traveler can go from rail to rail but will probably interfere with leads such as the spinnaker sheets, which will have to be routed around or over the traveler.

If there are no cockpit seat lockers that will be blocked, it is relatively easy to mount the traveler on the cockpit seats, with a length of teak horse underneath if the traveler is not built to span openings. (Harken makes a big-boat track and a small-boat track that are specifically designed to bridge cockpits and that do not require a supporting horse.) If the cockpit seats do not have adequate backing, use a backing board underneath, which can be bolted in place with the same bolts that hold the traveler, using large washers.

The bridge deck is another good location for a traveler, especially if the primary winches are not mounted too far forward so that the genoa trimming and mainsheet control are concentrated in the same place.

Modifications

If the traveler cannot be moved, there are other ways to get it to roll freely. Sometimes, adding another car and a doubling

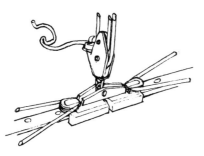

strap will spread the load over enough bearings to make the traveler free-running. Nicro-Fico, Ronstan, Harken, Schaefer, Kenyon, Mariner, and other manufacturers make travelers that can be coupled to spread the load. Another car and the strap to connect them are often not expensive. Even an entire new traveler may not be expensive if the mounting holes for the new track are the same as the one that is being removed. The difference between a low-friction traveler, like the Harken travelers, and the travelers that are usually supplied on production boats is striking.

Control Lines

A traveler without control lines isn't really serving the purpose of a traveler at all. On all but maxi-size boats, traveler control lines can be made up of tackles of from 2:1 up to 6:1 or even 8:1 purchase. Power to pull the traveler to weather in a lull is usually not the problem; it is being able to control the ease of the traveler in a puff. If the tackle is made powerful enough for a controlled ease, it will often have so many parts, and so much friction, that moving the traveler car back and forth on the track in light air is cumbersome. One solution is to use a small ratchet block somewhere in the tackle, usually at a 180-degree turn for maximum holding power. The extra holding power of the ratchet block will usually let you control the traveler with one or two parts less purchase, and the ratchet can be turned off in light air. The traveler control leads should be convenient to trim, cleat, and release for the crew member who usually handles the traveler. If the helmsman has to slide down from the rail or climb around the wheel

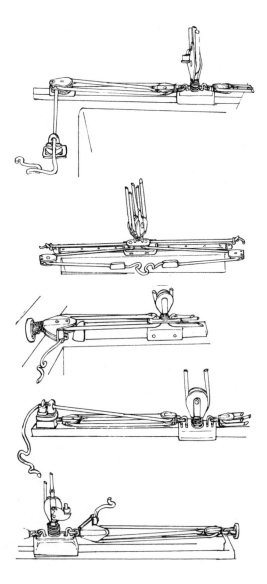

and brace himself in order to pull the traveler up, or if the mainsail trimmer has to stand in front of the helmsman and break his vision and concentration in order to ease the traveler, the boat needs a better lead or more purchase or both. In some cases, the best rig is to double-end the purchases, so that both the helmsman and a crew member forward of the traveler have access to the control line. Or swivel blocks can be used for the control lines to enable crew members in different positions on the boat to reach the lines.

Some of the simpler rigs, such as the self-cleating traveler, are suitable for moving the carriage to weather in light air but are not very responsive for quick dumps of the traveler in a breeze. It is an excellent rig for a boat with a powerful vang, where the vang can be used to control the leech tension of the main and the mainsheet used for control of the angle of attack in puffy reaching or on the wind.

On a well-rigged boat, the mainsheet, traveler, and vang will complement one another. A powerful vang can sometimes make up for a short traveler track, and a very long traveler track reduces the necessity for a high-powered vang. All three should be convenient and easy to operate, so that the helmsman can either control his helm or expect that someone else can control his helm swiftly in response to changing sea and wind conditions.

ADVANCED MAINSHEET CONTROLS

The mainsheet, vang, and traveler control the leech tension and angle of attack of the mainsail. To achieve its full power and effectiveness in a wide range of conditions, the mainsail also has to be adjusted into different shapes by changing the position of maximum draft in the sail, the amount of draft in different areas of the sail, and the size of the sail—functions that are controlled by the outhaul, cunningham, flattener, babystay, runners, and backstay. Some of these controls are thought of as adjustments for the grand prix racers, but cruisers and day sailers can also enjoy the remarkable control over mainsail shape and power, and the effect on heeling angle and helm, that these controls can produce.

Cunningham

Even with modern low-stretch sail fabrics and complex arrangements that align fabric panels precisely with the stress loads of the sail, the point of maximum draft in a mainsail will gradually shift aft as the breeze increases. It is possible to control the position of the draft with the main halyard or with a boom downhaul, but if the sail is made full size for light air, then the sail will be oversized when the luff is tensioned in heavier air. The cunningham, a tackle that pulls down on a cringle or pressed ring in the luff of the sail above the gooseneck, is a way of adjusting draft position without changing the overall luff dimension. Whenever the wind velocity changes or the shape of the sail is altered by mast bending, use of the cunningham is important to restore the position of maximum draft to the desired position in the sail.

Although a cunningham is a simple control, far too often it is neglected or set up as an afterthought. Most boats need no more than a 4:1 to 8:1 tackle, led aft to where a person can look at the sail and trim the tackle at the same time. The loads

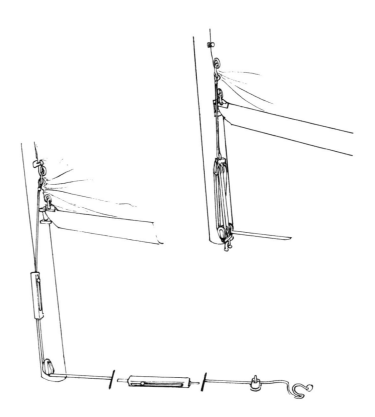

can usually be handled by bullet blocks or a magic box, and the cunningham cringle itself can be used as a sheave to double the purchase of a simple tackle.

Another option is a simple 2:1 purchase led aft through a stopper to a cabin-top winch. There are no emergency release requirements, and the load, even on a large boat, can be handled by a moderate-size winch. The important point is for

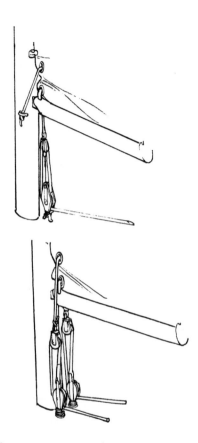

Outhaul

The load on an outhaul isn't great. Even on a large mainsail, the outhaul is reshaping the sail in an area of relatively light loading; the friction of the boltrope or sail slides, and especially of the slug that is sometimes used at the clew of the mainsail, constitutes much of the load on the outhaul. If the clew is fastened instead to a ball-bearing carriage on a track (a small traveler track is ideal), then the outhaul loads are modest. The lower the aspect ratio of the sail, the more important the outhaul will be. For fractional rigs and masthead rigs with a large mainsail, and for sailing conditions which will involve frequent changes in the mainsail shape, such as round-the-buoys racing, the outhaul should be easy to reach and control.

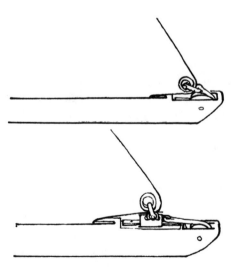

the control to be in a position where someone can look at the luff, and preferably the entire shape of the sail, to see whether it needs more or less tension. The base of the mast is rarely the best place for that assessment, and on a shorthanded boat, or a boat which is sailed with everyone on the rail, the cunningham is an adjustment that often doesn't get tended because it is inconvenient.

The travel of the outhaul is generally 5 to perhaps 15 inches, a range that is ideal for a magic box or for a small multiple-purchase tackle. A compound tackle, with the first purchase made of wire, can reduce friction and is often a simple improvement or addition to an existing outhaul system. For a new system built from scratch, it is simpler to use a straight 4:1 or 6:1 low-friction purchase. Watch out for small sheaves, bad leads, and poor-quality bearings on the blocks that are used to lead outhaul wires into the boom. The larger the sheave and the better the bearings, the easier it will be to trim the outhaul.

Even on a large boat a winch is probably not necessary, but if a housetop winch is available, a very clean and simple rig is a 2:1 or 3:1 tackle led to a winch and stopper on the housetop.

If the lead exits on the boom, the line can be run over a clam cleat and then through a bullet block on a pad eye. The outhaul lead can then be trimmed from aft or from either side, and it will automatically cleat itself. To release the line, pull down on the line between the block and the clam cleat. The setup is hard on clam cleats, which suffer from having line drawn through them, but annual replacement of the cleat is a modest price to pay for the convenience of being able to

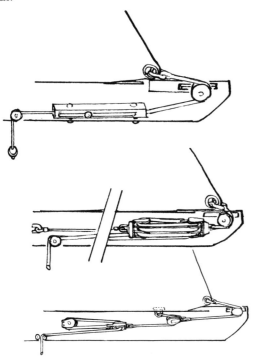

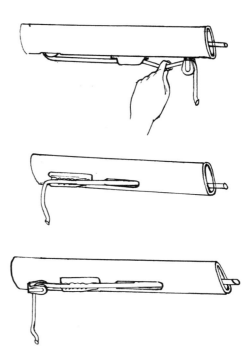

trim the outhaul from almost anyplace on the boat. For heavy loads, an aluminum clam cleat is a good idea. Be sure not to use a clam cleat with an integral fairlead, because it will be almost impossible to release.

An outhaul can also be fitted with a double-ended tackle that permits adjustment from aft when the boat is hard on the wind and from forward when the main is eased out.

Flattener

On most mainsails, the flattener* is an extension of the outhaul. When the clew has been pulled out to the black band on the boom, the only way to further flatten the sail is to take in the flattener, which can then be pulled as far as the black band. The area taken from the sail is not as significant as the change to a flatter shape. Combined with other adjustments, such as the running backstays, cunningham, backstay, and sheet tension, the flattener can open the leech and control the heeling and weather helm of the boat.

It has always been tempting to try to treat the flattener and outhaul as a single continuous control, and a few boats, such as the NY 36 and the Santana 30/30, are rigged with a control wire that goes from a block on the outhaul car up to the flattening reef cringle.

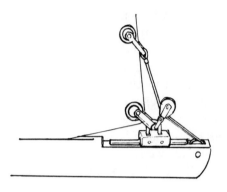

* Although it is often called the flattening reef and does shorten the leech of the sail, the primary purpose of the flattener is to reshape the lower portion of the mainsail, rather than shortening sail area. There is no corresponding luff reef point, and the cunningham ring should not be taken in with the flattener unless the flattened sail needs the draft pulled forward.

In theory, the block on the outhaul car converts the pull of the wire first into an extension of the outhaul; then when the outhaul is fully extended, it pulls down the flattener. The problem is that the geometry doesn't quite work on most sails. The friction on the outhaul car and the wide angle of the wire through the block mean that the flattener begins to come down long before the car has reached the end of its pull.

Most boats, instead, need a separate control for the flattener. If the design of the mainsail or the expected sailing conditions require only infrequent use of the flattener, one of the ordinary reef lines can be used. Taking in the flattener as though it were a reef is relatively slow, and if the boat has only two reef lines, the reef has to be tied off and the line rereeved to use the second reef, but it is a simple rig.

For sailing areas where a heavy #1 genoa and a main with a flattener, or a #3 genoa and a main with a flattener, is a common sailing configuration, the flattener should be more easily controlled. Unlike the deep reefs, it is not an all-or-

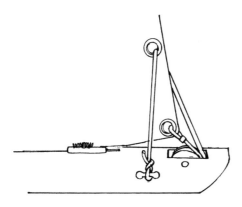

nothing control; sometimes taking in half of the flattener is just the amount of shaping the sail needs. The adjustments usually are not as critical as a cunningham or a mainsheet, and a little brute force with a smaller tackle may lead to economies of hardware. A more powerful version of the tackles that are used for outhauls is usually sufficient, although the hardware should all be stronger than would normally be used with an outhaul.

Large boats often use a hydraulic cylinder, either a special long cylinder or a smaller cylinder with a 1:2 purchase, that translates the short pull of the cylinder into the foot or more of pull that the flattener requires.

Hydraulic adjustment is simple, precise, and can be done without releasing the mainsheet. Like a hydraulic vang, a hydraulic flattener can tear apart the leech of the mainsail or permanently stretch the fabric if it is used incautiously. If you are installing the hydraulics yourself, make sure the base of the cylinder is attached to a strong welded or through-bolted point, and make sure that the hydraulic hoses are protected from chafe and are long enough to remove easily when the boom is taken off for winter storage. It's also a good idea to make sure that your overzealous crew members don't try to pump in the flattener when the main is sheeted hard; the result will be a severely stretched or torn leech.

For boats that do not require a hydraulic flattener, a compound tackle or a large magic box is a good choice. The Harken Duratron magic box is strong enough for the loads of a 300-square-foot mainsail, if the chafe in the line is watched and if the mountings of the box to the boom are secure. The largest possible sheave should be used in the end of the boom

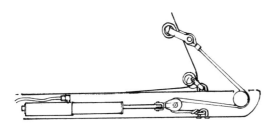

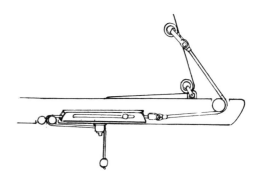

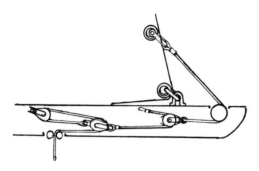

to reduce friction. With a large enough sheave, a Kevlar tail could be used instead of wire, which can be unpleasant whipping around. The shackle that fastens to the cringle should be very strong and big enough to fit over the cringle of the sail without distortion.

The easiest way to mount a magic box in the boom is to carefully drill and tap the base of the magic box for ¼ or even ⁵⁄₁₆ bolts, line up holes on the outside of the boom, then use pan-head machine screws from the outside of the boom. The dead-end tails of a compound tackle should be fastened to strong points, such as a through-bolt for the vang bail.

Although the tackle configurations for a flattener are similar to an outhaul, the loads are a whole different order. This is no place for flimsy aluminum rivets and small sheaves.

Finally, the backstay, babystay, and runners—all discussed in Chapter 11—are important tools for adjusting the shape of the mainsail. Almost every racing boat will have an adjustable backstay, and very few racing boats will not have either a babystay or runners or both. The more accessible these controls are and the more readily adjustable they are, the greater the control of the mainsail.

FURLING

The mainsail is not only the most-used sail, it is the sail that presents, in its own way, the greatest storage challenge. Roller-furling sails take care of their own storage, at least until it blows so hard that you don't want the windage of the sail on the headstay. Other sails fold up, or get stuffed into their bags or turtles. The main, because it is invariably going to get hoisted the next time out, is usually stored on the boom on boats over about 20 feet in overall length.

For some boat owners, the chores of flaking or furling mainsails are so onerous that they opt for roller-furling mainsails. There is no question that the devices are convenient, but they exact a substantial toll in reliability and mainsail shape. With all of them, it is impossible to have battens, which means a mainsail with no roach, a hollow-cut leech, and very little shape. With the external roller-reefing devices, it is impossible to avoid sag in the luff of the mainsail, which means that the sail must be cut extra-flat to compensate. And the internal roller-reefing devices, whether in a mast or boom, are subject to jamming, which would make reefing or furling the rest of the sail a tricky operation. Finally, there is the Zip-Stop system, which uses a rigid feeder and zipper devices to vertically furl the sail against the mast. Aside from windage and the possibility of a malfunction of the device aloft, the sail shape required by the furling device means either no battens or a weird, nearly vertical batten in the upper sections of the sail —neither of which is highly conducive to good sail shape. And while it is possible to build shape into a loose-footed mainsail, an exaggerated flat shape is required for smooth furling.

The in-mast systems require an unusual large mast section with a C-shaped latter half to accommodate the roller-furling rod and the sail. If the mast is not held straight when the sail is furled, it can jam, so running backstays are often fitted and needed to hold the mast straight while furling or unfurling the sail.

Most sailors opt for a conventional mainsail, attached to the mast by boltrope, slides on track, or slugs in a boltrope track. Boltrope presents the cleanest leading edge, but a large mainsail that is attached only with boltrope is tricky for a short-handed crew to lower and flake. Owners who buy large fractional rigs that are advertised as easy to handle for cruising are often surprised the first time they try lowering and furling a big mainsail in a breeze. The free luff blows aft and the battle for control ensues. One trick that does work is to hook the reef cringle of the luff onto its hook (you may need a loop of shock cord to keep it from falling off), and to stuff the sail into the pouch formed by the reef as it comes down. When it is down and under control, you can roll or flake it on the boom.

Slides and slugs make a sail more manageable for lowering and furling, although there is a less clean leading edge, the jacklines needed for reefing are messy, and the furled sail is trickier to cover than a flaked sail that hangs over the boom in a neat sausage. One option that some owners elect for boats that are raced and cruised is to use a racing mainsail with boltrope, then adapt an old mainsail to slugs for shorthanded cruising.

Lazy jacks and other devices to contain a sail when it is lowered are sometimes advocated for cruising boats, and they obviously have a place on boats like the Freedom designs. For most modern Bermuda rigs (as opposed to gaff rigs), lazy jacks are more affectation than genuine utility, and are rarely needed except in special circumstances, such as handicapped sailors.

9

GENOA
CONTROLS

A sailmaker makes certain assumptions in building a genoa or jib.

The clew is designed to be trimmed at a certain point on the deck, with a limited range of adjustments in the lead position to control the twist in the sail and the angle of attack of the sail.* If the sail cannot be trimmed at those points, either because there is no provision for lead blocks or because some detail of the rig and deck layout makes it impossible to achieve the lead that the sailmaker anticipated, the sail will work at far less than its designed efficiency.

The luff curve † built into the sail is designed either for the anticipated range of luff sag on the boat or for an optimized setting for some wind speed; if the boat cannot achieve the anticipated luff sag because the headstay tension cannot be controlled adequately, the sail will not take its designed shape. A sail built for a boat with a backstay adjuster may be much too full for a boat with fixed headstay tension, and a sail cut for a relatively flexible boat will prove too flat for a rigid boat

---

* Twist is the difference between the angle of trim at the top and bottom of the sail. Moving the clew lead block for a genoa aft increases the twist in the sail; moving it forward decreases twist. Angle of attack is the angle that the sail makes with the centerline of the boat. Trimming the sail to an inside track sharpens the angle of attack; trimming to the rail widens the angle of attack.

† To build shape into a sail, the sailmaker cuts the luff into a round, so that when the sail is hung on a relatively straight headstay, the extra fullness from the luff is "pushed back" into the sail. If the sailmaker knows that the headstay cannot be made taut, either because the hull is too flexible or because there is no backstay adjuster available on the rig, then the sail will be cut with less round, since fullness will be available from the sag in the headstay. If a boat is capable of achieving a wide range of headstay tensions, the sailmaker can choose a luff round that will achieve the maximum range of sail shapes for different sea and wind conditions.

that can achieve high luff tensions.* (There are boats that flex so much that some sailmakers' computer programs include a "banana factor" to use in designing sails for them.)

TRACKS AND LEADS

When a builder puts track down on the deck of a boat, he has to balance the ideal sailmaker's deck—which might have a grid of tracks spaced at 2-inch intervals over the entire surface—against constraints like the shape of the house or the appeal of "clean" decks. More often than not, the compromise is in favor of clean decks. Frequently the tracks are too short and do not lead far enough forward to trim a high-aspect #3 genoa or far enough aft for a high-clew light #1 or drifter. Or the tracks are set too wide, so that the sails cannot be trimmed close enough to achieve the optimum pointing angle for the boat on the wind.

There are even production boats that come from the factory with no genoa tracks other than a track along the rail. Except for boats with exceptionally inefficient keels, there are few boats that cannot profit from the ability to adjust the lead of a headsail to trimming angles much closer than those that were used years ago. Number-three genoas are now routinely built with leeches cut to clear the spreaders, so that the sail is positioned in front of the shrouds with the optimum trim point *inside* the chain plates of the yacht. Trimming one of these high-aspect sails outside the shrouds, or between the shrouds, is sacrificing the potential built into the sail. And the crews of many aggressively raced boats have discovered that the ability to move the genoa leads for the #1 genoas *in the course of a tack* adds substantially to the boat's ability to accelerate out of a tack. Even casual club racers and day sailors are learning how to use barber haulers to adjust the trim of their sails, and to make a limited inventory of sails responsive to a broad range of conditions.

Trim Angles

Depending upon the efficiency of the keel, the optimum trim position for the #1 genoas and the #3 genoa on most racer-cruisers will be somewhere between 8 and 10 degrees off the centerline of the boat. Boats with very efficient keels may profit from trimming the genoa as close as 7 degrees. Boats with inefficient keels or chain plates at the rail may need trim points as wide as 12 degrees. Number-two genoas (overlapping headsails with an LP of 120 to 140 percent) usually cannot be trimmed as close as the #1 genoas or the #3 because the sail would hook around the shrouds when trimmed close.

To determine the trim angle of a sail, you need two of the following measurements (illustrated on page 126):

A: stem fitting to centerline opposite clew lead block
B: stem fitting to clew lead block
C: clew lead block to centerline of boat

(See diagram on next page)

---

* It is not difficult to measure the flexing of a hull under backstay tension. Attach a length of thin wire to the pulpit (Kevlar line might work as well), stretch it the length of the hull, and dangle a weight on the end over the pushpit. Then fix a ruler vertically on the pushpit so the weight will move up and down the ruler when the boat flexes. Watch as you crank up hard on the backstay; the results are often surprising.

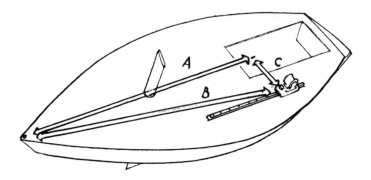

A: stem fitting to centerline opposite clew lead block
B: stem fitting to clew lead block
C: clew lead block to centerline of boat

SAIL TRIM ANGLES

Trim angle (degrees)	C / B	C / A	A / B
7.0	0.122	0.123	0.993
7.5	0.131	0.132	0.991
8.0	0.139	0.141	0.990
8.5	0.148	0.149	0.989
9.0	0.156	0.158	0.988
9.5	0.165	0.167	0.986
10.0	0.174	0.176	0.985
10.5	0.182	0.185	0.983
11.0	0.191	0.194	0.982
11.5	0.199	0.203	0.980
12.0	0.208	0.213	0.978
12.5	0.216	0.222	0.976
13.0	0.225	0.231	0.974
13.5	0.233	0.240	0.972
14.0	0.242	0.249	0.970
14.5	0.250	0.259	0.968
15.0	0.259	0.268	0.966

Measure the two distances that are most convenient (it is easiest to use feet and tenths of feet or a metric tape measure), then use the following table to look up the trim angle for the appropriate dimensions.

Barber Haulers

Your sailmaker can recommend a starting point for the genoa clew block (some sailmakers even draw lines on the clews of their genoas that are meant to point to an optimum trim point). The telltales on the leading edge of the sail are your first indication: they should break evenly, from the top of the luff to the bottom. Then use a barber hauler, which can be nothing more than a length of line with a hook at one end and a lead block, to experiment in different conditions.

Try using the barber hauler to trim the sail closer or wider. Your knot meter and compass (to measure tacking angles), a VMG (velocity made good) gauge, or best of all, another boat alongside will tell you what happens when you trim a sail closer to the centerline of the boat, or farther forward or aft. You will probably discover that in smooth water you can trim the sails much closer than the existing track, and that the boat will point higher (tack in a smaller angle) with little or no loss of speed. You may also discover other trim points that improve the performance or versatility of a sail. For example, many genoas are excellent reaching sails if the lead is moved forward and outboard. In heavy air some sails profit from having their leads moved aft to twist off the head of the sail.

Changing Leads

If you cannot trim the sails of your inventory where you and your sailmaker think they ought to be trimmed, it may be time to add tracks or other clew trimming devices. Sometimes a simple barber hauler, or even a different kind of car on the track, will do the trick. If you have a #3 genoa that needs to be trimmed farther forward than your track extends, it is worth trying a car with a low lead point, such as the Schaefer half-moon blocks. Changing the height of the sheave over the track has the same effect as moving the lead block forward or aft on the track. If the track does not lead far enough aft, you could try a higher lead block, for example a block on a slider instead of a regular genoa car, but usually a higher lead point will cause a bad lead to a winch or turning block. In some cases the easiest rig is to add a semipermanent barber hauler, using a pad eye for a tackle or the tail of a lead that will go to a spare winch.

The block or ring for a barber hauler should be as light and as friction-free as possible. If the change of lead angle is modest, a carabiner or a ring may work fine; otherwise a fairly wide

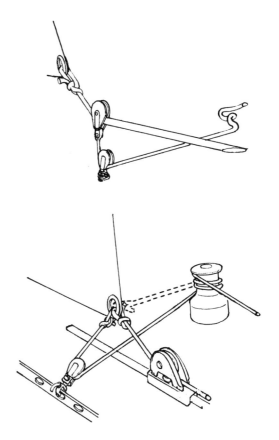

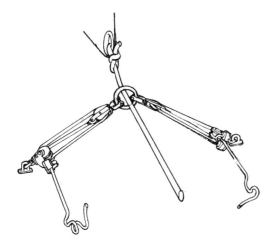

sheave block should be used. The Holt snatch blocks are good for smaller boats; a ball-bearing block with a lashing eye or a lightweight snatch block is good for medium-size boats. The pad eye for the lead should be strongly fastened, with a backup plate or block, and the line should lead to a winch on a large boat, to a tackle on a medium-size boat, or to a cam cleat on a boat the size of a J-24. On small boats, the same barber hauler lead can be used as a twing for the spinnaker guys.

The barber hauler arrangement is simple, and for occasional leads is probably preferable to removing headliners, drilling up decks, and installing toe-snubbing tracks and blocks. But if you find yourself needing a barber hauler or some other kind of jury-rigged system often, it is probably time to install either more track or well-placed pad eyes on the deck.

There are many options: new long tracks installed in place of or as extensions to the existing tracks, lengths of short track strategically placed, pad eyes for barber haulers or downhaulers, adjustable athwartship tracks, swinging tracks, and tracks with cars that are adjustable under load.

The choice depends on the level of sailing/racing anticipated, and the conditions. If you frequently race in rough-water conditions it may be important to be able to pull the lead forward on every tack, or to be able to adjust the lead in and out; in an area of generally flat water the boat may not need the added power in the genoa. The complexity of the system also depends on the size and weight of the boat and the skills of the crew. Athwartship tracks with downhaulers or tracks with adjustable cars offer the ultimate in flexibility. They also offer the ultimate in complexity: extra lines for a crew to master, extra lines to tangle in the cockpit spaghetti, and extra cleats and hardware to fail at the wrong moment.

Remember too that a short track might save weight, but it also presents two ends that can catch lines if they are not carefully rounded or fitted with track ends, and that short tracks do not distribute the load over as much area as a long piece of track. In any case, whether it is track or pad eyes that

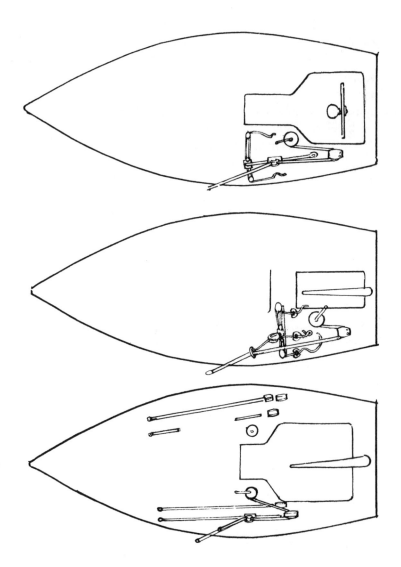

are being installed, the loads on the fittings will be in tension, and the installation will require some kind of compression tubes or epoxy fillers in the holes, plus backing plates or blocks, or at least large washers, to distribute the load under the deck.

Adjustable Leads

Finally, adjustable leads can range from the instantly adjustable lead that is meant to be used on every tack, to leads that can be adjusted under load with a winch, and finally to leads that can be adjusted only when the load is relieved by tacking or by the use of a temporary short sheet. Boats with an I dimension (height of foretriangle) of 48 feet or more will probably require ball- or roller-bearing cars (like the Harken or Penguin genoa track/car systems) to adjust easily under load by hand. For smaller boats, or for boats that elect to adjust under load with a winch, Delrin sliders in the cars will work. It is also possible to make adjustable car systems that are less expensive than the Harken or Penguin systems by fastening blocks to a mainsheet traveler block used on a length of mainsheet traveler track, but the Harken and Penguin systems have the advantage of a low deck profile. Because most genoa and traveler tracks have the same hole spacing, they can be swapped with minimum drilling and filling. Use the longest length of shock cord that will conveniently fit into the system to pull the cars aft when tension is released on the forward pullers.

The flexibility of a good adjustable jib lead system is remarkable. At the same time, if the system is too sophisticated it can lead to accidents, confusion, or mistrimming. Setting the genoa lead at position 14 on the track may not be as ideal as

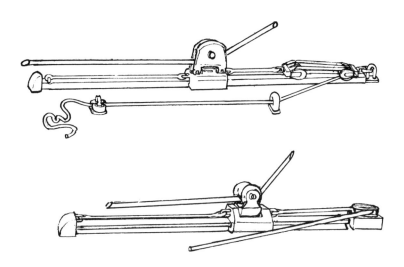

having instant adjustment between position 12 and position 16, but there is less risk of accidents (like someone tripping the adjustment line and letting the car slide all the way forward on the track) and less risk of catastrophic misadjustment.

Marking Leads

For any genoa system, it is essential to have clearly marked, repeatable settings for the cars. The most unambiguous markings are heavy clear ticks and labels on the decks, done with a waterproof marker pen; the marks can be removed later, but it takes some real scrubbing and polishing, or even fiberglass paint remover. The alternatives are tape and labels, or borrowing a die to stamp numbers into the tracks. Tape or other labels on the tracks will usually come off or get caught in the car. Die stamps are permanent, but require a chart to indicate which sail gets trimmed at which number, and whether the car is in front of or behind the number.

GENOA SHEETS

The usual formula for the length of genoa sheets is 1.7 times the overall length of the boat. If you have foot blocks sited well aft of the primary winches, you may want a longer sheet. If you have no intention of ever using a spinnaker or an overlapping genoa, you could get by with shorter sheets. A little extra length lets you cut the sheets off after they get chafed.

Cruisers and club racers will choose braided Dacron for the genoa sheets. The smooth-finished lines stretch slightly less and run more easily through blocks, but they do not hold as well on winches. More aggressively sailed boats may opt for Kevlar/Dacron blends for genoa sheets, especially for the long leads to the #3 and #4 genoas. By using low-stretch sheets with the heavier headsails, it is often possible to take a genoa trimmer off the leeward rail and put him to windward. Unless you are willing to replace the sheets often, all-Kevlar cored lines are not a good idea for genoa sheets, because the sail is almost always trimmed in so that the line chafes in a single spot, and Kevlar is not good at resisting chafe. Finally, grand prix racers often choose wire sheets with rope tails, which though hard on crew and hardware, provide the ultimate in low-stretch performance.

For most boats, a bowline is sufficient to tie the sheets to the clew of the genoa. For faster sail changes, and to avoid the hang-up of the genoa sheets on the shrouds when a closely trimmed sail is tacked fast, you can use J-locks or Presslocks on the genoa sheets.

If you are considering the use of J-locks or Presslocks, make sure that your sailmaker knows well in advance so that your sails can be built with webbed D-rings at the clew instead of pressed rings. For offshore sailing or any heavy-air sailing, Presslock and J-lock fittings should be either taped or held shut with a sliding piece of tubing.

What size sheets do you need? The table on page 58 is a good start. For heavy-weather sheets, there is no harm in using a larger size for a better grip, as long as the line runs freely in your blocks and your winch drums are large enough to take a full three or more turns of the sheet.

FOOT BLOCKS

The genoa sheet is the most heavily loaded line on the boat. It must lead fairly to the winch without chafe and without putting imappropriate loads on the lead blocks. If there is chafe on a coaming or housetop, or if the loads on the lead blocks are too acute, the boat will need foot blocks to turn the genoa sheet.

Some production boats position the sheet winches aft on the cockpit coamings to avoid the need for foot blocks, but if the J dimension of the boat (base of mast to stem) is large, the leads for a high-clewed #1 genoa will be so far aft that with either a wheel or a tiller the sheet winches end up next to the helmsman, just where a cockpit traffic jam is least needed. Installing a turning block where the winch is and moving the winch forward will end the traffic jam. Turning blocks also add the advantage of a consistent lead to the winch for every sail.

On some boats, the smaller genoas will lead properly but the #1 genoas lead too far aft to trim directly to the winch. On other boats, foot blocks are useful to permit cross sheeting, or to enable the use of the windward winch for a short sheet for sail changes or barber-hauling. Whatever the reason for the addition, a foot block can be easy to install if it is chosen carefully, positioned properly, and installed securely. But there is no piece of hardware that requires more caution in selection and installation: the load on a foot block is almost double the genoa clew load, depending on the angle of return of the sheet from the block.

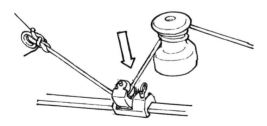

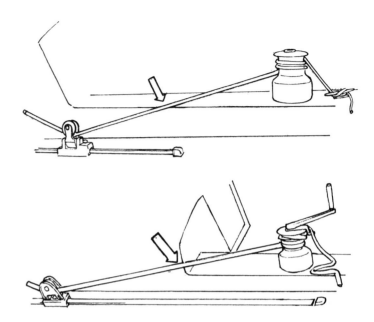

A foot block should have a safe working load at least double the MaxGenoa rating of the boat. Look for the largest and widest sheaves you can find (the smaller the sheaves and the narrower the swallows, the more likely you are to end up with jam-ups when the sheet is eased), reliable low-friction bearings, and large, strong mountings. A few large bolts may be stronger than many smaller bolts because if there is the slightest misalignment in the bolts, with one taking a disproportionate load, the bolt may distort and lead to mounting failures. Blocks are available in double and single configurations. You may need the second sheave for a spinnaker guy, short sheets, changing sheets, or barber haulers, but remember that the upper sheave of a double foot block is usually only half as strong as the lower sheave. If you will be using the upper sheave for your primary genoa sheet at all, select a block with a rating for the upper sheave equal to double the MaxGenoa rating for the boat. Frequently a single block will suffice and a secondary winch can be used without a turning block for changing sheets, barber haulers, and so on.

In positioning the block, make sure that it is at least 18 inches, and preferably 24 or 30 inches from the winch, in order to avoid tangles and hockles when the sheet is released. And above all, make certain that the lead from the genoa lead block to the turning block and then to the winch is absolutely fair, neither chafing the cheeks nor leading in or out of the turning block at an angle that will stress the sheave and bearings. If necessary, cut mounting blocks to position the turning block at an appropriate angle. (If you cut the mounting block from a large enough block of wood, the mating piece can be used under the deck to provide a backing block which will take the loads at the correct angle.)

The holes through the deck should be drilled out and filled with epoxy, which is in turn drilled for the mounting bolts. To prevent the block from creeping under extreme loads, the mounting block can be epoxied to the deck, or a powerful

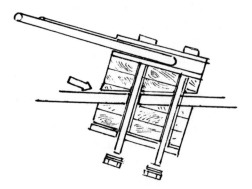

adhesive bedding compound like 3M 5200 can be used under the block. It will be hell to get off, but in this case the additional strength is worth the trade. Just make certain that you can remove the sheave for lubrication or servicing. There should be an aluminum or stainless backing plate under the block, or at least very large washers under the locknuts.

As an alternative to a foot block, it is possible to use a strong pad eye and a large single block to turn the genoa sheet. The advantage is that the block can be made to pivot and follow changing leads to housetop winches or for cross sheeting. The disadvantage is that you have to be careful to avoid hockles and tangles when releasing the genoa sheet, and the smaller footprint of the pad eye means that the mountings must be that much more carefully done. The pad eye and the block should be rated with a working load of at least double the maximum genoa clew load, and the block should have a large sheave with wide enough shallows not to snag modest line twists.

JIB TACK FITTINGS

Jib tack fittings have come full circle. Years ago it was popular to have either a pin in a channel or a simple hole for a tack snap shackle. Then open horn hooks were the rage, followed by closed horns with Wichard hooks on the sails. Now some boats are going back to snap shackles on the horn.

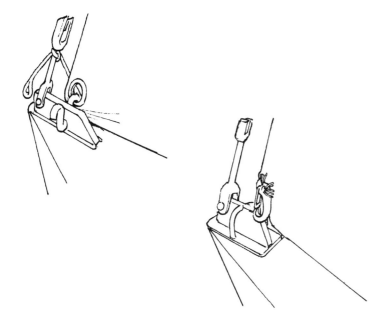
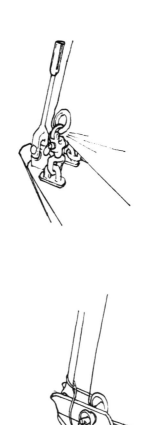
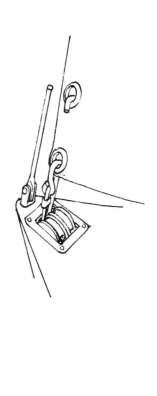

Open horns are fast and usually easy to hook on to, but they need a shock cord safety loop to hold the tack of the sail in place, and there is always a risk of catching a line on the horn (usually a spinnaker guy in the middle of a jibe!). Or a fold of sail can snag on the open horn. If you have trouble with lines snagging on a horn hook, try using large shock cord for the safety loop, or running a light shock cord line from the head-stay to the first upright of the bow pulpit to keep lines and sails off the horns.

The closed horn is safe and reliable, with nothing that will catch a sail, but it is difficult to get to when you are trying to set a heavy sail on the outside during a sail change. If the closed horn is close to the deck, it sometimes helps to use a strong swivel snap shackle webbed to the tack of the sail instead of the usual Wichard hook. (A shackle without a lanyard, such as a Sparcraft or Gibb shackle, will avoid the accident of snagging open.) Or you can use a snap shackle on the horn and have cringles put into the sails in place of the snaps.

Tack shackles fastened at the stem are reliable, but to make the foot of the sail sweep the deck it is necessary to set the tack cringle high in the sail, and the unsupported foot will sometimes be difficult to trim properly.

Finally, if you want to get fancy, and especially if your sails are cut with maximum length luffs that need a genoa cunningham, you can build a double hook stem fitting with two adjustable hooks led underdeck. One is the working stem fitting; the other serves as a genoa cunningham.

Genoa Cunningham

If your sailmaker has cut your sails full hoist, you may need a genoa cunningham to achieve full luff tension on the sail. Even if the sails are not full hoist, you may want to use a cunningham on the genoa because it is quicker to adjust the luff tension with a cunningham than with the halyard, and

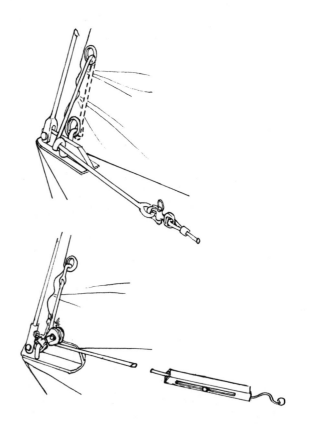

because the cunningham tensions the luff without requiring an adjustment of the clew lead car. (Tensioning the halyard raises the entire sail, so that it is sometimes necessary to move the car on the track to get the sail trimmed right again.) With Dacron sails, the tension adjustment is more important and much more effective than with Mylar and Kevlar sails, where the halyard tension adjusts only the leading edge of the sail and the entry angle, rather than the draft in the entire sail.

The simplest genoa cunningham is nothing more than a piece of line with a loop spliced into each end. One end goes over the genoa horn after the sail; the other end is led through the cunningham cringle, then down around the other horn and aft, where it can hook into the foreguy or even lead all the way aft to a winch.

If the friction against the horn is too great, a small block can be used, but it is often difficult to position a block with a decent lead. Using a hook on the genoa cunningham line is even more difficult because it will have a tendency to pull the luff of the sail aft rather than forward, distorting or even tearing the sail. For a closed-horn tack fitting, a small snap shackle can be spliced into the line, or the line can be tied onto the horn. Just be sure that one end of the line is small enough to go through the cunningham hole of the sail.

If you want or need a more permanent rig, you can either rig a small compound tackle along one rail or use a long magic box with a lead led aft. Because the lines are on the foredeck and subject to snagging, it is best to keep the genoa cunningham simple or, if possible, underdeck.

SPREADERS

In addition to supporting the panels of the mast, the spreaders put sharp constraints on a sailmaker in designing a genoa. The leech of a #3 genoa that is cut to be trimmed inside the shrouds can come no farther aft than the spreader. And even with the best of patches on the sails where they meet the spreader tips, an overtrimmed jib will soon have a hole in the leech. Some boat owners go to the extreme of cutting and fitting tennis balls to their spreader tips, or buying larger rubber jackets to cover the tip. What the large jackets add isn't really protection but friction, which not only slows down tacks but wears out sails.

All that is needed for most boats is a careful wrapping with tape. The newer stretchable tapes will make a neater job of it, but they are expensive. For a really easy job, get some "insignia cloth" from your sailmaker, which is the sticky-back cloth that is used for numbers on sails and for spreader and lifeline patches. Cut the cloth into dumbbell shapes, with the thin central portion long enough to cover the end of the spreader and with the wider ends long enough to wrap around the spreaders inside the shrouds. An extra-large patch is neither necessary nor desirable, and the extra windage of tape or a tennis ball is definitely harmful to the boat. A few boats that are specially prepared for closed-course racing use hockey pucks or other roller devices on the rod rigging to cut down on the friction of the sail over the spreader tip as the boat tacks.

One helpful addition to almost any boat is to put strips of tape on the lower side of the spreaders to mark useful trimming intervals, such as 3 inches and 6 inches in from the end.

When the genoa trimmer is trying to get the sail to a consistent position, "trim it as far from the tip as the first tape" is more reliable than expecting each trimmer's idea of "3 inches" to be the same. Reflecting tape is a good idea if you are sailing at night, when it is especially difficult to estimate distances.

HEADSTAYS

A mainsail is supported on the foot and the luff. A spinnaker flies free. Headsails are in between, supported on the luff, which makes the choice of a headstay system an important decision. There are roller-furling systems that can be converted to luff foil, and a few light-air headsails that are built to be raised free-standing on their own luff wires (sometimes Kevlar line is used instead of wire), but the conversion systems are rarely converted, you can't get along with only free-standing sails, and so most boats face the choice of a headstay system.

Hanks

Some boats still use hanks, and some owners argue the theoretical advantage that the sail is held in place when it is dropped so that it can be stuffed in the bag. True, and for offshore sailing in extreme conditions, a boat needs a secure means of fastening the sail to the headstay, such as hanks or the lacing holes that are required for offshore racing on heavy-weather jibs and storm sails used with luff foil systems. But for coastal cruising and racing, the time spent on the foredeck fighting with hanks is so long and exhausting, and the procedure for a sail change is so demanding, that hanks are mostly

slow inconveniences. In the spring and fall, grappling with cold fingers for the pins on hanks is enough to make you wish for a catboat. And even for the most casual evening club race, a bareheaded sail change with hanks will cost enough time to throw away any lead. On any boat large enough to need piston hanks or Wichard hanks instead of the cloth hanks that are used on one-designs up to the size of a J-24, the hanks are aerodynamically inefficient, interfering with the smooth flow of air over the entry of the sail. Hanks have their place in especially arduous sailing situations, or perhaps for single-handers or shorthanded sailing when there is almost no likelihood of sail changes. But for boats that are contemplating any racing, or for areas where an afternoon sea breeze fills in and requires a sail change, there are just too many advantages to luff foils to deny. If you do use hanks, it is worth exploring the Wichard hanks, which can be opened with one hand instead of the two that a piston hank requires.

Foils

Luff foils fall into two categories: over the existing headstay, like the Hood Gemini or the Headfoil II, and extrusions that replace the headstay, like the Stearns. Advantages and disadvantages are touted for both. The important points are that the over-the-headstay units can be installed by a boat owner without special tools and will generally require little maintenance beyond periodic inspections and some attention to the upper edges of the luff tape. The Headfoil II, in particular, chews up the heads of luff tapes, which should periodically be hot-knifed, stitched, or covered with very thin Teflon tape. The replacement extrusions, like the Stearns, require periodic attention to the bearings, which take the full load of the headstay. The bearing servicing (or replacement) is a job that an owner can easily do either during winter storage or at the dock with some help. Ignore the bearings for more than a season and the stay will probably stop turning because of corrosion.

With any luff foil system, there are some additions to the boat that can make life easier: a lubricator for the luff groove, a good prefeeder, lacing on the lifelines, and a system to hold the sail on the deck when it comes down.

Lacing the lifelines is a simple task with no special tricks involved. On boats with perforated toe rails, the holes in the rail can be used if they are smooth enough not to cut the lacing line. For other boats, tiny plastic or metal pad eyes can be installed on a toe rail or on the edge of the deck with self-tapping screws.

To hold the sail on deck, you can use a length of shock cord run between the stanchion bases with a plastic snap in the middle; when the sail is on the deck, the shock cord is lifted over the sail and snapped back onto itself or to the lifelines. A simpler system is to make sure that whoever goes to the foredeck carries a sail stop; on some boats the foredeck man and mast men wear sailstops like belts so that they are always available.

A lubricator is nothing more than a length, 6 to 18 inches, of the appropriate-size luff tape with a pair of grommets or pressed rings set into it. Goop the lubricator with Teflon or another colorless lubricant and hoist it on a halyard, with a downhaul, whenever the sails feel sluggish in the track. If you have a luff foil system that rattles around in the wind at an anchorage, the lubricator can be used to steady the luff foil at anchor; just set the lubricator in the luff foil, attach a line from one of the grommets to the deck or to the pulpit, and attach a taut halyard to the other hole in the lubricator.

A good prefeeder should be attached to the forestay at a height high enough to lead the sail from the deck without straining the luff, and low enough to hold the sail in line for the main feeder. The prefeeders on line or wire extensions, like the Gemini or Stearns prefeeders, work more easily than the Headfoil II prefeeder on the headstay; there is no reason why a different prefeeder cannot be added to a Headfoil system. It also helps to keep the foredeck clear of fittings that can catch on sails. The mooring cleats should either be positioned at the sides of the deck or covered with guards, and the chocks and any foreguy and other blocks should also be positioned to avoid snags, and should have their ring-a-dings and other potential snags taped.

The luff foil should be inspected periodically. Look for dings and bends, which are usually caused by a good hard slam from the spinnaker pole, and for obstructions and distortions in the track. With care, the track can be straightened, but if the stay has suffered a sharp bend, consider replacing the damaged section (in a sectioned system like the Gemini) or even the whole foil. The main feeder and the friction fastenings to the headstay should also be inspected. Check that all setscrews are tight, and that there are no unwanted gaps between sections of the extrusion or between feeders and the extrusion proper. Also, look for wear on feeders that could chafe or tear the luff tapes of the sails.

Roller Furling

The convenience of roller furling comes with a price. Unless the boat is designed with a special recess for the furling drum, the tack of the sail will be elevated 6 to 12 inches off the deck, which makes any kind of deck-sweeper cut impossible, and which usually means that a large genoa has to trim so far aft that it is impossible to achieve a decent sheeting angle. The loads imposed by furling and the requirements that the sail furl smoothly usually mean that the fabric will be heavier and the cut flatter than optimum. And the requirement for protection of the furled sail from ultraviolet radiation means either a heavy strip of acrylic fabric or sacrificial sailcloth on the leech—neither of which will add to the performance of the sail. There are some recent improvements in sail design for roller furling, including a return to miter cuts to permit the use of lighter fabrics for the central luff portion of the sail with heavier panels toward the foot and leech, and the use of soft padding at the luff to allow a full-cut sail to roll up smoothly. But no matter what efforts are made, the sail will never be as fast or as weatherly as a sail that can avoid the compromises of roller furling.

The systems that furl the sail around the headstay, whether by using a luff foil system on the headstay or by furling a hanked sail, can theoretically achieve the same luff tensions as a non-roller-furling system. The systems that furl the sail around its own luff wire, independent of the headstay (such as the Schaefer and Blue Water systems), rarely achieve enough luff tension to sail well to windward, even with multipurchase halyards hoisted tight enough to wear out the wire of the halyard in a season or two.

Despite its inherent aerodynamic inefficiency, there are times and situations when the sheer convenience of a roller-furling rig cannot be denied or refused. Without roller furling, someone has to drag a sail up to the foredeck, hook on the tack and halyard, and either lead the luff tape through the prefeeder and the feeder or hook on the hanks, then go aft to hoist the sail hand over hand, and finally use a winch to get enough luff tension on the sail. While this ceremony is going on, the boat with roller furling bears away, eases the furling line, pulls on the jib sheet and voilà! At furling time, if the wind isn't too strong and the boat can be brought to a smooth reach, and if the jib sheet is eased while the furling line is smoothly brought in, it's all done. There is no sail to fold or stuff into a sail bag, no berth taken up by a sail that instead sits out of the way on the headstay. In the right conditions, which usually means moderate air on the wind and moderate to fresh conditions off the wind, the roller-furling sail may sail slower, but it is the epitome of easy living.

Although most manufacturers are cautious about the claims they make of roller reefing, there are some boat owners who claim that their roller furlers also function as reefing systems, so that one sail can be made to function as two or three different sails. With a strong furling system that furls around the headstay, rather than on a freestanding luff wire, and with a properly constructed sail, it is possible to reduce the area of a sail so that it will sail adequately off the wind. But the sail shape and the general integrity of the system on the wind is questionable, if only because there is no way that the middle of the luff of the sail can be properly supported, and no way to properly tension what is effectively the "luff" of the reefed sail.

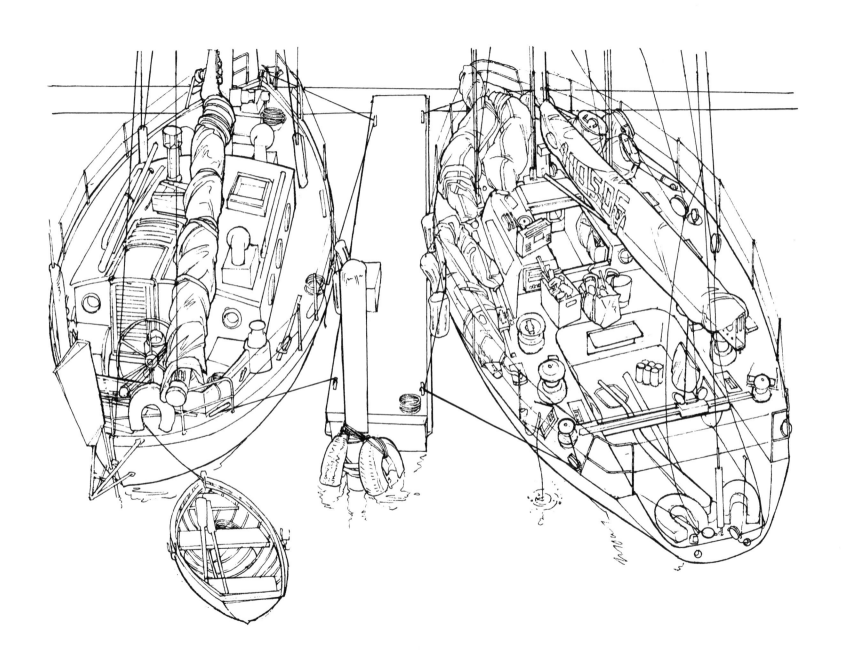

Finally, in heavy air, when it is time to hoist a #4 genoa or working jib, the roller furler is at a real disadvantage because the furling headsail has to be taken down before the jib can be hoisted, and with the over-the-headstay systems that means unfurling the sail to lower it. In light air the roller furler is also at a disadvantage, because most sails built for furling are cut flatter than a sail that is to be hoisted—both to give the furling sail increased range and to enable it to roll up smoothly. Thus it is common to see boats with roller furling missing out on a lot of sailing: motoring because the breeze is either too heavy or too light.

There are systems that can be converted to a luff foil system for racing, sometimes without detaching the headstay or disassembling swivels. Even the easiest of these conversions is not something you would want to do for the Tuesday night club race and undo again for an overnight cruise on Saturday. For a boat that races most of the year and takes a week or two for a cruise, the conversion feature might work; otherwise, the choice is really roller furling or a luff foil system, or for the diehards, hanks.

For boat owners who opt for roller furling, there are some ways around the problems inherent in the systems.

- First, while it is common to choose a #1 genoa as the roller-furling sail, it may make sense with many boats to choose a roller-furling #2 genoa with an overlap of somewhere between 120 and 140 percent. Many boats will sail well with a sail of that size in breezes from 8 to 20 knots, and the heavier weight and flatter shape that is best with a roller-furling sail is also appropriate for a sail designed for that range of breeze. To complement the sail, choose a drifter that can fly free on a Kevlar or wire luff. The drifter could be made of light Dacron or Mylar, or perhaps of heavy nylon; it can be hoisted on a spare halyard while the roller-furling sail stands furled.

Second, any roller-furling system will furl smoother and easier if the headstay is at high tension during the furling. Since you will want to ease the headstay tension for offwind sailing, for sailing to windward in light air, and while the boat is at its mooring or dock, roller furling is one more reason why even cruising boats should be equipped with a reliable, functional backstay adjuster. Before furling you pump up on the hydraulic adjuster or crank up on the mechanical adjuster; when the sail is in, the backstay can be eased to take the loads off the rig.

Roller-furling rigs are marvelous conveniences when they work; they are one of the most frightening devices on a boat when they fail, and there are many stories of jibs that couldn't be furled or dropped and finally either flogged themselves to death or had to be cut away. Some systems are inherently more reliable than others. Furling systems that depend on tiny internal halyards turning around small sheaves, or that put the entire headstay load on upper and lower thrust bearings, will naturally require careful maintenance of those parts. The halyards and the sheaves in the upper swivel units of designs like the Famet or the Cruising Center systems should be inspected frequently for wear. And the thrust bearings in units like the Stearns or the Hyde stays should be disassembled annually or even twice a year and lubricated or replaced as required. With any unit, be careful what grease you choose. Some units use hard steel bearings, which are fine in a marine environment if they are kept well packed with an appropriate lubricant, such as a good grade of lithium grease. Use the wrong grease, such as a Teflon lubricant which won't stick to the hard steel balls or rollers, and you will end up with a frozen mess in one season. The halyards of free-flying furling systems, like the Schaefer, are normally carried at extremely high loads, which tend to break down the wire of the halyard, the tail splice, and the sheaves at the masthead. Inspect them regularly and replace them early to avoid problems.

In many systems, problems are inherited from poor installations. Freestanding systems usually need a pad eye aft of the stem fitting, and if a 2:1 halyard system has been installed, a tang for the halyard may have been added to the mast. The pad eye should be strong, installed with a glassed-in backing block, or at least a wooden backing block and a backing plate. If the deck is not solid in the way of the pad eye, the mounting holes will need compression sleeves or the epoxy treatment detailed on pages 65 to 67. The tang on the mast should be attached with good-size machine screws. Sometimes in the press to install a system while the mast is standing, corners are cut that can lead to real problems later.

Extrusions that replace the headstay must be cut to an exact fit, or at least a fit that can be made exact with toggle plates. Extrusions that fit over the headstay often require that the headstay be cut and a new terminal fitting installed. If a Norseman fitting is installed on the headstay, as some of the systems require, make certain that the fitting has been installed very carefully. Norseman terminals are not as easy to install as some of the literature would make it seem, and the pointy end of a boat is not the best location for the painstaking (and in the case of heavy wire headstays, painful) work required to install the terminal.

The furling line itself must be led fairly and conveniently, which means blocks and fairleads all along the rail. Wire is usually unnecessary; prestretched line is often a better choice. Most systems should work without a winch in light air, and with perhaps a turn around a winch in a breeze. The continuous-line systems, which usually feature a smaller drum that allows the tack to be positioned much closer to the deck, are worth considering. With some clever thought beforehand, it isn't that much more difficult to lead two lines aft, and either a ratchet block under tension, or perhaps a Hood line-driver winch on a larger boat, can be used to tension the line.

When a boat is converted to roller furling, and especially when a sail is recut by a sailmaker to fit on a roller furler, it is important to recheck the position of the jib leads. A sail that trimmed just ahead of the primary when it was used with hanks may trim a foot aft of the winch after it has been converted to roller furling. You may or may not have track in the right place, and it may be wise to consult with your sailmaker before the conversion so he can compensate for any potential problems with a jib sheet lead.

10

TAMING THE SPINNAKER

Spinnakers evoke more excitement and prematurely age more boat owners than any other sail. No image captures the joys of yachting like the photograph of a fleet of billowing spinnakers, and no moment is as thrilling as the wild downhill ride when the knot meter hits the "teens." Yet to the beginning racer or shorthanded cruiser, the spinnaker sometimes seems an invention of the devil, a sail created to try his composure, pocketbook, and self-confidence. The approach of a windward mark, or the jibe mark, leaves some fledgling racers with trembling pulses and cold sweats, and there are cruisers who would rather motor or slat their way downwind than try to control hundreds or thousands of square feet of colorful nylon that they can only picture wrapped around the headstay or draped under the keel after some mishap or another.

On a well-rigged boat, a spinnaker should and can be easy to set, jibe, and take down. A cruising couple should have little trouble with a spinnaker in moderate breezes on a boat with an I dimension (height of foretriangle) of 45 feet. The same couple could handle the spinnaker on a boat with an I of up to 55 feet, except that jibing or taking down the spinnaker in anything other than light air would be tricky. With boats of I dimensions of 40 feet or less, it should be possible for two people to set, jibe, and take down a spinnaker in conditions up to a fresh breeze. And there are no special gadgets or devices needed—only sound rigging with well-positioned hardware.

Some boat owners, in mistaken fear of a spinnaker pole or a spinnaker, have turned to the so-called cruising spinnakers, which go under a host of splashy names like Flasher or MPS. Some sailmakers would have you believe that cruising spinnakers are their very latest invention, but the idea of a cross between a spinnaker and a genoa is really an old sail that has variously been called a ballooner, a genaker, and a half-chute. The latest versions feature a tack pennant and a variety of constructions from cross cuts to complicated radial cuts. On points of sail from a close reach to a beam reach, a cruising spinnaker or genaker is an ideal sail, easy to set and trim, and because of its asymmetrical shape, a more efficient sail than an ordinary spinnaker. But when the boat bears farther off the wind, the sail either falls inefficiently behind the main or has to be jibed over to the other side and flown with a pole, like a wing-and-wing genoa. It then becomes much less efficient and harder to control than a larger spinnaker. The cruising spinnaker is thus a rather specialized sail, and since it is illegal for racing in IOR, MHS, and most PHRF fleets, a regular spinnaker is probably a wiser and more versatile investment for most boats.

The only trick in rigging a boat for a spinnaker is to have reliable and easy-to-adjust controls for all three corners of the sail. Sound simple? How many boats have you seen where the sheets and guys had to be swapped from one winch to another when the boat hardened up from a run to a reach or before a jibe? Or boats where the spinnaker sheet grinder had to sit to leeward on a hard reach, just when you needed every bit of weight to weather? Or boats where the spinnaker sheets fouled the mainsheet tackle or the traveler whenever the spinnaker trimmer tried to find a position where he could really see the sail? Or boats on which a spinnaker hoist required at least two people on the halyard, and still happened so slowly that the spinnaker filled prematurely (or wrapped around the headstay, or fell into the water) before it was fully hoisted?

If all three corners are under control, a spinnaker can be docile in anything less than a fresh breeze. If any corner is out of control, or awkward to control, the spinnaker can be a beast. If the halyard gear slows a hoist or drop, sets and takedowns are likely to run into trouble. If the afterguy is awkward, led to an underpowered winch, or made of line that is too stretchy, or if the foreguy and pole lift are not convenient, it will be difficult to control the position and shape of the sail. And if the design and construction of the pole is not appropriate for the method of jibing used on the boat, jibes can turn the running rigging into a game of cat's cradle.

SECONDARY WINCHES

For most boats over 30 feet or so in length, a pair of secondary winches is one of the first additions of spinnaker gear. On a small boat, under 25 feet, a single set of primary winches can suffice for genoa sheets and spinnaker sheets. A larger boat with an experienced crew can get by with a single pair of primary winches for the genoa sheets, spinnaker sheets, and spinnaker guys, but it requires sheet stoppers or clam cleats with gates to hold the loaded lines, and careful juggling of lines during jibes or sail changes. For a less experienced crew, or for maximum flexibility, the answer is to install secondary winches. If the secondary winches are to be used only for the spinnaker sheets and perhaps a barber hauler or auxiliary sheet, with the spinnaker guys leading to the primary winches, the secondaries can be a size or two smaller than the primary winches. If the winches will be used for the spinnaker guys as well as the sheets, they should probably be the same size as the primaries.

Secondary winches are usually mounted on the housetop or the coamings, or occasionally a single secondary winch is located on the bridge deck. The housetop is an excellent location: the spinnaker trimmer will usually be forward, near the shrouds, and a grinder standing at the aft end of the house can easily hear the cry "Trim!" as the chute starts to collapse; on most boats, a housetop secondary will permit cross sheeting on a hard reach, which keeps all the crew weight to weather; and housetop winches are convenient for other uses, such as trimming a barber hauler or control lines.

Positioning the secondary winches aft of the primaries often doesn't work as well, because the person grinding the winch gets in the way of the helmsman, or the sheet leading from the winch to a trimmer standing on the windward rail fouls the mainsheet. Moving a winch is relatively easy, and it is worth experimenting with different positions so that the spinnaker can be trimmed on any point of sail from a reach to a run without traffic jams of arms, lines, or bodies in the cockpit. In particular, try to avoid winch placements that require sheet swapping. It is usually possible to hand-hold a sheet during a winch swap, at least on boats with an I dimension of under 45 feet, but the time lost and the potential for disaster during the swaps make it an ineffective setup.

SPINNAKER HALYARDS

The spinnaker halyard rarely needs adjustment, but it should be rigged so the sail can be hoisted quickly, with provisions for those inevitable situations when the sail fills prematurely and needs to be ground up to the masthead. There should also be an easy control for the lowering of the spinna-

ker, with provisions for both a quick dump of the halyard and a controlled release. A dedicated winch or a winch with a stopper in front will fill the bill for a larger boat; a smaller boat, with an I dimension of under 33 feet, can probably get by with a spinnaker halyard led through a ratchet block. The fastest rig for boats of J-24 size is to exit high on the mast with a good cam cleat directly under the exit.

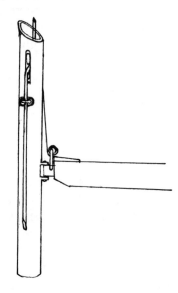

Halyards are often led aft to the cockpit, but the spinnaker halyard is a good candidate for the housetop or the base of the mast because it is rarely adjusted, and because it is frequently the foredeck man on a small boat or a mast man on a larger boat who will do the hoisting. The cockpit will already be crowded with sheets, guys, the mainsheet, and a helmsman, and one or two more pairs of flying elbows are hardly needed.

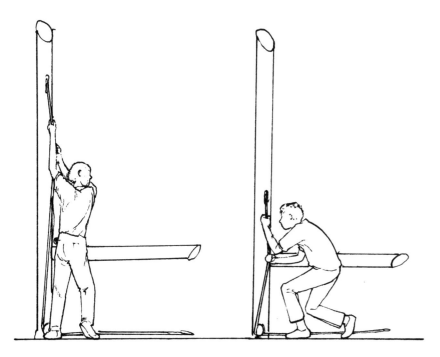

Wherever the halyard is ultimately located, it should be a position that allows the hoist to be done with long arm pulls. A high mast exit that allows the halyard to be "jumped" is ideal; boats with an exit at the base of the mast should allow sufficient room for a quick haul on the halyard.

For closed-course racing, where most roundings are to port, the spinnaker halyard should lead to the starboard side of the boat if possible. If there are two spinnaker halyards, it is traditional to put one on either side of the boat, but for closed-course racing and for spinnaker changes, it may be better to lead the two halyards to the same side of the boat so one man

can handle both the hoist of the new spinnaker and the drop of the old spinnaker.

SIZING SPINNAKER GEAR

MaxGenoa is a good working load for the sheet and guy blocks for a spinnaker. The actual loads on sheet and guy blocks are generally less than the maximum genoa clew load, but the shock loads on guy blocks, especially with low-stretch lines, and the acute turning angles of spinnaker sheet blocks suggest larger gear.

The manufacturers of spinnaker poles provide tables of recommended pole sizes, complete with columns for the overall length of the boat, the area of the spinnaker, and warnings about how they will take no responsibility for the breakage of the pole even if you follow the table recommendations scrupulously. The safest determinant for pole size is the J dimension of the boat (base of mast to stem).

SPINNAKER POLE SIZES

J Dimension	Spinnaker pole diameter
8–10 feet	2.0 inches
10–12 feet	2.5 inches
12–14 feet	3.0 inches
14–17 feet	3.5 inches
over 17 feet	4.0 inches

Boats with high-aspect rigs, and boats that will be sailed hard in conditions where dipping the pole end into the water is a real and frequent possibility, may need to go up one size of tubing. In moderate-air sailing areas an experienced crew may elect to go down a size in some cases, especially if the construction of the pole avoids cutouts and other "dotted line" break points, or if the pole is reinforced with carbon fiber or other specialized materials.

You can buy ready-made poles, with a variety of end fittings, from a rigger or from a manufacturer like Forespar or Nicro/Fico. A new spinnaker pole is also an excellent winter job for a boat owner, and if you are building a new pole from scratch, it is sometimes possible to buy sizes of tubing or pipe different from those advertised by the pole manufacturers. For example, it is possible to buy light-wall 3½-inch tubing which might be ideal for a 15- to 16-foot pole, especially in an area where the spinnaker will not be used for extensive heavy reaching or wild pole-in-the-water runs. The regular end fittings will usually fit; if not, the fittings can be shimmed with a thickness or two of stainless steel tape.

The crucial question in making or modifying a spinnaker pole and the associated gear is how you plan to jibe the spinnaker on the boat. Traditionally, boats with I dimensions up to 37 or 38 feet have used a loaded end-for-end jibe, with a single sheet/guy attached to either clew of the spinnaker; larger boats used a dip-pole jibe with separate sheets and guys on each clew. Recently, many boats with I dimensions of up to 48 feet have begun using unloaded end-for-end jibes, using separate sheets and guys on each clew, so that the foredeck man jibes the pole to an unloaded lazy guy while the chute is being flown on the two sheets. The advantages of the end-for-end jibe are that it is much quicker, at least for run-to-run jibes; fewer people are needed; there is only one person stand-ing in the bow of the boat; and there is no need to detach and reattach the babystay. If the boat is rigged right, the pole can still be dip-jibed for heavy-air reach-to-reach jibes. Boats with I dimensions of more than 48 feet will probably elect to use a dip jibe all of the time, and should be rigged accordingly.

End-for-End Poles To rig for end-for-end jibes, you need a pole with bridles for both the topping lift and the foreguy and with symmetrical ends, so that the pole will function indentically no matter which end is on the mast. Hence it is impossible to use a bayonet-type fitting on the mast. Instead, the usual fitting is a ring, or in some cases a toggled horizontal pin. The toggled pins are stronger, but they are less convenient for jibing, since they have to be pointed in exactly the correct direction if the pole end is to mate correctly when the pole is put back on the mast. For boats with I dimensions of less than 48 feet, there are ring fittings such as the strongest Schaefer or Nicro/Fico fittings, which are strong enough for most downwind conditions short of the Transpac. Poles shorter than 7 feet can get by with strong pad eyes for the foreguy or topping lift, but bridles are stronger and safer for any larger boat. One-eighth-inch wire should be strong enough for a bridle for an I dimension of up to 48 feet.

The end fittings for an end-for-end pole should be simple and reliable, either ordinary piston ends or a trigger with an external release. A single trip wire connecting the two pistons is the simplest rig, but it can sometimes release the wrong piston during a jibe. The solution is to fasten the wire down in the middle of the pole with a lashing or strong taping, or to use separate wires that will lead approximately three fourths of the length of the pole.

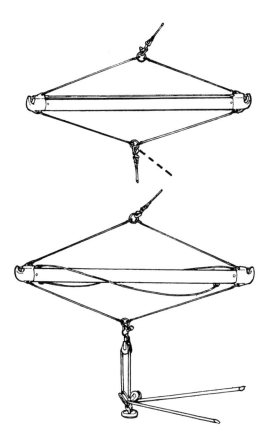

keep the pole from skying in some conditions. The middle of the foredeck position gives a good lead for all but the heaviest reaching. On any boat with an I dimension over 36 feet, a 2:1 foreguy is a good idea, both for the additional power, which usually means that no winch is needed, and for the simplicity of rigging. A double-ended control can bring the foreguy close enough to the spinnaker guy winch so that one man can control both, easing or tightening the foreguy as he trims the guy.

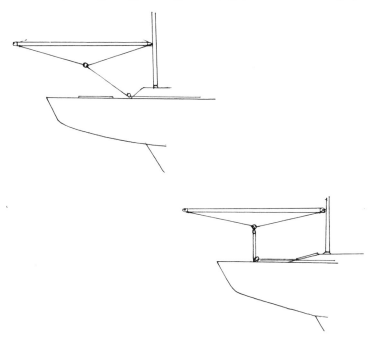

The foreguy of an end-for-end pole should lead either to the base of the mast on a smaller boat or to the middle of the foredeck on a larger boat. The mast-base position has the advantage that the foreguy does not have to be adjusted when the guy is trimmed or eased, but in heavy-air reaching the foreguy will be heavily loaded, and it may be impossible to

Some boat owners will object that the foreguy isn't next to the topping lift, but for most sailing the foreguy is adjusted far more often in conjunction with the afterguy than it is trimmed for adjustment of the height of the pole. It may make more sense to have the topping lift forward, where with a stopper it can share one of the winches used for halyards.

Dip-Jibe Poles   It is possible to use an end-for-end pole for a dip jibe, and many boats which normally end-for-end will use the dip jibe in heavy air or on reach-to-reach jibes. But for routine dip jibes, a very different kind of pole is far more effective. The dip pole should have an internally released trigger fitting with two release lines, one exiting the bottom of the pole near the inboard end and the other exiting the top of the pole near the outboard end. The inboard trip is used during a jibe to trip the pole off the guy; the outboard trip is used by the foredeck man to open the pole end when he is setting up or to stow the pole on its chocks. The two control wires (which could be prestretched ⅚₂ line instead) should attach to the piston independently, so that if one breaks or snags the other is still usable, and they should exit over small blocks that will permit a pull from any direction.

Because the larger pole will have to be set up earlier, it is common to use a retractable topping-lift bridle on a dip-jibe pole, which allows the topping lift to be attached early. The disadvantage of the retractable rig is its complexity and the fact that the shock cord makes it that much harder to hoist the pole with the lift. A simpler rig is to make no provision for the topping lift except for an eye on the end fitting or perhaps a separate pad eye a few feet inboard of the end fitting to allow the genoa sheets and/or the lazy spinnaker sheet to rest on the top of the pole. If the topping lift is then to be attached early, it can be held back at the mast with a looped sail tie or a length of shock cord.

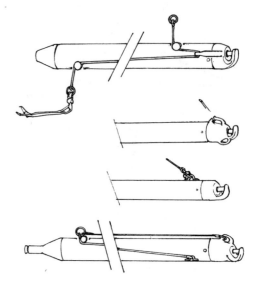

In building any pole, and especially for poles with internal trip lines or retractors, the end fittings should be fastened with tapped machine screws set in zinc chromate paste or silicone, so the end can be removed quickly to repair any tangles.

The foreguy for a dip-jibed pole should lead from the outboard end of the pole to a point well forward on the foredeck. A 2:1 lead can be used for additional power and to provide a double-ended lead, but it will require a lot of line. On a large boat, the foreguy should lead to a winch or through a stopper with a convenient backup winch for those occasions when a goof-up lets the pole sky, or when an unexpected death roll puts the pole end into the water. If the foreguy cannot be released quickly, the pole will almost certainly break.

The topping lift on a large boat will need a winch; a stopper with a backup winch—perhaps a halyard winch or a housetop

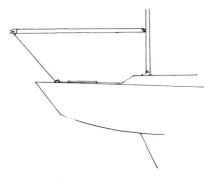

by with two strong eyes on the mast. For a larger boat, a track and sliding ring should be used; if the I dimension is over 40 feet, the slider should have Delrin inserts or roller-bearing surfaces and should be equipped with control lines. If the I dimension is over 48 feet, a doubled purchase will probably be necessary to adjust the car under load. Self-tailing tackles with clam cleats are the simplest rig. The cleats should be sized to the lines; use aluminum rather than nylon cleats if possible. If one or both cleats have fairleads, it will keep the tackle tidier and prevent accidental releases.

For larger boats, a Hood line-driver winch works well; the largest boats will need chain drives. It is also possible to lead the mast car adjustments aft, but the adjustment usually doesn't need to be made often enough to require aft leads. (If you calculate the difference in "projection" of the pole when the mast car is a foot too high or too low, it is hardly significant.)

utility winch—is sufficient. For fast closed-course racing, the topping lift can exit the mast high up and run over a strong clam cleat. Then for a mark rounding, a man can "jump" the unloaded pole into position and lock it off temporarily in the clam cleat until the topping lift is later loaded onto a winch for fine-trimming. Be sure to use a clam cleat with a gate so the line will not slip into the cleat later, when you are adjusting the topping lift from a winch.

The control of the end of the pole on the mast can be simple for any but a quite large boat. Some boats (J-24 size) can get

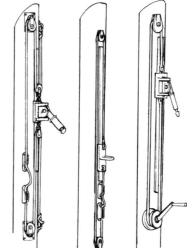

SHEETS AND GUYS

A sheeted-in genoa has less than 10 feet of line between the clew and the sheet winch—usually something like 5 feet. if the line stretches 2 percent of its length under load, the stretch will amount to around 1 inch. On a conscientiously sailed boat the stretch would be noticeable (especially if there were marks on the spreaders to indicate how far off the spreader the genoa was), and the genoa sheet would be adjusted to compensate. But 1 inch of stretch is tolerable.

If the spinnaker guy stretches 1 percent, it is a very different matter. On a 30-foot boat there may be 30 feet of line, or more, between the tack of the spinnaker (the pole end) and the winch. A stretch of 2 percent means the line will lengthen by 7 inches, which is enough to slam the spinnaker pole into the headstay. In light air, when the load on the spinnaker sheet may double or quadruple with each change in wind strength, the stretch in the spinnaker sheet with each puff yields the equivalent of tying your spinnaker sheet to a spring!

Unless it is forbidden by class rules, or infrequent spinnaker use makes efficiency a low priority, spinnaker guys should be made of the lowest-stretch material you are willing to use. The range of choices include Kevlar, Kevlar/Dacron blends, parallel-core Dacrons, and so-called low-stretch Dacrons, which covers a broad spectrum of cost, durability, convenience of use, and strength/stretch characteristics. The lower-stretch lines are so much stronger that it is usually possible to use a smaller line than would be needed with ordinary Dacron braid. In general, if a boat needs a ½-inch Dacron guy, it is sufficient to use ⅜-inch Kevlar or ⁷⁄₁₆-inch Kevlar/Dacron or parallel-core Dacron.

Pure Kevlar is ideal for a spinnaker guy. Diameter for diameter, Kevlar will match stainless cable in stretch and strength characteristics. The drawbacks are that Kevlar is expensive, unpleasantly stiff, and intolerant of chafe. Some larger boats avoid part of the chafe problem by splicing short wire tails onto the Kevlar to take the chafe in the pole end; for any but the largest boats this should not be necessary—and might be unwise, since each tuck of a tail splice puts the Kevlar core into a chafe situation against the wire. For smaller boats, with I dimensions of less than 55 feet, and for all but extended offwind racing under spinnaker, a good Kevlar splice with a plastic donut—and perhaps an elkhide wrapping to keep the pole end from chafing at the splice—should be sufficient. If you elect to use pure Kevlar lines (actually only the core is Kevlar; the covering is Dacron), make sure that you or your rigger does a proper Kevlar splice, that the sheaves on all of the blocks are large and appropriate for Kevlar lines, and that there is no possibility of chafe against the shrouds or the lifelines. With properly sized Kevlar, the spinnaker guy can be set just off the headstay on a reach and it will stay there even with a significant puff.

If Kevlar sounds too inconvenient and too expensive, the next alternatives are Kevlar/Dacron blends and parallel-core Dacron lines, which have similar stretch characteristics. Kevlar/Dacron blends, such as Yale Aramid 80 or New England Kevlar/Dacron 65, are made with Dacron covers over a core of 65 percent Kevlar and 35 percent Dacron. The Dacron in the core makes the line softer, more tolerant to chafe, less expensive, but stretchier than pure Kevlar lines. If the line is sized correctly and the splice is done carefully, an ordinary eye splice, rather than a difficult Kevlar splice, is sufficient.

Another alternative, with almost identical stretch characteristics and even more resistance to chafe, is the parallel-core lines, like Sta-Set X or Cup-Sheet. The parallel orientation of the Dacron core reduces the stretch dramatically but increases the stiffness so that these lines are as stiff as straight Kevlar. The parallel core also makes splicing the line difficult. The additional stretch of either of these over Kevlar is negligible at lower wind strengths or with a minor increase in wind strength; at higher wind speeds or with a sudden surge that increases the load by a factor of four or six, the increase in stretch is significant, especially on boats with less than ideal spinnaker pole geometry (narrow boats, boats with inboard guy blocks, and boats that do not use a reaching strut).

Finally, there are the so-called low-stretch or prestretched Dacron lines, which are usually advertised for use as halyards. They are actually ordinary braided, or in the case of Marlow, laid, Dacron lines that have been prestretched and/or heat-set to reduce the stretch. The treatments may make the lines slightly better than ordinary braided Dacron, but once the ordinary Dacron has been stretched in use, it seems to have almost the same characteristics as the prestretched Dacron. Unless spinnaker sailing is a very low priority or the budget is very tight, ordinary Dacron is a poor choice for the spinnaker guys.

For boats that use separate sheets and guys, Dacron braid is sufficient for the heavy-air sheet, which will probably be a fairly large diameter for grip on the winch and for the convenience of the sheet trimmer. For more aggressively sailed boats, a smaller-diameter sheet of one of the lower-stretch lines might be a good choice. For light-air spinnaker sheets, which are small-diameter for lightness yet need minimum stretch, either $\frac{3}{16}$-inch Kevlar/Dacron or $\frac{5}{32}$-inch Kevlar is a good choice. The smaller Kevlar is brutal on the spinnaker trimmer's hands, but it is lighter and has less stretch than any alternative.

Sizing Sheets and Guys

The table on page 58 is a good beginning for selecting the appropriate size of spinnaker sheets and guys. The usual formulas for length are to make the guy 1½ times the overall length (LOA) of the boat and to make the sheets twice the LOA, so the spinnaker sheet trimmer can lead the sheet well forward where he has a view of the entire sail. For boats that lead the spinnaker guy through a turning block instead of directly from the lead block to the winch, add 10 or 15 feet to the calculated length for the guy.

RIGGING THE SHEETS AND GUYS

Any boat with an I dimension of over 40 feet should have separate sheets and guys. Smaller boats can get by with a single sheet/guy on each clew if either a twing line or another means to bring the guy (the line leading to the pole end) down to the rail is added. It is possible to use nothing more complicated than a snatch block on the rail and go through the ritual of having a crewman step on the guy to get it into the snatch block, but a temporarily or permanently rigged twing line not only makes it easier to bring the guy down but is a versatile control for preventing collapses of the spinnaker in puffy air. When a sudden collapse of the chute threatens, it can often be saved with a quick tug on the twing instead of the long, slow trim of the sheet.

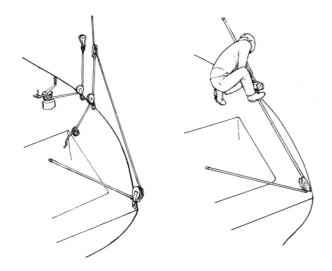

The carabiner twing is easy to snap on and off. A block, such as a Harken Big Bullet or one of the Schaefer ball-bearing blocks with a lashing eye, is more complicated but offers less friction. If the twing is to be used as a control rather than an all-or-nothing pull down to the rail, the short piece of line should be low-stretch material, and the block on the rail could be a ratchet block for increased control. On smaller boats, the twings and barber haulers can often be interchangeable.

The spinnaker sheet block on the aft quarter should have a large sheave to reduce friction on the almost 180-degree turn, especially if Kevlar sheets are used. Spreacher blocks, combining a large sheave for the spinnaker sheet and a smaller sheave for the blooper, reacher, or light spinnaker sheet, are popular, and for boats that routinely use a blooper or reacher they make a lot of sense. Smaller boats can substitute a large fiddle block.

For boats that do not use a blooper or reacher, a better rig is to use a snap block for the light sheet (either a snatch block or just a block with a snap shackle attachment; a small ratchet block is superb). The block can be moved forward as far as the shrouds when the wind is light and aft, which gives most spinnakers better shape in light air, and minimizes the length of the light sheet and the spaghetti in the aft end of the boat. If a ratchet block is used, there is no need to trim the sheet to a winch in very light air, which means there is no complicated ritual of swapping the sheets on and off the winch.

Positioning Guy Blocks

Positioning the guy block for a boat big enough to use separate sheets and guys is tricky, because the guy will invariably lead somewhere between the Scylla of the lifelines and the Charybdis of the shrouds. If the boat is beamy, with the chain plates set well in from the rail, the best location is usually inboard, aft of the shrouds. You can find the ideal position by putting the pole up and moving the guy around on the deck; when led through the block and to a winch or turning block, it should just clear the shrouds when the pole is a few inches off the headstay. Then try the same position with the pole pulled aft to where it would be on a dead run in light air. The guy will probably chafe the lifelines when the pole is low enough for light air, but the chafe may be tolerable, or the load in that situation can be taken by the lazy sheet.

If the boat is narrow or the chain plates are close to the rail, or if the lifelines slope inward rather than outward, a guy lead on the rail, outside the lifelines, will work better. The widest beam gives the best lead, but a position farther forward or aft may avoid chafe on the lifelines. If it is impossible to keep the

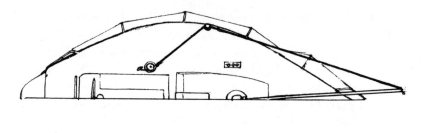

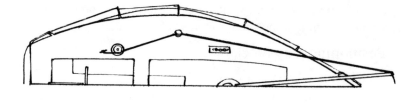

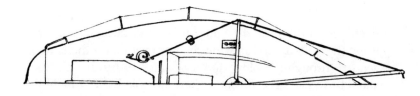

mounted with a length of hose to keep it off the deck. On the rail, use a pad eye or a strong car on a track, with shock cord from an eye or a becket to the lifelines. If you are installing a pad eye or deck block, make sure that the coring of the deck is reinforced with compression sleeves or the epoxy treatment, and that the block or pad eye is backed up and through-bolted with large washers and/or a metal backing plate.

SHACKLES

The spinnaker guy shackles (or the shackles on combined spinnaker sheet/guys) should be reliable and should release easily under load. For boats with I dimensions over 50 feet, pin shackles are not as reliable or as easy to release as latch-type shackles like the Sparcraft, Gibb, Wichard, or Lewmar shackles—all of which require a fid to release under load. Either the foredeck man must carry a fid with him to release the chute or there must be a fid strapped to the pulpit with shock cord. Smaller boats can usually get by with a pin shackle which can be released with a lanyard.

The shackles for separate sheets should be easy to release, so that changes to a light sheet are quick and easy. If you independently shackle your sheet and guy to the spinnaker, or shackle the sheet to the ring of the guy shackle, the shackles for the sheets can be one or two sizes smaller than the guy shackles. If your foredeck crew prefers to shackle the sheet to the spinnaker and the guy to the sheet shackle (which makes it easier to remove the lazy guy in light air), then the sheet and guy shackles should be the same size.

It is customary to tie in light sheets, but a small snap shackle is faster. The way to change quickly without a shackle is to

guy off the lifelines and the shrouds when the pole is forward, it may be necessary to use a reaching strut.

The block for the guy should be strong. Snatch blocks are not a good idea for any size boat, because if a snatch block isn't closed carefully it will explode under load, and because most snatch blocks have sheaves that are too small for Kevlar lines. If the block is positioned on the deck, it can either be a strong stand-up block or a pad eye with a separate block run a long bight of line through the clew and tie the bowline with the clew released; the bight of line probably weighs as much as the small snap shackle (the smallest Nicro/Fico and Merriman shackles weigh 1½ ounces).

POLE CHOCKS, TURTLES, AND SPINNAKER GADGETS

There are few screwups more annoying than genoa sheets wrapping around the end of a spinnaker pole during a tack. Even on boats with chocks for both ends of the pole, the pole is often supported off the deck in a position that seems calculated to plunge someone into an imitation of Chevy Chase doing a Gerald Ford fall.

Many boats keep the spinnaker pole on the track and ready to go for short closed-course races; to do the maneuver properly requires a mast track that comes almost to the deck, a foredeck that will permit the pole to rest out of the way, and efficient controls to raise the butt of the pole and the end. The alternative is to position the mast car where it will be when the pole is hoisted, and wait to put the pole up when it is needed. The process is speeded up if the pole is stored forward, so that one man can easily hook it up in position. For a spinnaker pole with reversible ends, the simplest stowage during a race is with the aft end hooked onto the shrouds at the deck. In that position, the pole is already forward, ready to be hoisted by one person; and with the aft jaws safely on the shrouds, there is little possibility of a line catching during a tack. For a bayonet end, secure stowage will require either a chock for the aft end or some arrangement of shock cord to keep the end from snagging lines.

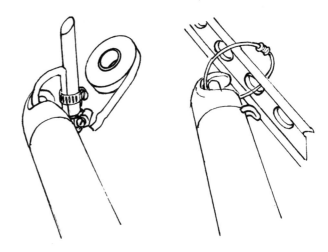

When the boat is not racing, or for stowage during distance races, the chocks can be as complex as the welded stainless or cast aluminum fittings sold by the hardware manufacturers—most of which keep a pole too high off the deck—or as simple as a D-ring fastened to the rail or to a pulpit or stanchion base with a hose clamp. For boats with perforated toe rails, it is easy to make a pole holder with a length of stainless cable and a Nicopress fitting.

Turtles are another device that can make spinnakers easier to use. They come in many flavors, from a sail bag with a loop of wire to hold it open to complex turtles with Velcro or shock-cord closures. Your sailmaker probably has preferences (mine admits that his preference for sail bags with loops is pure prejudice). Whatever kind of turtle you elect to use, make certain that it can be quickly and easily attached to the boat, preferably with Wichard-type one-handed snaps, and that there is a means of holding the two clews and the head of the spinnaker inside the turtle after the sheets, guys, and halyard are hooked on. One simple solution is two straps from opposite sides of the turtle with Velcro pads on the end; run the straps through the three cringles at the corners of the sail and push the Velcro pads together. A tug from the halyard or guy will pull the corners apart.

Various manufacturers advertise all sorts of gadgets that are supposed to simplify the use of a spinnaker. Most of these are some variation of a full-hoist turtle with a zipper or rings with halyards that are designed to allow the spinnaker to be hoisted completely before it is broken open, and which theoretically allow the spinnaker to be gathered into the device before it is lowered. The problem with all of them is that they are cumbersome and complicated, and while they will do what they are supposed to do in light air, there is really no difficulty in hoisting or taking down a spinnaker in light air. In a fresh breeze the plastic rings and zippers are likely to fail, or worse, to snag on something, so that instead of just a spinnaker to take down, you have a great tangle of lines and gadgetry up there. And once you take the beast down, instead of a soft turtle packed with a chute, you have a long, bulky snake.

An easier solution for hoisting a spinnaker in a breeze is to stop the chute, which is easily done with either the ready-made devices or a device you can make yourself out of a small bucket or a length of PVC pipe. If you are using a bucket, cut off the end and glue a strip of wood along one side of the bucket, which will let you get your fingertips around the rubber bands. The length of pipe needs only a strip of wood. Then line up enough rubber bands and snake the chute through, with the leeches together and untwisted, popping off rubber bands at regular intervals. The chute is then ready to be hoisted and broken open with a smart trim on the chute, unless you have used too many rubber bands or rubber bands that are too strong for the breeze. If you have stopped the chute and want to hoist it in lighter air, break off every other rubber band before you hoist. A stopped chute is easier to hoist than a chute in one of the fancy gadgets, and once it is up there are no lines or rings or other gadgets hanging off the mast.

There are also tricks to facilitate take-downs. With a practiced crew, a belly-button line sewn to a strong eye in the middle of the chute allows you to drop the chute and pull it in without easing or tripping the guy. If the procedure is done swiftly, and if there is enough breeze to keep the chute blowing out from the boat as the halyard is dumped, the maneuver is spectacular and allows you to carry the chute all the way to the mark before the chute is dropped. Some boats are able to do the same take-down without a belly button by having two or more crew members with fast hands gather the chute as it comes down under the genoa.

For boats with less virtuoso crews, the greatest aid to a take-down is the lazy guy or a twing line. If you normally don't use a twing or lazy guy and just push the sheet into a snatch block when it is functioning as a guy, try hooking a piece of line into the clew of the spinnaker and using it to pull the spinnaker down behind the main. If the halyard is set to run smoothly and the helmsman keeps the chute blanketed behind the mainsail, two people can drop the chute on a quite large boat without hassle.

11

UPGRADING
A SPAR

A custom-built spar, designed and constructed for low windage and weight and optimum bending characteristics, can cost ten times as much as a simple production spar. The differences go beyond the choice of a lightweight section with tapering, chemical etching, and stiffeners, and the controls built into the spar for adjustment of luff and foot tensions and spar bend. There is often a level of detailing in the custom spar that most production spar makers rarely try to equal. Fortunately, there is no reason why a production spar cannot be upgraded to the level of detailing seen in the best custom spars. The work is not difficult; much of it can be done by a boat owner or at modest cost during the off season by a rigger.

Modifications to the running rigging of a boat are generally simple and straightforward. Internalizing halyards and reefs; improving systems like backstay adjusters, topping lifts, and outhauls; installing spinnaker gear; and releading halyards or reef lines are modifications that usually can be made without affecting the integrity or structural design of the rig. Modifications of the standing rigging, and modifications that are designed to improve or alter the bending characteristics of a rig, on the other hand, should not be attempted without some consultation with a sailmaker, a spar builder, or a naval architect. It is not difficult to add mast bend controls or to change a rig with double lower shrouds to a single lower shroud and babystay configuration; frequently such changes will add to the structural integrity of the rig and the boat. But it is important not to set off on such changes half-cocked.

Any adjustment of the mast bend will directly affect the shape of the mainsail, and it is wise to at least consult with the sailmaker before going ahead, so that the luff curve of the mainsail can be matched to the bending characteristics of the mast. Substituting single lowers and a babystay for double lowers will change the loading on those shrouds, and depending upon the positioning of chain plates and tie-rods will change the loading on structural members of the hull and deck; it is wise to consult with the naval architect who designed the boat, or at least with an experienced rigger or spar designer, before leaping into the change. Most spar builders put their labels on the sides of the spars, and many naval architects will welcome a phone call if you aren't trying to get them to design a new rig for free. Frequently there are engineers or experienced rig designers at the spar builder's plant or the naval architect's office who can suggest modifications or can caution you away from modifications that they don't think will add much, or that may even be dangerous. Many times they are remarkably candid, letting on that it was the manufacturer who insisted on the oversized rigging or the omission of a babystay in the first place, and that the first thing they would have done would have been to rig the boat the way you are planning.

Finally, replacement of a spar with a different section is a job to be undertaken with the guidance of a spar designer or naval architect, although there is no reason why a boat owner should not work closely with the spar designer and the spar builder, making sure that the rig really suits the intended use of the boat. Spar builders have their own styles of rigging, and the experience of the builder should be important in the choice of that person to do the work. A rigger who is terrific at low-windage marginal racing spars may not be experienced in building a spar with an internalized roller-reefing mainsail system.

INTERNALIZING LINES

There is little excuse for external halyards, reef lines, outhaul controls, flattening reef controls, and topping lifts on any boat. The symphony of external halyards slapping against a spar is charming for a night or two, but when you realize that the music is taking a toll in chafe and wear on both the spar and the halyards, it loses its charm. There is a myth that internal halyards are somehow unsafe, that it is too difficult to rereeve a halyard after it breaks, or that the halyards cannot be inspected inside the mast. The same observation could be made about an engine; that it is easier to inspect and service if it is left uncovered, perhaps in the middle of the salon. In fact, the protection offered by the mast will generally extend the life of halyards, and with messengers it is a simple job to partially or completely remove a halyard for inspection, repair, or replacement. Reef lines, outhaul and flattening controls, and topping lifts can also be run internally, avoiding snags with lines hanging off the boom and leaving a boat aerodynamically cleaner.

Internalizing halyards is not a difficult job, and in many cases gear built into a spar for other purposes can be used for the internalization. There are essentially two separate jobs: the masthead, and exits lower on the mast.

Main and Genoa Halyards If a masthead is built with double sheaves to lead the genoa and main halyards externally, you can use the single sheaves to lead the halyards internally and have an extra sheave for a second genoa halyard. If the smaller sheaves wear the wire halyards excessively, it is worth considering the next larger size of wire for a replacement hal-

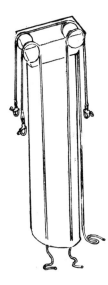

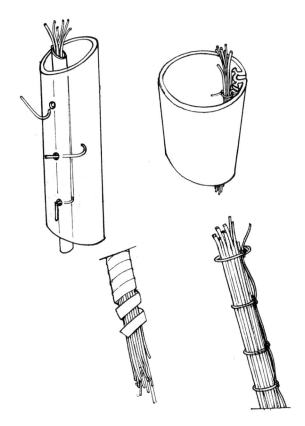

yard. The halyard tail, after exposure in the sun for so long, may be due for replacement anyway.

Internal halyards should run fair from the entrance point to the exit point. Check carefully inside the mast for spreader brackets, compression sleeves, loose wiring for a deck light, masthead lights, electronics, or foam disks that are used to keep internal wiring from slapping around. It is usually possible to route the halyards around compression sleeves and spreader brackets, but make certain that there are no sharp edges, which should be filed or taped. The wiring will have to be secured, which can be done with PVC tubing, cable wrapping, or cable ties. Many spars have grooves built into the extrusion to hold clamps or tubing that is designed for internal wiring.

The easiest tool for stringing the halyards is an electrician's snake, which you can borrow or rent. An alternative is to use long sections of small PVC tubing, which might later be used to hold the wiring. The other essential tool is a powerful light that can be held at one end of the mast. (After a session of stringing halyards you will find that the expression "light at the end of the tunnel" will have taken on new meaning.)

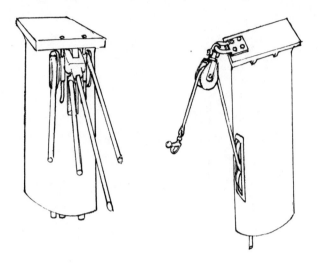

masthead, but it is often just as easy to through-bolt the crane. Make certain that you use a lock washer or a Nylock nut on any through-bolts, especially those that are aloft where you can't see the nut come loose until the spinnaker crane tumbles off the mast and onto the deck.

When fitting a spinnaker halyard, make sure you hold the headstay out in the position it will be in when the mast is up, so that you can see whether the lead is fair and will not chafe on the headstay after the spinnaker is jibed.

Pole Lift The spinnaker pole topping lift is also easy to internalize. It's important to remember in installing a topping lift that it must swivel approximately 180 degrees. The simplest exit is a sheave box, which may need a small pad eye fitted to make certain that the line or wire doesn't jump off the sheave when the pole is square on either jibe. It is also possible to exit through a slot to an external block on an eye or crane, an installation which offers a fair lead but more windage.

The higher a topping lift is placed on the mast, the better the angle for raising the pole, especially if the lead is to the

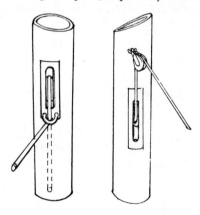

Spinnaker Halyards To add a spinnaker halyard or internalize the spinnaker halyard leading from an external crane, use an exit slot a few feet below the masthead. If you put the slot too close to the masthead, the lead will chafe. If you cut a slot carefully, and if it lines up perfectly with the halyard, you won't need an exit block for the halyard; in fact, a plain slot or a slot with a cover plate such as those made by Schaefer or Kenyon has less friction (if the line is led fairly) than a double-sheave exit block. In any case, make certain that there is no chafe of halyard against spar; a wire halyard will quickly leave a raw enough edge on the aluminum spar to rip up your rope tails and create meat hooks on the wire halyards.

If the masthead does not have a crane for the spinnaker, there are semicustom fittings made by some riggers, or you can get a fitting made up by a local metal fabricator with heliarc welding equipment. It is possible to drill and tap the outer end of the pole instead of to a bridle. If the topping lift is also to be used as a staysail halyard, be sure to consult with your sailmaker as to where it should exit the mast.

Spar Exits

To lead an internal halyard out of a spar, you can use an exit slot, a straight-line exit block, or an exit turning block. The exit turning block is used to exit lines which will not need to be "jumped." In general, for halyards it is better to use a slot or a straight-line exit block and a separate turning block, because the exits can be staggered to avoid weakening the mast, and because the external run from the exit slot to the turning block enables a crewman to "jump" a halyard faster than it can be pulled hand over hand on a winch.

The only trick with exits is to make sure they line up from the entry point of the halyard (usually the masthead sheave) and that the order of exit blocks around the mast corresponds to the order of the lines within the mast. Any crossing of lines will eventually cause trouble. It may feel free when you first put the halyard into the mast, but when the mast bends, or if a line ever goes slack, your crossed halyards will become

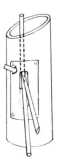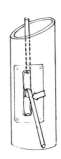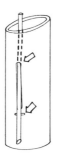

wrapped halyards. It usually happens on a dark, rainy night when the wind is blowing between 25 and 30 knots!

Deck Blocks

If you exit from an in-line exit block or a slot, make sure that the turning block on the deck is exactly in line with the exit. Kenyon and Schaefer make blocks designed for mounting on the mast, which avoids the problem of the turning

blocks lifting the deck. If the turning blocks are mounted instead on either the deck or a mast collar, the loads should be spread by substantial backing plates, or transferred to the mast or to the keel, to prevent the halyard loads from lifting the deck. On a smaller boat, a good backing block or plate will spread the load. On a larger boat, bolting the mast to the mast collar, or using some kind of tie-rod or cable from the mast collar or from the base of the turning block, will make sure the deck stays on the boat.

One simple setup is to use a pair of matching pad eyes, bolted back to back, for each turning block: one on deck for the block and a second below deck for a cable or rod, with a turnbuckle, to the keel and/or mast step. If there is a mast collar, the turning blocks can be hooked on or fastened to the collar with strong pad eyes, then pad eyes on the bottom of the deck can be used for a cable or rod to the mast step, keel, or to a pad eye or tang on the mast.

It is a good idea to mount small pad eyes, or perhaps a straightened boom bail, on the deck in front of the mast to hold halyards when they are not in use. At a mooring or anchorage, you will probably want to keep the halyards forward, on the pulpit or deck pad eyes, to avoid the noise and wear and tear of halyards slapping against a mast. But while sailing, the halyards should be aft, and it is a good idea to provide a place for each one, preferably in order around the base of the mast so that they can be stored untwisted.

A good trick for halyard storage, and for mounting small blocks at the base of the mast, is to use eyebolts in place of the bolts that hold down the mast collar. Small turning blocks for a cunningham or outhaul line can be shackled onto the eyebolts, or the eyebolts can be used to hold unused halyards.

If your boat has halyard winches on the mast, this is a good time to move them to the deck. With a careful choice of exit blocks and turning blocks, the lead from the mast to the winch can sometimes be done with a single block.

BOOMS

The lines on a boom are even easier to internalize than mast lines, and with the reef lines, outhaul, flattener, and topping lift controls safely inside the boom, there are no dangling lines to catch on people, winches, cleats, or the furled or flaked mainsail.

Reef Lines   When slab or "jiffy" reefing first began to replace roller reefing as the norm on cruising boats, it was widely believed that the reef lines had to lead from a special spot on the boom that required careful measurement of the sail. Now, most boats lead the reef lines from the boom end, wrapping the reef line around the boom and letting the sail find its own spot on the boom.

For booms that do not have fabricated end fittings, Kenyon and Ronstan make fittings that can be adapted to many booms with sheaves for reef lines, outhaul, flattener and/or topping lift tails. An alternative for reef lines is to use an external cheek block, either fixed or on a track, with a slot forward of the boat to internalize the line. A boom topping lift can enter the boom through the boom end, through a centerline sheave aft of the outhaul or flattening reef sheaves, or through a small cheek block ahead of a slot. At the forward end of the boom, lines can exit through internal turning blocks or slots.

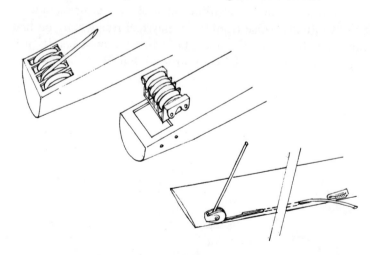

For an outhaul with sufficient internal purchase, or for a boom topping lift, an exit block or a slot and cleat on the boom is probably sufficient. For reef lines that will need the power of the winch to snug up, the lead should be through turning blocks with built-in stoppers, or down to the deck and then through stoppers or over clam cleats to the winch.

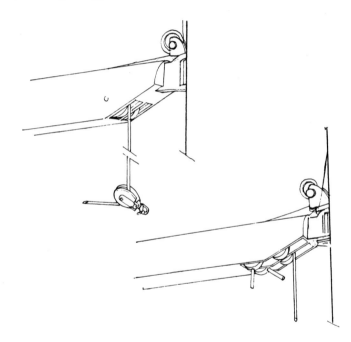

Boom Topping Lift While you are improving the boom is a good time to clean up the boom topping lift. Too often a heavy line, or a wire leading to an inconvenient tackle or even lashing, is used instead of a proper topping lift. The heavy line or

wire is excess windage and usually means excess chafe on the leech of the mainsail, with no real advantages.

There are many choices, both for internal and external control and for removable topping lifts. If you are replacing the topping lift because it is chafed, worn, or just too big, a good choice is small Kevlar line (⅛ or 5⁄32 inch), which is lighter, stronger, and less likely to chafe the leech of the mainsail; or 1 x 19 wire, which is stronger and smoother than the usual 7 x 19 wire and less likely to kink around a headboard shackle or other obstruction aloft. Kevlar should be terminated with large thimbles unless a large sheave is used at the end of the boom to lead the line inside to a tackle. Most booms will not require more than a 3:1 tackle on the topping lift, and for booms under 12 feet in length, 2:1 should be sufficient. Use a horn cleat or a good jam cleat to secure the topping lift; a cam cleat or clam cleat can slip and drop the boom on someone's head.

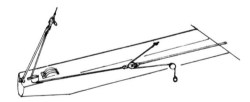

In light air, a topping lift slapping against the leech of the sail is annoying and detrimental to the life of the sail. One solution is to run a length of shock cord up the backstay to take the slack out of the topping lift; it works, but the long length of shock cord is sloppy, especially when the boat is well off the wind. If the boom is long enough and the topping lift can be made to clear the roach of the sail, the slack can also

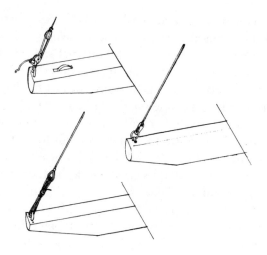

BENDING THE MAST

It is safe to bend most masts, within limits. Almost any section can be safely bent up to one half of its fore and aft depth, and even that amount of bend can do wonders to control the depth and power of the mainsail. If the mainsail is cut like a board, mast bend will only make it flatter, but any mainsail with shape in it can be improved with control of mast bend. In light air and off the wind, a full powerful shape can be carried in the mainsail. On the wind in a breeze, the shape

be taken out with a length of shock cord led directly from the topping lift to the boom, either externally or inside the boom.

The simplest and most direct solution of all is to put a snap shackle in the topping lift rig, so that it can be unhooked after the mainsail is hoisted. Or the entire topping lift can be nothing more than a length of Kevlar line (or wire) with a small snap shackle tied at the end. If the main halyard is inspected on a regular schedule, there is little likelihood of a failure that will drop the boom on the deck; for reefing or lowering the sail, either the topping lift can be rehooked or the boom can be lowered onto the lifelines. If the boom was manufactured with an internal sheave for the topping lift, as many are, and if the sheave is large enough and strong enough, it can often be used for a flattener—which needs critical adjustment more than a topping lift.

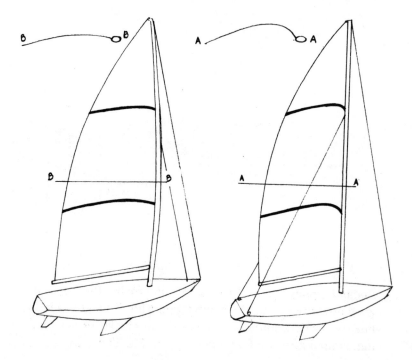

of the sail can be flattened by bending the mast—reducing the power of the mainsail as effectively as a reef, with the advantage that the sail can be "powered up" almost instantly in response to changing wind or sea conditions.

Backstay Adjusters

The first step in controlling mast bend is to have an adequate backstay adjuster. There was a time when the difference between a racing boat and a cruiser was that a racer had an adjustable backstay. Now, as more and more cruising boats are realizing the benefits of being able to control the sag of the headstay and the shape of the mainsail, some kind of adjustable backstay is becoming standard equipment on most boats. Even owners of boats with roller-furling headsails are learning how much easier and neater it is to furl the headsail when the headstay is pulled taut with the backstay adjuster.*

For a small boat, up to 30 feet, blocks and tackle, used in either split bridle or a compound purchase, are the simplest adjuster to rig and the quickest to adjust. The bridle is often easier and less expensive to rig, especially if the boat already has a split backstay. With strong, easy-rolling blocks, the compound purchase can be effective on a boat that does not have a split backstay. Either rig can be set up with double-ended controls.

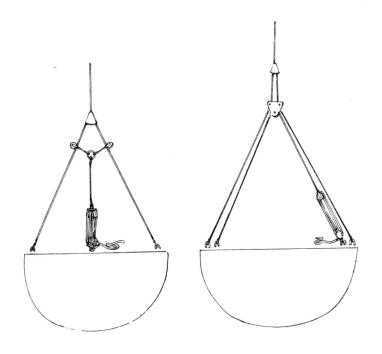

A 4:1 or 6:1 tackle is usually adequate for a bridle control. For the compound purchase, the tackle can range up to 16:1 or more on a fractional rig, and 32:1 or even 48:1 on a masthead rig. To make the control work effectively, the sheaves should be as large as possible and the wires and lines should all run clear and free. The breaking strength of the first block in a compound purchase should equal the breaking strength of the backstay wire. The loads will then divide with each stage of the tackle, but make sure that the sheaves are kept as large as possible for all wire purchases. Some kind of stopper, which

* On boats with aft-swept spreaders, such as the B&R rigs, tightening the backstay has limited effect on mast bend, and while the backstay adjuster will control the sag of the headstay, it will also slacken the upper shrouds. In many cases, a headstay adjuster (usually hydraulic) is a better choice for a boat with aft-swept spreaders.

can be nothing more than a thimble too large to clear a sheave, will keep the adjuster from "running away" if the line should be released too far.

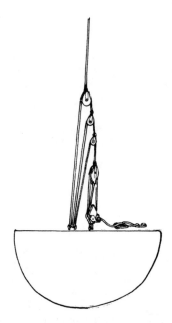

Mechanical adjusters, such as the Navtec, Ronstan or Maritox adjusters, can be used for boats from 30 to 35 feet; they are generally reliable and relatively maintenance-free, but they are slow and cumbersome to tension and to release. A bridle or compound tackle or a small hydraulic adjuster is much faster, and with the introduction of compact and relatively inexpensive self-contained hydraulic units, they are a better choice. The important thing to ascertain is whether adjustment at the backstay will be convenient. For boats with

travelers across the cockpit, or boats in which the entire crew sits ahead of the helmsman, an adjustment to the backstay would mean either someone climbing over the helmsman or the helmsman himself reaching back. In many cases it would be better to use a remote hydraulic panel, which is not difficult to install.

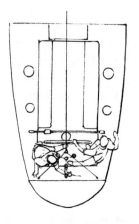 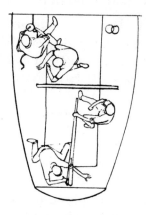

Improving the Bend

If reasonable amounts of backstay tension (up to one third the breaking strength of the backstay) do not produce the required bend, there are several simple modifications that may help. The first, if the mainsail is not too flat and the rig is keel-stepped, is to induce prebend in the mast by blocking the mast forward at the deck or by pulling the mast step aft. In some cases, a mast step can be modified or the base redrilled and retapped to move the fitting. Most boats have room for play in blocking the mast at deck level. Sometimes the blocks or rubber wedges can be swapped, or a thicker or thinner wedge

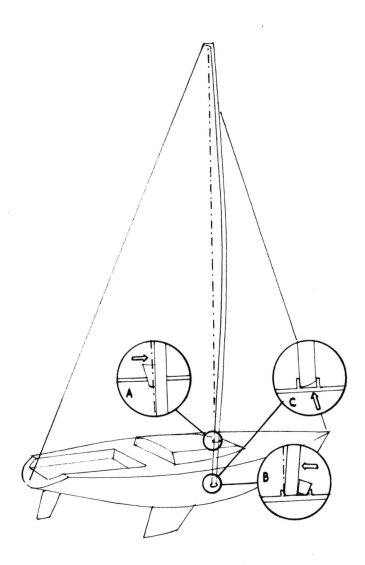

can be substituted. Boatyards often use wood wedges, which are cheap and easy to cut to size and shape. Hard rubber is a better choice if it is available. Auto-body repair shops are one source, or some sophisticated riggers may have hard rubber in ¼- to ½-inch sheets.

On a deck-stepped mast, the base of the section can be ground or cut off at an angle, so that compression from increased backstay tension will rock the section forward and produce bend. The cut should be modest, on the order of ³⁄₁₆ inch or less, and the bottom of the mast should be carefully shaped so that the loading is not on a single point.

Babystays

If the mast section is extremely stiff, the next step is to consider the addition of a babystay. Usually the forward lower shrouds can be removed if a babystay is added. (Don't worry about the mast falling down with a single babystay instead of two lower shrouds. The babystay actually provides more support. Chances are the manufacturer didn't go with a babystay in the first place because his market research told him that potential buyers would be frightened by it.) In some cases it may be necessary to beef up the remaining lowers if they are small. On a single or double spreader rig, single lowers should be at least as large as the uppers; if they aren't, consider beefing them up.

In addition to inducing mast bend in the lower sections of the mast, a babystay can steady the mast in a seaway, and it will prevent the spinnaker pole from inverting the mast on a hard reach. The advantage of the babystay is that it does not have to be adjusted on each tack or jibe (except that it may have to be released and reattached after a dip-pole spinnaker jibe), and that it provides a simple and powerful means of controlling mast bend. The disadvantage is that the farther forward the babystay is on the foredeck, the more it can interfere with the skirt of the genoa during a tack. And if the lower spreaders are swept aft, it will be difficult to affect the shape of the mainsail with a babystay pulling in opposition to those spreaders.

The placement of the attachment point for a babystay is a tricky decision: too close to the mast and the pull is too vertical, compressing the mast and lifting the deck instead of bending the mast; too far away and the babystay will have to be eased or released in order to tack the genoa. On most boats, it becomes a choice between the housetop and the deck in front of the house; and the placement of a hatch may narrow those choices. The attachment point will have to be blocked or backed up, and probably will need some connection to a bulkhead or the keel to transfer the babystay loads from the deck.

To control the babystay you can use a tackle, a track, or hydraulics. The simplest is to use a strong tackle with the tail led aft to a winch. The pad eye to which the tackle is attached should be strongly backed up, preferably with a tie-rod or cable fastened to the hull or the keel. If the forward cabin is used for cruising, the cable can be made removable with a pelican hook or a Fastpin.

The drawback of a block and tackle for the babystay is that the clew of the genoa or the genoa sheets may catch on the tackle, which generally must be fairly large to withstand the shock loads imposed by the pumping of the mast in a seaway.

A second choice is to use a track and car, with a 2:1 or 3:1 lead to a small winch, or to a magic box, to pull the car out on the track. Many traveler manufacturers produce special cars for babystay use, or an ordinary car can be adapted. The babystay should release from the track, either by having a tack snap shackle as the end fitting on the shroud or by modifying a shackle with a Fastpin.

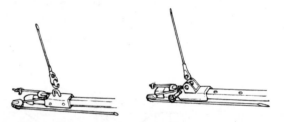

The track will spread the load on the deck, but the point of maximum load should be bolted to the pad eye or plate which in turn is fastened by a cable or tie-rod to the keel, mast step, hull, or floor timbers.

Finally, boats with hydraulic systems often use a hydraulic cylinder for the babystay. The cylinder can be above deck or

below, or a self-contained integral adjuster could be used. In general, it is a better installation to have the babystay controllable from the cockpit, so that the mainsail shape can be seen while the babystay is being adjusted. On aggressively raced boats, the babystay can be eased on tacks to power up the main. If the babystay is to be adjusted that aggressively, it is a good idea to make the lead a magic box, dedicated winch, or a winch that is not used for anything else on the wind.

Because of the vertical loads and the potential shock loads when the boat comes off a wave, every aspect of a babystay installation should be strongly designed and carefully exe-

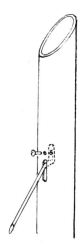

cuted. The stay should be attached to the mast with a carefully aligned tang or welded eye, and there should be sufficient toggling to allow the babystay to move forward on a track if one is used. An easy and strong attachment to the mast for smaller boats is to bend and tap a marine eye, which is then inserted through a slot and bolted. Use Loctite on the screw.

Runners

Running backstays can be the most powerful and effective device for controlling the shape and power of both the headsail and the mainsail on a sailboat. They can also break booms, get in the way of tacking, jibing, and sail handling in general, and can cause cockpit traffic jams that suggest choreography as a necessary racing skill.

Runners serve different purposes on masthead and fractionally rigged boats. On a fractional rig, runners control the sag in the headstay in much the same way that the backstay does on a masthead-rigged boat. In flat water ("pointing") conditions, the runners are tightened; in lumpy seas, when the boat needs power in the headsail, the runners are eased.

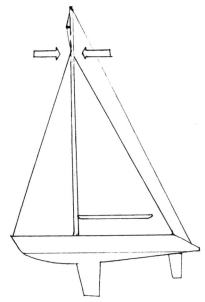

The runners on a masthead-rigged boat, and the checkstays or lower runners on a fractionally rigged boat, are used to limit mast bend and to steady a limber mast. Runners permit separate control of the shapes of the genoa and mainsail: tightening the runners will pull shape into the mainsail; easing the runners will flatten the mainsail. On the wind, easily adjusted runners can be used as a throttle to power up and depower the sail. Separate lower runners ("checkstays") enable a sail trimmer to alter the shape of the mast bend.

Runners are tricky to rig because the runner must be eased enough to clear the mainsail when the boat is sailing off the

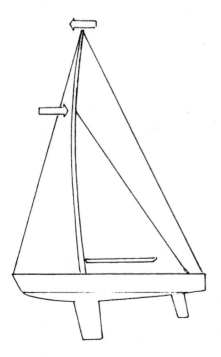

wind, yet a great deal of power is required to hold the headstay straight on a large fractional rig, or to control the bend on a big masthead rig. The trick to avoiding tangles and problems with runners is to set them up so that the slack can be quickly trimmed in, and to have a means of applying sufficient power to control the runner at the end of the trim. If the primary purpose of the runner is to steady the mast section, it may be effective to have the runners attach near or at the rail in the cockpit, limiting the amount of line that has to be eased when the boat bears away. For maximum control of the mast, and especially for sections that need the runners for support, it is more effective to have the runners as far aft and as close to the centerline as possible.

Simple 3:1 or 4:1 fiddle tackles are often used on small fractional rigs (under approximately 28 feet) or on masthead rigs of up to 36 feet. The amount of line required to ease the runner all the way off can be daunting, so some boats make the runners detachable, put the tackles on slides that can be eased forward when the boat is off the wind, or use small (3/16 inch) tails on the larger line that is used in the tackle.

A better rig for runners on small fractional rigs is to use double-ended runners, with one end for quick trim and the other end leading to a small tackle or magic box for fine-tuning. Depending on the deck layout of the boat, a single fine-tune can be used for both runners, as long as the tails are long enough.

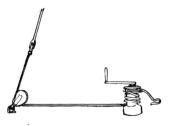

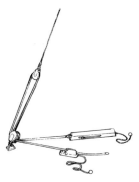

For larger boats, the runners are usually 2:1 or 3:1 tackles led to a winch. A becket block is simpler for the lower block, but if a pad eye and a separate single block are used at the deck to split the load, it is possible to use a smaller block and to distribute the loads on the deck. As an alternative, the tail of the runner can be led to a hydraulic cylinder or cylinders, giving fingertip hydraulic fine-tune control. If the runners both lead aft, a single hydraulic cylinder can be used for the fine-tune of both runners.

For a fractionally rigged boat of 30 feet, or for masthead-rigged boats of 40 feet, the simplest rig is to lead a single-part runner to an unused secondary or primary winch. Self-tailing winches are often used for this purpose. Or to save weight and cost, the runner can lead through a rope clutch to the unused primary winch. The rope tail should probably be Kevlar or at least Kevlar/Dacron or straight-filament line. Unless you have a practiced crew, using the unused primary winch for the runner may lead to confusion in tacking duels, because the windward genoa sheet cannot be "loaded up" in advance while the runner tail is on the winch. If the boat is light, and if the runner will be used for more than steadying the mast, a 4:1 tackle with an easy-to-release clam cleat will probably be a quicker rig.

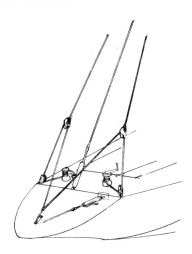

Sizing Runner Hardware The loads on a runner cannot be calculated as easily as theoretical genoa or mainsheet loads. The stiffness of the mast section, the sail-carrying ability of the boat, and the anticipated sea conditions are all significant in evaluating the potential shock loads on the runners.

For modifications to an existing runner, the size of the runner is a good starting point. Except on the smallest boats, the rig designer will probably have chosen a wire size with a breaking strength approximately three times the maximum anticipated loads. (On the smallest boats, sizing runners that way might lead to unacceptably thin wires. Even ⅛-inch wire can seem like spaghetti when it is whipping around. Hence runners are sometimes larger than they need to be.) If the runners are 3⁄16-inch 1 x 19 cable, then the safe working load for the runner blocks should be somewhere in the neighborhood of 2300 pounds. If you are adding runners to a masthead rig that was designed without runners, a good starting point is to make the safe working load of the runners at least equal to the maximum anticipated mainsheet load (MaxMain). For runners on a fractional rig that was designed without runners, a good starting point is the maximum anticipated genoa load (MaxGenoa). Runners are usually made of 1 x 19 stainless cable, fastened to the mast with Gibb T-ball terminals. The breaking strength of the wire should be three times the anticipated loads.

Checkstays and Lower Runners Checkstays or lower runners are usually fastened to the runner block through a small tackle, with the tail dangling into the cockpit. An option is to have the checkstays adjustable from within the mast by magic boxes or tackles. Lower runners are generally one or two sizes of wire smaller than the runners.

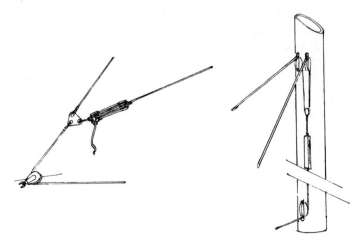

The same rig details apply to running backstays that are used on cruising boats to oppose the load of an inner forestay on a cutter rig. A little time and thought will yield a rig that is convenient enough to be used. Too often, the runners on cruising boats consist of fiddle tackles that are carefully wrapped up in their tails and permanently trimmed at the shrouds. The result is that whenever the staysail is used, the loading on the staysail halyard bends the mast forward, making the staysail too full and the mainsail too flat.

Runner Pullers One reason that runners are sometimes feared on boats is the question of what happens to the slack leeward runner: how do you keep it from slapping against the belly of the mainsail, scraping the boom, or just getting in the way of the grinders and tailers on the genoa winch and any other activity to leeward?

There are several solutions, depending upon the location of the runner. If the runner leads aft, to the corners of the tran-

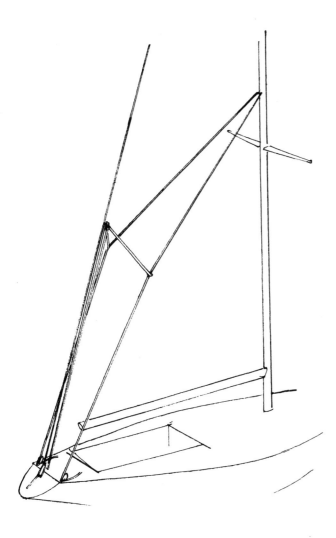

som or to the centerline of the boat, the best solution is to run a length of shock cord from the runner up to a bullet block halfway up the backstay, and then down to the other runner. As one runner is tightened forward, the shock cord will pull the other runner aft and up, keeping it clear of the main. The problem with this rig is that the runner will invariably cut into the leech of the main on a run, and in light air the runner and shock cord are actually strong enough to pull the leech of the sail in unless a preventer (rigged or human) is used. The rig can be improved somewhat if a double block is used on the backstay and the shock cord is led through the block, down to another block at the base of the backstay, then up again. The longer shock cord is more effective in pulling the runner up without exerting too great a pull.

If the runners lead to the toe rail on the quarters, the easiest rig is to run a piece of shock cord from one runner, around

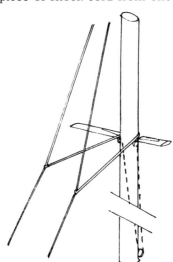

the mast near the lower spreaders, and back to the other runner. Pulling one runner tight will then pull the other runner forward. If the length of shock cord doesn't provide adequate tension, the shock cord can be run to a block on the mast, down the side of the mast, through a cheek block somewhere below the gooseneck, and up the other side.

The shock cord can be knotted around the runners, but a better attachment is to wrap two turns, then use two shock-cord clamps. If you don't have the special crimping tool, Vise-Grips will work in a pinch.

Whatever improvements you decide to add to your spars, it is important to keep them scaled to the sailing you will be doing and to the crew available for your boat. Upper and lower runners and a babystay might add the ultimate in mast bend controls, but if you frequently sail with inexperienced crew, you may look up from the helm someday to find the babystay and runners both on hard and the mast looking like the product of a pretzel shop.

12

HYDRAULICS

Not many years ago, hydraulics were thought of as the special curse of a racer. The early systems, adapted from industrial devices with little thought of the special requirements of a marine environment, were delicate and dangerous, a potential quagmire of dripping fluids, dangling hoses, and complex controls. But hydraulics have come a long way, and with improved materials and designs, modern marine hydraulic controls are simple and reliable, requiring no more upkeep than a winch or other traditional marine gear.

ADVANTAGES

For a racer, hydraulics are the fastest and most accurate means of tensioning short-throw, high-tension rigging to a repeatable setting. With gauges that read not only system pressure but actual tension, it is possible to repeat the backstay setting of 3200 pounds that was found to be fast in flat water with the heavy #1 and 12 knots of true wind speed.

Cruisers too are discovering the advantages of hydraulics. A roller-furling genoa system can enable a couple or even an individual to furl the headsail on a large boat. But the furling operation is much simpler if the headstay is straight, and the only way to straighten the headstay is either to keep the backstay tight all the time with a turnbuckle or to use a backstay adjuster. The tight headstay (within limits) won't hurt the rig, but since roller-furling headsails are normally cut flat to furl smoothly with the expectation that a sagging headstay will put shape into the sail for light air, the sail will be too flat in light air if the backstay is kept straight. The answer is hydraulics, which can be simple to install, simple and quick to operate, and reliable.

LOCATION

Another advantage of hydraulics is that it permits the control of large forces from a convenient position on the boat. Backstay tensions of 4000 or even 10,000 pounds are easily controlled from the cockpit, and by placing the hydraulics controls carefully, a sail trimmer can be watching the effect of a control as he uses it. Unfortunately, on many boats this potential advantage is lost because the hydraulics panel is tucked away in a "convenient" unused location, with the result that the trimming has to be done "by the numbers." Instead of being able to watch the sail, the trimmer has to ask, "How much backstay do we want?" or "Enough?"

Another problem with many hydraulics installations is complex or multi-function panels which in panic situations can lead to disasters. When a switch valve and a single pump control the vang, backstay, flattener, and babystay, it is only a matter of time before someone reaches for the handle to pump up the backstay and finds that instead the vang has been pumped down so hard that the leech of the main is torn or permanently stretched. Multi-function panels should be placed where they can be seen easily; they should have big labels, color-coded or even coded in some equivalent of braille; separate gauges for each function can help keep things sorted. If there is no convenient storage for the hydraulic pump handle—such as room in a convenient winch handle holder, or perhaps a special holder for the handle—it will quickly find its way to the cockpit sole or a seat top, where it will either be stepped on, get wrapped in a line, or slide overboard.

Complex hydraulic installations—such as push-pull cylin-

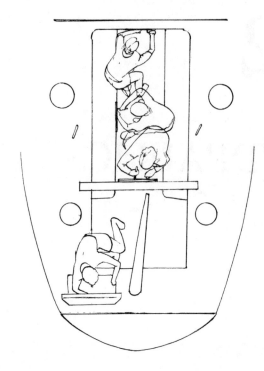

ders for centerboards, two-speed pumps, four-way valves to simultaneously pump and release vang and flattener cylinders or runner cylinders, and multiple-control panels or quick-release buttons—can all speed up sail trim and control on a grand prix racing boat. The trade-off is the risk of breakdown of a complex system and the increased maintenance required. A complex system is a job for a rigger, or even for the manufacturer of the hydraulic components. But there is no reason why a boat owner cannot install a simple hydraulic system

himself. There is nothing required that cannot be done with a saber saw, a drill, and patience.

INSTALLATION

Before you contemplate a hydraulics installation—whether you are doing it yourself or having a boatyard or rigger install the gear—ask who will control the hydraulics and how often. If it is a backstay for a cruiser and adjustment is a sometime thing, consider an integral adjuster: there is no plumbing required and the installation is simple. For a club racer with a wheel, or even with a tiller and a cockpit and weight distribution that allows a man to be behind the helmsman, the integral may also be effective.

On a weight-conscious racer or a boat that will be aggressively sailed, meaning that the backstay will be adjusted frequently in response to changing sea and wind conditions, the adjustment should be convenient to the genoa trimmer. Especially with Mylar and Kevlar headsails, the halyard tension is less effective in controlling the draft of the sail, and the backstay becomes more important as a sail shape control. The control panel for a hydraulic vang should be convenient to whoever is in charge of the panic button for reaching. When a boat begins to broach under spinnaker, it takes too long to ease the mainsheet; easing the vang, which dumps the top of the mainsail, will get the boat under control more quickly. As an alternative, a special quick-release button can be included in the hydraulic plumbing for the vang.

The panel should be securely bolted in place, with storage for the handle nearby. The valves on many of the systems are unfortunately small and difficult to read. Sometimes redline tapes can help to control an overenthusiastic pumper.

The connections between the pump and control panel and the cylinders can be either stainless tubing or Kevlar-reinforced hose. The tubing is more compact and can be run inside hull and deck sections, but it requires a tubing bending tool and either a flaring tool or expensive flareless fittings. Hose is easier to install and offers flexibility for changing the installation. Stainless swage fittings for hose are expensive; to save money, cadmium-plated fittings can be used below deck and plastic glands, available inexpensively from electrical suppliers, can be used instead of the expensive through-deck connections offered by the hydraulics manufacturers. If the local rigger is either unfamiliar with hydraulics or overpriced, the swage fittings and hoses can be made up by a hydraulics supplier. Just make sure they understand that when you specify stainless steel for an external fitting, you mean it. Be sure to leave plenty of slack in the hoses to make large-radius turns. The hoses should all be fastened down with plastic holddowns, and the reservoir should be installed where it can be reached for filling and checking the oil level.

Measurements

The most important measurement is the length of the cylinders and/or the rigging attached to the cylinder. Plan carefully, measure, measure again, then go away, come back later, and measure a third time. If all three are right, go over the whole plan, make sure you have thought of everything, and measure a last time. Then order the rigging or cut off your rigging or make what changes you need. The most common disasters are vang cylinders that are too long, so that trimming the main too hard bends the vang, and backstay cylinders that are too short and need multiple toggles.

Precautions

Every hydraulic cylinder should be toggled to avoid any bending action on the shaft. In a backstay this will mean either a toggle at the base or a toggled fitting to attach to the backstay itself. In a headstay cylinder (used instead of a backstay cylinder on rigs with swept shrouds, like the B&R rigs), the cylinder should be toggled top and bottom because of the side loads of the headstay. A vang cylinder should pivot vertically on the boom, and both vertically and laterally at the base of the mast. The vang gooseneck should be directly under the boom gooseneck.

When installing the system, cleanliness is essential. A single speck of dirt can clog a valve, destroy a seal and/or score a cylinder wall. New hoses and the fittings on cylinders and pumps should be covered with tape at both ends until they are installed, and the entire work area should be swept clean before the tapes come off.

The connections are straightforward: low-pressure hose to and from the reservoir, and the Kevlar-reinforced hose or stainless tubing to and from the cylinders.

The hoses are tough, but loops of hose should not be exposed in locations where they get tripped over or stepped on. Check with the manufacturer first about the oil to use. For most systems, hydraulic jack fluid works fine.

Budget Hydraulics

On a budget? You can put together your own hydraulics system cheaply. Buy a good marine cylinder, or even shop the marine flea markets or ask riggers about used cylinders. Then get an Enerpac pump and gauge from a hydraulics supplier. It isn't marinized, and you should spend some time carefully painting it. But it will work as well and as fast as the beautiful panel, and for some boats it can be put in a lazarette for a compact and trouble-free installation.

MAINTENANCE

The maintenance for hydraulics is not difficult. Wiping the shafts of cylinders clean and making sure that no dirt gets into the system is the most important single step. If dirt does get into the system, rapid wear of the hydraulic pumps and valves will ensue, and you may experience a temporary failure, usually a cylinder that fails to respond to pumping. For a temporary cure, try opening the valve wide and pumping, which may move the offending particle. Then at the earliest possible opportunity have the pump and/or cylinder serviced. The other potential problem is a leaky seal at a cylinder. The seals are not expensive to replace, but it should be attended to quickly.

As a last caution, watch out for hydraulic hoses and connections during winter storage. If you have hydraulic cylinders mounted inside your boom, or a hydraulic vang, make sure that they are carefully disconnected and the hoses sealed properly when the boom is removed. And make certain that cylinders on deck are carefully stored for the winter. There is no danger in leaving a hydraulic cylinder on the boat during winter storage, as long as no special bending moments are put on the hoses, the plumbing connections, or the cylinder itself.

13

BELOWDECKS

When a tourist on the dock asks, "Mind if I come aboard for a look around?" it is rarely to study the deck layout. The attraction is belowdecks, where the berths are counted, the joinery is admired, and the facilities in the galley and head are totaled up like so many features on a house tour. Even for boat owners who rarely, if ever, spend a night aboard and whose use of the galley is limited to storage of sandwiches, the facilities belowdecks are important —as symbols of luxury, fine craftsmanship, clever design, or the unmistakable status of "yacht owner" they convey. No matter how unmanageable life can sometimes seem, the cabin of a boat is small enough that order and even perfection are achievable in the lovingly fitted dovetails, carefully aligned bungs, laminated moldings, and the glowing finish of seven hand-rubbed coats of varnish.

At a dock, and especially at a boat show, you rarely see the interior of a boat in sailing trim. The most obvious omission is the sails, which on many boats fill most of the berths or the entire forepeak. The storage space—in lockers, under settees, in the galley shelves, over the navigation station—seems vast at the show, where the only thing stored is a stack of brochures on a shelf. The head seems bright and private, the berths roomy, the vents more than adequate. Indeed, the interiors of most boats are adequately equipped, even superbly equipped—for boat shows or dockside duty.

It's in use, on a weekend cruise or an overnight race, that the inadequacies begin to show up. The lockers that seemed so spacious are suddenly tiny, wet, and inconvenient. The shelves that looked perfect for spices turn out to have fiddles so low that the bottles tumble off as soon as the boat heels 20 degrees. The head that seemed so private begins to seem claustrophobic. And the eight berths that seemed to define the craft as "big" now take up the space that is needed for sails, gear, and people.

It's only in use that the buzzwords of the boat shows and the fantasy sailing magazines begin to sound hollow. The cozy interior of the double-ended deep-bilged passage-maker feels claustrophobic on a hot, still day; the deep bilges that were supposed to hold months of tinned goods offer little usable storage space for the weekend trip out to Catalina. The gimbaled stove swings when someone accidentally leans on it at the anchorage, spilling the pot of soup that has been sitting there for two hours trying to come to a boil on the pitiful heat of an alcohol burner. And the vents that were supposed to provide cross-ventilation provide only leaks—spray and occasional seas when they're open, the steady drip of rain when they're closed.

The irony of interiors is that they seem so often to be marvelously mismatched to the actual use of the boat. The cruising boat that cruises mostly across the sound, which needs a few quick hot meals in an anchorage and storage for a weekend for two or four people, has a full galley with three burners, an oven, an ice chest big enough to hide a stowaway, storage space for tinned goods for six months at sea, and fuel and water tanks sufficient for a passage around Cape Horn. Yet amidst all the furniture and facilities, there is a desperate lack of room: room for sails, room to stretch, to read a book, to get away from other cruising companions, to enjoy a moment of real privacy.

At the next dock, a sleek racer which carries a crew of ten or twelve, sometimes in races that extend for three or more days, has as its total cooking facilities two swinging burners, which if pressed can provide instant coffee in two shifts of heating water. The rest of the menu for a 300-mile race is sandwiches—breakfast sandwiches, lunch sandwiches, dinner sandwiches, and by the third day out, desperation sandwiches. The special treat of lukewarm Kentucky Fried Chicken the first night out is the last hot meal the crew will see.

The head of the racer consists of the stern rail, since the required Porta-Potti is taped shut. The owner trusts that the usual ocean-racing plague of severe constipation will strike the entire crew and last the duration of the race, lest they end up in what the crew members would call "deep ____." Crew storage consists of an area where duffle bags are piled. There are plenty of berths, but never enough on the high side, so the sole of the cabin is a wet tangle of sails, sail bags, blankets, and bodies. By the second day out, dry clothes and hot food must join sex as a forbidden topic of conversation, in the interest of preserving crew morale.

Walking from one boat to another, or sailing on one and then the other, it is hard not to wonder if some kind of swap wouldn't make sense.

BERTHS

At a boat show, there is one question you hear more often than any other. It's the same question you will hear from friends who don't know boats, the question that seems, for some reason, to be the ultimate classifier of boats: "How many does she sleep?" When you reply "six" or "eight" or whatever, your friends are impressed, imagining staterooms with attached private baths, or at least elegantly appointed berths like the belowdecks shots in movies, and having no idea that some if not all of the berths included in your count (1) are suitable only for individuals with tiny or peculiar body dimensions, (2) can be used only in a calm anchorage, unless the sleeper is willing to wear a hard hat, (3) require preparations comparable to opening the locks in the shuttle for a spacewalk, (4) have somewhat less privacy than a phone booth in Grand Central Terminal, and (5) have substantially less ventilation than the Grand Central Terminal phone booth.

There are two kinds of berths that you can have on a boat: sea berths and port berths. If you do your sleeping in an anchorage or at a dock, you want a wide, comfortable berth, preferably one that is easy to get into and out of—a seaborne adaptation of your bed at home—with room to roll over, stretch out, or whatever else suits your fancy. For sleeping during a race or an offshore passage, that same wide, comfortable berth is an invitation to black-and-blue marks over much of your body. As the boat heels you will roll back and forth, slamming into the sides of the hull or bulkheads, or you will simply roll out of the berth and onto the cabin sole. And berths that might have pleasant privacy in port, such as a berth in the bow or a quarter berth, will have the most violent motion at sea. Once again the problem for a boat owner is to answer, honestly, how the boat is to be used: how many will actually sleep aboard, and under what conditions?

If your primary need for berths is room for you and your family, and perhaps an occasional guest, on overnight cruises, then you want port berths, with maximum comfort and privacy. If your main use is distance racing, you will need usable sea berths, enough to sleep an entire watch, preferably with all of them on the windward side. Most racer-cruisers will elect a compromise between the extremes, with some berths

that are usable for racing or passage-making and others that are usable only in port.

Most production boats come through with a V-berth forward, one or more settee berths and/or a convertible dinette in the main cabin, and one or more quarter berths. At the boat show, the boat is said to sleep seven, which is true if you can find two short people or people who don't mind sharing athletes' feet in the V-berth, and if the rest of the quota don't mind confined and poorly ventilated quarter berths or the setup ritual of the convertible dinette berth. If you put two children in a V-berth, it is only a matter of time before they are fighting about who kicked whom first. Adults might not fight, but few of us have learned to sleep in the point positions that are used for ballet training. And with a V-berth, the entire forepeak, which would be a useful storage area for sails, inflatable dinghies, or Windsurfers, is instead given over to under-berth storage space that is inconvenient, oddly shaped, and so difficult to reach that the usual effort ends up with a bunk board falling onto your neck. The quarter berths are used as sail stowage, and the dinette ritual becomes a nightly necessity. For the occasional passage or overnight race, or just a lazy afternoon when someone wants to catch some sleep while others sail the boat, the average production boat has few, if any, berths that are suitable at sea.

Sea Berths

The berths that work at sea are pipe berths, root berths, and pilot berths. All are narrow enough to keep a person from crashing into bulkheads or hull sides when the boat rolls; they provide either built-in retainers so a person will not bounce or fall out of the berth onto the cabin sole, or are adjustable to the angle of heel of the boat; and if they are situated close enough to the middle of the boat, they will have a motion gentle enough to allow restful sleep, soothed by the sounds of water flowing by the hull instead of jolted by the crash of oncoming seas or the whine of winches turning on deck. Concentrating the weight of sleeping bodies in the middle of the boat is also better for the performance of the boat. A boat with broad stern sections can tolerate the weight of sleepers in quarter berths, but the bow of any boat is not only uncomfortable or impossible for sleep at sea but also noticeably harmful to the sailing performance of the boat.

Pipe Berths One easy way to gain storage space and comfortable berths is to replace the V-berths forward with folding pipe berths. Pipe berths are lightweight, comfortable, take up little room when they are not being used, and leave the entire area open for storage of sails and other bulky items. Children adore both the privacy of the berths and the idea that they can raise and lower their own berths.

Unless there is major plumbing to be moved, changing a V-berth into pipe berths is not as complicated as it might seem. If you elect to remove built-in berths, make certain that you do not remove a bulkhead or longitudinal supports which are being used to stiffen the hull. In most boats the bulkhead and/or stringers will be glassed in with a plywood platform screwed to the top. It is probably wisest and simplest to leave the stringers and/or bulkhead in place, unless you plan to replace them with an equally stiff reinforcement. And remember that while pipe berths are lightweight, the weight of a sleeping person requires strong, through-bolted pad eyes for the tackles that

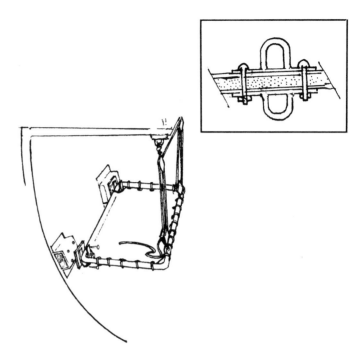

hold up the berth and for the supports on the sides. A pad eye that is to be installed on the overhead should be bolted from above. Sometimes a foredeck fitting, such as a fairlead for the foreguy, will be in the ideal position, and then the fastenings for the fairlead can also be used for a pad eye to support the pipe berth.

Root Berths Pipe berths can be added above settees or above spacious quarter berths, but a better installation for an occasional berth in the main cabin or above a quarter berth is some variation of the root berth, which can be folded away to take up almost no space, and which is surprisingly comfortable for sleep in port or at sea.

Aluminum tubing or stainless pipe can be used for the side of the berth, and the inside edge can either be fastened to a cleat along the inside of the hull or can be another tube or pipe fitted into brackets. A thin mattress (2 inches of foam in a comfortable cover) adds to the comfort of a root berth. It might be possible to adapt cockpit cushions to do double duty in the berths.

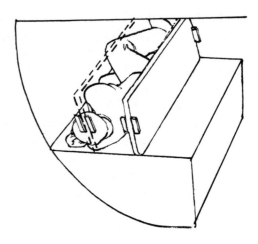

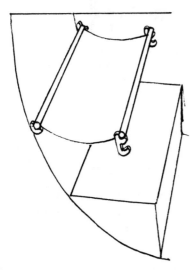

Pilot Berths A pilot berth tucked up above a settee is the classic sea berth. You can achieve almost the same coziness on a boat with wide settees by adapting the backs for two positions, like the J-35 berths. The area behind the movable back is a snug sea berth, and the edge can still be used by crew members for eating, resting, or changing clothes.

Finally, with minor modifications settee berths can be used as sea berths. They will lack privacy, and a sleeping person on the settee is effectively in the middle of the cabin where sails are stored for racing and where anyone moving through the boat drips from wet foul-weather gear or dirty dishes, but with lee cloths the settee can be made into a secure and comfortable berth.

Lee Cloths Lee cloths are easy to add to a boat, and are essential in a sea berth unless it is an adjustable pipe berth, a semi-enclosed pilot berth, or a root berth. The easiest way to make them is to secure a number of ties on the overhead, but an extendable tube or pipe, or a heavy line with a small snugging tackle, leaves better access to the berth and a more open feeling in the cabin.

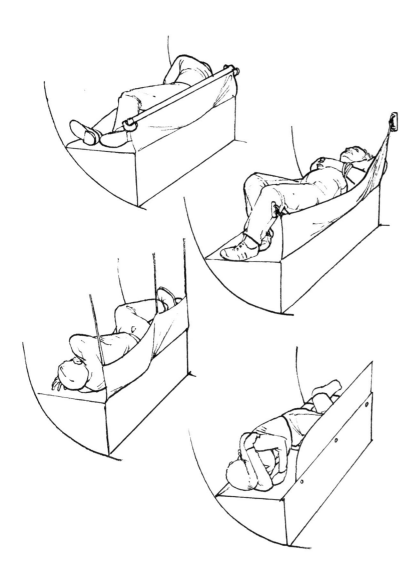

AIR AND LIGHT

Think of a yacht interior and you probably imagine hand-rubbed varnished joinery, shiny brass or bronze fittings, a teak and holly cabin sole. Wood has become so much a convention belowdecks that even lightweight trailable boats are displayed at the boat shows with signs proclaiming their "full teak" or "teak trimmed" interiors. But the key to a livable, comfortable, and practical interior isn't joinery; it's light, air, and space. The finest joinery in the world looks gloomy in the dim interior of a flush-deck boat. The coziness of a snug cabin on a rainy night turns to claustrophobia when you first sniff the musty odor of mildew or the faint leafmold odor of dry rot. And when two stir-crazy children begin crawling the cabin sides after a day inside in the rain, or a racing crew of seven or eight sleeps on piles of sail bags because there aren't enough sea berths, or you bang yourself black and blue on the edges of that joinery while trying to navigate or cook as the boat sails to windward in a seaway, the drawers and cabinets and lockers that fill up that cabin are suddenly less charming and appealing than they once were.

It's almost impossible to have too much air or light in the interior of a sailboat. The trick is to balance the placement and use of hatches, ports, prisms, and the companionway with the needs of a deck layout and sailing plans. Vents and hatches that are terrific at a mooring or anchorage can be unusable at sea. A hatch over the center of the cabin can be great for light and air during meals, but if it interferes with the use of the vang, it cannot be used as the source of ventilation during overnight races. Prisms can admit marvelous soft rainbows into the interior of a flush-deck boat; but if the

prism is carelessly situated, the crew will need hard hats belowdecks. Opening ports are great for ventilation at anchor,
permitting cooling breezes to blow through the boat, but
while sailing, even in a moderate sea, an open port will invariably take a wave. Ultimately, every form of vent presents the
expected trade-off: if it readily admits air, it will also let in rain
or the occasional sea; if it is baffled against water, it admits
much less air.

Ventilation

How much ventilation do you need? Some of the naval
architects use formulas, such as one 5-inch vent per sleeper,
but for all but grand cruising boats that number—or the classic diagram with dorades over the main cabin, an exhaust vent
over the head, an electric exhaust vent for the galley, engine-
room clamshells, vents for each berth, a cowl vent for the
forepeak—is hard to achieve. But it should be possible to use
a combination of vents, hatches, and ports to achieve enough
ventilation to control mildew and musty smells at dockside or
a mooring and to mitigate the locker-room smell that can take
over a racing boat on the second night out.

The most effective vents for a mooring or anchorage face
forward; cocked open, a hatch can function as a wind scoop.
Hatches that face aft are safer for offshore sailing, because a
rogue wave will close rather than open a partially open hatch.
A good combination is to have a main hatch that faces forward
and smaller hatches over the head, galley, or main cabin that
face aft and that can be left partially open when sailing. A
lazarette hatch can be left open to ventilate quarter berths if
holes are cut through from the end of the quarter berths to
the lazarette.

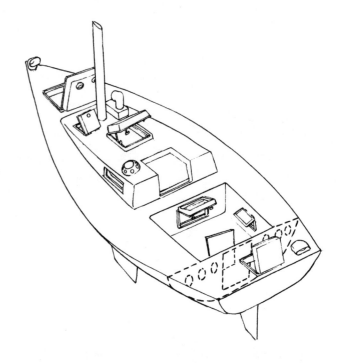

You can improve any berth with decent ventilation. A quarter berth without a vent port feels like a coffin, but it is easy
to install ports into the cockpit. Clamshell vents in the lazarette with vent holes cut high up into the quarter berths will
also help, and will provide a good air passage for ventilation at
a mooring or dock. Whatever kind of vents are used, they
should not be installed directly over a berth; any vent that
allows a decent airflow will leak at times, and there is nothing
worse than waking up to a drip on your face.

Vents are available in every size and configuration, and most are easy to install. Basically, they fall into two types: cowl vents (including clamshell vents) and exhaust vents (such as mushrooms or domes). The cowl vents are far more effective at admitting air to the boat; either a reversed cowl or an exhaust vent can be used to circulate the air back out. Whatever kind of vent you are considering, remember that the effectiveness of a vent increases by the square of the radius of the effective area; in other words, a 4-inch-diameter cowl vent admits four times as much air as a 2-inch vent. A single 5-inch vent has an effective area close to that of three 3-inch vents.

The engine compartment and bilge of any boat need vents, for safety on a gas-powered boat and for efficiency and livability on a diesel-powered boat. The Coast Guard requirements for ventilation plus an adequate blower are the minimum for a gas-powered boat. The vents should not be removed or blocked, above decks or below. It is legal, but unwise, to remove the vents on a gas-powered boat for racing. There are situations, such as a man overboard, when the engine will have to be started, and it is unlikely in the panic of an emergency that someone will suggest that the vents be replaced and the engine compartment blower turned on. The rough weather that precipitated the man overboard is exactly the condition that will stir a tiny fuel leak into the magic cupful of vapors that destroys boats.

Although there is no Coast Guard requirement for ventilation for diesel-powered boats, diesel engines have an incredible appetite for clean air and will run sluggishly or unevenly if they are not given enough. And even the most careful diesel installation usually results in some tiny drips of diesel fuel into the engine pan or the bilge from time to time. Belowdecks will be far more pleasant if the smell of the fuel and lubricating oil is shared with the world instead of being reserved for your crew.

Bilge and engine-room vents can also contribute to the general ventilation of a boat. If there are openings or ventilation ports forward in the bilge, the airflow will go a long way toward removing the mystery smells—usually caused by some unduplicatable combination of mildew, bilge crud, oil, and part of a sandwich—that trouble many boats.

If the galley is near the companionway and most cooking is done in mild weather, a galley vent may not be necessary. The usual problem in a galley is heat from the stove or a lack of fresh air, and for most coastal cruising and racing boats, a combination of general ventilation of the main cabin—from open hatches in port or vents at sea—and an open companionway will suffice. For larger boats, boats cooking with diesel stoves, boats with galleys not adjacent to the companionway, or boats on which extensive cooking will be done in heavy weather, galley vents are necessary and should probably be powered exhaust vents like the Aeolus vent imported by J. Stuart Haft.

The head, even if it is nothing more than a Porta-Potti in the forepeak, needs ventilation if it is to remain usable. For coastal cruising, a small hatch over the head is a superb source of light and air, and in calm weather it can usually be left open while sailing if it is positioned so that it will not catch lines. For racing or offshore cruising, where a hatch is likely to be dogged most of the time, an exhaust vent is a better choice. A carefully sited mushroom or dome vent will present a minimum deck obstacle, will entangle few lines, and can be left open in all but the most severe weather. It will also ensure that a modicum of ventilation is available even when the boat is bolted up tight in heavy weather.

Dream about extra vents and hatches during the winter, if you want, but try to delay the installation until the boat is fully rigged, with foreguys, jib sheets, halyard tails, boom vang, and the other control lines in place. You may discover that what looked like a vast expanse of open deck suddenly seems less promising when it is crossed with lines. A hatch placed in the inviting spot over the center of the main cabin will frequently interfere with a vang. Raising the vang attachment point on the mast in order to clear the hatch is possible but usually will put undue loads on the gooseneck and the boom; it may be better to situate the hatch to one side or the other, or to move it aft and have it face aft. Hatches or cowl/dorade vents over the head often catch on jib sheets during a tack. Forepeak vents will interfere with sails and will admit a lot of water in any but calm conditions. They should be removable. Large foredeck hatches can interfere with the foreguy, and if placed too high off the deck can snag jib sheets and sails on deck. It is often possible to move leads to clear a place where you want a hatch or vent, but remember that every fairlead and block adds friction and the chance for a hockle and a snag.

Installing Vents and Hatches

It is not complicated to install a vent or hatch. Cover flanges at the deck and a corresponding cover ring for the headliner mean that the hole you cut with your saber saw—if you are not lucky enough to have access to a large hole saw—need not be perfect. Aesthetically, the flanges and cover rings make the job look neat, but the more important concern is integrity. If you cut the initial hole small and patiently file or hand-saw

the edge to fit—somehow resisting the temptation to make the quick cut that inevitably comes out too big—you will be thankful later when you enjoy years without leaks. Even with a careful cutout, the edge of exposed deck must be sealed. Brushing the exposed core material with two or three coats of epoxy is sufficient if you are careful to make certain that there are no "holidays" in the coating. Never try to make a hatch fit by bending the frame. If the deck in the area of the hatch is not flat, either choose a hatch that matches the deck camber (Bomar makes two different cambered hatches and will send a template to check the fit beforehand) or build up a frame for the hatch. Trying to draw the hatch down to the deck with bolts, or trying to fill the gaps with a sealant, will invariably result in leaks.

Dorade boxes are popular on cruising boats, and while they are a real shin-bruiser on deck, a good dorade will admit air and exclude water. For inshore cruising, or for boats that alternately race and cruise, a better choice might be removable vents with or without spray guards (which cut down on the airflow) or proprietary water traps.

Dorade boxes can be purchased or built out of teak or mahogany; the books on accessories to build for a yacht have good drawings and specifications. A Lexan top will admit light, and the larger the box, the more air it will admit. Some of the compact boxes may not leak, but they also admit so little air that they are nearly useless. And if they are carelessly installed, without proper drain holes or with the drain holes angled improperly, they will either leak or rot. If you are buying or building a dorade box, try measuring the area of the air passages that wind up and through the box. If there is any point where the passage has less area than the opening of the cowl vent on top, it is an inefficient dorade.

The same measurements are appropriate for the proprietary vents that supposedly baffle out water but admit air. Check the size of the passages for air before you buy a vent. In some cases, a 4-inch vent will have the efficiency of a 2-inch vent.

Opening Ports Opening ports come in every price range, from the very expensive bronze or aluminum ports to very inexpensive plastic ones. For protected ports, like those installed in quarter berths, the plastic are often sufficient, especially when they are installed on a flat surface. For exposed ports on the house, and especially for any port installed on a surface that is even slightly cambered, the plastic ports usually end up leaking because the frames bend easily to fit the camber of the house and then the port never closes properly, even when dogged tight. The larger the port, the more likely the problem. Temporary solutions, such as more gasketing material, rarely work. The only real solution is to remove the port and remount it with shims and proper bedding so that the frame is not bent.

LIGHT

Hatches and some kinds of vents admit light. It is also possible to modify a companionway, substituting a Lexan panel for the slider or for the boards. Be sure to use Lexan or a substitute polycarbonate, not acrylic or Plexiglas for a companionway. The acrylic, even in thicknesses as heavy as ⅜ inch, can crack under the weight of a man; Lexan is close to bulletproof. It takes patience, but Lexan can be bent into a curve, either with heat from a heat gun or a high-powered hair dryer, or under slow, steady tension. It should be held in place with wood or aluminum forms and carefully through-

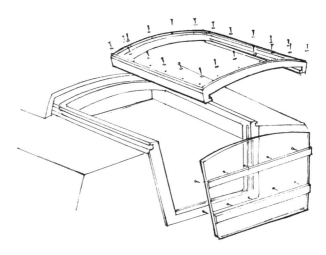

bolted. The supplier can usually cut it to shape for you or will sell you special saber-saw blades and drill bits that help to avoid splitting the plastic sheets. Any straight span broad enough to bend under moderate load should be stiffened with wood stringers, which can be through-bolted on both sides and bunged, or fastened from one side with large washers. With plastics always use round- or pan-head screws, or oval-head screws with finishing washers; countersunk screwheads will eventually crack the plastic. And remember that the smoked plastic which seems so private in the daytime will turn your boat into a glass house when interior lights are on at night. The way to admit light and still maintain privacy is with fiberglass laminations without gelcoat, which are used by some builders for hatch covers, or by using a textured Lexan.

Prisms are easy to install, requiring no more than a careful cutout, bedding, and screws. They admit a lovely diffuse light, with rainbows that will play across the inside of the cabin in direct sunlight. The elegant Simpson Lawrence bronze and glass prisms are appropriate for a traditional cruising boat; the lighter aluminum and plastic Bomar prisms might be more appropriate for a racing boat. The trick in placing a prism is to put it in a location where it will not result in permanent creasing of heads. Warnings or red tape won't work, and a guard will cut down on headroom and the light admitted. Over a centerline table, or next to a deck beam or carlin, is a good location. Too much interior trim around the prism cuts down on the light admitted, so the simpler the better: a thin wood molding or even nothing at all for interior trim.

THE CHART TABLE

Whether the primary navigation tools are a full complement of electronics, a chronometer and sextant, or a protractor and a pair of dividers, a boat needs a place where charts can be studied, plotted, and stored.

If nothing better is available, under a berth cushion is a fine storage area for charts. And a chart table—which if at all possible should not double as a dining table—need be nothing more than a space on a counter, with good light and a place to store a protractor or parallel rules, dividers, and a pencil.

Boats larger than 30 feet will usually have a permanently installed chart table or navigation station, often with storage, shelves, drawers, installation panels or compartments for electronics, and a seat for a navigator. For boats smaller than 35 feet, where a full-time navigator is unlikely for racing or cruising, a full nav station with a seat may be less convenient than a standing station, because it is easier to glance at a chart or plot a quick course at a standing station and because most sitting stations run athwartships; when the boat is heeling the navigator may have to struggle to keep him- or herself in the seat and over the chart unless a special harness or belt is available.

The navigation stations which use the front edge of the quarter berth as a seat look like a clever double use of space, but if the berth is being used at sea, it is tricky to use the chart table without sitting on the sleeper's head. And when sails are stored in the quarter berth, as they often are, dragging a genoa or spinnaker out usually manages to thoroughly disrupt the chart table.

If possible, the chart table should have easy communication to the helm. In a smaller boat, the skipper may often be darting down for a glance at a chart; in a larger boat, the helmsman will have questions for the navigator and will look forward to frequent updates on position, tides, weather, and other information. In many boats the chart table is next to the companionway, which is ideal for communication in mild weather. In heavy weather, some juggling of hatches or companionway boards may be necessary, or a heavy plastic curtain can be used to keep down the spray. On boats that have the chart table under the cockpit or behind the companionway, a small hatch or opening port lets the navigator communicate easily and directly with the helmsman.

Whatever the configuration of the chart table, there should be a provision for pencils, dividers, and a choice of plotting tools ready to hand. For a few dollars it is possible to make or buy a rack for pencils and dividers. A length of shock cord on two tiny pad eyes or a secure shelf space for the protractor or parallel rules will make it possible to do plots or checks of a chart without the annoying rigamarole of digging up the appropriate instruments. If the fiddles on the chart table don't keep the charts there, another easy addition is a roll of masking or drafting tape to tack down the corners of the charts. The fancy chart weights in the shape of a whale are fine as paperweights on a desk, but they would be likely to slide off and stub a toe or bang a knee on a boat.

The chart table should have a secure shelf or cupboard for miscellaneous instruments and books: tide tables, light lists, a hand-bearing compass, binoculars if they are not kept in a rack near the companionway, stopwatches for timing lights and race starts, erasers, spare leads for the mechanical pencils or a sharpener for regular pencils, a guide to code flags if you haven't memorized them. A deep fiddle on a shelf will work, but for neatness and security, sliding doors that convert a shelf to a cupboard are even better. Three-sixteenths- or ¼-inch acrylic doors sliding in upper and lower wood channels will do the trick.

For night sailing, and especially night racing, the navigation station needs lights that make it easy to read a chart but do not interfere with the vision of those on deck. Red bulbs are traditional, but the dim light makes it difficult to see. The newer halogen-bulb lights that are made for use in cars and boats, and which include dimmers, may be a better choice; they provide a bright, well-focused light. If you have room, try installing both a wide-range light to illuminate the entire navigation station and another gooseneck light that can be swung down over a chart or tide table.

One feature that should be incorporated into every navigation station is a small bulletin board, which can be anything from a section of bulkhead used for 3M sticky-back notes to a small corkboard and pushpins. It is a place to post the race instructions, course, and the times of tide change for a day

race; to put up a loran "idiot sheet" so that inexperienced crew can quickly get a bearing to the next mark for the helmsman; to post a list of marine operators and their channels; or to display the menu and the watch schedule on a distance race. It is also an obvious place for notes about needed upkeep and repairs, which have a way of getting forgotten in the usual post-race or post-cruise hubbub.

Another useful feature on nav stations that are close to the companionway is a spray shield, which can be anything from a section of Plexiglas to a roll-down canvas and plastic curtain. In heavy weather it is easy for spray or the drip from wet foul-weather gear to make a real mess out of a nav station, and for night racing the curtain can also permit brighter light on the nav station without disturbing the crew on watch.

Finally, the instruments—from a compass or chronometer to loran, sat nav, or radar—should be mounted for maximum visibility and utility for the way the boat is normally sailed. If you usually sail distance races with a full-time navigator, it is fine to install the instruments so they can only be read by a person sitting at the navigation station. If, instead, most of your navigation is a quick glance at the instruments and the chart by someone coming off the deck, the placement of the instruments should not require a person to sit down just to check on a pair of TD lines off the loran. Matched instruments installed in a panel are attractive, but too often the effort at symmetry means that the most needed instruments are the least visible, that buttons and controls are awkward to use, and that service for the electronics—whether checking the tightness of a connection or removing an instrument for a trip to the shop—means dismantling half of the navigation station. The LCD displays on some instruments can be read only at a limited range of angles, and installing them for appearance or symmetry may mean that in bright daylight a person will not be able to read the loran or the depth sounder without a cock of the head.

Elaborate navigation stations are invitingly high tech, but on boats that are not used for long-distance racing or passage-making, the navigation station may see less use for its dedi- cated purpose and far more use as an adjunct to the galley, as a storage space for reading material, or as an "office." Keeping the actual use in mind as you plan and equip a navigation station may have it looking less like Mission Control in Houston, but it will probably save you money and give you useful space in the interior of the boat.

14

GALLEYS

Whether a mug of coffee on deck on a cold wet night, a lavish meal served on a tablecloth with wine glasses, or a breakfast after a storm that revives a crew and makes the rest of the passage possible, food is an important part of sailing. And like every other aspect of buying and equipping a sailboat, the galley poses choices. A boat that is used for weekend cruising or gunkholing has galley needs very different from those of a racer or an offshore passage-maker.

Usually the racer has a minimal galley—a corner of the cabin with a lightweight stove or swinging burner, an ice chest or perhaps only a portable cooler, and enough storage to stash a few paper plates and mugs for the instant coffee that will be sloshed up in the middle of the night. The cruiser in the slip next door is equipped with a gimbaled range with three or four burners, large cabinets that can hold full sets of dishes, condiments, dry foods, liquor, and enough pots and pans to keep the burners busy. Both galleys are usually selling points for the boats: the racer's minimal galley is praised for its light weight and the cruiser's galley is praised for its completeness, "just like home."

In fact, the priorities are almost exactly reversed. The cruiser galley that is used for weekends has to feed two, four, or perhaps six people; there is little rush or press of conditions while the galley is being used; and provisions can usually be bought fresh at almost every overnight stop. The galley of the coastal cruiser is rarely, if ever, used for cooking at sea, and because the interior of the boat is also a living room, playroom for children, dining room, dressing room, and bedrooms, the space taken up by the large U-shaped galley is space that effectively cannot be used for other purposes.

If the cruiser galley is underutilized, the racer galley has to provide three hot meals (four if you count the hot drinks and snack that are usually provided for the midnight change of watch) to a hungry crew of six, eight, ten, or more people. The meals have to be prepared in whatever conditions come along; unless the boat is large enough to have a full-time cook, the act of cooking takes the time of a person who could be used on deck or who at least could be sleeping, so there is a premium on efficiency; meals have to be timely if the watches are not to be disrupted, which means the galley must be adequate to prepare meals for an entire crew all at once; and for a race of any distance, provisions have to be carried to feed the entire crew for the full haul, which on a race longer than a single night constitutes an enormous task of provisioning and a challenge to storage facilities. Passage-making presents the same galley demands as racing, except that cooking is usually for a smaller crew and provisions must generally be stored for a longer period.

STOVES

The real problem with most boat stoves is that they don't produce enough heat, and the reason usually stems from the choice of fuel. The Coast Guard has declared alcohol a safe fuel for onboard cooking, and because alcohol stoves are cheap to build and install, many production boats come equipped with coppertone or brushed stainless steel alcohol stoves which are elegant, attractive, stylish, and have only three disadvantages: (1) by the end of the first sailing season the coppertone stove will have taken on a patina best described as rust-tone, (2) the average weekend cruise is not long enough for a cook to do any cooking which involves boiling water, baking at a temperature over 300 degrees, or searing meat, and (3) sooner or later the stove will reward the cook with a flare-up, which though it can be put out with water (the great claim for the putative safety of alcohol stoves) is likely in the interim to singe the eylashes of the cook and the headliner of the boat, if it does not ignite the entire galley.

There are a few alcohol stoves that work adequately. The Shipmate alcohol ranges are well built, reliable, and have large burners and a well-constructed oven that can hold a constant temperature of over 400 degrees. The Origo ranges have the convenience of using a wicking material instead of pressurized fuel, and since they do not require priming or tank pumping, they make up in convenience and freedom from flare-ups for the lack of heat and inefficiency of the alcohol fuel. But on the whole, the disadvantages of alcohol—low heat, expense, inconvenience, the danger of flare-ups, and the invisibility of the blue flame—suggests that for most boats an alternative fuel is a better choice.

Fuel Choices

There are a few yachtsmen in the northern corners of Maine who argue for wood- or coal-fueled stoves, and there are passage-makers who swear by diesel stoves that run off the main fuel tank of the yacht. If you're gunkholing around forests or coal mines, a wood- or coal-burning stove may provide coziness, warmth, economy, and a satisfying snugness. If you are sailing offshore for extended passages in which the difficulty of gimbaling a diesel stove and the need for a forced draft matter less than the convenience of fueling both the stove and the engine from a single tank, a rugged, reliable diesel stove built by one of the commercial boat stove builders, such as Dickinson, or perhaps a diesel stove from Taylor in England or Force 10 in Canada, may be the ticket. But for most yachtsmen the choice of fuel "boils down to" kerosene, LPG (liquid petroleum gas—propane or butane), or CNG (compressed natural gas).

Kerosene Kerosene stoves are simple, relying on a burner design that has been in use all over the world for years and on fuel that is available everywhere. Kerosene burns with an intensely hot flame and is highly efficient (a gallon or so will get most boats through an entire season of cooking). The installation is generally inexpensive and simple, the fuel is quite safe, with a visible flame and a high ignition point, and kerosene stoves are available in compact, lightweight models that will fit into even a small galley with a minimal addition of weight and bulk. The disadvantages of kerosene are that it requires priming (usually with alcohol); if the burner is misadjusted or if impure fuel is used, the stove can be smoky or smelly; the flame is so hot that hot-top (cast plate) burners or asbestos pads are sometimes required to achieve a slow, simmering flame; and if you spill the kerosene while refueling the tank it can seep into porous surfaces and leave stains or unpleasant smells.

For a racing or cruising boat that requires a hot, effective stove with minimal space and weight requirements, kerosene is an ideal fuel. The kerosene stoves made by Taylor in England, Force 10 in Canada, and Shipmate in the U.S. are well built, reliable, and effective ranges. The Taylor stoves, which combine brass, stainless steel, and heavy enamel cooking surfaces, are among the most attractive galley implements available for a yacht. Priming a kerosene stove is generally easier than priming an alcohol stove, especially if the alcohol is kept in a long-nozzled squirt bottle. If the priming flame is allowed to almost burn out, the burner will start every time.

Another advantage of kerosene is that it is simple and economical to add a kerosene heater to a boat with a kerosene stove. The same pressure tank can be used for both stove and heater, and kerosene heaters are small and efficient. Although diesel heaters are sometimes recommended on the argument that the heater will use the same fuel as the engine, most diesel heaters require a gravity day tank that must be fueled by pumping from the main fuel tank. By contrast, the kerosene heater requires only a tiny copper line from the pressure tank.

For boats that are equipped with alcohol stoves there are conversion kits available from Force 10 which make for an easy changeover to kerosene fuel. The same pressure tank and plumbing can be used, and the refitting is a simple wrench and screwdriver job.

Gas Both LPG and CNG stoves are convenient because they require no priming. Turn the gas on, strike a match, and you're cooking. Some gas ranges even include electronic ignition and special sensors to turn the gas off if the flame is extinguished. Gas cooks with a hot flame; it can readily be adjusted to a low simmer; except for the wretched smell which is added to the propane or CNG so that a leak can be detected by a human nose, it is odorless; it does not cause sooting or stains when it is spilled. But, with the possible exception of gasoline, LPG (propane or butane) is the most dangerous fuel you can carry on a boat for cooking. LPG is heavier than air, it is stored under pressure, and if even a tiny leak develops, the escaped gas will gather in the bilge of the boat, awaiting a single spark from an electrical connection—something as innocuous as a loose terminal on a bilge pump switch—to turn your boat into a bomb.

The Coast Guard and insurance company specifications for the installation of an LPG fuel system are stringent: the fuel tanks must be either on deck or in a separate, sealed compartment with drainage overboard; and there must be a shutoff valve at the tank. The tank storage requirement imposes a real performance penalty on a sailboat because the tanks are heavy and bulky, and storing them in a separate compartment usually means the stern, where the extra weight hurts the performance of the boat and where space that might be used for fenders, dock lines, and other gear that needs to be kept convenient to the deck is given over to the dead weight of propane tanks. Unless you are willing to go back to the tank to turn the master valve on and off with each use of the stove, the installation will also require a remote electric solenoid valve on the tanks. Finally, for safety, the boat needs a fume detector system and a bilge ventilator. Add them all up and it is a complex, expensive, and heavy installation.

CNG, which is lighter than air and will thus not settle into the bilges of the boat, does not require quite so stringent an installation. Although the tanks are even heavier than LPG tanks, they can be secured in the bilges of the boat, which will center the weight. (They *must* be secured, because the first-step pressure is enough to put the tank into orbit!) The two-step regulator is expensive to buy, and repairs are inconvenient and expensive, but the plumbing of the installation is simple, because flexible hose and slip-on connections can be used instead of copper tube and flared fittings. (In fact, copper is not compatible with CNG and should not be used in a CNG installation.) Finally, the big caution for anyone contemplating a CNG installation is that CNG refills are available from only a few dealers on the two coasts. If you are not near a dealer, the tank must be mailed to the refiller for refilling. And while many excellent stove makers now build stoves with CNG-compatible burners as replacement, in order to get the original regulator and equipment for a CNG installation, you need to deal with Gas Systems, which sells the regulators and tanks and which also requires that you select from their line of stoves, which may or may not suit your requirements.

Thus LPG and CNG are not instant cures to the problems of boat stoves. For any permanently installed stove, the installation of gas tanks and plumbing will be complex and costly, and the danger of the fuel means that there is no possibility of shortcuts.

Portable Gas Stoves One alternative which can be attractive when most of the cooking is done at anchor, and for boats that do not require a gimbaled sea stove, is to use a portable gas stove with fuel in disposable cartridges. The Coleman or Sears camping stoves, or the Lytham Mariner stoves imported from England, use the kind of propane cylinders that are sold for use with torches. Although they are frowned upon by some insurance companies and should certainly be safely secured when not in use, the very simplicity of the plumbing, with tanks that attach directly or perhaps through a short length of flexible hose—no concealed plumbing running through the bilge—makes the installations inherently trouble

free. The DeGill Corporation of Claremont, New Hampshire, manufactures pot rails for the Coleman and Sears stoves. The stoves will probably rust after a few seasons' use, but they are so inexpensive that they can be replaced. The Lytham unit is built for a marine environment and would probably last much longer than the cheap alcohol stoves it could readily replace. Either will provide quick, reliable heat for cooking and is an excellent stove for weekending or casual coastal cruising.

There are also smaller, swinging gas stoves which use tiny butane camping cylinders or larger propane cylinders. Butane is even more volatile than propane, but with a secure installation and care taken that partially depleted canisters of butane are not left around, the Forespar stove, the modified Sea Swing stove sold by James Bliss and other dealers, or the swinging propane stove sold by DeGill can make an excellent stove for a pot of coffee or soup while sailing. The heat is quick, operation of the stove is simple, and fuel canisters are readily available from camping equipment suppliers.

Stove Installation

If you need a permanently installed stove, the installation is not difficult as long as it is done carefully. Stove installations, no matter what the fuel, are not a place to cut corners, since the consequence of a breakdown could be not only inconvenience but fire or explosion.

Stoves are heavy, and the gimbal mountings require both precise alignment and secure mounting. If they cannot be through-bolted to the sides of the stove opening because the backs of the bulkheads are inaccessible, they should be fastened with heavy screws, preferably into mounting blocks that

are glued in place on the bulkhead. The room needed for swinging a gimbaled stove is usually drawn on the installation instructions, but remember that you need the same swinging room in front of the stove to avoid black-and-blue shins for the cook. Every installation should be provided with a crash bar in front of the stove, so that no one is pitched into a hot stove by a roll of the boat. Crash bars can be made out of powerboat stanchion fittings: usually two 90-degree bases and a length of stainless tubing will suffice. Mount the bar with some clearance; when the stove swings, it should not hit your fingers if you are holding on to the crash bar.

The stove compartment should be lined with a fireproof or fire-resistant material. Sheet stainless steel over thin asbestos sheet is lightweight, but asbestos has its own dangers, espe-

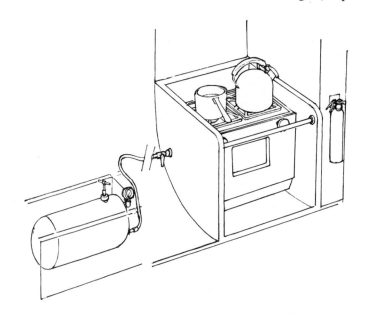

cially for installation in the confined space of a yacht. For a boat that can afford the weight, tile is attractive and easy to clean. Plasterboard would provide adequate fire protection, but will not survive a marine atmosphere. Most boats will probably leave the compartment unlined, in which case there should be plenty of room between the sides and bottom of the stove and the surrounding woodwork. Make certain that flameproof paints are used for the surfaces.

Alcohol and kerosene stoves generally require a pressurized tank; find a location for the tank which allows access to the pump and the filler cap. It is sometimes tempting to try to install the tank under or behind the stove, because the swing of the stove often leaves an area that is otherwise difficult to utilize. Don't! No matter how careful your installation, there will come a moment when you will want to refill the tank while the stove is hot, or when you need to turn the fuel off in a hurry—and the last thing you will want is to have your fuel lines and shutoff valve too close to the stove. A better installation is under a berth on one side of the galley, with the fuel cutoff valve located somewhere outside the stove compartment.

The easiest and safest installation is to use copper tubing (3/16-inch tubing works well) for the plumbing from the tank to the cutoff valve, then flexible hose for the last run to the stove. The copper tubing resists abrasion and crushing, is thin and unobtrusive to string through cabinets or under berths, and is safe and easy to install. Use compression fittings for the tubing and electrical wire clamps to hold the tubing down against bulkheads. Cut the tubing off cleanly and file off any burrs. (A small tubing cutter makes the job easy and is so inexpensive that it is worth buying even for two or three connections; or borrow one from a service station.) If you cannot find the right

size of compression fittings in a plumbing supply store, try an air conditioning supply store. Insert the end of the tubing into the sleeve, and tighten the fitting with a wrench until it stops leaking.

For a cutoff valve, there are many small gas or fuel valves which will work well with kerosene. Valves that are intended for use on gas lines often will not work with alcohol, because the alcohol dissolves the packing. A small Teflon-bushed ball valve is probably the best choice for alcohol. A plumbing supply store will sell you brass or bronze step-up and elbow fittings if you need them.

Liquid fueled stoves operate at such low pressure that simple barb end fittings will work for the hose. Make sure that whatever hose you choose (automobile fuel hose is readily available in short lengths) is resistant to the fuel you are using. Hose clamps over the barb fittings are not necessary, but they are a good idea. And a metal-clad hose with swaged end fittings, if one comes with the stove or can be made up by a supplier (aircraft and motorcycle stores are good sources), will make the safest possible installation. Mark the shutoff valve with clear "open" and "closed" labels.

Gas Installations Gas stove installations are not so easy. LPG plumbing can be done with copper tubing, but flare fittings are needed instead of the simpler compression fittings. And the entire installation should be checked with soapy water, fume detectors, and careful inspection to make certain that there are no potential weak points, unsupported fittings, lines, hoses, or electrical connections. The remote solenoid must be a fail-safe device which closes when the power is off (Marinetics and other marine electrical fitting suppliers make solenoids with galley control panels), and the fume detector should be on whenever the master valve is open. It is a good idea to use a bilge blower and to double check every electrical connection anywhere near the bilge of the boat.

For added safety, install a pressure valve between the shutoff (solenoid) valve and the stove. If the reading on the valve ever drops when the shutoff is closed (it should be closed whenever the stove is not in use), it means that there is a leak in the system. If the pressure is ever above normal, it means the regulator is bad and should be replaced before the system is used.

The usual tanks are the same metal tanks that are used for campers and home barbecues, and they do not take well to the marine environment. Paint helps, but in time the tank will deteriorate and require replacement. If you do not have double tanks, or an auxiliary propane bottle with an adapter to connect in place of the regular fixed tanks, you should carry a fisherman's scale to periodically weigh the tanks to determine how much fuel is left.

If the boat does not have a ready-made tank compartment, there are prefabricated plastic tank compartments that can be installed in a lazarette and hooked to a small through-hull fitting for overboard drainage. Whatever the installation, make sure the tanks are securely strapped or locked in place.

Despite the safety claims of CNG advocates and the fact that the fuel is lighter than air, most insurance companies will demand the same safety precautions with CNG as with heavier-than-air LPG fuels. In addition, the tank must be secured carefully, lest a leak propel it into orbit, and the plumbing must all be of materials that are certified for CNG compatibility. Flexible hose is generally used and should be protected against abrasion of any kind.

ICEBOXES

The difference between a good icebox and a mediocre one is not the quality of the shelves or the convenience of the double-hinged top or the butcher-block cutting board that the builder has provided as an "extra." What matters is insulation, and unfortunately it is in the provision of insulation that most iceboxes are weak. Insulation takes up space. Less than 4 inches on all sides of the icebox is probably not enough, and that space is robbed from the interior of the icebox, from storage space, and from general interior room. It is also difficult to install insulation without gaps and with proper overlapped joints. Since the work is completely hidden from the boat owner, and few owners think to ask about or try to inspect the quality of the insulation, many boat builders save money by using poured foam instead of sheet urethane or sprayed foam. Under ideal conditions, the poured foam can produce effective insulation, but usually it is uneven, with large bubbles that destroy the effectiveness of the insulation. Tops are often built with more concern for appearance than insulation. Butcher block doesn't hurt; hinges do. Without several inches of insulation the top will function with the effectiveness of a sheet of cardboard.

There are tests that can be performed to measure the insulation effectiveness of an icebox.* For most boat owners, the real measure is subjective: Does your ice last long enough? Or are you always scrounging around for more because the

* *The Perfect Box: 39 Ways to Improve Your Boat's Ice Box*, by Spa Creek Instruments, Annapolis, MD 21403, is a complete reference on boat iceboxes, with descriptions of measuring techniques and suggestions for building new iceboxes from scratch.

blocks never seem to make it through a weekend? If you find that ice just doesn't last, the usual culprits are inadequate insulation, leaky gaskets and drains, side-opening doors, and icebox installations too close to stoves or engines. Sometimes the layout of a boat requires that the icebox be placed next to the stove or engine; if so, the insulation requirements are even greater—probably close to 6 inches of good urethane foam on the side that faces a heat source.

If your icebox is less effective than you want, the first test is to determine how much insulation has been installed. Begin by measuring the interior of the icebox. If the sides are sloped, as they usually are, measure as many points as you need and use your high school geometry to determine the actual dimensions.

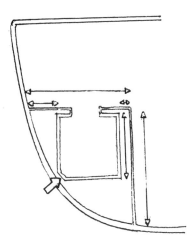

Then, measure the exterior dimensions of the area where the icebox is installed, subtracting for the thickness of plywood counters and bulkheads. The trickiest part is to estimate

or extrapolate for the section of an icebox that is built against the hull. Often there is minimal insulation at some of the corners of the icebox: if you calculate that there is only an inch between the interior of the icebox and the inner skin of the hull, chances are that the only way to keep your ice from melting quickly is to sail in the Antarctic.

Once you know how much room there is for insulation, you can measure the quantity and quality of the insulation. If panels on the sides of the icebox enclosure are removable, you may be able to disassemble part of it and peek inside. You will probably find either urethane sheet insulation or sprayed foam insulation. If you cannot disassemble the enclosure, you will need to do some careful drilling and probing to check the insulation. Begin by finding areas where you can probe without marring interior surfaces. Next to a berth cushion, inside a stove comaprtment or sink cabinet, or inside a drawer compartment are obvious choices. If there are no obvious choices, you will need to drill inspection holes in an exposed surface. As long as the holes are neatly spaced in a straight line, they will not affect the beauty of your interior. Indeed, a neat row of finished bungs may improve the appearance by breaking up a bleak panel. If you absolutely cannot bring yourself to drill through the oiled or varnished teak panels, you can drill access holes from the inside of the icebox. A row of neat holes can afterward be covered by ordinary vinyl tape; or you can patch, sand, and paint the holes to match the rest of the interior of the icebox; or you can install a shelf bracket over the row of holes.

You can drill inspection holes as small as ¼ inch, but ⅜ is probably a better size. Use a sharp bit, preferably a brad or Forstner bit, and drill slowly so that you will not chew up the insulation that you hope to find on the other side. A single probing hole won't really tell you much, because many iceboxes are nicely insulated on some surfaces (the easy ones!) while there are gaps or even no insulation at all on other surfaces. To probe, use a length of wire or a pusher fid. Try to determine how thick the insulation is, what gaps if any there are in the insulation, and by pulling out tiny chunks of the insulating material, determine what the insulation is. You will probably find either green or brown urethane sheet material or brown sprayed foam insulation. If you find Styrofoam or rock wool, you will need to replace the insulation completely. If you find urethane or foam with some gaps or open areas (you can feel them when the probe suddenly goes through easily), you can repair the gaps fairly easily.

Improving the Insulation

The easiest repair to the interior of an icebox is to spray additional foam into the gaps. What you need is a careful survey of the areas that need additional insulation, a row of holes large enough to take the nozzle of the foam sprayer, a careful plan to inject foam from bottom to top, and either bungs to fill the holes you have drilled from the outside or a repair technique to close up holes you have drilled from the inside. The larger the access holes you drill and the deeper the empty space that you are filling with foam, the fewer holes you will need. Three-quarter-inch holes, the largest you can comfortably bung, can be spaced a foot apart because the larger hole will allow you to turn the nozzle from side to side; smaller holes will need closer spacing; ⅜-inch holes are the smallest that will still accommodate the nozzle of the foam container.

The idea is to pump foam into one of the bottom holes until it appears at the holes to the side and above. When you have worked across at the bottom level, you shift to the next row up.

There are large foam machines that can be rented (Insta-Foam Froth-Pak is one brand name), but for most amateur work the small urethane foam canisters that are sold in hardware stores are more manageable. Most come with a short length of hose that can be used as an extension for the nozzle. You will probably need more than the optimistic capacity labels on the can suggest. And since you won't want to stop in the middle of the project, try buying twice as many as you think you will need; you can always return unopened cans later.

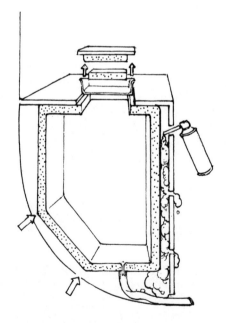

Remember that the foam can only be sprayed down, and that once you start a can you cannot stop for more than five seconds without clogging the nozzle. If you have to stop, you can keep the can active by shooting a short burst into an empty paper bag every five seconds. Good planning and the help of an assistant will make the project run more smoothly. The foam can get messy if you slop it around, so drop cloths or lots of newspaper is a good precaution.

If any of the panels that enclose the icebox are flimsy, you might want to put in some temporary braces to hold them while the foam expands and cures. The expansion of the foam is strong enough to distort panels or pop weak fastenings, but in any but an excessively lightly constructed interior the adhesive foam will ultimately add to the strength of the ice chest and joinery.

Once the foam cures, which happens quickly in summer but may require a heat lamp in the spring or fall, you can go ahead with the bunging of the holes in joinery, or the filling or covering of holes in the interior of the icebox. (Chapter 5 has hints about installing bungs.) For the interior of the icebox, epoxy putty will fill and fair the holes. Don't try gelcoat repairs inside the ice chest, because gelcoat is porous enough to absorb odors. An acrylic lacquer paint can be sprayed or brushed over any interior repairs, will dry quickly, and will not absorb odors. An even neater repair is to install a shelf batten over the holes. Countersunk screws or oval-head screws on finishing washers will hold the batten in place, and a Plexiglas shelf can be cut to fit.

The other areas to improve in an icebox are the cover, which should have adequate insulation and a good gasket, and the drain, which can be a real cold leak. Hinged covers are convenient but difficult to insulate. If the cover insulation is inadequate (less than 3 or 4 inches thick), urethane foam panels can be cut to size, glued in place, and covered with fiberglass, or you can shop around and find a ready-made vinyl or fiberglass box that can be filled with insulation and fastened to the bottom of the cover.

Icebox Drains

Drains are important to keep the ice chest from turning into a pool of floating labels, lettuce leaves, and Baggies. But icebox drains also cause problems in boats, ranging from huge heat losses in the ice chest to wretched bilge odors to severe rot problems in wooden boats or in the joinery of fiberglass boats.

Unless you will *never* have milk or any other potential disaster in the icebox, and you will *always* keep the bilge pumped down to the last drop, iceboxes should not drain into the bilge. On a wooden boat an icebox drain is a certain invitation to rot, both around the drain fitting and in frames, floors, and planking in the bilge area. On a fiberglass boat the joinery around the icebox drain will probably turn black and ultimately rot; long before the black spots begin to annoy you, you will accidentally spill milk in the icebox, which will find its way to the bilge before souring and leaving your boat uninhabitable.

If your ice chest is located high enough on the inside of the hull to allow drainage overboard—even if the through-hull is close to the waterline so the drain can only be used when the boat is level or heeling with the icebox up—an overboard drain is the obvious choice. Install a sea cock on the through-hull, open it when the boat is level or heeling the right direction, and you're set.

Unfortunately, few boats have ice chests located high enough to allow overboard drainage. The alternatives are to provide a reservoir that can be pumped or carried overboard, or to provide plumbing that will allow the ice chest drain to be pumped into the sink. A reservoir can be as simple as a plastic "jerry jug" which is periodically dumped overboard. Or with a little more time and trouble, you can install a simple plumbing arrangement, with or without a reservoir, to pump the drain into a sink. If the ice chest is kept clean, the drain water can be used for dishwashing or for a bracing wake-up splash that will make a cold shower seem soothing.

Using an electric pump or a dedicated pump is the fanciest system, but for a simple installation you can use a single sink

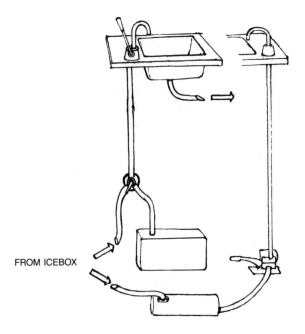

FROM ICEBOX

pump with a Y-valve. Ordinary clear vinyl hose is adequate for the installation (⅝- or ½-inch hose usually will fit the valves and sink pumps), and a periodic pump-through with chlorine will kill any accumulated crud in the hose.

If you have a side-opening icebox, or if there isn't sufficient room for additional insulation around your icebox, the only solution is to install a new icebox. *The Perfect Box* has instructions on how to build a new box from scratch; it is not a simple project. As an alternative, you could buy an icebox liner from one of the boat manufacturers and install it yourself, using cut urethane panels and spray foam to fill the gaps in the insulation. It is not a job to undertake unless you are experienced in joinery.

Refrigeration

Installing refrigeration does nothing to solve the problems of inadequate insulation. If you install one of the do-it-yourself refrigeration units in an inadequately insulated box, instead of making trips to the dock for more ice you will make trips to get dead batteries recharged, or to get more fuel for your engine which will have to be run overtime to keep the cold plates of the refrigeration unit adequately charged.

A powerboat, which has engines running much of the time that it is in use, or a boat that is kept plugged in to shore power at a dock for most of its life, with only short excursions under sail, can use low-capacity refrigeration systems—most of which run on 110-volt shore power. There are also solid-state heat-pump systems which draw modest current and require no plumbing. The problem with heat-pump systems is that they are effective only if the air in the boat is cool, which means that they are most successful in cold-water areas. (Usually they are placed so that the fan draws air from the bilges.) A good heat-pump system will keep food frozen, but it may draw up to an amp per hour. Heat-pump systems generally cannot freeze food.

At the other extreme of refrigeration are high-capacity systems with efficient cold plates that can store the cold in an easily frozen brine solution. Cold plates are rated in BTUs; the higher the BTU factor, the more heat the plate can absorb before needing to be refrozen by running the refrigeration unit again. The less you are willing to run the engine or generator of your boat, the higher capacity (in BTUs) you will need for your refrigeration system.

A refrigeration system can be owner-installed. The popular models from Spa Creek, Adler/Barbour (now International Marine), Crosby, and Grunert all provide installation kits and instructions. There are two basic choices for refrigeration: a self-contained unit that is driven from the battery, or an engine-driven until that works off a belt driven by the boat's engine. The self-contained units are simpler to install but less efficient, since the energy goes through more stages (engine to alternator to battery to refrigeration-unit motor to compressor, instead of engine to compressor). All that is required is a secure mounting for the compressor unit, copper piping to the icebox, and the cold plate mounted in the icebox. Engine-driven units have substantially higher capacity but require trickier installation, and in the crowded engine compartments of many boats it may prove almost impossible to fit the compressor to the engine. Depending upon the complexity and capacity of the unit, you may need an additional seawater intake for cooling water, which could turn a simple installation into a complex one.

STORAGE

Few galleys have enough storage room. In addition to the pots and pans that even a stripped-out ULDB racer needs for overnights or distance racing, the galley needs storage for dried and canned food, the inevitable jar of peanut butter that usually constitutes emergency rations, dishes or paper plates, flatware, mugs, glasses or paper cups, pot holders, liquor or "emergency" spirits, electronic or mechanical matches, a bottle of priming alcohol for a kerosene stove, and the gadgets

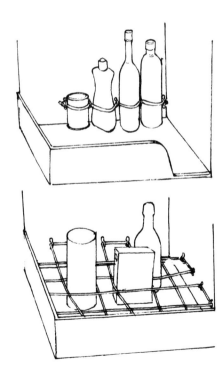

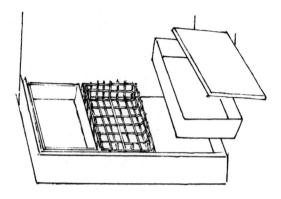

that every experienced shipboard cook soon accumulates to simplify the tasks of cooking and serving food at 27 degrees of heel.

Dedicated storage—whether in the form of built-in plate and mug holders or the ready-built cabinets that can be bought unfinished—can be attractive and functional, but it is heavy, bulky for the amount of stowage it provides, and inflexible if storage needs change from season to season, or even during a season when a boat is used alternately for cruising and racing. Some alternatives are plastic restaurant storage bins, which can be loaded with pots and pans, dishes, or food and conveniently loaded onto or off the boat; and shock-cord stowage, which while less elegant in appearance than fitted bins for mugs, bottles, or flatware, is lighter, less bulky, and far more versatile.

Whatever the choices made for a galley, the most important decision is always to build a galley for its real use. If you are cooking an occasional meal during a weekend cruise across the sound, you probably don't need galley belts, gimbaled ovens, and the rest of the paraphernalia that is sometimes advocated for cruising boats. At the same time, if you are going to keep a racing crew or a passage-making crew going at top efficiency, you need adequate ice-chest, cooking, and storage facilities to provide the prodigious quantities of food that a crew can devour.

15

PLUMBING

Whatever the brochures may say about "fully enclosed" heads, there is no way a marine head can offer the privacy of a home toilet. On smaller boats, the effort to fully enclose a head can leave a space so confined that a person using the toilet has to ask him- or herself permission to reach for the toilet paper. And even on a fairly large boat, the lack of sound insulation and adequate venting makes the head a more public space than many owners, families, guests, and crews would like. Many grand prix racing boats today go to the opposite extreme: the head consists of a fully exposed Porta-Potti (often taped shut to make sure that no one will use it) and a bucket, which is the actual facility. It is simple, lightweight, and reliable, but if you plan to have women crew, or you plan to use the boat for activities other than racing, you may find yourself single-handing whether you like it or not.

HEADS

The first requirement for a good head is air and light, which means either a hatch or a ventilator—the larger the better. If the head is fully enclosed, there should be louvers in the door, an opening port, or other venting to assure a flow of air through the head. Without adequate ventilation in every kind of weather, the head will be unusable. Opening ports are generally a bad idea, since they must be closed in rain or any kind of a seaway (just the conditions when the head seems to get increased usage).

Next, the head should include a reliable, functioning toilet, installed securely and with first-class plumbing. If you have the luxury of designing or specifying a head from scratch, or are modifying an existing head, it is worth considering the possibility of installing the toilet to face fore and aft, to avoid the high side–low side problems of using an athwartship toilet under sail.

There may be a few small boats that will elect the simplicity of a portable toilet, but a few tries at the emptying procedure should be enough to deter anyone from trying to cruise or distance-race with one. The smaller and less expensive marine heads are reliable and simple as long as they are installed well, which means that they are securely bolted down, the discharge goes through a vented loop to prevent back-siphoning (even if the head is above the waterline, it will probably be below the waterline on one tack or the other), both the discharge and the intake go through reliable sea cocks, with the intake far enough down on the hull to pick up water no matter what the angle of heel, and high-quality hoses with marine-grade clamps are used throughout the plumbing. Tapered-plug or ball-valve sea cocks are reliable and quick to open and close with a simple quarter turn; for the highly optimized racer, one of the flush-exterior sea cocks, though slower to operate, does eliminate the drag of the through-hull fitting on the skin of the hull.

It helps to educate crew on the proper use of the head and the importance of keeping the intake valve closed when the head is not in use, in case the check valve on the intake line fails. For maintenance and safety, it also helps to have the sea cocks accessible. Sea cocks that cannot be reached easily will be left open all the time and will eventually get stuck open, usually just when a split hose, torn or jammed joker valve, or broken check valve leaves you with a first-class mess that can only be cleaned up and straightened out by closing the sea cock.

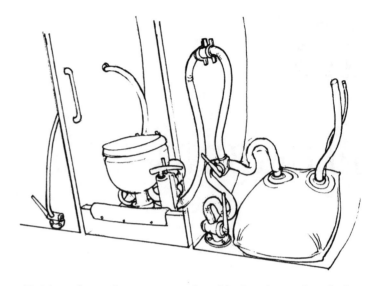

Raising the toilet to a comfortable height and including strong handholds make the head safer and more convenient. It is easy to install a handhold on a bulkhead, but make certain that it is through-bolted, because the loads on a handhold when someone standing at the head is thrown back by a sudden pitch of the boat are more than enough to tear wood screws out of a block of teak. Another valuable addition is a kneeling block: an elevated block, usually covered with carpet or padding, that enables men to improve their aim when using the head in rough seas.

Storage space, such as a simple cabinet with sliding doors or canvas pockets, can make good use of the otherwise wasted space above the head. It is also easy to add a small sink, which can drain into the head to cut down on through-hulls. Jay Stuart Haft imports an elegant and expensive folding sink. It would also be easy enough to build a small counter, fixed or folding, and include a small marine or RV sink with a flexible drain. Brushing your teeth or washing your face uses very little water, and it is as easy to flush it down as to reach in and open a through-hull. Another idea is to change the fitting on the sink to a shower head. There are kits sold for home showers that can be adapted, or you can use a dishwashing hose and head. Even without pressure water and/or a hot water system, a foot pump and a shower head can be welcome for after-swim showers.

If you have a shower sump, you will need a shower drain pump, which is usually a modified bilge pump. It is also possible to drain a shower into the bilge of a fiberglass boat, although the soap scum that inevitably develops does little for the freshness of the bilge. In either case, a raw teak grating makes an excellent floor for the head and will stay dry enough for good footing even through showers, splashing from the sink, or the dripping of foul-weather gear that is tossed there to dry.

Holding Tanks and On-board Waste Systems

The law is controversial and still under debate, and with the exception of areas like the Great Lakes or Nantucket, if you aren't guilty of other infractions, it's unlikely that your boat will ever be inspected for a treatment system or holding tank. But the law is still there, and for some areas of the country observance is a must. Anyone who has tried to swim in the Salt Pond during Block Island Race Week can understand why the law exists.

New boats usually come equipped with a Y-valve and a holding tank, with the plumbing set up to permit either direct overboard discharge or pumping out through the deck. The problem with this setup is that if the Y-valve leaks, as many of them do, or if someone accidentally sets it incorrectly, you will have a full holding tank very quickly, and in most areas of the country the lack of pump-out stations makes a full holding tank a poignant and piquant problem. Even if the tank is only partially full, the flexible tanks that are used on many boats seem to be odor permeable, and in many installations the tank vents are installed so that odors come wafting into the cabin or back to the cockpit.

One solution is to install a bilge pump or waste pump that will permit you to discharge the system yourself (outside the 3-mile limit, of course). Another option is to use two Y-valves, so the tank can be bypassed or emptied. Be sure in any system to use only hose that is manufactured for waste (either flexible hose with a smooth-lined interior or heavy-wall reinforced rubber tubing); if you use flexible hose, you will need to ce-

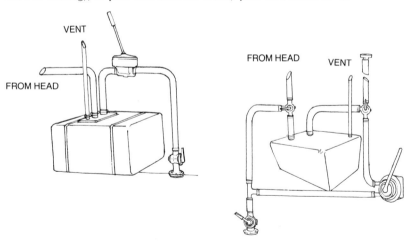

VENT

FROM HEAD

FROM HEAD VENT

ment end collars on with PVC cement. The Y-valves should be carefully labeled, and if they are in a position to be accidentally flipped, should be either taped or wired. And in any case the holding tank should be checked periodically to avoid surprises.

Treatment systems are easy to install. They all require heavy-duty electrical circuits (usually #8 or larger wire), large battery and charging capacity, and some means of bypassing and/or pumping out the treatment tank in case of blockage or breakdown.

If the law changes, sailors in areas where the water is regularly cleansed by tidal action will probably elect to eliminate the excess weight and complexity of plumbing in favor of straight-discharge installations.

SEA COCKS

One topic that is never omitted from buyers' checklists for purchasing a boat is the caveat about sea cocks instead of gate valves in the underwater plumbing. Sometimes the warning will go on to insist that the fittings be heavy-duty, through-bolted bronze sea cocks, as the only fittings adequate for offshore sailing. For extensive offshore sailing, or sailing where hard grinding of the boat bottom on coral reefs or rock piles is a real possibility, solid bronze through-bolted sea cocks are stronger. They are also expensive; heavy; demand a regular maintenance schedule including frequent lubrication, replacement of leather seals, and lapping; and are subject to electrolytic and galvanic corrosion. If your real sailing plans are less far-ranging, it may be wise to consider some of the alternatives to traditional sea cocks.

The real criteria for a sea cock or valve on a boat are: (1) that it be easy enough to use that it will get turned on and off instead of being left open all the time, and (2) that it be reliable, so that when you discover a ruptured or burned hose you can depend on the sea cock to shut off the flow. Leaving a sea cock open, especially when a boat is left at a mooring or on an anchor, is an invitation to a surprise. A corroded hose clamp, a weak spot in a hose, a worn check valve in a head, or a clogged anti-siphon vent in a bilge pump system can result in an astonishing flow of water, enough to greet you with a close-up view of the masthead instead of the topsides as you motor out in the club launch. And even when you're aboard, there is nothing as frustrating or frightening as discovering a leaky hose, reaching for the trusty sea cock, and finding it frozen in the open position. There are alternatives to bronze sea cocks in preventing those surprises.

Alternatives

The cheapest alternative, and the easiest to install, is a gate valve, which is generally not a good fitting for underwater use on a boat. Gate valves require many turns to open and close, instead of the quick quarter-turn required by a sea cock or ball valve; the stem of a gate valve is narrow and easily weakened by corrosion, often to the point where the torque necessary to free up a sticky valve will snap the stem off; the internal parts of a gate valve are often made of brass and subject to dezincification or rapid galvanic corrosion in a marine environment; and it is difficult or impossible to drain a gate valve for in-water winter storage. If you have gate valves, it may be wise to replace them with ball valves, especially if you can buy bronze ball valves with no-maintenance Teflon seals.

Ball valves turn on and off in a quarter-turn, have no especially vulnerable interior parts, and require no maintenance beyond periodic use. Like gate valves, they do not have drain plugs and must be cleared of water with compressed air or filled with antifreeze for winter use in a boat afloat.

The chief advantage of a sea cock, as opposed to a valve, is that the sea cock is fixed to the inside surface of the hull. If your boat uses separate valves instead of integral sea cocks, you should be especially cautious in protecting and inspecting the through-hulls and any exposed plumbing between the through-hull and the valve. In particular, watch for accidental impact to the plumbing and for stray-current electrolysis, which in a matter of days or even hours can corrode through a pipe or a plumbing fitting. And be careful that leverage on a sticky valve does not weaken or break the stem of the through-hull fitting.

Sea cocks which bolt to the hull, or can be glassed to the hull, and which accept a threaded through-hull are available today not only in the traditional tapered plug construction but also in ball-valve and rubber-plug constructions. A manufacturer, or a boat owner ordering or installing additional equipment for a boat, has the option of bronze or various reinforced nylon and plastic construction materials. The advantages of the nylon or Zytel sea cocks is that they are lightweight, do not require lubrication, and are not subject to corrosion. The disadvantage is that some plastics are subject to weakening if they are nicked or scored. A scratch in a bronze sea cock is nothing more than a scratch. Even an accidental blow to the sea cock, though it should be avoided, will probably not result in hidden damage. With plastic sea cocks, the threads and the body of the fitting should not be subjected to scoring or to accidental blows. Finally, be careful in choosing a bedding compound to use with plastic plumbing fittings: a few of the plastics are incompatible with certain polysulfide or polyurethane compounds.

Sea Cock Installations

Sea cocks are not always installed properly. On a wooden hull, the sea cock should be backed up and securely bolted to the hull. The threaded through-hull fitting should be cut short enough so that threading it all the way in does not put pressure on the sea cock. The block on which the sea cock is mounted should be securely fitted and bedded to the hull and should not form a water trap (because the sea cocks are often fitted later, or replaced, boats which have the top of every butt block carefully beveled will sometimes have a perfect little rot trap on the backing blocks for the sea cocks). In fiberglass boats the sea cocks are sometimes glassed to the hull, which can be satisfactory if the assembly is built with an adequate backing block. Again, the through-hull should be cut short enough so it does not apply pressure on the sea cock, and any holes through a cored hull should be thoroughly sealed with epoxy. On metal hulls, a bronze sea cock will have to be insulated from the hull, which makes the installation complex and expensive.

Some boat builders use through-hulls which are not flush with the surface of the hull, usually to save the cost of cutting and fitting a countersunk hole for a flush through-hull. They can be replaced with flush through-hulls, which will have a marked effect on the performance of a boat. On an uncored hull, a flush through-hull will need a substantial backing block, because the countersink penetrates so deeply into the hull. On a cored hull, it is important to seal any core material and to make certain that the installation of a flush through-hull does not crush the hull.

Maintenance

Ball-valve sea cocks and sea cocks made of Zytel or nylon generally need no maintenance beyond use, but tapered-plug sea cocks need regular greasing, periodic replacement of the leather or synthetic washers, and occasional lapping with valve-grinding compound. If your sea cock develops leaks where the tailpiece joins the valve, the usual problem is the washer, which either dries out and cracks or is damaged from too-energetic tightening of the tailpiece nut. Take it apart, clean out the pieces, and clean off the mating surfaces. You can usually buy replacement washers from a chandlery or from the maker of the sea cock; you could make a replacement from rubber gasket material, but without the old one as a model it is hard to get it exactly right. Be careful not to tighten the nut any tighter than needed to stop the leaking.

If the sea cock leaks around the ends of the plug, try removing one of the drain fittings, putting on a grease nipple, and pumping the valve full of waterproof grease. Do the whole operation with the valve in the open position, and pump in grease until it is forced out of the ends of the plug. Then tighten the nut on the end of the plug until the leak stops. If it doesn't stop, you probably have corrosion in the sea cock and it needs lapping or replacement.

BILGE PUMPS

Almost every boat needs two bilge pumps. One is to clear away rainwater that leaks down the mast, the drip from the shaft log, the occasional water that comes through the companionway or an open hatch in foul weather or when a wave sweeps over the deck, the puddles from wet sails or foul-weather gear, and the water that comes in when you remove the knot-meter transducer for cleaning. The other pump you hope you never use.*

For rainwater and other nuisance water, either a manual or an electric pump is fine. It is usually neither necessary nor desirable to install an automatic switch for an electric pump, and not having an automatic switch will save you from the surprise of a leak that shows up only after your battery is dead and you discover a foot of water in the bilge. Most leaks begin with hints, and regularly monitoring your bilge will give you advance warning.

Submersible centrifugal pumps are inexpensive and easy to install. All that is required is to find a low point in the bilge, screw the pump to a convenient floor timber or sole support, and run the hose and wiring connections. The pumps are generally reliable, the built-in filters are easy to clean by snapping out the pump mechanism, the current draw is generally

* There are many wooden boats, and not a few fiberglass boats, which need constant pumping to keep up with known, limited, but seemingly incurable leaks. Usually owners keep the exact frequency of operation of the pumps which handle that leakage somewhat more secret than their extramarital affairs. If you have a "leaker," you have probably already developed techniques to use automatic bilge-pump switches, timers, extra batteries, and alarms to keep up with your routine problems. Whatever system you rely upon to keep up with a regular leak should be completely independent of the systems you rely on in emergencies.

modest, and the capacity of even the smallest models is usually sufficient for a "puddle-clearing pump" for most sailboats. Most can be run dry briefly, but it is a good idea to watch how long it takes to pump the bilge dry. If you suddenly find that what used to take two minutes, even after a heavy rainstorm, now takes ten minutes, it is probably time for some troubleshooting.

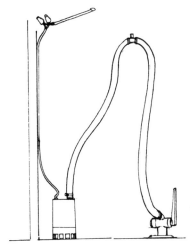

The disadvantage of a submersible centrifugal pump is that it won't pass even small debris from the bilge, so that the inevitable crud that accumulates in the bilge tends to stay there. A diaphragm pump can pass small debris but is less efficient and must be mounted outside the bilge, which means a more complex installation. Diaphragm pumps are noisy, especially if they are mounted on a panel or bulkhead, which can serve as a resonating sound box. Flexible mounts will help, but you will probably need to move a pump to several locations to find a satisfactory spot.

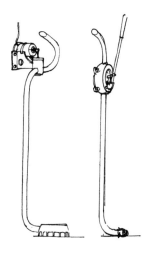

With any electric pump, make certain that the polarity is not reversed on the wiring. On some pumps the only problem will be pumping in the wrong direction; on others, the reversed polarity could introduce severe stray-current electrolysis to metal fittings in the boat. Whether the pump is submersible or mounted high in the boat, make certain that the wiring is kept as dry as possible, and that any junctions or connectors in the wiring are kept clear of the bilge water.

For best efficiency, any bilge-pump installation should be checked for leaks with soapy water. Even the tiny leak from a loose hose clamp will severely degrade the effectiveness of a pump. For the little pump that cleans up the puddles in the bilge, an air leak will mean that the pump runs longer and that you don't get the last little bit of water. For the more important pump that you rely on in an emergency, an air leak may prove more costly.

There are high-volume impeller and centrifugal pumps that can be driven by electric motors or by a direct drive off the engine, but no boat should rely on anything except a high-volume manual pump for emergency use. The schemes of using the engine intake or the head as an emergency pump are terrific for adventure stories, but the reality of an emergency that requires a pump is usually far more mundane than the stories of collisions with whales, attacks by swordfish, or holings from small-arms fire unleashed by pirates.

More often, someone goes below and discovers water in the bilge, sometimes enough to lap over the floorboards. It might be nothing more severe than a loose hose clamp that has allowed a hose to slip off a sea cock or through-hull. It might be a through-hull fitting that has broken, a hose that has cracked or burned, a shaft log that has shed its packing, a clogged anti-siphon valve that has converted a pump into a siphon, a jammed check valve with the head on the leeward side so that water is flooding in through the toilet bowl. Whatever the cause, it will take time to find and fix, and it is during that search for the source of the problem that you need a reliable, efficient emergency bilge pump. It is possible that there will be so little water that the engine will run perfectly, and that an engine-driven pump or the engine intake could handle the water while you calmly fix the problem. But it is also possible that the engine cannot be run, that the batteries are dead, the ignition is wet, or water has contaminated the fuel supply. Whatever the problem, you want to be able to reach for the handle and start pumping.

Navy (plunger) pumps can be made to handle high volumes but are generally tiring to operate, requiring a long stroke instead of the short pumping action of a diaphragm pump,

which is what most boats will choose for an emergency pump. The actual capacity of most pumps is far less than their rated capacity, and most boats will want a pump larger than the usual recommendations. The large Edson or Gusher pumps are not too big for even a modest cruiser. The pumps are often shown mounted on boards for temporary placement wherever they are needed, but in an emergency it may be difficult to dig down into a locker under a seat, find the pump, and set it up. In any case, every boat should have a permanently installed manual pump which can be operated efficiently from the cockpit with all hatches and lockers closed. A pump mounted so that the pumper has to lie on his back or be hit with the tiller, or which requires that the pumper kneel under the feet of the helmsman, cannot be operated efficiently. The handle should be stored nearby, and if it does not lock in place in the pump, there should be a spare handle. The run of hose from the bilge should be as short as possible, and should run clear of dangers like a galley or engine fire or a loose anchor in a locker that can pinch the hose. The pump and hose should be protected from blockage by a strum box or a simple bar or cross grate at the end of the hose, which should be accessible for clearing. The pump should also be accessible for repairs, and should be used often enough to make certain that the valves are not clogged or held open and the diaphragm is not punctured or leaking.

Pumps can drain overboard over the waterline, or below the waterline. The advantage of an above-waterline drain is that you can see the water coming out, which is reassuring, but unless the through-hull is on the transom, it will be submersed on one tack and needs to be treated as an underwater drain. The problem with an underwater through-hull as an outlet for a bilge pump is that like any through-hull it should be protected against breakage or damage by a sea cock, but if the pump is to be available for instant use, the sea cock must be left open. And depending upon the type of pump used, the outlet, if not protected by an anti-siphon device, can begin to function as a siphon. The hose and through-hull which are large enough to serve as an outlet are large enough to bring water into the boat with truly astonishing speed.

A check valve in the intake hose of a pump will keep the water sucked up into the hose from rolling back into the bilge. The check valve will also degrade the efficiency of the pump, presents another spot where a blockage can sneak in just when you don't need it, and can cause problems in the winter if the hoses are not disconnected so that the entire system can be drained.

The discharge for any bilge pump should loop safely above the waterline, and if the outlet is below the waterline on either tack it should be protected with an anti-siphon valve as well as a sea cock. Any bilge pump through-hull which is below the waterline should have rigid pipe or very-heavy-duty hose for the section that leads to the anti-siphon valve. And make certain that there are no bottlenecks anywhere in the pump discharge. An elbow, a sharp turn, or a pinch in a hose can sharply reduce the efficiency of a pump.

HOSES AND PIPES

There are so many different systems in a boat—the engine, electronics, lights, fuel, water, stove fuel, refrigeration, heat, bilge pumps, pressure water, head, showers, sinks—that the basic priorities sometimes get forgotten in the urge toward lightness or in the desire to conceal plumbing behind and under attractive joinery and ceilings or clever furniture. The stakes are usually high in a plumbing failure. If a hose cracks or slips off an engine intake or a bilge-pump outlet, before you know it you discover water over the floorboards. If a head waste line cracks or slips off a holding tank, you will for a long time regret the use of cheap hose instead of the strongest and most reliable hose available for the job.

Wherever plumbing is concealed, there is the possibility of a leak that cannot be fixed. A sea cock that is partially inaccessible, that cannot be reached without dismantling the engine compartment or the galley joinery, is next to useless. And while it isn't necessary to expose all of the plumbing for easy repair, any plumbing that cannot be reached easily should be assembled to last and to resist impact, puncture, and the other dangers that lurk below in a boat. For example, the hoses from cockpit scuppers to underwater or transom through-hulls are often made of flexible (accordion-style) tubing. If the through-hulls lead out through the transom, above the waterline, or if they are protected by sea cocks, a crack or break in the hose will not sink the boat. But what if that break or crack comes when you are taking occasional waves into the cockpit from a following sea?

As a general rule, the less accessible the plumbing is, the more reliable the materials used should be. Every hose coupling below the waterline should use double hose clamps, and if you make certain that you buy marine hose clamps instead of automotive hose clamps, you will be more secure. Solid rubber or vinyl hose reinforced with webbing or nylon is safer and more reliable than lightweight plastic hose, including those that are metal-reinforced. Although more connections are involved, using rigid plastic (PVC) elbows instead of bending the hose results in less fatigue to the hose and less risk of pinching if the hose should shift in position. If you do have bends in the hose, use enough tie-downs or hose clamps to keep the curve gentle.

In some cases specialized hoses or pipes may be advisable or necessary. If the bilge-pump plumbing must run directly under the stove, a length of exhaust hose could be used for the section of hose that is vulnerable to fire accidents from the stove. Super-flexible polybutylene tubing can be used instead of most of the water hoses in the boat, including hot water lines. It is stronger than most hoses, more resistant to vibration fatigue than copper tubing, and cheap. With the variety of compression fittings available, is easy to install with nothing more than a sharp knife and an adustable wrench. If your local plumbing supply house does not carry polybutylene tubing and fittings, try a recreational-vehicle dealer. The only

drawback to polybutylene is that it is susceptible to damage from freezing if the water systems are not carefully drained and/or treated with appropriate antifreeze in the winter.

Next to fire, plumbing accidents are the most common problems in a boat. Vibration, neglect, and corrosion take a real toll on plumbing, and much of the hardware installed in a boat is designed for lighter usage requirements. And even the strongest-looking plumbing fittings can fail without warning. Fortunately, temporary repairs are easy to make if the right equipment is aboard. A few lengths of nylon-reinforced vinyl tubing of various sizes and a box of hose clamps of different sizes are often enough to repair almost any part of the plumbing for long enough to finish the race or the cruise.

Plumbing is a mundane topic, far less interesting than the newest gadgetry in electronics or deck hardware, but plumbing, like the basic integrity of the hull, keeps everything where it belongs.

16

VHF

A VHF radio is a top electronics priority for most boat owners. And with the recent advances in LSI and microprocessor technology, VHF radios—with all the bells and whistles a pleasure-boat owner could ever want —are cheap. For under $300 it is possible to buy a radio with eighty-eight channels, auto-scan, dual watch, programmable memory, auto-revert to channel 16, U.S., Canadian, and international frequency usages, a built-in hailer, keyboard entries for channels, and a score of other features. You may or may not want some of these features; if reliability and dependable communications are your main concern, you may elect instead to buy a radio with fewer features and a more rugged construction.

FEATURES

Auto-Scan   It is sometimes called scanning or programmable scanning. What it does is pick its way through the full range of channels, or a selected number of channels, stopping for a few seconds on each one before going on. If you're an avid fisherman and want to listen to the commercial chatter or the gossip from the boats that are clustered around buoy 15, or if you are a compulsive telephone caller and want to scan all the public channels to find one that is free, or if you like to spend your time at home listening to police and fire calls with a scanner, auto-scan might be useful. If you go out on the water to get away from telephones, or if simplicity and reliability are something you want in your electronics, a scanner is the last feature you want.

Dual Watch   It is sometimes called "sea watch" or "dual monitoring." For a commercial boat, which must by law maintain a watch on channel 16, this is a useful feature. It means that they can use one radio instead of two. But unless you want your own radio conversations interrupted by people calling for "radio checks," you may find this a seldom-used feature.

Auto-Revert to Channel 16   Again, for commercial vessels which establish contact on channel 16 before switching to another channel, and which must maintain a radio watch on channel 16, this is a useful feature. But most sail- and power-boat owners use channels like 9, 68, 70, 72, or the public channels for direct calls. The auto-revert may in fact prove annoying if it cannot be turned off, because every time you put the microphone back into its holder, the radio switches to 16 and must then be switched back to the channel you usually use.

International Channels   In many areas of the world, especially Europe, the channel allocations are different, with duplex frequency assignments for channels that are used for simplex communications here.* If you really will be sailing in Europe or other waters that require the different frequency assignments, the ability to switch and thus cover all 61 or 78 or 90 channels might be important. Otherwise, there is only added complexity and the possibility of confusion or panic

---

* In simplex operation, both transmit and receive are on the same frequency. In duplex operation, the transmit and receive are on different frequencies, which ostensibly would allow simultaneous conversation, as on a telephone. The public channels in the U.S. are duplex, except that the procedures permit only semi-duplex operation, which is why you have to explain to your mother-in-law that you and she cannot talk at the same time on the marine radio.

when the "domestic/international" switch is accidentally set improperly. For Canadian waters it is usually sufficient to install the one or two channels required for Canadian weather stations.

Hailer   If the radio has provision for an external speaker, it can be adapted to blast your voice from the microphone to the speaker. Of course if you really need a hailer you can buy one quite cheaply and have the versatility of pointing it wherever you want, and of not having to disconnect and reconnect the speaker and reset the various switches to disable and enable the hailer option. On many radios, if the hailer option is accidentally enabled the radio doesn't work; it can take minutes of valuable time to figure out what is wrong. Both radios and loud-hailers are used in close quarters where you don't usually have time to switch back and forth from one setting to the other.

Keyboard Station Entries   Keyboard data entry is essential on a computer or a loran, and push-button phones are certainly faster. But phone numbers are at least seven digits, as are TDs and latitude or longitude positions. VHF channel selections are only one or two digits. Ask yourself which is easier for you: (a) press 6, press 8, press "enter" (three steps); or (b) turn a dial to 68 (one step)?

The feature count is not the most important difference between VHF radios. The important differences are reliability, frequency stability, sensitivity, selectivity, and power output. Fancy features are relatively cheap to include: a chip can give you scanning, and a few resistors and diodes can expand a synthesized radio to more channels. On the other hand, reliability, stability, and sensitivity are expensive to build into a radio: they require expensive oversized power transistors and heat sinks, hard-wired construction (that one is rare now), or commercial- and/or computer-grade components. A list of features often won't mention such things as a heavy-duty microphone and cable, and at first glance a well-made microphone and cable doesn't look very different from a cheap one. But the cheap one will begin to wear out when it is pulled at the wrong angle—as they all are. And you can be fairly certain that the moment when it chafes through will be the moment when you have lost all power and are drifting toward a breakwater. That is precisely the moment when multiple channels and scanners and dual watch and all those buttons matter much less than just being able to get on that VHF and reach someone.

Radios don't all perform the same. Today almost every radio is rated at the legal maximum of 25 watts. On a test bench, with a steady input voltage of 14 volts, most radios will produce close to that rated 25 watts of output in an intermittent test of ten seconds on and one minute off. A really good radio will put out close to 25 watts after fifteen minutes of transmitting, even when the input voltage drops to 12 volts or less.

The difference between the good radio and the cheaply built radio is that the former will probably have oversized power transmitters and large heat sinks to dissipate the heat from those transistors. The smaller unit is rated for intermittent usage. Most boaters actually use the radio for intermittent usage, but there may come a time when the mast has come down, the engine won't start, the batteries are low, and you have to call over and over again to raise the Coast Guard. That's when you want the unit that keeps up its output.

There is also a great difference in "punch" between differ-

ent radios. Many times one boat in a raft-up can reach a distant station that no one else can raise. Some boats have no trouble reaching the New York marine operator from Stonington, Connecticut, a distance of some 90 miles. Sometimes the difference may be power output or the quality and height of the antenna installation. More often it has to do with the cleanliness and stability of the radiated signal, a lack of spurious radiation that puts all of the available power into useful signal. And many times the difference in effectiveness is not in transmitting but in reception. A more sensitive and selective radio can pick out the weak signal that another set will miss. After all, if you can't hear the other station you really can't communicate with them. They may hear you call for help, but you won't know.

For most boat owners, the prime consideration in a VHF radio should be reliability, which means more than not needing frequent service and repairs. It means knowing that when you pick up the mike and squeeze the button, it will transmit and be heard—even on low voltage, with an emergency antenna, and in an unfavorable location. You can find this kind of reliability in crystal-controlled radios, diode programmed radios, and synthesized radios. In general, it does not come cheaply, especially in the synthesized VHFs.

Synthesized radios are in fact cheaper to build than a high-quality crystal or diode programmed radio. But unless the components and circuit design are especially robust—which is expensive to engineer and manufacture—the synthesized radio is neither as reliable as the crystal or diode radio, nor as likely to stay on frequency and produce a clean signal. And if a component in the synthesizer fails, you are left with no channels, unlike a crystal or diode set which may get off frequency on one channel (rarely, actually) and remain functional on the others. There may be some bargains among the cheap, feature-laden synthesized radios, but in general, if the manufacturer has put so many features into a cheap radio it is likely that he has skimped on some of those basics, like sturdiness, frequency stability, sensitivity.

How much radio do you really need? How many channels will you use? You can get radios with as many as ninety channels, but do you really need or use more than twelve or twenty-four?

Few pleasure boaters will ever need more than the following channels, and most boat owners can get by with a smaller selection.

6	Intership emergency (required)
9	Commercial and private, ship to ship, ship to shore
13	Commercial bridge-to-bridge standby channel
12, 14	Port and bridge operations
16	Calling and emergency (required)
22	Coast Guard
24, 25, 26, 27, 28	Public channels (telephone)
68, 70, 72, 74	Ship-to-ship channels
84, 85, 86, 87	Public channels (telephone)
WX1, WX2, WX3	Weather

If you rarely make phone calls from the boat, you need only one or two of the public channels. In some areas channels 12 and 14 are rarely used, and noncommercial traffic may be so light that one or two channels from 9, 68, 70, and 72 suffice for ship-to-ship and ship-to-shore contacts. If you sail near ship traffic, 13 is a good idea; commercial skippers are often responsive to your requests if you call on *their* intership channel, especially if you respect the fact that they are on the water for a living.

Most boaters could get by with twelve or twenty-four channels, but it is getting difficult to find high-quality crystal-controlled or diode programmed VHF radios, like the Horizon Standard 25 or the ICOM M-25D. An inexpensive synthesized radio that is limited to twenty or twenty-four channels is not a good choice, because with most synthesized radios it is difficult or impossible to change the channel usage, and changes in channel assignments or your own plans may leave you with a useless unit. You will probably find that there are few special features you really need, so the real criterion among the many synthesized radios is quality.

How do you choose? A few radios have achieved legendary reputations, like the Horizon Standard 25, the ICOM M-25D, the ITT Decca STR-25, the Raytheon commercial-grade units, the Sailor RT 144AB, and the Modar Tritons. Some of these radios were so expensive to produce that they are no longer manufactured, so if you find one on a used boat, treasure it.

Among the newer radios, models are introduced, upgraded, and canceled so quickly that it is difficult to name outstanding radios. The published output, sensitivity, and selectivity figures on each radio won't really tell you much, because there are no standards governing how such measurements are made. You can learn a lot about a radio by asking marine electronics repairmen whether they know the unit.* Most repairmen are ornery and highly opinionated, but it's opinions

---

* Don't try the technique with a discount dealer. They will invariably give a great rating to the unit they are currently pushing, and since most discounters do no repair work and little warranty handling, it isn't clear what basis they have for their ratings.

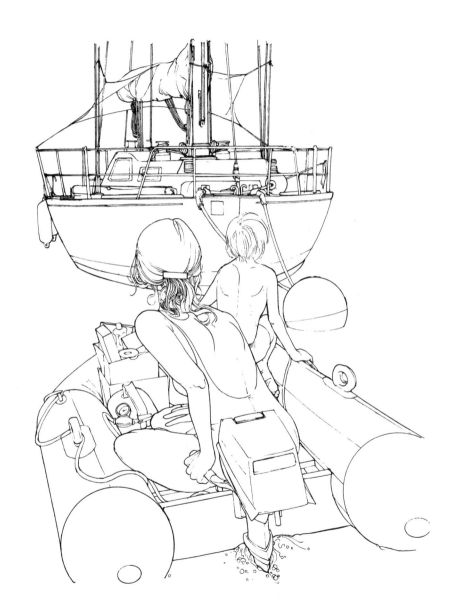

that you want. Ask which units break often, what breaks, and how difficult or easy they are to repair.

You can also learn something by examining a unit. Is the case sturdy, either metal or heavy plastic? Are the controls convenient to use, with knobs or buttons that are big enough to see and push or turn even when you're tired or it's dark? Can you read the dial? Try it under bright light and at odd angles. Examine the connection of the microphone cable. Is it a plug and socket or a sturdy strain relief? The cheaper units often have nothing more than a rubber grommet. After enough tugging, and when you least suspect or need it, the cable wears through. If you can get a peek inside, look at the heat sinks and the power transistors. Compare the size and the sturdiness with a unit like the Horizon 25, which has the heat sink mounted externally. Is the wiring neat? Are the component boards securely mounted?

For certain locations on a boat, or certain types of boats, there may be more specialized requirements. If the radio is to be mounted close to the cockpit, look for a radio with gasketed controls, like the ICOM or some of the Cybernet units. There is a difference between the water resistance of most radios and a unit like the ICOM that can take a hose turned on it. If the radio is to operate in a boat with loud engines, look for 3 to 5 watts of audio output and a noise-reducing microphone. Tone quality isn't important, but you want to be able to understand plain speech against the loud background noise. Finally, there is the question of mounting flexibility and, for some boats, anti-theft mountings. Most radios come with reversible front panels and mounting brackets, which makes them suitable for overhead and bulkhead mounting as well as shelf or under-shelf mounting. Make sure the radio will fit your boat and still leave enough room to remove it when you want to.

Finally, for the VHF radio and for all other electronics, make certain that the controls are easy for *you* to use. If your fingers always seem too big for small buttons, select a unit with a dial selector for stations. If the radio will probably be used by other people (family, crew, guests), it may be better to select a unit that is straightforward (turn it on and twist the dial to the station you want) instead of a radio that requires a sequence of commands. And if you have a special need for reliability (such as potential medical problems that would require immediate attention), it may be worth paying for a commercial-grade radio with features such as a separate crystal-controlled channel 16 that will function even if the synthesizer fails.

INSTALLATION

A VHF radio is one of the easiest items of electronics to install. It is also an item that is absolutely dependent upon a good installation if it is to function well. The best radio coupled to a lousy antenna with cheap coaxial cable, or with shoddily installed cable connectors, will be substantially less effective than an inexpensive radio in a good installation.

Antennas The choice of an antenna is not a difficult decision. Unless there is some special reason why the antenna cannot be mounted at the masthead, the choice for most sail-boats is a masthead whip, preferably a stainless whip with a base-loaded coil, such as those manufactured by Metz or Phelps-Dodge. The antennas are lightweight and low windage, and the range advantage of a masthead antenna is so great that any other location seems an unwise trade-off. There are cheaper masthead antennas available, such as the fiberglass whips that are sometimes offered in packages by discounters. The fiberglass whips are heavier, with much greater windage than the stainless whips. The claims of greater gain made by the manufacturers of the stainless whips are probably not correct, and in any case a high-gain antenna would not be desirable on the masthead of a sailboat.*

Coaxial Cable   For coaxial cable, unless the run is 20 feet or less, which is unlikely in any sailboat, stay away from the small RG 58U cables that are offered in package deals. Instead choose either RG8U, which is about ½ inch in diameter, or RG8X (sometimes called RG8M), which is slightly over ¼ inch in diameter. Be careful where you buy: all RG8U or RG8X cables are not the same. The quality is determined by the density of the copper shield and by the stability and effectiveness of the core material. The smaller RG8X cable actually has better statistical ratings in the VHF frequency range than the larger RG8U cable, but only because in ideal laboratory conditions the foam dielectric material of the smaller cable tests better. The problem is that the foam is heat sensitive, so that after long exposure to the sun, it can change shape and electrical characteristics. The larger cable is thicker-skinned and more rugged, and it is heavier and harder to thread through mast conduits and through interior joinery. Whichever you choose, make certain that the cable has not been kinked or coiled too tightly before you buy it.

* Gain in an antenna is obtained by concentrating the radiation of the signal. High-gain antennas broadcast a narrower angle of radiation, with an output pattern that looks more like a horizontal donut than the ball of a zero-gain antenna. Steerable antennas can concentrate the pattern even more. On a sailboat, and especially at the top of the mast where the motion of the boat is accentuated, an antenna with too much gain would produce a radiation pattern so flattened that as the boat rolled, pitched, and heeled the signals might be lost. Stick with a 3-decibel-gain antenna for masthead use.

The cables can be freely combined and joined together with coaxial connectors, as long as you confine yourself to 52-ohm cables.† You can use the smaller and lighter RG8X for the mast and the larger RG8U for the interior of the boat, as long as the connections are made with proper coaxial connectors. For the larger cable you need only the familiar Amphenol PL 259 male plug. To use the smaller cable you also need a UG176/U adapter for each plug. Make absolutely certain that it is a UG176/U, which fits RG8X, and not a UG175/U fitting made for the RG58U cables. The no-solder connectors are not adequate for a VHF radio.

Soldering Coaxial Cable   To attach one of the connectors, begin by doing a very careful job of stripping the end of the co-ax. Measure carefully and use a sharp knife to cut away

† Be careful not to confuse the widely available RG59U, a 75-ohm coaxial cable that is often used for cable TV installations and is almost exactly the same diameter as RG8X. The designation of the cable should be stamped or printed on the outer covering. Check for it.

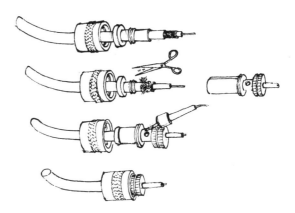

the outer cover. The easiest way to cut the braid without injuring the dielectric is with sharp scissors. Then the proper length of dielectric can be cut away with a sharp knife. A razor is too sharp for any of this work and will probably nick the inner conductor. Your goal is to strip the co-ax so that there is no possibility of a short between the inner conductor and the shell of the connector, and so there is enough inner conductor and braid to make good solder joints to the connector.

Solder with a low-wattage gun. Do it quickly, but be sure that you get a real solder joint, not a cold joint with a drop of solder on it. Then check with a VOM (volt-ohm meter) or a continuity checker to make certain that you have no resistance between the braid and the shell of the connector, and between the inner conductor and the pin of the connector. There should, of course, be no short between the inner conductor and the shell. Be sure to check both ends of a cable before it is installed with the antenna, because many antennas read a DC short from the inner conductor to the shield when checked with a VOM, and you will not be able to analyze the cable in place without disconnecting the antenna.

Connections Every installation should have a disconnect at the base of the mast, or perhaps at deck level, so that the mast can be removed for winter storage or for rigging work. If possible, the connection should be made under the deck, rather than above deck. It is possible to waterproof a coaxial connection, and there are special (and expensive) dry-plugs made for the purpose. If you must have an above-deck connection and need to waterproof it, Radio Shack sells a gray mastic for the purpose which, though messy, does work. Otherwise, try to keep the wiring inside the mast until it gets below deck. And

if you have a deck-stepped mast, try to lead the connection inside so that it can be safely tucked up into the mast when the mast is stepped.

In threading cable up a mast or through the interior of the boat, avoid sharp turns and avoid pulling the cable through small holes. Any strain on the cable can dislocate the dielectric, and cable that is exposed to heat can quickly lose its effectiveness if it is pulled in a sharp turn. The exit at the top of the mast requires special care. The best installation is to exit through a slot, which can be covered with silicone and/or tape. If an anti-drip loop is put into the cable where it joins the antenna, you will prevent a steady flow of water down the cable into the spar.

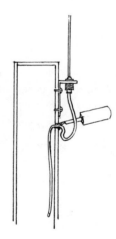

It is sometimes a trick to juggle the VHF antenna, masthead wind vane and anemometer, Windex, and masthead lights, especially if you also try to fit a burgee halyard. For security and to cut windage, the VHF antenna bracket should be fastened directly to the mast either with stainless pop rivets or with drilled and tapped machine screws. The connection between the cable and the antenna can be covered with heat-shrink tape or Navtec Rig-Rap tape, but a little grease will do a better job of keeping down corrosion and maintaining the electrical integrity. Ordinary black electrical tape doesn't really do anything for the connection.

Many boat owners like to carry a spare emergency antenna in case the vessel is dismasted. The tiny rubber-ducky antennas like those used on portable VHF radios are not as efficient as a simple quarter-wave antenna which rolls up for compact storage.

Power Finally, the VHF radio should be supplied with adequate DC power. The current draw of the average set is high enough on "transmit" that 14-gauge wire is the minimum for the connection to the electrical panel. If the wire run is more than 10 feet, use 12-gauge or 10-gauge instead. The power wires should be long enough to make removal of the unit easy.

There is no need for a separate ground with a VHF radio, unless you have an unusual electrical system. There is rarely an interference problem with VHF-FM radios.

Have a hardware store make up a tiny plastic or brass plaque with the station call letters to mount over the radio, and if your radio is frequently used by guests or others who are not familiar with the operation, type up a list of instructions to post on the navigation station bulletin board or to mount under a plastic sheet.

MAINTENANCE

VHF radios require very little maintenance. Most boat owners ignore the requirements for periodic frequency checks and retuning, but with synthesized units in particular, especially if the radio is seldom used and changes in effectiveness may go unnoticed, it is a good idea to take the radio in once a year to have a technician run through the channels and make certain that each channel is putting out a clean signal on the correct frequency.

17

LORAN

Although there are many claims and promises for the next generation of navigational electronics, including the Global Position System which is so accurate that the Defense Department is degrading the accuracy for civilian use to 100 meters (the absolute accuracy is said to be on the order of 10 meters!), for the next decade at least, Loran C will remain the primary navigational tool for coastal navigation in U.S. waters and other areas serviced by loran chains (generally waters which are of strategic importance to the U.S. Navy and the Coast Guard). Loran does not replace a sextant and chronometer for offshore navigation, and it is not a substitute for accurate and careful piloting in inshore waters, but it is a generally reliable, easy-to-use, and increasingly inexpensive navigational tool.

Loran C is based upon extremely accurate measurement of time intervals and the wide propagation of low-frequency (100 Hz) radio signals. Three or more transmitters, widely spaced, make up a loran chain, and each chain has a GRI (Group Repetition Interval) which serves as a signature and allows a loran receiver to identify the master station and "slaves" of a given chain. The signals of the different stations in the chain are coordinated so that they are transmitted together, and the loran receiver includes circuitry which not only identifies the different signals but measures the time differences (TDs) between the arrival of the signals. Since radio waves travel at the speed of light* and the position of the various loran stations is known, measurement of the time difference in the arriving

---

* Actually, the signals are slowed down by passage over land masses and by other factors. Through measurements of actual versus theoretical positions, the TD lines on charts are calibrated to incorporate the propagation differences.

signals from any two stations places the boat on the hyperbolic curve which is "proportionally" spaced between the two stations.

Add another line of position from two other TDs, and the intersection between the two lines is a loran fix. Unless the signal strengths are weak or are distorted by the use of sky waves instead of direct signals, or one of the lines of position is on that portion of the hyperbolic curve which extends from the "baseline" of the station, the system is remarkably accurate. Depending upon the geometry of the fix, the repeatable accuracy of a loran fix can be as precise as 50 feet.*

When Loran C receivers first came onto the market, it was thrilling to have a display of the two TDs in steady digital numerals. Compared to the complexity of tuning a Loran A receiver, the idea of picking off two TDs and plotting their intersection on a chart seemed simplicity itself. Now, even the most inexpensive loran receivers offer positions in latitude and longitude coordinates as well as TDs, programmable waypoints, range and bearing to the next waypoint, cross-track error and time to go to the waypoint, true course, ground speed, VMG (velocity made good toward the waypoint), automatic selection of secondaries, autopilot interfaces, and programmable or automatic latitude, longitude, and magnetic variation corrections. So ubiquitous have the features become that manufacturers have begun competing and advertising on the basis of miniaturization and teak cases, or sometimes unjustifiable claims of extreme accuracy or reliability.

With the exception of a few shoddily engineered and constructed units, most of the Loran C receivers on the market today are accurate and reliable. The more sensitive units are sometimes capable of settling more quickly on a signal, or perhaps picking out signals in marginal reception areas, but for cruising and racing in North American coastal waters, most receivers have adequate sensitivity. Where the units differ is in versatility, ruggedness, current draw, stability under changing electrical supply, and most important of all, ease of use.

FEATURES

Versatility   If you are planning to sail offshore, or to race or cruise in areas served by loran chains different from the loran stations serving your usual sailing area, the versatility of the loran receiver may be important. Most lorans have their notch filters factory-set for the area in which they are sold—East or West Coast—and will perform adequately under normal circumstances.† Many of the more expensive loran receivers have user-adjustable notch filters, multiple self-adjusting notch filters, and automatic selection of master and secondary loran stations—which could be valuable features if you sail out of the range of one loran chain and into another, or if you sail in the vicinity of a powerful military or commercial transmitter which might not have been filtered by the regular notch filter settings on your loran receiver.

* Repeatable accuracy is a much more useful concept with loran than absolute accuracy. The absolute accuracy of a loran fix depends upon the quality of the charts used (if the fix is from TDs) or the quality of the algorithm used to convert the TDs to latitude and longitude. In both cases, the fix depends upon how well the actual signals in a given area have been calibrated against the theoretical signals. Repeatable accuracy is a factor only of the geometry of the signals; many lorans will display an estimation of the repeatable accuracy of the loran fix at any location.

† Loran receivers are subject to interference from very-low-frequency transmitters, such as those used by the U.S. Navy in Annapolis or by the Canadian Navy in Halifax. Notch filters are included in loran receivers to filter out this interference.

Automatic Selection of Chains and/or Secondaries If you sometimes wake up and find yourself more than 1000 miles from where you expected to be, it is comfortable to know that your loran can automatically choose the appropriate chain of stations for position finding. Otherwise, automatic selection of the chain is an interesting, harmless, but not terribly useful feature. Automatic selection of secondaries is also harmless, if you can manually program the secondaries you want instead. In some cases the loran will choose secondaries that you know to be less useful in your area, whether because the geometry of the intersection of the TDs is bad or because experience has told you that one or another of the secondaries is unreliable.

Automatic Corrections The TD lines on most large-scale charts have already been corrected for the secondary path variations that affect loran signals.* When the loran is used with the built-in algorithms for converting TDs to latitude and longitude coordinates, the secondary path variations may introduce errors as large as a mile or so in position. Most lorans allow you to enter corrections for a given area, which you can determine by comparing the loran longitude and latitude figures for a known location with the charted figures. As you travel, you may need to recalculate the corrections every 20 or 30 miles, an operation which takes a minute or so when you are at a charted location. (A buoy, unfortunately, is not a

good location for measuring corrections, since the swing in location of a buoy on its mooring may be larger than the correction you are trying to introduce.) A few lorans, including Trimble, Micrologic, and some of the Northstar units, automatically calculate the secondary corrections; for the highest possible accuracy, you will need to add a final correction manually. If you sail over a wide area and frequently use the latitude and longitude readouts, or other loran functions which are computed on the basis of the latitude and longitude computations, automatic corrections may be a good idea.

Automatic Magnetic Corrections Lorans which offer such data as Course Made Good or Bearing to Waypoint need the local magnetic variation to complete their calculations. Some require that you enter the magnetic variation every time the loran is turned on; others will either store a figure in memory or calculate the local variation on the basis of a hard-coded algorithm. Because it is easy to forget to enter the magnetic variation, a loran that stores the variation or calculates it is a good choice. The algorithms to calculate the variation are sometimes off by as much as 1 degree, but usually allow a manual entry for fine correction.

Alarms Many lorans offer a variety of alarms, such as an anchor watch, off-course alarm, or arrival alarm, in addition to the basic alarms or lights to indicate a blink status at the loran transmitting station or a dangerously low SNR.† The

---

* In general, there are two corrections that need to be made to the theoretical TDs that could be plotted as hyperbolic curves on a chart. First, signals travel at a different speed over land and water, so the TD lines have to be corrected to account for the slowing of signals that travel over land. Second, major obstructions, such as mountains or prevailing atmospheric conditions, can affect the timing of the arrival of signals enough to require corrections.

† SNR (signal-to-noise ratio) is the strength of the loran signal over the ambient radio "noise." A loran manual will advise you of the minimum SNR for reliable tracking or signal acquisition on the loran. Unfortunately, each manufacturer uses a different measuring system. The figure should be easily accessible with a button push or two, so it can be checked from time to time, especially when the loran appears to be acting up.

anchor watch is supposed to beep or shriek or whatever if you drift away from the initial position programmed in when you anchored. In theory, as soon as you are dragging your anchor the alarm wakes you. The problem in most instances is that if you put in a large enough figure to avoid false alarms from a harmless change in the tide or the wind, you will probably have dragged into a rock pile before the alarm goes off. The waypoint alarm tells you that you are within a certain distance of a programmed waypoint. If you generally sail shorthanded in foggy conditions, a waypoint alarm could enable you to "listen" to the loran while you are on deck steering. Another alarm on some units signals that you are a certain distance (in miles or TDs) off the rhumb line to a waypoint. The last alarm would presumably wake a helmsman who fell asleep. On the whole, alarms are not the most useful features on a sailboat.

Routes Some lorans group or chain waypoints into routes, the idea being that as you approach one waypoint, the loran automatically switches to the next waypoint on the route. For a lobster fisherman who has programmed his pots into a morning collection route, or a cruising sailor who must frequently thread a long channel, it is a superb feature. For most sailors, it is more convenient to be able to switch easily and quickly from any waypoint to any other waypoint. Unfortunately, on some lorans the organization by routes makes it less convenient to select or program waypoints in the random order of the average race around the buoys or point-to-point cruise. The last thing you want is to be fighting with your loran in the minutes before the start of a race or as you approach an unfamiliar harbor.

Sensitivity Some advertisements and some dealers make a great fuss about the superior sensitivity of one loran receiver over another. In fact, except for marginal reception areas like the Caribbean or Baja California, the sensitivity of most loran receivers is more than adequate. Indeed, oversensitivity, rather than inadequate sensitivity, is a common problem. There are some loran transmitters, such as the station on Nantucket, which are well within normal cruising and racing waters. An oversensitive unit will sometimes go bonkers if it is too close to a transmitting station.

Accuracy Except for the difference in the quality and extent of automatic corrections that a loran may apply to a received signal, the accuracy of a loran is a theoretical rather than a qualitative measurement. The fact that some lorans read out in hundredths on TDs or in tenths of a second on latitude/ longitude is not really a reflection of accuracy, since the last digit is rarely steady or repeatable, and it is impossible to plot to that kind of accuracy on most charts. It may be satisfying to think that the loran is locating itself not only in the anchorage but at the right end of your boat, but even with the best possible signal reception and station geometry, repeatable accuracy closer than 50 to 100 feet is nearly impossible to achieve. The geometry of the stations determines the repeatable accuracy of the loran, and unless a loran is faulty or is being used for marginal signals or sky-wave signals, which is not generally the case for most sailing in U.S. waters, all lorans have acceptable accuracy. If you are using a loran with latitude and longitude and are too lazy to apply the corrections to positions, or if you use old charts on which the TD lines have not been corrected, or if you are sailing out where the loran signals are marginal, you will be off. Otherwise, any decent loran will come up with the right answers, eventually.

Acquisition Time   Some lorans acquire and settle very quickly; others can take five minutes or even longer, especially in weak signal areas. If you generally sail in weak signal areas, or if you frequently turn your loran off to save electrical power, a unit with fast acquisition time makes sense.

Stability and Current Draw   Stability is nothing more than the ability to hold on to signals in changing conditions. Depending upon the quality of the receiver and filtering circuits, some lorans are far more able than others to filter out interference from sources like the big U.S. government transmitting facilities in Annapolis or the Canadian government facilities near Halifax. If you sail regularly near powerful low-frequency transmitters, stability of reception may depend upon the quality of the tunable or automatic noise filters in your receiver.

The other stability problems in receivers come from voltage drops, especially when the engine is started, and from internal interference from fluorescent lights, televisions, alternator noise, and gasoline ignition noise. Some units can tolerate low voltages and keep tracking. Others falter when the voltage momentarily drops. If you frequently start the engine with the loran on (for example to charge batteries in a distance race or on a long passage), stability at low operating voltages might be important. Sets also differ in the amount of current they draw. Generally, the current drawn by the receiver and loran computer is modest, but some displays, and especially units with remote displays, can draw a lot of current. If you will be using the loran for long sails, distance racing, or passage-making, a low-draw unit may be a better choice.

USER CONVENIENCE

A loran is the closest most boats come to an onboard computer, and the abysmal computer software terms of "human interface" and "user friendliness" are certainly appropriate for lorans. In the contest to distinguish their units from one another, the manufacturers have come up with all sorts of knob, button, dial, and command options. The cute tricks, like units that acknowledge every entry with "Aye, aye, Skipper!" may ultimately prove more annoying than engaging, especially when you find yourself screaming at the seemingly intelligent unit because any command more complicated than "display TDs" requires endless sequences of keystrokes that have to be memorized or looked up.

Some lorans seem to have been designed by sailors, or at least by people who took the time to see what information sailors would want from their lorans and the conditions under which the unit would usually be used. Other units seem to have been designed for the convenience of the programmers who encoded the system EPROMs, with little or no regard for what happens on a boat. If you have the luxury of a full-time navigator on your boat, almost any unit can be made to yield the information that is generally useful for sailing. Otherwise, you want to look for a loran that gives you quick and easy answers to the questions you most often pose. And in any case, make certain that the buttons are large enough to find easily, and easy to push when you have fairly complex sequence of figures to enter. If you sail at night, a backlighted keyboard may be a convenience.

Where Am I? It shouldn't require more than a single key to get a present position in TDs or in latitude/longitude. Whether the two lines of position are displayed alternating in one window or simultaneously in two is much less important than the ease of retrieving the information. Watch out for units that interrupt the display with repeated reminders of what you are looking at, sometimes so frequently that you cannot concentrate long enough to plot the position.

Range and Bearing Most lorans allow you to program in from ten to a hundred or more waypoints, and offer a readout of the present range and bearing to the currently selected waypoint. The information is useful for cruising or racing, passage-making or around the buoys, and should be readily accessible with a minimum of button pushing.

Course Made Good and Ground Speed An averaging function that tells you the course and speed over the ground you have made during the last averaging period (the period is adjustable on the better lorans; you can use a longer period for rough water, which will keep gyrations of the boat from distorting the readout). If you have been steering 110 degrees, which is the bearing to the mark, and your course made good on the loran is only 104 degrees, you know that leeway, current, or a combination of the two* is affecting your course. Contrasting your speed through the water (from your knot

* Or a badly adjusted compass or a carelessly programmed loran . . .

meter, assuming the meter is correctly calibrated) with the ground speed on the loran will tell you if you have current helping or hindering you. Course made good and ground speed should be accessible with a minimum of keystrokes.

Changing Waypoints Whenever you round a mark or pass a waypoint on a cruise, you will want to change to another waypoint. It should be a simple sequence of keystrokes, and if there are enough waypoints you can often assign them numbers that correspond to buoy numbers (Waypoint #2 is Red Bell Buoy #2, etc.). A few lorans offer the option of assigning alphanumeric names to the waypoints, but if the keyboard doesn't include a full complement of alphabetic keys, the sequence for entering a name becomes so cumbersome that this feature is really designed mostly for the advertising photograph that shows "HOME" in one window and the course in the other.

Programming To use the waypoint feature, you have to be able to enter the waypoints into the computer, usually in TDs or latitude/longitude. Extrapolating the exact position of a buoy in lat/lon requires nothing more than a pair of dividers. Extrapolating TDs is a little trickier, because the TDs are hyperbolic curves, not straight lines. If the algorithm used by the loran to convert lat/lon to TDs works well, lat/lon entry is usually easier. But just as important is the sequence of buttons required to enter a waypoint position. Is the sequence "natural," like [waypoint lat] [4][1] [2][6] [0][9] [enter]? Or is there a bizarre set of entry codes that you will probably forget from one weekend to the next?

Display As important as all of these features are, they are useless if the display of the loran isn't large enough and bright enough to read quickly and easily. Most manufacturers are now using liquid crystal displays, but the LCDs vary widely in their readability, especially at acute angles or with bright sunlight shining on the display. Try to check the display before you buy a unit; take it out in the sunlight or to a window that will imitate the conditions on a boat. Otherwise it may be necessary to mount the unit in a less than desirable position, just to make the display readable. Also, the display should be simple, rather than cluttered. In the sanctity of a marine electronics showroom, displays that tell you everything from the distance to Shanghai to the course to Lisbon are impressive. On a boat, heeling at 30 degrees and with water dripping off your sou'wester onto the loran, the only thing you want is a quick, clear readout. You want keys that you can find effortlessly and press when your fingers are wet and swollen. And you want a unit that can tolerate spray, knocks, or the slam of the boat falling off a wave.

INSTALLATION

A loran is not difficult to install, but the difference in performance between a properly installed loran and a carelessly installed unit is marked. If the ground connection is inadequate, if the antenna and preamplifier are thoughtlessly positioned, or if simple precautions are not observed in checking for signal strength and interference, a potentially accurate and sensitive instrument may become marginal in performance.

The electrical connections are simple. If the loran is near the distribution panel, 14-gauge wire should suffice. Other-wise, increase the size. The instructions will probably tell you to connect the loran directly to the battery, but if the circuitry leading from the batteries to the distribution panel is adequate, it is neither necessary nor desirable to connect the loran directly to the battery.

Then, ground the receiver. The ground wire should be 10-gauge stranded wire or larger. Green-jacketed wire is traditional for a ground, but it will certainly work just as well with any other color of cover. Just be sure you label the wire if it is another color so you or someone else won't be confused someday. A ring terminal should be crimped and soldered on the end and securely fastened to the ground screw of the receiver.

Then, lead the wire to either a keel bolt (if you have external ballast) or a bronze through-hull fitting. Do not try to hook into a bonding system or to use the engine block as a ground; if possible, your ground should be isolated from the bonding system that probably does tie to the engine block.* If you are using a keel bolt, which is probably stainless steel, you can clean an exposed end of the bolt with bronze wool and clamp the stripped ground wire to the bolt with a hose clamp; or you can drill and tap the end of the exposed bolt and use a small machine screw (8-32 is big enough) to fasten a soldered terminal to the keel bolt. The hose clamp is easier but less reliable, since the exposed copper wire will corrode in contact with salt water and the stainless fitting, and in time the contact will be less than ideal. You can try tinning the wire first (coat-

---

* If you have any problems with galvanic or electrolytic corrosion on the boat, or if you cannot find a decent ground which is isolated from the bonding system, you may want to wire a 50-volt 100-microfarad nonpolarized capacitor in series with the ground lead. The capacitors are stocked by the larger radio/electronics dealers.

ing clean copper wire with solder), but even a tinned wire will corrode in the bilge. On the other hand, it is no simple task to drill the keel bolt for a machine screw. Use a powerful drill, a very sharp bit, and plenty of cutting compound. Solder the wire to a ring terminal of the correct size, make certain that the terminal and the mating surface of the bolt are clean and bright, and use a locknut for the screw.

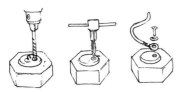

To use a bronze through-hull fitting as a ground, look for one of the mounting bolts long enough to extend beyond its nut. If one does, get a bronze nut to fit, solder on a ring terminal, and make sure the surfaces are clean. If none of the bolts are long enough, you can either fasten the clean wire to clean bronze with a hose clamp; find a grounding fitting at an electrical supply house (it looks like a hose clamp with a screw on it for the wire, and is probably made of copper), which should be more compatible with the bronze fitting than a stainless hose clamp; or you can drill and tap a thick part of

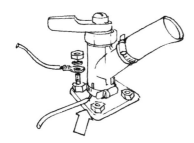

the base of the through-hull for a bronze machine screw. The bronze will be easy to drill, but be careful that you don't damage the through-hull.

A few units also require a separate grounding wire from the coupler to the receiver. A covered, stranded 14-gauge wire is usually sufficient. Any connections should be soldered rather than relying on crimp-on butt connectors.

Once you have a good ground, the next problem is finding the right position for the preamplifier and the right kind of antenna. In most locations, a simple whip antenna, usually an 8-foot CB antenna, is optimum. Some lorans, like the Micrologic units, come with a shorter whip instead, and there is no advantage to installing a longer whip. If you are using a whip, the best place to install it is usually on the stern pulpit (pushpit). Most couplers can be fastened to the pushpit with a pair of hose clamps, and nothing more complicated is needed. Another option is to buy one of the extenders that mount on a ratchet VHF mount and put the coupler and whip on top of the extender. Unless you are in an area of marginal reception, the extender probably won't be necessary.

To find the optimum location, mount the antenna temporarily, turn the loran on, let it settle, then push whatever sequence of keys is needed to read SNRs (signal-to-noise ratios) for the master and the secondaries that you usually use. Then try different positions for the antenna until you find a position that yields the highest SNRs. If the cable from the coupler is too long, it can usually be shortened. Many units now use a multiplexed coaxial cable to connect the coupler to the receiver; there is no harm in cutting off the excess cable and installing a new coaxial cable fitting on the loran end.

If you have a ketch or a yawl, the pushpit won't be usable.

Mounting the coupler and whip on the top of the mizzenmast will work, although you will have a long feed in cable and may in some cases need an extension. Most units now use ordinary RG58U coaxial cable, and an extension can be bought or made. If the coupler is wired with special cable, you will need to obtain an extension from the manufacturer.

If you have an insulated shroud or backstay that you are not using for any other purpose, such as a shroud that once served as an AM or Loran A antenna, it may be usable as a Loran C antenna, especially if your usual sailing area is not near any loran transmitters. To use a long wire antenna, position the coupler (preamplifier) as close to the antenna as possible and connect the antenna socket on the preamplifier to one end of the insulated stay with a length of insulated stranded wire. A small hose clamp is adequate to connect the wire to the stay, and a correctly sized machine screw and terminal will connect the wire to the coupler. The coupler can even be mounted belowdecks and the wire run up through a waterproof through-deck connector such as the ones sold for use with small coaxial cables.

A long wire antenna (stay or shroud) will probably work for most locations, and may work very well in low-signal-strength areas. If you get too close to a loran station, such as the station in Nantucket, you may find that the additional signal strength blocks your receiver. The solution is simple: just undo the connection between the coupler and the backstay or shroud, leaving only the little pigtail from the coupler as an antenna. You will probably find that it works just fine without the antenna, although the set may take longer to settle. When you get 25 miles away from the offending station, you can reconnect the pigtail to the antenna.

Once a unit is installed and working, check it with every possible combination of engine and electrical accessory. The usual offenders in loran interference are the alternator, gas engine ignition systems, fluorescent lights, and televisions. By turning each accessory on and off with the loran running, you can usually determine which is the guilty offender. Another way to check is to take a beacon-band radio direction finder, or if one isn't available, a broadcast-band receiver tuned off of a station at the bottom of the band. Use the receiver as a "snooper" to find where the offending interference is strongest. The hiss or static from the receiver should get louder as you approach the fluorescent fixture or other noise generator.

Interference problems can often be cured by moving units and/or wiring. If not, the next step is to try a filter, such as those made by Marland. Make certain that the filter you purchase is large enough, and if necessary experiment in locating the filter in different places in the wiring. Sometimes a filter in the wiring to the offending light or television will help, but often it is necessary to put the filter directly into the wiring to the loran and close to the loran receiver, because the wires between the filter and the loran will pick up interference.

There is almost never an interference problem that cannot be cured, so you shouldn't settle for an installation that requires you to not use the engine while the loran is on or to make some other compromise.

There are two accessories that can make loran use far more convenient and pleasurable. First, if you are using TDs rather than latitude and longitude for your position fixing, get one of the laminated interpolating cards that are usually given away free by electronics dealers. Using the card to plot your positions is much faster than using the interpolation table on the charts. Second, if you ever have anyone else use the loran, make up an "idiot sheet" that lists the steps necessary for typical usage: position finding, selecting waypoints, finding range and bearing, true course and ground speed, course made good and velocity made good. If the loran is simple to use and the steps are listed at the navigation station, it will be possible for anyone to step below—no matter how busy you are—and to give a quick fix or a quick piece of information that you, at the helm, may need in a hurry. Add another list of pre-encoded waypoints for race marks or cruising points that you commonly use, and you will find that the loran ceases to be a magic black box and instead becomes a tool that everyone can use.

18

BLACK BOXES

L oran and VHF are generally the first two electronics units bought for a boat, but there are many other devices that can be effective for navigation, entertainment, or communication. Depending upon sailing area or style, a boat might find one or more of the following "black boxes" indispensable: radio direction finder, auxiliary receiver, satellite navigation, Omega, single sideband transceiver, radar, radar detector, Weatherfax, Navtex, autopilot, dead-reckoning navigator, stereo.

RADIO DIRECTION FINDERS

With the widespread use of loran, radio direction finders have been relegated to backup status in most U.S. coastal waters. Yet there are many areas of the world where RDF is the primary coastal navigation system. Even in areas where strong and well-placed loran stations are available, RDF is a useful auxiliary navigation system for those times when a loran station is suddenly, unaccountably on "blink" status, or when a Navy experiment presents an unexpected strong interfering signal that temporarily zaps your loran reception, or when your normally trustworthy loran decides to take a brief vacation to electronic limbo.

Three kinds of RDFs are available, generally with coverage of the marine and aircraft beacon band, the AM broadcast band, and sometimes the marine 1.6 to 3.0 MHz band: automatic radio direction finders, fixed units with rotating antennas, and hand-held units. There are also many units that are sold as radio direction finders but which in fact are little more than entertainment receivers with rotating antennas. These units may provide passable reception of Michael Jackson, but they rarely yield any navigation information more useful than the direction of New York City from the western end of Long Island Sound.

For a commercial vessel or a large motor-sailer that has a frequent need for radio bearings, the automatic units—which require a fairly large external antenna—are incomparable. Si-Tex, Newmar, and King, among others, make units which with a few pushes of the buttons will give you a bearing; in England and Europe there are units on the market that will actually calculate a position from the bearings. These units should not be confused with the receivers that are automatic only in that there is an antenna on top turned by a small motor inside. A real automatic receiver will have an external antenna that must be mounted on the housetop or somewhere up in the rig and does its tuning electronically rather than by turning the antenna.

Most of the tabletop units with rotatable antennas are built to double as both entertainment receivers and RDFs, and unfortunately they do a poor job of both. The old Benmar 555 and the current Newmar receivers are sensitive and selective enough to provide useful radio bearings; the Benmars can sometimes be picked up cheap secondhand and make a good auxiliary receiver. Few of the other brands of tabletop radios are very useful for real direction finding, although they can be used to get aviation weather or sometimes to get time ticks or weather bulletins.

The easiest units to use on a sailboat are the hand-held receivers, such as the excellent Locata units made in England. The new Epsco digital finder is also a sensitive unit, and the Brooks & Gatehouse RDF units, either the older model or the RDF finder for the new Homer receiver, are reliable and easy to use. The advantages of a hand-held unit are that they give bearings to the sending station directly, without requiring a simultaneous reading of the steering compass; with a headset and/or a visual null indicator, it is usually easy to know exactly when the station is zeroed in; and the portability of the unit means that the readings are less likely to be affected by the rigging or the lifelines of the boat—both of which can throw a reading off by enough to put you on the rocks. The only disadvantage of the hand-held units is that some of them do not receive frequencies outside the beacon band, which means that they are less useful as auxiliary receivers for aviation weather or SSB (single-sideband) broadcasts.

VHF-band radio direction finders are now available, either as stand-alone units or as add-on accessories for a VHF radio. For a fisherman who wants to home in on another boat that is reporting successful catches, or for a Coast Guard rescue team homing in on a boat making a distress call, they may be very useful. For position finding they are all but useless, since there are almost no VHF stations in calibrated locations and position finding on VHF frequencies is inherently less accurate than position finding on HF (beacon- or broadcast-band frequencies).

AUXILIARY RECEIVERS

In coastal waters, a boat rarely needs more than a VHF radio with weather channels and perhaps a broadcast-band receiver for news and as a thunderstorm alert.* For offshore

* An AM radio will pick up the static from a nearby thunderstorm, or a large distant thunderstorm, long before the VHF stations get around to issuing a thunderstorm warning. On days when the clouds look threatening, it is sometimes useful to leave an AM radio on with the dial set between stations. FM radios, including the marine band VHF, will not pick up the same static, which is why they are more reliable for short-range communication than the old 2–3 MHz AM band.

sailing, a receiver that covers the frequency range from 1.6 to 30 MHz can be used to pick up time ticks to recalibrate the chronometer for celestial navigation as well as offshore weather bulletins, facsimile broadcasts for a Weatherfax machine, shortwave news and entertainment broadcasts, ham broadcasts, and SSB marine-band broadcasts. There are many excellent receivers made by companies that produce ham radio transceivers, such as Drake, Yaesu, Kenmore, and ICOM, and the Brooks & Gatehouse Homer is a superb all-band receiver. There are also less expensive units available from Radio Shack and from Sony and some of the other Japanese electronics companies which may prove adequate. Frequency stability, ease of acquiring a station (which means either digital or smooth vernier tuning), and reliability should be the main criteria for the selection of an all-band radio. Most radios, even those with built-in antennas, will require a long wire antenna for optimum reception; an insulated backstay or lifeline is excellent, but a wire strung around the interior along the hull/deck joint is often adequate.

SATELLITE NAVIGATION

Satellite navigation is not a substitute for loran. Sat nav is a worldwide system with extraordinary accuracy, but under the current system (the new GPS system will change things), satellite fixes can be as much as six hours or more apart in many waters, which means that a sat nav unit requires careful dead reckoning between fixes. Most of the better units incorporate interfaces to electronic compasses and the knot meter, and automatically calculate the DR position between fixes, but for coastal sailing loran is simpler and more accurate because the fixes are continuous. For offshore sailing, especially beyond the range of the loran chains, sat nav is a splendid system in a boat that can maintain the power required to keep the sat nav unit on twenty-four hours a day. If the sat nav is being relied on for offshore position fixing, there should be a provision for auxiliary power, a second battery or even dry cells, and an alarm to report that the system has switched to secondary power. The reliability and accuracy of sat nav should not be considered an excuse to leave the sextant, tables, and chronometer at home.

Because the current satellite navigation system is due to be replaced by the promised GPS system, there is no government commitment to repair or replace the current satellites. Hence a sat nav receiver may not be a wise investment today.

OMEGA

Omega is a very low frequency long-range navigation system with worldwide continuous coverage, but with substantially less absolute accuracy than satellite navigation. Most yachts will opt for sat nav instead, since the dead-reckoning computers in modern sat nav receivers provide accuracy comparable to Omega for the intervals between satellite passes, along with the high precision of the position finding during the pass itself.

SINGLE SIDEBAND

The maximum reliable range of a VHF-FM radio for communication with land stations is about 50 miles. There are exceptions: when the antenna on the boat is at the masthead and the land station antenna is elevated, it is sometimes possible to maintain communications as far out as 100 miles. For reliable communications beyond the range of VHF, SSB is the answer.*

There are essentially two kinds of SSB radios. The larger units, with power in the 100- to 150-watt range (or up to the 1000-watt range) and with keyboard or dial selection of thousands of frequencies in bands from the 1.6 MHz band up to the 20 MHz band, are built for twenty-four-hour worldwide communication. The wide choice of frequencies is necessary because the frequency bands from 2 to 30 MHz are fickle in their effectiveness at different times of day, different seasons of the year, and different intervals in the cycle of sunspot activity. A band that yields reliable communications in the range of 3000 to 5000 miles during the daytime in May may be worthless for more than line-of-sight communication on a December evening. Propagation charts are available that indicate a good frequency range to try for various times of year and times of day, but during various cycles of sunspot activity, the propagation of SSB signals can be surprisingly unpredictable.

A good installation of an all-band SSB transceiver requires a separate tunable antenna coupler and a very good ground, usually in the form of a substantial area of copper mesh laid

up in the fiberglass or installed inside a lazarette.† It is not an installation for an amateur, and FCC regulations require that a licensed technician certify the installation. Much of the expense of an SSB installation can be saved by mounting the unit and the antenna coupler, and perhaps installing the DC wiring, before the technician is summoned to complete the installation and tune the unit.

For communications in the range from 50 to 1000 miles, there are now a number of less expensive SSB transceivers available, many of which can be owner-installed. Typically these units offer crystal-controlled frequency selection of nine to twelve channels in the 1.6 to 9 MHz bands and power ranges of 25 to 100 watts. They use half the current of the bigger units, require less tuning, and are somewhat more forgiving in their antenna, antenna coupler, and ground requirements. In many cases a keel is adequate as a ground, and if the antenna can be located close to the transceiver, it is possible to get away with a total installation cost of under $1000.

The caveats that apply to a more complex installation should still be observed: (1) keep the wiring from the antenna coupler to the ground as short and as heavy as possible; use #4 or larger twisted copper wire, or flat copper strap; (2) use a vertical antenna, either an insulated section of the backstay or a 23-foot (or 35-foot) antenna mounted as far as possible from other antennas and rigging, and as close as possible to the antenna coupler; (3) make certain that the DC wiring from

---

* For very-long-range communications, ham radio is an alternative, and there are networks of ham operators who regularly monitor certain frequencies for contact with yacht-based stations. The operators also have the ability to "patch" a ham call through to the phone lines. But direct emergency communication with the Coast Guard, long-range communication with the marine operators, and reliable twenty-four-hour communication in coastal waters beyond the range of VHF require SSB on the marine frequencies.

† A steel or aluminum vessel can use the hull itself as a ground for an SSB installation, but extreme care has to be taken to make certain that the entire electrical system is insulated from the hull, and that no other systems, such as the loran, share the ground.

the switch panel is large enough to carry the amperage required while transmitting without any significant voltage drop.

RADAR

It has often been joked that an enterprising dealer could make a fortune selling radar domes to boat owners who aspire to the look of a boat equipped with radar. No other electronics is as visible on a boat. And no other electronics presents as much windage and weight aloft, or makes power demands as great, as radar.

For coastal cruising in areas of heavy fog, extensive traffic, and dangerous coasts, radar can make the difference between relatively easy piloting and the anxiety of poking along a fog-shrouded coast, trying to pick out horns, lights, and the sounds of ships that seem close enough to run you down momentarily. But radar is not easy to use. Clutter from rain or dense fog, the ambiguity of shape of many objects, the difficulty of interpreting coastlines, and the confusing signals reflected from poor radar targets, such as a low beach, can make the interpretation of a radar screen a nerve-racking challenge. Radar requires hours of practice, comparing the radar image with a chart of the appropriate scale, before it is more than an entertaining toy.

The figures that are issued in conjunction with various units are more confusing than illuminating. Should you buy a 24-mile unit or a 48-mile unit? Raster screen display or rotating sweep trace? What features are useful?

Range   The theoretical range of a radar is approximately line of sight plus about 15 percent.

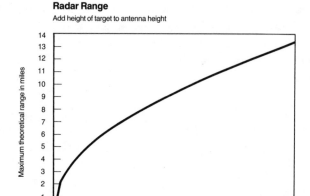

Radar Range
Add height of target to antenna height

Maximum theoretical range in miles (y-axis, 0–14)
Height of antenna in feet (x-axis, 0–120)

Along the Atlantic and Gulf coasts of the U.S. the coastline is low enough that shoreline features will not show up on radar until you are within a few miles. On the Pacific coast, where high mountains come close to the coastline, the longer-range radars will pick up the coast from farther off, but at the speed at which a sailboat maneuvers, it isn't clear that the added warning time is important. For piloting, a more important consideration in selecting a radar is the *minimum* range, which is determined by the length of the transmitted pulse.*

* Radar waves travel at the speed of light. Since the signal bounced back from the buoy or the coast cannot be heard while the radar is busy sending out a pulse, short-range reception is limited by the pulse length of the transmitted signal. In theory, a 0.1 microsecond pulse could pick up a target as close as 50 feet away; a 1.0 microsecond pulse could pick up a target as close as 500 feet away. Although most marine radar units use a pulse length of approximately 0.06 microseconds on short range, the theoretical performance is rarely achieved, and targets much closer than ¼ mile cannot be resolved well.

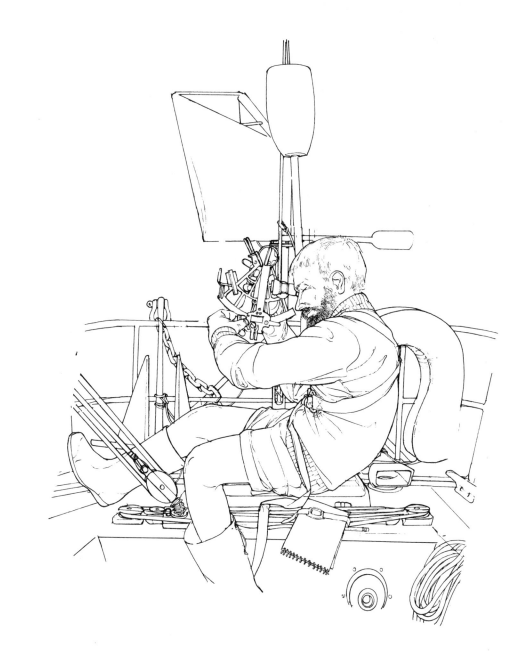

The working range of a unit is dependent upon the height of the antenna off the water as well as the elevation of the target that is being acquired. At the same time, the weight and windage of a radar antenna mounted on the mast of a sailboat has a clear effect on the performance of the boat. A 50-pound antenna mounted 25 feet off the deck is the equivalent (in righting moment) of removing 250 pounds of ballast from a point 5 feet below the center of gravity of the boat! And the windage of the radome is considerable. Most large racing boats that have radar for piloting and collision avoidance elect instead to mount the unit on a vertical pole at the stern, cutting down on the theoretical effective distance, and on the windage and heeling moment.

Resolution   Resolution, or the ability to separate targets, is determined by the span of the antenna. Whether in a radome or exposed, a short-span antenna (20 inches) will not be able to resolve targets closer than 5 degrees; a longer-span antenna (48 inches) can resolve targets within 2 degrees. The vertical beam of any unit used on a sailboat should be 25 to 30 degrees, so that the unit can function as the boat rolls and pitches.

Displays   There are two display types. The conventional sweep trace provides a circular display, which is swept at a rate that corresponds to the rotation of the antenna, usually twenty-five to thirty times per minute. The persistence of the display may be less than the two seconds taken for a full sweep, so that parts of the display are constantly fading and being refreshed. For most sailboats, the displays are either 5 or 7 inches in diameter, although the apparent diameter is greatly increased by the magnifying hoods that are available.

The advantage of the sweep trace is that the echoes are proportional to the actual size of the boats, buoys, and objects; shorelines are shown as continuous lines, with cliffs or bluffs returning stronger echoes than sloping beaches. Most features are sharply defined on a sweep trace display, with the resolution dependent upon the radar definition of the objects.* The disadvantage of sweep displays is that they cannot be seen without a viewing scope, which means that they cannot be used by a helmsman, except perhaps in a pilothouse boat.

A raster scan display works on the same principle as a video game or computer graphics display. The signal is digitized and displayed as a series of small dots (actually squares or rectangles) on a rectangular screen. Depending upon the unit, there will be from 250 to 750 squares or pixels in the horizontal and vertical axes. The display is illuminated at all times, with no fade-out on each rotation of the antenna. The brilliant image is bright enough to see without a hood in all but direct sunlight. The disadvantage of the raster scan display is that the images are limited in resolution in much the same way that the images of video games or crude computer graphics are limited. Straight lines that are not exactly vertical or horizontal come out looking like the edge of a saw blade, and the images are not exactly proportional to the size of the boats or other features that are seen by the radar. The end of a breakwater or a headland will not be as sharply defined as on a

---

* Objects which are sharply defined to the naked eye can be indistinct to radar. A large sailboat with full sail may hardly show up on a radar; a buoy with a radar reflector on top will be clearly defined. The solid planes, their reflective angles, and the material used determine the radar reflectivity and definition of an object. Spend a little time on a radar set near a fleet of fiberglass and wooden sailboats and you will be eager to buy and use a radar reflector for any sailboat you own.

sweep trace display, and it requires a little more practice to correlate the radar images with the chart. Generally, digital raster scan displays are easier for a beginner to use, but until higher-resolution digital displays become available, the raster scan units cannot match the detail and resolution of a sweep trace.

Features Useful features that are available on some radars are an electronic bearing marker (EBM), a variable range marker (VRM), and proximity alarms. The EBM is an electronically generated line on the radar screen which can be controlled to mark a desired bearing from the center of the display (the position of the boat) to any point on the azimuth. The relative bearing of the line is displayed numerically. The VRM is an electronically generated range circle that can be moved to a desired object on the screen. The range to the object is then displayed to $\frac{1}{10}$ mile. The proximity alarm projects a circle at a desired range from the boat; if any object—boat, buoy, or coastline—is picked up within the circle, an alarm is sounded.

Radar, unlike most position-finding instruments, requires more than a quick glance. It is possible to lash the helm or lock the wheel on a boat and scoot below, take a fix off the loran, plot it, punch up the range and bearing to the next waypoint, check the true course made good and ground speed, and get back to the helm before the boat has gone astray. On the other hand, radar requires either someone to take the helm, or an autopilot or self-steerer, because the display will rarely reveal all that you want to know without a careful comparison of the radar image and the chart. The display is analog, not numbers, and while the scales on the screen will help discern the distance to various items, it is far less precise than the digital readout of a loran or sat nav. Hence radar is not for the casual user and is certainly not a unit to acquire and install "just in case we need it sometime."

Installation Although the mechanical work for a radar installation can be done by a boat owner, FCC regulations require that the final check-out and initial tuning be done by a licensed technician. The receiver should, of course, be mounted away from any spray. Sunlight is usually not a problem, because raster screen displays are bright enough to be seen in the sun and tracer displays are usually equipped with viewing hoods. The usual problem is to find a location that allows an operator to glance back and forth from a chart to the screen.

For piloting, as opposed to collision avoidance, a transparent chart overlay that matches the mileage ranges on your chart lets you compare what you see on the radar with what is shown on the chart. You can make one out of a Mylar sheet by drawing rings (on the dull side of the Mylar) based on the latitude scale of the chart. If you add a compass rose (cut out of an old chart or perhaps from an old protractor), you can plot the bearings of objects on the radar screen.

RADAR DETECTORS

One reason for radar is collision avoidance, and for boats that sail offshore or in coastal shipping lanes, an alternative to radar is a radar detector. There are several units available which will sound an alarm when radar signals are detected, generally from a ship or tug maneuvering with its own radar on. The units are similar to the radar warning devices that are sometimes installed in cars. Most cannot precisely identify the direction of the signals, but they are sensitive enough to warn you to maintain a very sharp lookout for a vessel and perhaps to indicate whether the vessel is getting closer. Even with a good radar reflector in use, a sailboat does not represent a large target to most radars, so the security of knowing when someone is tracking you can be good insurance against collision.

WEATHERFAX

Weatherfax machines are neither complex nor difficult to use. Some are completely self-contained, with built-in receivers that require no more than a whip or long wire antenna. Others are easily hooked up to an auxiliary communications receiver or even to an SSB transceiver. There are dozens of stations transmitting weather maps, and for the offshore passage-maker the constantly updated maps can give important warning of disturbances or changing wind patterns. Some of the charts even present data in forms especially convenient to the mariner, with arrows (like those in pilot charts) to indicate predicted wind directions and velocity in addition to the usual symbols for fronts, convergence lines, and air masses.

For the coastal cruiser or racer, who is usually within range of VHF weather stations and for whom refuge from storms is usually only a matter of a few hours' sailing or motoring time away, Weatherfax makes little sense. The scale of the weather maps available won't tell a racer which side of the weather leg is favored, and the kind of weather information a cruiser needs to plan the next few days of his cruise is usually available from the weather maps in the newspaper and from a little interpretation of the patterns reported on VHF weather stations.

NAVTEX

Already popular in Europe and now undergoing testing by the U.S. Coast Guard, the Navtex system allows a boat to receive continuously updated weather and navigation messages which are automatically printed out on a compact self-contained printer, so that a message is received even when the navigator or skipper is not monitoring broadcasts. Anyone who has read the stories of missed weather forecasts during the Fastnet disaster will appreciate the automatic features of the Navtex. The receivers, which work on a frequency of 518 KHz, near the universal safety frequency of 500 KHz, are reliable in most weather and atmospheric conditions. All you need to do, once Navtex transmitters are operating in your area, is buy a suitable receiver, hook it up to a power source and an antenna, and you will get a regular printout of weather reports, navigation and hazard warnings, air-sea rescue alerts, ice reports, shipping forecasts, pilot warnings, and navigation alerts (such as inoperative loran stations). The set stores messages as they are received, using serial numbers to make sure that its memory is not cluttered with repeat broadcasts of messages that are already stored. The operator can use coding to select which categories of messages are to be printed out later. The units have a very modest current draw in the receiving mode and a tolerable current draw in the printing mode, and for many sailors who contemplate occasional offshore sailing,

Navtex may be a simple and inexpensive alternative to Weatherfax, and an alternative to constant monitoring of Coast Guard broadcasts on the HF bands.

AUTOPILOTS

Many of our images of sailing shape themselves around the excitement of a racing start or mark rounding, or the peaceful moments of a passage or an anchorage, but the reality of sailing is that hours and hours are spent tending the tiller or wheel. Before and after the excitement of a race there is the trip out to the start and back from the finish. And for every hour spent in quiet contemplation at the helm, there is another hour when you wish you had a hand or two free to hold a beer and a sandwich, or when you wish you could read on deck and let the boat steer itself. With an autopilot, you can.

Wind vanes were very popular years ago and are still seen both on offshore passage-making craft and on local cruisers that wear them as badges of honor, declarations of the seriousness of their credentials and intentions. The advantage of the wind vane, of course, is that it requires no electricity to operate, and for lengthy passages in steady trade winds it is reliable and effective, especially if the wind is not light and aft. The problem with wind vanes, aside from their size, weight, windage, and vulnerability to damage, especially around docks or other boats, is that in coastal cruising the wind is rarely steady enough for long enough to make full use of a wind vane.

The alternative is an autopilot, and with the availability of microprocessor-controlled sensing circuits, flux-gate (electronic) compasses, induction or photocell sensors for card compasses, and low-current, high-power servomotors, electronic autopilots have come into their own as highly reliable units.

The earliest autopilots worked by measuring course deviation and compensating with a course correction. The result was a see-saw course as the boat zigged and zagged across the course dialed into the compass, compensating one way and then the other, and in the process draining even the largest batteries in a few hours of use. Today's autopilots use deadband and sometimes proportional-response technology to cut down on the zigging and zagging and the corresponding power drain. A dead band is simply a band, usually of adjustable width (from 1 to 4 degrees), on either side of the selected course in which the autopilot will not take a corrective action. In smooth water the dead band can be narrow, to keep the boat very close to the desired course. In rough water, a narrow dead band would have the autopilot trying to correct for every wave, so the dead band is set broader and the boat is allowed to correct its own course, which many boats will do. Only when the boat strays beyond the dead band will the autopilot counter with a movement of the rudder. Proportional response, which is used on only a few autopilots, alters the rudder angle in proportion to the measured deviation from the desired course, producing a sharper rudder angle for major deviations and a much smaller correction for a minor deviation. All of the corrections made by an autopilot are relatively small. Indeed, experienced helmsmen are often astonished to see how well an autopilot can follow a course.

Autopilots come in two basic configurations—add-on units and permanently mounted systems—and with a variety of features that, like so many marine accessories, require a glossary to understand. The simplest units will have few of these adjustments. The most sophisticated will have many. Which you will choose or need depends on the use of your autopilot.

Adjustments

Sea state   Sea state, sensitivity, dead band, and yaw are different terms to refer to the adjustment of the width of the dead band. In some autopilots it is an internal set-and-forget adjustment; in most it is available on the unit or on a remote control, so that it can be adjusted to compensate for changing sea states.

Gain   Gain, rudder, ratio, and proportion factor (P) refer to the amount of rudder that is applied to correct a course error. A light boat with a spade rudder needs very little rudder to correct a typical deviation; a heavier boat with an attached rudder may need much more. In some autopilots the control also, or instead, regulates the speed of response of the rudder to the course change.

Counter Rudder   Counter rudder is the adjustment of how much the rudder is turned back to keep the course correction from oversteering. Watch a good helmsman steer a boat back to course and then make a minuscule correction to "steady her down" and you are seeing counter rudder. In some autopilots it is calibrated and forgotten. In others there is circuitry that sets the counter rudder proportional to the correction.

Bias   Bias, trim, and offset are various names for a control which allows you to set the autopilot to compensate for a persistent heading error, such as that caused by extreme weather helm. You can try to use bias to compensate for leeway or current, but it requires continuous refinements of the course.

The ultimate in sophistication is to couple the autopilot to the loran, so that the course steered can itself be corrected for the effects of current or leeway. Most lorans now have outputs that follow a standard protocol and can be read by autopilot circuitry, and many autopilot manufacturers offer optional control units to interface the loran signals to the autopilot. For a lobsterman who is making a circuit of pots in the morning, and who needs both hands free to hoist the pots while the boat steers itself to the marks, the link of loran and autopilot is ideal. If you are tempted to try such a setup, remember that neither the loran nor the autopilot will pay any attention to rocks, land, shoals, or other boats that are on the course.

The output of the autopilot unit can be linear, rotary, or hydraulic. The linear units use an aircraft control motor to turn a long threaded shaft; a collar rides on the shaft and converts the motion into a push-pull motion to steer the boat. The units that fit onto a tiller are linear controls, and some of the permanently attached units can use a linear control on an arm fastened to the rudder shaft.

Most permanently attached units are rotary controls, which use chains coupled into the drive mechanisms of the pedestal unit. Finally, for the few sailboats—usually motor sailers— that have hydraulic steering, there are special actuators which couple into the hydraulic steering controls.

Both temporarily attached systems and permanently mounted systems can be purchased with an auxiliary wind-angle sensor which can be used to steer a steady angle off the wind instead of a compass course. If you are planning to use the autopilot on upwind courses, or even very close reaches, the wind vane attachment is a good idea.

Choosing an Autopilot

For a boat that uses an autopilot on delivery runs, an occasional long passage, or the long run out to the start of a race, a removable autopilot that attaches to the tiller or wheel makes sense. Motor sailors will be more inclined to choose a permanent installation. Whichever you choose, make certain that the unit has adequate power for your boat and your needs, and that your boat can supply the current which the autopilot draws. The manufacturers' recommendations ("for boats 30 to 45 feet") are not very useful, because a 30-foot, heavy, full-keeled cruiser will often need much more autopilot power than a 45-foot lightweight racer. And steering in heavy seas or ocean swells will require more power from the unit and draw far more current than an easy run or reach in flat water.

The best way to choose a unit is to measure the actual tiller or rudder loads on your boat in the conditions in which you will probably use the autopilot. Don't pick a storm, in which you would probably take the helm anyway; but don't shy away from wind and sea conditions that are typical or perhaps slightly windier and rougher than typical. Then overtrim your sails slightly so that the boat is overpowered and the helm is at the point where you would normally begin to ease sheets. That will probably represent the maximum tiller or wheel load on your boat. Use a fisherman's scale with a hook to measure the tiller or wheel load in pounds. With a tiller, make sure

that you measure the load at the point where the autopilot will attach to the tiller, which is usually well aft of the point where you hold the tiller. With a wheel, you will have to hook the scale onto a spoke and pull against it enough to turn the wheel while keeping the scale perpendicular to the spoke. Then use the following equation to come up with foot-pounds of torque needed:

$$\text{Torque} = \frac{\text{Pull} \times \text{Radius} \times \text{Turns}}{12}$$

Pull is the pull on the wheel measured in pounds, *Radius* is the measurement from the hub of the wheel to the attachment point of the scale in inches, and *Turns* is the number of turns the wheel makes from lock to lock.

Most temporarily attached units are calibrated in pounds of tiller load. Permanently mounted units are calibrated in foot-pounds of torque required. You may want to consult with the manufacturer to assess how much safety margin you should allow.

The current draw of an autopilot can be significant, especially if you are planning long passages under sail. The manufacturers' indications are not reliable, not because they lie but because it is difficult to relate their specifications to one another or to actual sailing conditions. If you can find a boat with a similar installation, ask how much current the unit draws in normal use. If that question draws a blank or an answer like "not much," ask how often the engine has to be run or how frequently the batteries go dead.

If you can't get advice, a rough guideline is that a tiller-actuated unit will draw roughly ¼ to ⅓ amp in normal use. It doesn't sound like much, but multiply by the hours of a long passage and you can see why boats that use autopilots for long passages often have solar cells or other auxiliary power-generating equipment.

Wind Vanes

Wind vanes are the subject of serious debate among offshore cruisers, with hours and pages of debate devoted to the merits of direct vane, trim-tab, servo-rudder, and auxiliary rudder systems, and the storm survivability of the wind vanes manufactured by the different companies. The real question for the debate is not the superiority or inferiority of one system or the other but the suitability of one system or another for a particular boat. Heavy boats, and boats with considerable weather helm, need the steering power of powerful systems like the servo-pendulum wind vanes. Whatever system is chosen, it is weight and windage at the stern of the boat, and the auxiliary or servo-rudder in the water is drag—both of which will slow the boat, often measurably. And any kind of auxiliary or servo-rudder left in the water will make the boat less responsive when you are motoring or taking the helm yourself. If you already have difficulty making a long-keeled boat spin the tight circles that are needed in a crowded anchorage, a self-steering apparatus on the stern will double your woes. Finally, the mechanism on the transom seems to have an almost magnetic attraction for docks, other boats maneuvering around docks, and Windsurfers sailing around an anchorage.

In selecting a unit, look for strength of construction, simplicity of repair, minimal corrosion potential, and simplicity of operation. If you are buying a wind vane, you are buying it to sail offshore, which is no place for flimsy mechanisms and super-light materials. The combination of wood, plastic, and a variety of metals; the position of the mechanism, half in the water and half out; and the expectation that the wind vane will be used for extended cruising suggest that you need to pay real attention to the potential problems of galvanic corrosion. Aluminum is a fine metal to use at sea, but aluminum in the water next to a copper-painted bottom is asking for trouble. And when the wind vane breaks (everything at sea breaks!) you may have to effect repairs not in some calm lagoon but with the transom of the boat pitching up and down, the boat sailing in circles, and the boom crashing back and forth, which is no time to try to sort your way through thousands of tiny parts, at least some of which will undoubtedly roll overboard just before you can reach them. And while it is always fun to fiddle with a mechanism which looks so invitingly like a Rube Goldberg contraption, you want fairly simple and reliable controls to adjust the dampening of the rate and amount of correction to allow for different sea states, and a very simple mechanism to disengage the vane to allow you to take over the steering to avoid floating objects or collisions.

Tiller and Wheel Locks

Autopilots and wind vanes conjure up the images of hour- or day-long passages, the boat sailing herself while you and your crew relax in the sun, sipping cool beers and casually watching for passing ships. For many sailors, the reality of self-steering is a need expressed not in hours or days but in minutes. You want to step below to look at the loran, or to grab a sandwich from the icebox. Or you need to go forward and snug up the tension on the genoa halyard. With pedestal steering, if there is a wheel lock on the pedestal the task is easy; you find the setting of the wheel that will allow the boat to hold her course, tighten the lock, and you're free. If the helm of a boat is well balanced and the wind and seas steady, the boat can be made to steer herself for minutes or even hours with the wheel locked.

On a tiller-steered boat, the same task requires a little engineering, or jury-rigging. There are all sorts of devices sold that mount on the tiller to cleat or clip lines that are led from the sides of the cockpit, and for small boats there are devices that allow you to use an adjustable tiller extension as a wheel lock. The problem with most of these systems is that pad eyes and cleats have to be mounted on the tiller and the coamings, usually exactly in the position where the helmsman sits. An alternative is lashing the tiller with a special piece of line or with the tails of the traveler adjuster lines, the mainsheet, or a genoa sheet tail. It works, but it takes too long to do, leaves the varnish on the tiller with the equivalent of the "Indian rope burn" that kids give one another on the wrists, and takes too long to disengage when you rush back out to the cockpit.

An easier solution, especially for boats that can balance the helm to neutral, is to use shock cord for a tiller lock. Use either a long piece with loops to fit over winches or cleats and a central loop to fit on the tiller, or fix a pad eye on the sole of the cockpit (if there is a foothold cleat on the centerline, a hole through it will serve as the pad eye) or the bottom of a traveler bridge, and use a vertical link of heavy shock cord to hold the tiller. It will not correct for a weather helm, but it will keep the tiller in the middle of the boat, will not present an obstacle to crawl over or around on your way back aft with beer or chart in hand, and is quick and easy to disconnect when you once again take over as master of your ship.

DEAD-RECKONING NAVIGATORS

The steps you follow in keeping your own dead-reckoning plot on a chart, marking known positions and drawing new positions based on calculations of course and speed, can be done instead by a small computer which uses as inputs the output of an electronic compass and the knot meter. Usually DR computers are used in combination with, and as a backup for, satellite navigation to track the position of the vessel between satellite fixes. They can also be used as a backup for loran or as an electronic backup to the DR chores of routine navigation. The only caution in using the units is that they are only as accurate as the knot meter and compass inputs that are fed into them. On most sailboats it is difficult to get a single knot meter to read exactly the same on both tacks. And a good location for an electronic compass is no easier to find than a good location for a cockpit compass.

STEREOS

Although it serves no navigational purpose, except perhaps to pick up commercial weather broadcasts, a radio and tape deck is a frequent installation on many boats. Sensing a gap in the market, some electronics companies have begun selling what they advertise as "marine" radios. If a stereo could be made weatherproof, so that it could be mounted in the cockpit and keep playing even after taking a few seas, the "marine" label might be appropriate. It would be possible for a radio; the problem of putting cassettes into the receiver makes weatherproofing an elusive challenge for a tape deck.

A few of the higher-priced "marine" radios may be rugged

units, and they may have additional corrosion protection that is roughly equivalent to the installation of an inexpensive anti-moisture pad or spraying the circuit boards with one of the moisture-eliminating sprays. But there is no reason why a high-quality automobile stereo unit cannot be used in a boat, yielding performance that is at least as good as, and in many cases far superior to, the marine units. The same criteria of sensitivity, selectivity, power, frequency range, flutter and wow that are applied to any stereo receiver are applicable to units used in a boat. Certain features that are desirable in a car are less desirable in a boat. For example, in a car, where your eyes are on the road, autoscan tuners may be important if you are a radio station hopper. Station selection on a sail-boat is usually far less frenetic.

In general, boats require a lot of power from the receiver and may even require auxiliary amplifiers if you are planning multiple speaker installations or the deck-blasters that are pop-ular on grand prix racers. If your installation is simpler and you don't need to play hard rock at intercontinental decibel levels, 15 or 20 watts per channel is probably sufficient. Be-cause most sailboats have limited power available for the radio, check on the current draw if you are planning to install a 150-watts-per-channel super-power amplifier.

Installation

The installation of a car or marine stereo in a boat is simple. If you have an enclosed area in the joinery and a panel that can be cut out for the speakers, flush-mounted car speakers can convert otherwise wasted space into a good speaker enclo-sure. Otherwise, small self-enclosed speakers will work better for the interior of a boat, which in terms of bouncing sound

around is comparable to a small room rather than an auto-mobile interior. For cockpit speakers, you can use the water-proof speakers that are manufactured for poolside or other outdoor use. The fidelity is roughly that of elevator music, but they will keep playing in the rain or with water sloshing off the deck and onto the face of the speakers. The wire run to the speakers is usually longer on a boat than in a car, and to avoid trouble it is a good idea to substitute two-conductor marine wire (16-gauge is fine for any unit under about 200 watts) for the miniature zipcord that is packaged with the speakers. Solder the connections in the wires (be very careful soldering to speakers), and you will avoid the problems of corrosion, which eventually turns automobile-type plug con-nectors green and mysteriously drops hard rock to whispers.

One problem that sometimes comes up is an antenna for the FM radio. An automobile antenna would work fine, but there is no convenient place to mount a whip on most sail-boats, on which the VHF and loran antennas already consti-tute a crowd. The alternative is to put the antenna inside the boat. The antenna can be as simple as a 31-inch-long piece of wire soldered to the center conductor of a plug that fits the antenna jack at the back of the receiver (most use a so-called Motorola plug which can be purchased at Radio Shack), or as complex as an electrically powered collapsible whip antenna with a built-in preamplifier. You can also use a dipole antenna like the ones that come with home stereos. Just solder one conductor of the parallel-wire feed to the center of the Moto-rola plug and the other conductor to the shell of the plug. Then drape the antenna wherever it works well; under a berth or inside a locker will often work satisfactorily.

There are no special electrical requirements in hooking up

a car or marine radio to work in a boat, except that most car radios are built for single-wire electrical service in which the ground (the car chassis) serves as the negative return. To install the unit in a boat, if it does not have a negative power terminal, connect the negative wire of the power feed from your switch box to the chassis ground connection. Then make certain that the case of the radio does not come into contact with other instrument cases. If the radio is mounted flush in a bulkhead, or if a panel is cut to mount the radio under a shelf, there is usually no problem, and the installation will be more compact and much more economical than most of the units that are sold for marine use.

19

INSTRUMENTS

Microchips have revolutionized sailboat instruments. A compact, reliable instrument, driven by the same simple sensors that once yielded nothing more than speed through the water and apparent wind speed and direction at the masthead, can now produce accurate digital readouts of boat speed, distance traveled, apparent and true wind speed, apparent and true wind angle, and VMG (velocity made good to windward or downwind). Add an electronic compass and the appropriate interface, and the readouts can include true wind direction, time and distance to lay lines, and a dead-reckoning position. The question for the boat owner is: how much of this information do you want and in what form? Most owners will opt for a selection of instruments somewhere between the seat-of-the-pants and back-of-the-neck sensors of the one-design sailer and the full instrumentation and a navigator and tactician to interpret the readouts of a 12-meter or a maxi-class boat.

For some instrumentation, such as depth sounders, it is still easy to understand what information is coming from the instruments. With wind and speed instruments, the myriad readouts available from modern instruments require a glossary.

DEFINITIONS

Boat Speed: the speed of the boat through the water. Boat speed does not compensate for current. Thus if a boat is sailing down-current in a 2-knot current, the speed over the bottom might be 7 knots but the boat speed indicator would read only 5 knots.

Apparent Wind Speed: the speed of the wind measured at a wind sensor on the boat, without compensation for the speed and direction of movement of the boat. If a boat is sailing downwind at 5 knots and the speed of the wind measured at a fixed station is 20 knots, the apparent wind speed on the boat will read only 15 knots.

Apparent Wind Angle: the angle between the bow and the direction a wind vane on the boat points. The apparent wind angle is a sum of the vectors of the boat's motion and the wind direction. When the boat is sailing upwind (on points of sail closer than a beam reach), the apparent wind angle sensed on the boat is closer to the wind than the true wind angle; when the boat is sailing downwind (on points of sail farther off the wind than a beam reach), the apparent wind is farther off the wind than the true wind. On a digital display, apparent wind angle is given in degrees off the boat's bow, usually with an "S" or "P" to indicate which side of the boat the wind is on.

True Wind Speed: the speed of the wind as if it were measured from a fixed station.

True Wind Angle: the angle between the bow of the boat and the direction that the true breeze is blowing.

True Wind Direction: the compass bearing of the wind as if it were measured from a fixed station.

VMG: velocity (or speed) made good. On instrument systems without an electronic compass, VMG is the component of the boat's movement toward or away from the wind. If a boat is sailing hard on the wind, with an apparent wind angle of 29 degrees off the bow and a speed through the water of 6.8 knots, the VMG might be 5.1 knots, which is the effective speed that the boat is moving directly upwind. Off the wind, VMG is a measure of how fast the boat is sailing directly downwind. Thus a boat might be heading up to increase its speed and find that the VMG downwind will increase because the increased boat speed more than compensates for the fact that the boat is sailing a longer course. On boats with a compass incorporated into the instrument systems, VMG can indicate the speed made good toward a mark or toward a compass course that is programmed into the instruments.

The other functions that are sometimes available on advanced wind and speed instruments, such as time and distance to the lay line or distance lost in tacking, are self-explanatory. There are also advanced instruments which measure the angle of attack of the keel to determine stalling, lift, and drag factors for the keel.

True wind speed, angle, and direction and VMG are derived, rather than measured, functions, and each calculation is subject to a multiplication of errors in the sensors. The more sophisticated the system, the more complex the interaction, which can yield subtle data for the helmsman, navigator, and tatician and can also lead to complex problems when even one of the sensors is miscalibrated. For example, if the knot meter transducer is not reinstalled correctly after cleaning, the erroneous knot meter readings will affect not only the readings of speed but also the derivative readings of true wind speed, true wind angle, wind direction, VMG, and dead-reckoning position. If the system is sophisticated enough to include an algorithm to calculate leeway from speed and angle of heel, that calculation will also be off and will affect the VMG and dead-reckoning calculations. The more sophisticated wind and speed instruments incorporate sensors and software to approximate corrections for heel, leeway, upwash from the sails on the wind instruments, and mast twist to minimize errors in the readings, as well as RS232 outputs which allow the interconnection of a computer, plotter, and disk or tape drive to analyze or record data.

What information do you want or need? The grand prix "rock stars" can often get along with almost no instrumentation because they have an instinctive feel for wind direction and boat speed that has been developed in years of competitive sailing. To be competitive against that kind of sailor, a less experienced sailor may need the help of instruments which can electronically feed out the information that the more experienced sailor can feel on his face, ears, or the seat of his pants. An experienced cruiser who has sailed his boat for years may develop an instinctive feel for true wind strength and the ability to discern between shifts in velocity and shifts in the direction of wind. True wind instruments can provide the less experienced sailor with the same information.

DEPTH SOUNDERS

Before the availability of Loran C navigation, depth sounders were used as much for position finding as for piloting. It was common to mount a depth sounder belowdecks, usually over the chart table, where a navigator could use contour lines on the charts as a primary position-fixing line. Now depth sounders are used primarily for piloting—to tell a helmsman when he is straying off the channel as he pokes his way into a gunkhole, or to tell a tactician or helmsman how much longer he or she can continue to sail toward shore to catch favorable lifts off the beach.

Depth sounders are made in dozens of configurations, from the simplest digital or flasher readouts to complex video displays and recording sounders which will feed out a contour of the bottom, along with schools of fish, for as long as you are willing to pay for the paper. For most sailboats, the choice is between flashers and digital sounders. There are analog sounders, which show the depth on a dial, but depth is one measurement where imprecision and a quick glance are often insufficient, so digital readouts have squeezed the analog sounders to a tiny portion of the market.

Flashers have the advantages of low cost and great sensitivity (many can be read to extreme depths by following the flasher on the second rotation). They have a relatively low power drain, and many models can be powered with an internal battery that will last through the season. The disadvantage is that in general a flasher must be mounted belowdecks, both for visibility and for protection against spray. It is possible to build a Plexiglas, wood, or aluminum bracket that will swing a flasher sounder into the companionway for visibility from the cockpit, but the arrangement is less convenient than a bulkhead or other mounting for a digital sounder. And with rare exceptions, flashers do not include alarms, which can be a useful feature. In selecting a flasher, remember that a unit that operates at a low frequency (50 KHz) will read deeper depths and have a broader beam width than a unit that operates at a higher frequency (200 KHz), but the low-frequency units are less accurate at piloting depths. Unless there is some special need for extreme depth readings, the higher-frequency units are more appropriate for sailboat use.

Digital sounders come in all sizes, shapes, and prices. Although some are laden with dozens of features and enough bells and whistles to make the operation a mystery to all but the initiated, there are few features beyond an alarm that are really important to a boat owner.

Alarms come in three flavors: low, high, and shoaling. A low-water alarm tells you just that: that the water under the transducer is less than the preset alarm value. On some depth sounders there is only a single range or a choice of ranges; others let you key in whatever figure you want for the alarm. Although keying in a value is more flexible, the simpler alarms will probably see more use, because it is so quick and easy to switch on the alarm to a preset value of 6 feet or whatever. High-water alarms are used when you are following a bottom contour, say the 10-fathom line. If you stray from the line to deeper water, the alarm will sound. The high- and low-water alarms can be used together as an anchor watch, blasting off with a loud alarm if the boat drifts off position to an area of higher or lower water. Naturally, if there is any tide, the range set on the alarms will have to be large enough to encompass the tide change, which generally makes the alarms less than useful as an anchor watch.

Finally, there are shoaling alarms, which are sometimes called "forward-looking alarms." Only a true scanning sonar looks forward and can actually detect the contour of the bottom in front of the boat. What the shoaling alarms do is calculate the *rate* of shoaling by measuring changes in depth against an internal clock. Thus if you are sailing over a gradually shoaling bottom toward shore, the depth sounder can calculate that in thirty seconds the depth under the boat will be only 6 feet, which will be time to tack. Of course the depth sounder has no way of knowing that a badly placed rock will spoil its calculations. A few units allow programming of the alarm, or have the alarm connected to the knot meter so that the rate of shoaling is calculated at your present speed. The shoaling alarm is useful, but on anything other than a steadily shoaling bottom, close reliance on the alarm may result in some unanticipated expenditures for keel fairing and bottom painting.

In addition to the features, there are other considerations that are important in the selection of a depth sounder. Display brightness and readability should be chosen with two considerations in mind: current drain and planned location of the depth sounder. LED displays that are highly visible inside a boat are difficult to see in sunlight. LCD displays have a low power drain but are sometimes difficult to see inside the boat and may have blind angles. Gas tube displays have a high current demand and may have reliability problems.

The controls on a depth sounder must be waterproof and foolproof if the sounder is mounted in the cockpit. Membrane push buttons are usually reliable; tiny toggle switches with rubber boots can leak and corrode, and the sharp edge can hurt someone or get tripped accidentally; rotary switches are difficult to waterproof.

Installing Depth Sounders

The transducer for a depth sounder will usually be in one of three forms: a puck, which is made for internal mounting in a solid fiberglass hull; a bronze through-hull mounting; or a plastic/nylon through-hull mounting. If you have a solid (non-cored) fiberglass hull, or if you have a cored hull which has an area of solid bottom that was put there by the builder for the installation of depth sounders or other transducers, you have the option of mounting the transducer inside the hull. The sensitivity of the depth sounder will be reduced, but there is no hole to drill in the hull and no problem of fouling of the transducer. If you have a cored hull, a wood hull, or an aluminum or steel hull, the transducer must be mounted through the hull.

There are two ways to mount a depth sounder inside a solid fiberglass hull. The simplest is to find a flat spot in a suitable location (away from the keel and away from the heavy vibration of the engine), make sure the inside of the hull is clean, spread a heavy layer of clear silicone seal on the hull or on the face of the transducer, and press it in place. If you want to make sure the location is suitable, try the depth sounder with the face of the transducer pressed down on a plastic bag filled with water over the desired spot. If you get decent readings, the location is all right. The silicone mounting is quick

and dirty; it works, and for a depth sounder that is installed during the season, without a haul-out, it is fine. For a more permanent installation, either buy one of the ready-made plastic bubbles for in-hull installation or build a water or oil box from PVC plumbing parts. A short length of 3-inch PVC pipe with an end cap and a screw-in plug for a filler hole will do.

The bottom of the box should be cemented to the inside of the hull with epoxy or a polyester fairing compound. You can saw or sand the pipe to make a close fit. Then install the transducer so that the face is always immersed in the liquid. Water will work to fill the box, but mineral oil doesn't evaporate and is easy to buy in a pharmacy.

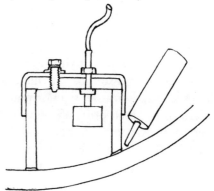

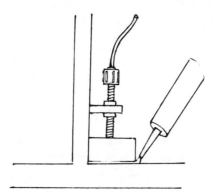

If you do not have a solid fiberglass hull, or if you do not want the sacrifice of sensitivity that an inside installation entails, the transducer will have to be mounted through the hull. Unless you have a hull with such an extreme wineglass shape that there is no flat underwater area, the transducer should be mounted flush with the exterior of the hull, usually well forward of the keel, and with the face of the transducer aimed as close to straight down as you can manage. The through-hull hole should be cut carefully, either with a special cutter tool made by the manufacturer of the transducer, or with hole saws and then filing or grinding. Any exposed core should be sealed with epoxy, and the transducer should be backed up inside the hull with a suitable backing block cut to fit the inside of the hull.

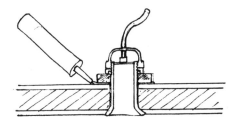

The cable for any depth sounder should not be cut or spliced, because the capacitance of the cable is part of the transducer circuitry. If you need to remove the end plug to go through cutouts, try to cut off as little as possible; and if you need an extension cable, buy one directly from the manufacturer.

If you find that your depth sounder is inaccurate or not as sensitive as it should be, the problem is usually either fouling on the transducer face or a slight mismatch between the transducer frequency and the circuitry of the depth sounder. Some brands of anti-fouling paint work fine on the face of a transducer; others have enough copper content to effectively shield the transducer. You can ask around your boatyard or experiment; in general, more than a single coat of paint isn't a good idea. If you suspect that a mismatch of the depth sounder and

the transducer is the problem, you will have to take both into a marine electronics shop that is equipped to test them. It is fairly common for 200 KHz transducers to actually resonate at 205, 210, or 195 KHz; the circuitry of your depth sounder can be tuned to match, which will greatly increase the sensitivity of the unit. The job shouldn't take more than an hour if you do the hard job of removing the depth sounder and transducer.

KNOT METERS

"Is that really how fast we're going? How do you measure it?" Knot meters are no longer a curiosity. Except for one-design racing, where it is possible to monitor your own boat speed by watching your competitors, on well-sailed boats the knot meter is monitored constantly by the helmsman, tactician, sail trimmers, and navigator; and even the most casual of cruisers will use the knot meter to estimate his arrivals and to decide whether it is indeed time to start the engine or put up the spinnaker.

Although an analog knot meter may give a faster initial indication of speed, just as an analog watch gives you the general time of day quicker than a digital watch, digital knot meters have become more and more accepted for their accuracy and readability in measuring incremental changes in acceleration and speed. A calibrated digital knot meter will register the change in speed that comes from tweaking the genoa sheet or easing the backstay. If the true wind speed is monitored at the same time, it is possible to know whether the change in trim or a change in wind caused the boat to speed up or slow down.

There are some fancy accessories available for knot meters, such as fine-scale acceleration meters and LED indicators which show the rate of change of speed, but the bells and whistles are no substitute for a high-quality instrument and a careful installation. For cruising or distance-racing navigation, you may want to add a log that works off the same transducer; or many knot meters have a log readout as part of the circuitry.

Some distance cruisers still use taffrail logs that are dragged behind the boat. For real offshore passage-making the taffrail log may be accurate and offers the advantage of no current draw. For inshore cruising a taffrail log is more suitable as fishing gear than as an instrument, although your likely catch is seaweed and flotsam rather than aquatic species.

Installation

A few knot meters use Doppler or other high technology to avoid an external paddle or turbine transducer, but most still rely on a transducer, which must be mounted in the right position and with the right alignment if the knot meter is to give reliable and accurate readings. The transducer should always be mounted well in front of the keel (approximately one third of the way from the keel to the bow is a good starting guess) unless two transducers and a gravity or manual switch are used. The reason is that there is a difference in the speed of the flow on the two sides of the keel, especially when the boat goes to windward. Thus if the knot meter is mounted to one side of the keel, it will read low on one tack and high on the other. The transducer must also be aligned precisely with the fore and aft axis of the boat. If it is turned, it will read differently on the two tacks. If the transducer does not include

pins which lock the alignment (the Signets do, the Kenyons don't), mark the barrel and the locking nut to guarantee that the transducer is always replaced in the same position. If the finish of the bottom is changed, or if the bottom is faired, the knot meter will have to be recalibrated.

The same mounting practices that are used with a depth sounder transducer can be followed with a knot meter transducer. The transducer cable is sometimes coaxial cable. More often it is a twisted pair with a shield. The cable can be shortened or spliced, as long as the shielding is maintained and carefully grounded. And if the wiring involves add-on logs or repeater instruments, the wire can be split either with Y-cables or by soldering two cables in parallel into a single plug or socket. Most digital instruments have no practical limit to the number of instruments that can be hooked in parallel to the single transducer. With some analog instruments there may be a limit because the transducer is actually generating an AC voltage which is measured at the knot meter.

If you cannot get accurate readings on both tacks from your knot meter, and the location of the transducer meets the criteria of being forward of the keel, as close to the centerline as possible, and precisely aligned, the options are to prepare a correction chart for different points of sail on either tack, or to install two transducers, either with separate instruments for port and starboard or with a manual or gravity switch that automatically switches the correct transducer to the knot meter. Manual switches are obviously not very convenient for closed-course racing, since they must be changed with every tack. Gravity switches depend upon a ball or a blob of mercury; they can be reliable, but if possible should be avoided as another gadget that can break. If there is any reasonably flat hull area forward of the keel and you are willing to position the transducer where it must be for efficiency—even if it means that cleaning the transducer will require lifting floorboards in the head or hanging locker or wherever—it should be possible to get acceptably accurate readings from a single transducer.

Calibration

Calibrating a knot meter is nowhere near as simple as the terse instructions from the manufacturers would have you believe. It is possible to follow their guidelines and time two runs past a measured mile, but boat owners with a full-function loran may find it easier to use the loran to calibrate the knot meter. Just remember to make all measurements at calm water in the tide cycle and to allow for differences between the two tacks, which are often amplified when the boat heels. And if you calibrate with the transducer clean, remember that any fouling on the transducer will foul up your readings later on.

Maintenance

In general, there is no maintenance for knot meters besides keeping the instrument dry, the connections clear of corrosion, and the transducer clean. Especially in the warmer months, the transducer should be removed from the hull when the boat is at its mooring. If you forget, it will foul with algae, tiny shrimp, barnacles, and general crud. A toothbrush or a toothpick can be used to clean it, and an occasional bath in chlorine will remove embedded crud. Be especially careful

and thorough in cleaning around the rotor shaft and bearing points, which often have such close tolerances that a slight buildup of growth inside the transducer through-hull pinches the bearings so that a rotor that spins easily in your fingers stops working in the hull.

WIND INSTRUMENTS

The wind at the top of your mast is different from the wind you feel on deck. Usually it blows harder aloft, and the direction may even be different from the direction of the wind on the water. Compound the problem with the movement of the boat through the water and the interaction of the sails and the wind, and it sometimes seems that what you measure at the top of the mast has little connection with the wind you feel on deck. You can measure wind speed at deck level with hand-held wind-speed indicators that can be very accurate. If you test one by holding it outside the window of a moving car, the readings will correlate with the speed of the car. On a boat, the instrument is of limited utility.

Many yachtsmen can get along with no wind instruments beyond a simple Windex at the masthead. The angle of heel or the feel of the helm is enough to tell them whether there is too much or too little sail on the boat, and the telltales on the sails or the rigging, or the feel of the wind on ears, the back of the neck, or the cheeks, is enough to indicate the direction of the wind. Indeed, there are many good helmsmen who consider wind direction instruments a distraction; except perhaps in the chaos of a tack or a jibe around a mark, they rarely glance at the masthead wind indicator. The only addition they might want to consider is lighting for the masthead indicator for evening and night racing. The tiny lights that are sold for use with Windex indicators use an 18-volt bulb, presumably to yield long life in 12-volt service. Replacing the bulb with a 12-volt bulb will give brighter light, although the bulb may have to be replaced annually.

Apparent Wind Instruments

If you use an apparent wind indicator as a substitute for or supplement to a masthead indicator, whether to prevent a permanent crick in your neck or because you prefer the damped action of an electronic display, an analog wind direction display provides the quickest and easiest readings. Some of the less expensive units use indicators that do not travel the full 360 degrees and instead race the long way around the indicator when the boat is sailing dead downwind or tacking. On a large indicator like the Combi instruments, the racing of the arrow around the dial can prove distracting. Most of the better analog indicators provide a full 360-degree indicator, and it is possible to obtain either an amplified scale indicator or an auxiliary digital readout for critical decisions such as "can we carry the spinnaker or is it too close?"

Apparent wind speed indicators are also available in analog readouts, a simple dial that reads from 0 to 60 knots or some other scale. Although an analog instrument does provide the quickest general indication of wind speed, the decision of when to change sails or whether to reef often depends upon precise wind speed readings. An analog instrument is difficult to read with the precision necessary to prevent destruction of a delicate "angel's hair" spinnaker or Mylar headsail at the top of its range.

True Wind Instruments

The other use of wind instruments is for tactical and strategic decisions by a skipper, tactician, or navigator. "What sail should we use when we round the next mark?" is the most common question, and it is a question of importance to the cruising skipper or the racer. Recognizing the actual ("true") direction and strength of the breeze is tricky even for the most experienced sailors. Upwind or on a close reach, especially in cool air, or at night when you cannot see the surface of the water well enough to read the wind strength, a 10-knot breeze can feel like 20 knots. Off the wind, especially in warm air, a 10-knot breeze can feel like 5 knots. The direction of the true breeze can be even more deceptive, especially as a boat comes to a course well off the wind or close to the wind. The unanticipated effect of the apparent wind explains why when the Windex or apparent wind indicator seems to suggest that a spinnaker could be carried, you sometimes discover after hoisting the chute that the wind has suddenly gone forward and you cannot carry the spinnaker comfortably. What has really happened, usually, is that the spinnaker has so increased the boat speed that the apparent wind angle has moved forward.

Calculating True Wind

You can calculate the true wind speed and direction from readings of apparent wind angle, apparent wind speed, boat speed, and course. You will need either a calculator that can handle trigonometric functions, and preferably with one or two levels of memory ($12 to $15 should buy one today) or a small computer that can be programmed in BASIC. A battery-powered computer like the Radio Shack Model 100 or Model 200 is ideal.

Simple formulas for a calculator are:

$$TS = \sqrt{BS^2 + AS^2 - 2 \times [BS \times AS \times \cos(AA)]}$$

$$TA = AA + \sin^{-1}[BS \times \frac{\sin(AA)}{TS}]$$

$$VMG = BS \times \cos(TA + \text{leeway})$$

where TS is true wind speed, TA is true wind angle, AS is apparent wind speed, AA is apparent wind angle, BS is boat speed, and VMG is speed made good in the direction of the wind (a negative VMG is speed "away" from the wind). Leeway is an optional variable which will depend upon the boat type, angle of heel, and point of sail. All speeds are in knots, and directions in degrees.

If you have a small computer with BASIC which includes sin, cos and arctan (usually atan) functions, you can calculate true wind information with the following program. The program will prompt you for the compass course, boat speed, apparent wind speed and angle, and whether the boat is on port or starboard tack. It will then give you the true wind speed, true wind angle, VMG to/from the true wind, and the true wind direction (compass bearing of the wind).

```
10  'TRUEWIND.BAS copyright 1985 Ronald Florence
20  CLS: PRINT "APPARENT → TRUE": PRINT
30  INPUT "compass course"; C
40  INPUT "boatspeed"; BS
50  INPUT "apparent wind speed"; AS
60  INPUT "apparent wind angle"; AD
70  INPUT "wind (p/s)"; W$
80  L = 0              'leeway factor*
90  PI = 3.141593
100 R = PI/180         'convert angles to radians
110 TS = SQR(BS^2 + AS^2 - 2 * AS * BS * COS(AD * R))
120 S = BS * SIN(AD * R) / TS
130 TA = AD + ATN(S/SQR(1-S^2)) * 180/PI
140 V = BS * COS(TA * R + L)
150 IF W$ = "p" THEN TD = C-TA ELSE TD = C + TA
160 IF TD<0 THEN TD = TD + 360
170 IF TD>360 THEN TD = TD-360
180 PRINT: PRINT "true wind speed = ";
190 PRINT USING "##.##"; TS;
200 PRINT " knots"
210 PRINT "true wind angle = ";
220 PRINT USING "###"; TA;
230 PRINT " degrees"
240 PRINT "vmg (to wind) = ";
250 PRINT USING "##.##"; V;
260 PRINT " knots"
270 PRINT "true wind direction = ";
280 PRINT USING "###"; TD;
290 PRINT " degrees"
```

* For indications of *relative* VMG, you can try the program with no leeway factor. For optimum accuracy, L should incorporate values for angle of heel and point of sail and a constant value corresponding to the effectiveness of the keel of the boat. If you want to experiment to get closer to the actual VMG of your boat, try L = X/AD (apparent wind direction), with an initial trial value of anything from 2 to 5 for X.

For regular use by a navigator or skipper, the hand or computer calculations are too slow, which is why more and more skippers are relying on wind and speed instruments with built-in microprocessor capabilities. Although there are theoretical limits to the accuracy of true wind data (your compass is a better indication of a wind shift during the daytime, especially upwind), the availability of continuous readouts of true wind speed and direction can greatly simplify the choices for a helmsman, navigator, or tactician. And in night sailing and any downwind sailing, the true wind direction and speed instruments will pick up and display changes that most sailors cannot detect with the backs of their necks or the seats of their pants. If you trim a sail and the boat speed goes up while the true wind speed stays the same, you know you did something right. If you are sailing a compass course of 015 degrees and the true wind angle is 90 degrees off the starboard bow (a true beam reach), you know the true wind direction is a breeze from 105 degrees. If the next leg is a compass course of 060 degrees, you know that you will be sailing 45 degrees off the true wind, and if you also know the true wind speed, you can know exactly what sail combination to use.

Velocity Made Good

Upwind, VMG tells you whether it is more effective to point and go slower or foot and sail faster; offwind, VMG tells you whether it is more effective to sail straight downwind or to tack downwind. The instruments are generally accurate, but only if used correctly, which means if the VMG readings are averaged over time. If you are sailing upwind and you suddenly point the boat high, the VMG will quickly rise, then only slowly fall back. This is because changes in apparent wind angle are read instantly; changes in boat speed take time to record and average. So VMG works best for picking an average course. Most helmsmen use a knot meter in conjunction with the VMG indication. A slavish attempt to sail by the VMG indicator will not make a boat fast.

The real trick to making the most of wind and speed instruments is to use them in combination with other information to maximize the sailing potential of a boat. If you have polar speed curves for your boat,* sophisticated wind and speed instruments can tell you whether you are sailing your boat at its optimum speed, or whether you should head up or bear away to take advantage of the sailing characteristics of your boat. For distance racing or passage-making, the use of a polar curve with sophisticated information can lead to some surprises: often it is much faster to sail the optimum point of sail of your boat, even if the course does not lead directly toward the mark or the next waypoint of your passage, because the distance back to the mark is insignificant in comparison to the speed (and distance) gained by sailing fast. And for charting the progressive shifts in wind strength and direction, no amount of scribbled notes on the coamings in the hectic minutes before the start can compare to the printed record of wind direction and velocity that a portable computer and printer can provide from the input of true wind speed and direction.

Even if all you have is a list of optimum upwind and down-

---

* Polar speed curves show the speed potential of a boat on various points of sail in various wind strengths. They are available with velocity prediction programs that are sold by naval architects and some sailmakers, or for boats that have been measured under the MHS (Measurement Handicap System) rule (or a sister ship of a boat that has been measured for MHS), from USYRU.

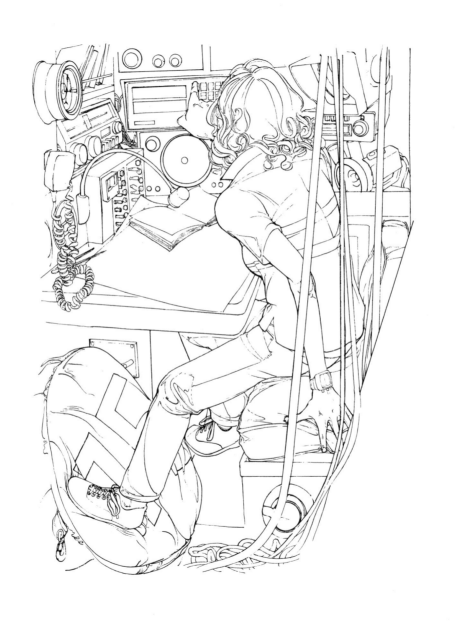

wind speeds for your boat in different true wind strengths, you will find yourself sailing faster and more efficiently if you occasionally glance at the boat speed, the true wind speed, and the chart. Instead of that uncomfortable, inchoate feeling that "the boat's not moving well," you will *know* whether the boat is moving as well as it should. And if you have a list of optimum wind strengths for the sails in your inventory, you don't have to ponder sail choices.

Selecting True Wind Instruments

True wind speed and direction instruments are almost always digital readouts, because the numbers are used more for navigational and tactical information than as guides for steering the boat. The thing to look for in buying new wind instruments, besides reliability and ruggedness, is clarity of display and an arrangement of displays that will allow you and your crew to monitor the information you will need as often as you need. If you use the instruments only occasionally, for example to decide on sail changes, a display that requires switching or button pushing to go from true wind direction to true wind speed to VMG, like the Signet 2000, is fine. If you or your crew monitor instruments continuously, if for example you like to watch the AWI and your crew like to watch the true wind speed while they trim sails, you should select instruments that offer multiple simultaneous displays, like the Rochester instruments or a large set of B & G instruments. The ultimate in separate readings comes from modular instruments like the Ockam instruments, with individual displays which can be keyed by the insertion of a chip to whatever readout is desired.

Installing Wind Instruments

There are no special tricks involved in installing wind instruments. The vane should be precisely aligned with the centerline of the boat, and the vane and cup or other wind-speed mechanism should be level when the boat is level. If possible, the unit should be mounted on the centerline of the mast crane. The mountings should be rigid. There are constant arguments whether the instruments should face forward or aft. On the East Coast, instruments forward is common; on the West Coast most installations point the instruments aft. The upwash from the sails can be corrected for either installation on the most sophisticated units; otherwise it may be wise to favor the most common points of sail (hence sensor aft for West Coast sleighrides, sensor forward for East Coast upwind sailing).

Most units come with a waterproof plug for the masthead fitting but leave no provision for detaching the wiring at the base of the mast, or at another location belowdecks, when the mast is unstepped. Boatyards and marine electricians usually install a terminal strip for the wires, but a better solution is to buy a cheap plastic plug and socket from Radio Shack (they are available with six, nine, and twelve connections); crimp and solder the pins on, then "waterproof" the plug with liquid vinyl or the mastics that are sold for outdoor wiring. Come spring, instead of trying to read the color codes of eight wires while you are on your knees in the bilge (or paying a rigger $35 an hour to read the fading colors of the wires), you slide the plug in and don't have to worry whether the instrument will read 180 degrees off course or not read at all.

ELECTRONIC COMPASSES

The primary reason for having an electronic compass is that it can be interfaced with sophisticated wind instruments to give a reading of true wind direction in compass coordinates, and to permit electronic tracking of a dead-reckoning plot by combining direction and distance inputs. The output can be either cumulative, with a continuous reading of a dead-reckoning position in latitude/longitude, or on a chart recorder or plotter that can keep track of the jigs and jags you have taken in getting to a present position.

A few skippers are also using electronic instead of magnetic compasses for steering and to read wind shifts, but it is a moot question whether the digital readout of an electronic compass is more effective than the large analog display of a magnetic compass. If an electronic compass is installed, it should of course be backed up with a magnetic compass, and the flux-gate sensor unit should be very carefully aligned with the fore and aft axis of the boat and carefully compensated. And remember that when instruments are interconnected, the failure of any one can cause a chain-reaction failure of others. Make certain that the installation allows you to isolate instruments so that if the electronic compass fails, you can still use the wind and speed instruments.

MOUNTING INSTRUMENTS

There are no special tricks to mounting instruments in a cockpit, except to make certain that the people who will most often read the instrument can in fact see it. Too often the aesthetics of symmetry or the appealing image of steam gauges lined up on the bulkhead or on a pod over the companionway replaces the utility of instruments mounted where they can be seen and are not routinely blocked by crew or sailing companions. Before cutting holes in bulkheads or letting an installer plop the instrument into a companionway or pedestal pod, stand or sit at the helm in all the positions you assume while sailing, with lines draped around the cockpit the way they are when you're sailing, and with crew lined up against the house bulkhead or wherever they generally position themselves. Then check: Can you see the instruments? How much do you have to cock your head? On larger boats there is a real advantage to multiple instruments ("repeaters"), and aggressively raced boats profit from the use of large instruments

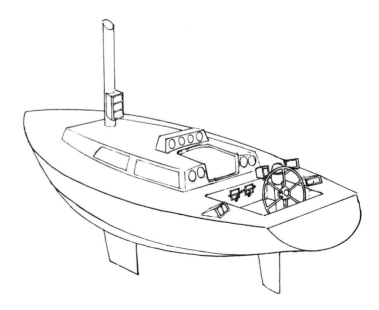

mounted in a location (such as the aft edge of the mast under the gooseneck) where they are visible to headsail trimmers as well as the cockpit afterguard.

It is rare that instruments will not need periodic servicing, so make certain that the wiring cables are long enough to enable you to remove the instruments, and that whatever bedding compound you use to install the instruments is not only compatible with the plastic cases but also sufficiently non-adhesive to enable you to remove the case with the instrument. The cables themselves should be securely fastened to bulkheads with cable clamps. Unless you are very handy with a soldering iron and have superb vision for the minuscule numbers on connectors, it is often easier to leave the cables full length and coil the excess in an out-of-the-way spot rather than to attempt shortening the cables.

COMPASSES

For any boat larger than a dinghy, the compass is the most important instrument. Whether you are following a course off the wind or under power or are sailing upwind, you will glance at your compass constantly—to make certain of your own steering, to check for wind shifts, to take bearings, or to re-orient yourself after a confusing maneuver in close quarters. If a compass is large enough and well placed, a helmsman can glance at it without losing his or her concentration on the sails, the water ahead of the boat, or a distant star or point. Unfortunately, the compasses on many boats are too small and too awkwardly positioned to be used properly.

What size compass do you need on a boat? Figure out how much you can afford to spend for a compass, then buy a unit one or two sizes larger! It is difficult to have a compass that is too big. A 6-inch compass on a one-design racer might be overdoing it, but there is nothing absurd about a 6-inch compass on a 30-foot cruiser-racer, and a compass smaller than 5 inches on a boat over 35 feet is generally too small. The big compass is steadier, easier to read, easier to take bearings from, and permits individuals other than the helmsman to quickly glance and note a wind shift.

The trick with large compasses is mounting them. The binnacle is traditional on wheel-steered boats, but except for casual offwind sailing or motoring, the binnacle is not a good place for a compass. To see a binnacle compass the helmsman has to look straight down, which usually means not only lowering his eyes but turning his head down. By the time he raises his eyes again, he will have lost track of the seas ahead of the boat, or the star or point of land he might have been steering by. And on the wind, when the helmsman is sitting to leeward, the binnacle compass either cannot be read at all or has to be read from a hard-to-interpret 45-degree or 90-degree lubber line.

In general, the best location for a compass is the side deck, the house bulkhead, the housetop, or the bridge deck.

The choice depends on how the boat, and especially the cockpit, is used. The best way to position the compass is to get on the boat with the kind of crew you usually sail with and scatter them to where they will normally be. Put whoever will grind and tail genoa sheets on the winch. Put the mainsheet trimmer where he usually stands. If you cruise with children and they usually hang around the bridge deck or lean back against the house bulkhead, put them there. Now, where would a compass work? Remember that lines will hang off a

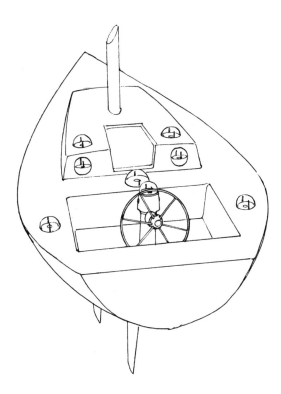

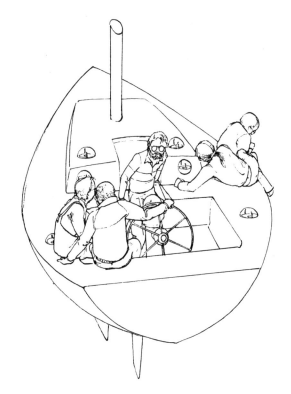

housetop in front of a bulkhead compass, that traffic through the companionway may block a bridge deck compass, that a spinnaker trimmer or someone trimming a housetop winch may block a housetop compass, and that feet or rear ends lined up on the rail can block a deck compass. Sometimes, any location is a compromise. But the compass is used so much that you need the best compromise.

The bridge deck is the only location that permits a single compass, and it usually has to be large if a helmsman well aft

is to be able to read it. Compasses used on the side decks or the bulkhead can be smaller, but must be carefully mounted to achieve proper alignment with the fore and aft axis of the boat. And unless the compass is internally gimbaled to compensate for a nonvertical mounting (the Danforth polyaxial compasses are), the compass should be mounted on a backup block so that it is absolutely vertical. Deck or housetop compasses should be level. And any compass that is even close to feet, elbows, or winch handles should have a guard. Nonmagnetic stainless guards are made by some of the compass companies and by fabrication shops. Because the guard looks like an inviting handgrip, it should be strongly built and through-bolted.

Some boats tackle the compass problem with multiple compasses: a large steering compass in the binnacle for offwind sailing and smaller tactical compasses on the side decks for upwind sailing, or compasses on the side decks and bridge deck. It may seem like a large investment, but the convenience and racing and cruising efficiency of a good compass or compasses is a wise investment, more important for most boat owners than a lot of the instrumentation that gets sold and put onto boats.

Another useful location is on the chart table, where a small flush-mounted or bracket-hung compass can eliminate the incessant shouts up the companionway: "What course have you been steering?" There are some hand-bearing compasses that supposedly double as chart table compasses, but a permanently mounted compass is probably more reliable. For boat owners who discover that the regular compass on the boat is too small, a good move might be to substitute a larger compass and move the regular compass to the chart table.

Installing Compasses

Install your compass the way porcupines make love: very carefully. The axis of the compass should be exactly parallel to the centerline of the boat. Eyeballing it rarely works. Either use taut wires and a steel measure to draw lines on the deck parallel to the centerline, or use a hand-bearing compass to sight down the centerline of the boat while someone else turns the main compass into the exact same alignment. If possible,

mount the compass with a single screw (and without any adhesive bedding compound) until after it is compensated. Sometimes after a frustrating half hour, a compensator will discover that the compass is misaligned and that no amount of sailing back and forth and tweaking of the compensator magnets will get things right. If the mounting is not too permanent, it can be realigned. If possible, the compensating magnets, for compasses with built-in magnets, should be readily accessible to the compensator. If not, he can use external magnets.

The internal lighting on most compasses provides excellent illumination, but the bulbs are often either too dim for use at dusk and dawn or too bright for use at night. A simple rheostat will cure the overbright bulb. A rheostat combined with a larger bulb would cure the too-dim light, but call the manufacturer before you install a bigger bulb. The heat from the bulb might damage plastic parts of the compass.

Compensators

There are yachtsmen who will spend $100,000 on a boat, with vast inventories of sails and electronics, and then never get around to hiring a compass compensator for $100. It is possible to compensate a compass yourself, but by the time you build the pelorus or sundial, find someone to motor back and forth with you, and learn how tiny the adjustments to the compensating screws are (you adjust only half of the error out each time), you may conclude that the fees of a compensator are a worthwhile investment. A compensator will not only get your compasses as close to zero deviation as he can, he will also recognize when compasses cannot be perfectly compensated and will prepare a deviation chart. It is especially important to have paired compasses swung. Few things are more annoying or dangerous than two compasses that give different readings. A periodic servicing of a compass is also a good idea. It is usually not necessary or a good idea to remove compasses from the boat in the winter. But a compass is affected by light: the plastic dome will eventually grow cloudy if it isn't scratched first, the exterior metal or plastic parts will fade, and eventually the seals may deteriorate. It is usually a fairly simple and inexpensive job to replace seals, top up the compass fluid, or install new lubber lines. If the compass is remounted in the exact location, it may not need recompensation after work has been done.

20

WIRING

The wiring in a boat looks twice as complicated as the wiring in a car, for the simple reason that boat wiring requires two wires where an automobile electrical system requires only one. In an automobile, the chassis functions as the return wire of the system: lights, radio, and accessories are wired between a single "hot" wire and the chassis.* Because most boats are not made of a conductive material, and because using the hull of a boat as the return path for electric current would turn the hull of a metal boat into a galvanic sandwich, boats are wired with a two-wire system, with both the positive and negative wires of the DC wiring leading to every fixture, light, electronic device, and accessory.

The second reason that boat wiring needs to be more complicated than automobile wiring is that the marine environment—with constant moisture, the threat of periodic dousing, and the galvanic and corrosive atmosphere of salt— puts electrical fittings, connections, and components to a continuous harsh test. Crimp terminals, wire, insulation, and screw fittings that would last indefinitely on land can fail suddenly and mysteriously in a boat.

High-quality marine-grade electrical components are expensive, and the best techniques of installing wiring and circuitry are labor intensive; hence many boat builders and marine electricians save time and money by using materials and techniques that are perhaps adequate, but which in time will deteriorate or fail, leaving the usual electrical mystery of

* Most boats, and most cars, have a negative return system. If you have an odd boat with a positive return system, reverse the polarity references in this chapter and be especially careful if you are trying to install an automobile accessory, such as a radio, in the boat.

a light that is intermittent, a fuse that blows, a circuit breaker that trips, or electrolytic corrosion that rapidly destroys zincs, fittings, keel bolts, and the market value of the boat.

Even boats that are built with impeccable electrical wiring, using commercial-grade components, neat mechanical and electrical connections, and careful planning, can be degraded into electrical messes by a single shoddy installation of an accessory. One badly wired bilge pump will send enough electrical current through the hull fittings of a boat to turn bronze sea cocks into a material that more closely resembles pink bath sponges. One corroded crimp terminal deep in the electrical guts of the boat can put the navigation lights, instruments, engine, or radios out of order, and like most marine mysteries, the connector will fail not on a spring Saturday in the boatyard when you are checking out the electrical system, but on a rough, wet, and foggy night when you really don't have the time or the inclination to troubleshoot with a flashlight to try to get the radio, navigation lights, or loran working again.

COMPONENTS

Magazines and boat advertisements are filled with photographs of large-boat electrical panels, the rows of multicolored wires neatly bundled, coming off the terminal blocks at right angles and leading through the boat in labeled bundles. The most extreme wiring jobs dispense with the bundles and mechanically fasten the wires in parallel lines, like chemical pipes in a refinery.

By contrast, the electrical wiring in most boats looks more like a bird's nest or a serving of linguini. Boatyards, marine electricians, and owners have often added lights, instruments, and gadgets, running new wires into the switch or circuit breaker panel, doubling up on fuses or circuit breakers, piling multiple terminals onto a single screw connector, and lacing zipcord and dozens of other varieties of wire into a tangle that can only be analyzed by hours of work with visual or electrical tracers. Trying to repair that kind of wiring when you need navigation lights and can't get them to work, or when you are desperate to get the VHF back on the air and it is dead or weak, is an unforgettable experience. Color coding and superneat parallel wiring may not be necessary except for sales brochures, but if wiring isn't electrically and mechanically sound, a boat will almost certainly develop problems, and if the wiring cannot easily be traced, it will take that much longer to track down and correct the problems.

Corrosion

Water, especially salt water, is pernicious. Don't let anyone ever tell you that it's "only" water, an inert substance. Just as water will find the tiniest possible leak in your deck, water will find its way to electrical connections, no matter how tightly you think they are sealed. And water or moisture will leave its calling card, usually in the form of corrosion, which can range from a fine white powder that only looks annoying to classic galvanic and electrolytic corrosion that can turn once strong metal into a substance with the strength and electrical properties of toilet paper.

The favorite spot for corrosion is a crimp terminal connection, either at the end of a wire or at a butt junction of two wires. The worst offender is using a crimp connector of the wrong size. Doubling over a wire in a large connector, or stuffing several wires into a single terminal, is usually an invitation to disaster somewhere down the road. Even with the right size connector,* if the wires are not absolutely clean and free of all corrosion, and if the crimp is not strong enough to allow no room for moisture or corrosion between the terminal and the wire, eventually the connections between the wire and the terminal will break down. Extra pressure in the crimping process doesn't work because the fine wires in stranded wire will break when they are squeezed too hard. Indeed, some of the larger boat builders use special fail-safe crimping tools that make it impossible to under- or overcrimp a connector. But if the sole electrical bond between the connector and the wire is mechanical, moisture will eventually corrode the connection, weakening if not destroying it. And a weak connection often means a voltage drop, which can diminish the performance of lights, instruments, or devices; a voltage drop also creates a potential differential in the wiring of the boat which can all but guarantee electrolytic corrosion of components or fittings.

Soldering Connections

The answer is solder. A hot-soldered joint is electrically secure. Add the mechanical security of a crimp behind the soldered connection and you have an electrical connection that will not fail within the lifetime of the average boat. Fortunately, it is not a difficult task to solder electrical connec-

tions when you are installing new devices or electrical fittings, and if the terminals in your boat are not already corroded, they can be soldered to prevent future corrosion or electrical deterioration.

All you need is a small soldering iron, rosin-cored electrical solder, a scrap of sandpaper, needle-nosed pliers, and three hands. It is possible to buy 12-volt soldering irons, or cordless soldering irons that can be charged on shore and carried out to a boat, but the easiest technique is to solder many terminals in a single session, which is probably best done in a boatyard or dockside with an inexpensive soldering iron plugged into shore power. A 25- to 40-watt iron, which costs less than $10 at Radio Shack or a similar store, is more than sufficient for all but the largest terminals. And if you have any terminals too large to solder with a small iron, they can be soldered with a propane torch.

If you are soldering a terminal that has already been crimped, make certain that the wire and terminal are not corroded. If you're in doubt, it only takes a minute to snip off the old terminal, strip the wire, sand with two swipes if the copper isn't bright and shiny, and crimp on a new terminal. Then apply the fully heated soldering iron to the surfaces that are to be soldered, give it a few seconds (a larger terminal may take up to a minute), then touch the solder to the hot terminal, not to the soldering iron. If the terminal and wire aren't hot enough to melt the solder by themselves, you will not get a properly soldered joint. If they are hot, the solder will run into the joint and cool to a shiny finish. You don't need a blob, just enough so the soldered surfaces are shiny and effectively "tinned."

* The crimp connectors are color-coded with a standardized code, at least for the smaller sizes. Blue connectors are for 14- and 16-gauge wire; yellow connectors are for 10- and 12-gauge wire; and the red connectors are for 18- to 22-gauge wire. Generally, wire smaller than 16 gauge is too small to use on a boat, except perhaps for stereo speaker wires. Hence most connectors on a boat should be blue or yellow.

Wire

Soldering every connection in the boat won't help if you don't use decent wire for the wiring. Zipcord—the plastic-covered wire that is seen on the lamps and radios in your home—has no place on a boat. What you want on a boat is double-insulated wire, with a separate outer shield of plastic and individual insulation of the two connectors, which should be in different colors (usually black and white or brown and white). The wire is not only safer (because the insulation is more rugged than zipcord of comparable gauge), but the polarity of the wiring is much easier to read than trying to identify the ridge on one conductor of a zipcord. If you are planning any electrical work at all, it makes sense to buy a 100-foot roll of #14 or #12 marine electrical wire. In time, as you install electrical devices, extra lights, or instruments, or replace shoddy wiring, you will discover that the monstrous roll quickly disappears.

For the best possible connections use tinned wire, which is wire that has been coated with solder during manufacture. Many electrical suppliers will tell you it doesn't exist, or that you don't need it; ask for Alpha #1892 and you will win the argument. Tinned wire not only lasts longer without corrosion but is easier to solder. Whatever wire you use, make certain that it is stranded, as a protection against fatigue from bending or vibration. When you prepare the terminal or the end of the wire, it should be clean and shiny. You may want to take a swipe or two at the surface of the terminal with sandpaper or emery cloth to remove any surface corrosion before you solder.

Don't worry if the yellow or blue insulation on the terminal melts back from the heat of the soldering iron. You shouldn't use the terminals so close to one another that they need the insulation in any case. In fact, you can save money by using uninsulated terminals, which will crimp more securely. If you want the terminal shaft to be insulated, you can slip a length of heat-shrink tubing over the wire before you make the connection, then slide it down and heat it with a hair dryer, or even a match, to shrink the tubing into a tight fit over the exposed connector. Black electrical tape just doesn't work in a marine environment; it will eventually turn into a slimy mess that will not stick to itself or the wire.

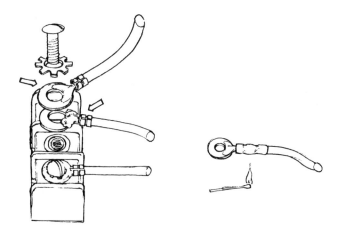

Butt Connections

Trying to upgrade a crimped butt joint with solder usually doesn't work. The best connection of two wires, if they are not connected at a terminal block, is to strip the wires, twist them together, and solder the twist. Electrical twist connectors can then be put on to insulate the joint. An alternative is to solder and crimp terminal connectors and use a machine screw, lock washer, and nut to make a compact and reliable connection that can still be disconnected relatively easily. For neatness or insulation, heat-shrink tubing can be used over the connection.

If wiring connections are exposed to weather, even on the inside of a navigation light fixture, or are located in the bilge, you need extra precautions to seal the connection against corrosion. It is difficult to totally seal a connection, but using liquid electrical tape, which is a vinyl mixture that seems to be the same as the whip-end dips that are sold for the ends of rope, followed by heat-shrink tubing will make a connection that is close to waterproof. Remember to slide the heat-shrink tubing onto the wire before you make the connection, and don't try to use heat-shrink tubing that is too large; a snug fit before the shrink is best. Make your solder and/or mechanical joints, and when the solder joints are cool, coat the connection with two or more coats of the liquid electrical tape, then slip the heat-shrink tubing over the cured liquid vinyl and shrink it down.

All wiring should be mechanically fastened with either cable ties or wire clamps. The fastening job usually takes more time than the actual electrical installation, and boat owners are sometimes tempted to hook up the wires and "tuck them away" out of sight.

One way to save time when you are installing wire ties or cable clamps is to use short plasterboard screws to fasten the clamps under stringers, shelf supports, or berths. The screws will eventually rust, but they are a great time saver, because they can be safely driven in without a pilot hole. Just get a matching Phillips-head bit for your slow-speed, portable electrical drill.

It is sometimes tempting to tie a new wire onto the bundle of old wires with a small cable tie, but when it is time to trace or replace wiring you will find yourself cursing the hodgepodge of ties. It is usually easy enough to remove and replace the cable tie, or to remove and reinstall the wire clamp, perhaps with a larger size if necessary. For neatness, insulation, or to prevent snaring of wire, it is sometimes a good idea to add spiral wraps to clumps of wiring, or even to run exposed wiring through PVC tubing that in turn is fastened with special clamps. If you do elect to run wiring through PVC tubing, make certain that the wire is mechanically fastened at the ends of the tubing so that a snagged wire will not pull out a terminal connection.

Control Panels

All circuit wiring should run to a master control panel, and each circuit should be wired through a fuse or circuit breaker. The panels can range from fancy panels of circuit breakers to simple fuse boards. Circuit breakers are reusable, and are generally installed in better-quality marine electrical panels, but especially in the low amperage sizes, circuit breakers can induce a voltage drop. If you elect to wire with fuses, make certain you have a large supply of the commonly used sizes, because when you do get a short, you may run through a lot of fuses trying to track it down.

It is tempting to wire several circuits onto a single fuse or circuit breaker, both for economy and for the convenience of

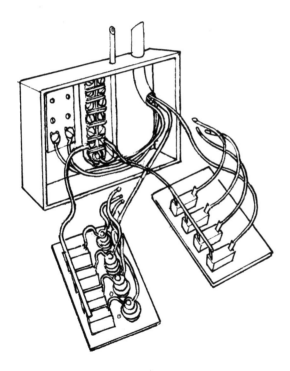

flipping one switch to turn on the navigation lights, the masthead light for the Windex, and the compass light, or one switch for all of the navigation instruments. The problem with multiple circuits on a single switch is that if one circuit shorts, you lose them all: if a navigation light on the pulpit shorts because one wave too many has come over the bow, you not only lose all of the navigation lights, but until the lights are repaired, the helmsman has neither a compass light nor a light for the wind direction indicator. Putting all of the interior lights in a boat on a single circuit can mean a boat plunged into total darkness inside if a single fixture shorts.

The best wiring is to have a separate switch and fuse combination, or circuit breaker, for each circuit. If you run out of circuits, or if you discover on inspecting your electrical panel that someone—the builder, a boatyard or marine electrician, or you—has already doubled up on the circuits, you can add a supplementary panel. The major marine electrical component manufacturers—Marinetics, Bass, Perkins—make a variety of panels which can be built into a simple wooden box and connected in parallel with the main circuits leading to the original electrical panel. If you are adding more than a few extra circuits to the wiring of a boat, you may want to consider the addition of a second (parallel) wire from the battery or battery switch to the distribution panel, or the substitution of a wire one or two sizes larger. It may also be appropriate to install a larger ground wire and/or a new return wire terminal arrangement for new circuits. The return wiring doesn't have to be complicated. An aluminum panel, drilled and tapped for machine screws and mounted on a block of plastic, is sufficient to tie the return wires together.

If you are reluctant to install a new panel with switches or circuit breakers for each circuit in the boat's electrical system, it is possible to use one switch for several independently fused circuits. For example, a single switch could turn on the navigation lights, the masthead light, and the compass binnacle light, with each of those three circuits running through a separate fuse so that a short in any one will not kill all three. A small fuse block installed inside the master control panel will handle the additional fuses, and is generally neater than pigtail fuses. Just make certain that as you add gadgets, even apparently harmless gadgets like another interior light or two, you provide adequate fuse protection and a sufficiently orderly system of wiring so that a failure doesn't require days of troubleshooting.*

BATTERIES, METERS, AND SWITCHES

The best of wiring and components won't keep your battery from going dead. Batteries are ornery, demanding devices, and the special needs of a sailboat electrical system, which puts a steady drain on a storage battery for a long period and expects to replenish the charge in a short time of engine-running, can lead to regular and unwelcome surprises from batteries that don't hold the charge you anticipated. In the midst of an overnight race you can suddenly see your run-

ning lights dim or your loran begin spewing out bizarre blink or low SNR (signal to noise ratio) signals; at anchor in a quiet overnight anchorage, after an evening of music on the stereo, you can discover that your battery doesn't have enough juice to turn over the engine. Or after a long motoring run that should have left your batteries fully charged you can discover that your battery can hardly keep the lights burning with more than a romantic glow. Fortunately, there are several minor changes you can make to the wiring of a boat which will prevent or at least minimize the risk of dead batteries.

Batteries go dead because they are undercharged, or because an unnoticed load is placed on them for too long. A voltmeter or battery charge indicator, which is a simple and inexpensive addition to the wiring system of a boat, will tell you if batteries are undercharged. Danforth, Perkins, Marinetics, and other marine electrical device manufacturers have a whole line of battery indicators with expanded scales and markings in green, yellow, and red to tell you that a battery is okay, undercharged, charging, or overcharged. You can get the same information from a simple expanded scale voltmeter or LED battery charge indicator. West Marine and Radio Shack, among others, sell inexpensive voltmeters; Spa Creek sells LED battery charge indicators, which give you a quick indication with "idiot" lights to tell you when you are low or undercharged.†

Wiring a battery charge indicator is easy. You can either wire the indicator permanently across the live circuit, so that

---

* Boatyards are often the worst culprits in installing "maze" wiring. If you order additional electrical gadgets from a boatyard, ask them to sketch the new connections for you and to explain how and where they tied a new circuit into the electrical panel. The fact that you care enough to ask may be sufficient to keep the wiring orderly.

† If you are afraid that you won't notice the low-volt indications on a meter, *The 12 Volt Doctor's Practical Handbook*, by Edgar J. Beyn (Annapolis, 1983), has a number of schematics for simple low-voltage alarms and indicators.

it shows the condition of the battery in use, or you can use an SPDT (single-pole, double-throw) momentary switch which will allow you to flick back and forth to check the condition of either battery. If you have more than two batteries, you can install a rotary switch with enough poles to use a single charge indicator for all your batteries.

The wiring schematic is straightforward. Just remember that the voltmeter is wired across the 12-volt circuit, with the positive terminal connected to the positive terminal of the battery or battery switch, and the negative terminal connected to the ground return.

The other indicator that can be installed in a boat to prevent dead batteries is an ammeter, wired in series with the hot lead to your accessories. The ammeter on your engine control panel indicates whether or not the alternator is charging; it

will not tell you if or how much you are discharging your batteries through accessory load when the engine is not running.

A 0–20 or 0–30 amp, 12-volt ammeter, wired in series with the hot lead to your master distribution panel, will tell you exactly how much load is on your battery at all times. As soon as you hook it up you will discover some secrets. Watch the meter when you turn on the interior lights, or push the transmit button on your VHF or SSB, or plug in a vacuum cleaner or other motor-driven device, or push the button on an electric head, and you will learn what devices are likely to exhaust your batteries in a hurry. After some experience with the ammeter, you can develop guidelines for which devices can or should be run for how long.

An ammeter is easy to install. The hot lead from the battery switch goes to the positive terminal; the negative terminal goes to the main distribution panel. The easiest installation is to break the wire from the switch to the panel and install the meter. If the wires are not long enough to locate the meter in a convenient location, you will need to extend them or use new wires; make sure that the wire you add is at least as large as what is there; if you lengthen the wiring by more than 5 or 10 feet, you should probably go to a larger size of wire.

If you still have trouble with dead batteries after installing a voltmeter and ammeter to monitor your charge and load on the batteries, chances are that you are not charging your batteries sufficiently, usually because you do not run the engine enough to keep the charge you need on them, or because your alternator/voltage regulator charges your batteries too slowly for the running time you allow. The obvious solution is to run the engine more, but if like many sailors you don't

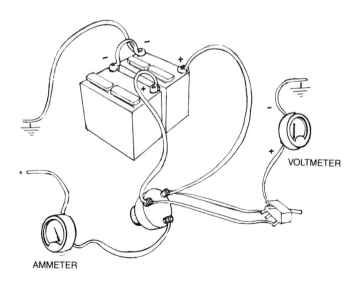

VOLTMETER

AMMETER

like to run the engine more than you need, the alternative is to increase the alternator output by installing one or more resistors in parallel with the voltage regulator. (In effect, you will be fooling the regulator into thinking that the alternator is putting out less charge than it really is.) If the resistors are carefully chosen, and if you watch to make certain that you do not overcharge the battery on long engine runs, the bypass scheme will work. One or two 6-ohm, 20-watt resistors in series, or a 10–20 ohm, 150-watt rheostat, can be used as a variable alternator output control, wired across the voltage regulator in the altenator field lead.*

Keeping two batteries evenly charged is sometimes a problem. Diodes, which are available in ready-made devices for either marine or recreation vehicle use, will split the charging current from the alternator to the two batteries without draining the charge from one to the other.† The problem with diodes is that they have a voltage drop (around 0.6 volts), which is dissipated in the form of heat. Thus if you use a diode device to charge both batteries at the same time, you will need to run your engine more to achieve a proper charge on the batteries.

TROUBLESHOOTING

It happens to every boat: a light suddenly fails and you know the bulb is good; an instrument goes dead or behaves errati-

cally; the battery ends up dead after an evening of light use following a day of heavy motoring; or—and this discovery can ruin the end of the sailing season—you inspect the bottom of the hull after a haul-out and discover that one of your bronze through-hulls has the texture and appearance of finely grained pink Swiss cheese. What do you do?

There are three tools you can use for testing and trouble-shooting the wiring of your boat. Two—a continuity tester and a test light ‡—you can make for about $1. Or you can buy an inexpensive VOM (volt-ohm meter), which will do all the testing you will need. Unless you're doing fancy troubleshooting inside electronics units, you won't need much more than the $10 to $15 VOMs that are sold at places like Radio Shack.

Most electrical problems on boats fall into one of three categories: (1) bulbs that don't light, or instruments that refuse to work or are erratic; (2) batteries that mysteriously go dead long before they're supposed to; and (3) corrosion.

Bad Wiring

If the problem is bulbs that don't light or instruments that don't work, use the test light or the DC voltmeter scale of the VOM to see whether there is a break in your circuitry somewhere. Try the 12-volt leads coming into the device or light socket. If you don't get a full 12 volts (depending on the battery charge, it could read anywhere from 12.0 or even 11.8 up to 13.6 or higher), then track back toward your distribution

---

* *The 12 Volt Doctor's Practical Handbook* contains dozens of ideas for alternator output controls, including ready-made controls that are sold by Spa Creek Instruments.

† The device is really nothing more than a heat sink for the two diodes and some convenient terminals for the wires. Hence there is little reason to spend more for a "marine" version.

‡ A test light is nothing more than a 12-volt bulb wired with a pair of alligator-clip leads; automobile wiring testers are the same gadget wired with a single-clip lead for the ground (negative chassis) and a probe for the hot wire. A continuity tester can be the same bulb hooked up in series with a 12-volt battery to test the continuity in circuits, or you can use a flashlight battery and bulb to accomplish the same check with 1.5 volts instead of 12.

panel and from there back to the battery switch. If you get the 12 volts at the socket or the wiring coming into the instrument, your problem is in the bulb, socket, or instrument.

If you suspect that the problem is a break somewhere in the wiring (which usually means a loose or bad connection rather than an actual "break" in the wire), you can test by looking for 12 volts with the power on, or you can turn the power off, preferably at the master switch, and use either the ohm-meter scales of your VOM or your continuity tester to see if there is a bad connection. The ohm meter should show 0 ohms resistance, or very close to 0 ohms, between any two points that are supposed to be connected.* If there is more resistance, and especially if the resistance of the circuit changes in different humidity or temperature, you probably have a bad connection somewhere, such as a loose screw in a terminal block, a bad solder joint, or corroded switch contacts. You may discover that if you keep turning a switch in the circuitry on and off, there is measurable resistance on the circuit sometimes and none other times, or that the repeated switching during the diagnostic procedure suffices to clean the contacts. Keep narrowing the measurement and you will isolate the bad connection.

The repairs to breaks in the wiring, corroded contacts, or intermittent switches are obvious. A squirt of WD-40 or CRC 666 may temporarily cure the problem, but to avoid future problems, it would be wise to resolder the bad wires, tighten the connections and make sure there are lock washers on the

---

* If the ohm meter is extremely sensitive and you have it set on a very low scale, you may see measurable resistance along extended wire runs. Try zeroing the meter again (by connecting the clips or probes to one another and adjusting the zero control).

terminals, or use fine emery paper to clean the corrosion off the switch contacts. If the problem is a broken or breaking wire, it is probably due to severe corrosion of some kind or fatigue; make sure the replacement wiring is securely fastened, and try to avoid the bilges or other wet areas that can lead to corrosion.

Dead Batteries

The more common problem for troubleshooting is batteries that seem to drain too quickly. If the battery is good (a simple matter of testing with a specific gravity tester that you can buy in any auto supply store), then the probable cause is either a battery drain from some device in your wiring or an electrical leak. Excessive drain can best be monitored with an ammeter installed in the circuitry. Watch as you turn on each device or light: one of them will make the ammeter jump. Or do a little quick arithmetic, measuring the drain of different devices and lights and multiplying by the hours in use to get amp-hours. And remember that the rated capacity of your battery in amp-hours, usually somewhere from 65 to 105, is substantially greater than its actual usable capacity.

If there doesn't appear to be any substantial drain from any device in the wiring, it is time to check for a leak in the circuitry. Begin with the main battery switch off, and measure the voltage differential between the hot lead to the master distribution panel and one of the battery leads coming into the main battery switch. Connect the positive lead of the voltmeter to the wire from the battery, and the negative lead of the voltmeter to the hot lead. With the voltmeter set on a 15 VDC (volts-direct current) or 50 VDC scale, the reading should be 0. If you are using a test light, the light should not glow when it is hooked between the two points.

If the meter does not read 0 with all switches off, or if your test light glows, it is time for more serious diagnostics. Begin by disconnecting the hot lead to the master distribution panel at the battery switch, and measure from the hot lead to ground with your ohm meter. If the reading is under 100 ohms, you have some switch on, or some item that is wired directly to the hot lead is on. Common culprits are electric clocks in instrument panels, car-type radios with built-in clocks, or even lorans and other instruments that have been installed with direct leads. Keep checking and switching devices off, or if necessary disconnecting devices that have been wired directly. If you cannot get the meter to show an open circuit (infinite resistance), move along the wiring and keep disconnecting wires from switches or circuit breakers until you track down the circuit that is showing a leak. Any resistance under 10,000 ohms is going to cause trouble, and by probing long enough and spending enough time disconnecting circuits, one after another, you will find it.

After one troubleshooting session of tracking your way through wires and connections, trying to guess which gray wire leads where, you may decide that a decent wiring diagram is worth the tedium and time that it takes to compile. There is no trick to a wiring diagram other than careful notes, clear schematic drawings, and labels on the wires that correspond with the labels on the drawings. If you have trouble with electrical schematics, you can also try drawing the actual connections or numbering the terminal strips, but you may discover that the drawing will quickly become complicated. If you do take the time to compile a wiring diagram, keep a copy of it, and your VOM, on the boat for those times when mystery problems develop.

21

CORROSION

Most boat owners regard electrolysis and galvanic corrosion with about the same friendliness they reserve for herpes or AIDS. If a boat has the electrolytic pox, other boat owners will stand clear, even refuse to moor or dock alongside, lest they catch the dread disease which will eat away propellers, shafts, fastenings, struts, through-hulls, and anything else that gets in its way. The fact that a boat has "electrolysis" is mentioned in a hush, as if even the word could convey the contagion.

Although many of the myths about corrosion and electrolysis are false, the fear is well placed. Any metal, in a marine environment, will corrode. Sometimes the corrosion is nothing more than the attractive patina on exposed copper or bronze, or the protective oxidation that develops on the surface of raw aluminum. The "stainless" steel used in standing rigging develops rust stains, which are a form of surface corrosion. If metals are placed in unsuitable environments, the effects of corrosion can go far beyond surface patinas to pitting, dezincification, impingement corrosion, poultice corrosion, stress corrosion, crevice corrosion, cavitation erosion, or the rapid and horrifying ravages of electrolytic or stray-current corrosion, which can reduce a new fitting to scrap in less time than it takes to describe the process.

The good news is that severe types of corrosion are generally preventable, and most other forms of corrosion are controllable through careful shipbuilding and maintenance practices. There is no black magic to the process of galvanic and electrolytic corrosion. But despite hundreds of years of experience and research, there are no sure-fire procedures that will work for the potential problems on every boat.

To begin, it is important not to confuse galvanic corrosion, which is the interaction of dissimilar metals in an electrolyte, with electrolytic corrosion, which is the same process accelerated by the introduction of an electrical current, usually a stray current. In general, galvanic corrosion is slow and steady, and while the ultimate corrosive effect of dissimilar metals on one another isn't going to do your boat any good in most situations (there are exceptions!), the process is slow enough that you probably won't lose the boat overnight or even over the season because of a galvanic mismatch. Electrolytic corrosion, on the other hand, can cause startlingly rapid decay and deterioration of fittings. A propeller or shaft or through-hull can disintegrate so rapidly that you could leave the boat one weekend, come out the next weekend, and in trying to open a head sea cock find that the body of the fitting snaps off, leaving a 2-inch-wide hole in the bottom of your boat.

The way to avoid galvanic corrosion is to keep metals that are far apart on the galvanic scale away from one another, especially in environments where the mutual effects of the metals on one another are accentuated by the presence of seawater. Most boat owners are familiar with the galvanic scale.*

* Nigel Warren, *Metal Corrosion in Boats* (Camden, ME, 1980) and Edgar J. Beyn, *The 12 Volt Doctor's Practical Handbook* (Annapolis, 1983) are excellent references on corrosion and corrosion prevention.

The important thing to note on the scale is not the exact position of each metal, but the relative positions. You want to avoid "sandwiches" of metals that are far apart on the scale. For example, stainless steel is near the top and aluminum near the bottom of the galvanic scale. If you use a stainless steel fastening in an aluminum mast without insulating the metals

GALVANIC SCALE

NOBLE (anodic, passive)

Platinum
Gold
Graphite
Silver
Stainless steels (passive)
Titanium
Monel
Bronzes
Copper
Brasses
Tin
Lead
Stainless steels (active)
Iron
Mild steel
Aluminum
Cadmium
Galvanized steel
Zinc
Magnesium

LESS NOBLE (cathodic, active)

from each other, the aluminum around the fastening will quickly corrode.

In general, galvanic problems can be avoided by selecting only those metals that are suitable for use in a marine environment, and by not juxtaposing metals that are far apart on the galvanic scale, especially in the presence of seawater. Certain metals, in particular, should either be avoided or used carefully.

Stainless Steel Stainless steels appear twice on the galvanic scale. In their "passive" state, stainless steels are just below the precious metals. In their "active" state the stainless steels are below lead, just above iron and mild steel. The difference between those two states is the reason that stainless fastenings are superb for deck and mast fittings and generally unsuitable for underwater fittings.

Stainless steels are normally in the passive state when a continuous supply of fresh oxygen is available at the surface of the metal; when oxygen is denied to the surface, the metal will revert to its active state. The danger in the use of stainless steel comes because in some fittings part of the metal may be in one state and part in the other; for example a chain plate which is partially sealed into the deck with sealant and partially exposed to the air, or the end of a stainless steel cable which is swedged into a terminal fitting. At the joint of the sealed and exposed sections you will frequently see rust stains, which are a consequence of the two states being next to each other—almost as though they were different metals—and reacting galvanically with each other.

Stainless fittings and fastenings are excellent for deck and mast fittings, especially if they are kept isolated from aluminum and other incompatible metals by zinc chromate paste, mica washers, or even silicone sealants. Underwater, stainless steel is a less than ideal material, because an underwater fastening or fitting will frequently be partially or totally deprived of oxygen and will turn "active," for example under a barnacle, or in the case of a keel bolt, in the section that is enclosed by sealants. Once the "active" and "passive" parts of the stainless begin to react with each other, the result is surface or crevice corrosion, which in time can turn keel bolts waspwaisted and leave a shaft with deep crevices that in turn invite cavitation and other forms of corrosion.

The answer is to avoid stainless steel fittings and fastenings underwater whenever possible, in favor of Monel or bronze. If you do have stainless fittings underwater, make certain that (1) they are type 316 stainless, which is substantially more resistant to corrosion than the commoner type 304 stainless, and (2) that they are frequently inspected for telltale pitting that may be an indication of serious corrosion. Ideally, shafts for propellers and keel bolts for lead keels should be made of Monel or bronzes. If your boat instead has stainless bolts in a lead keel, check it from time to time. If the bolts loosen, if there is bad rust streaking on the keel bolts, or if there are leaks around the keel bolts, you may want to carry out a thorough inspection, including backing off a keel bolt, before real trouble develops.

Brass   On a boat, brass is not a good choice for any fitting more structural than a screw holding up an interior trim molding. Because of the relatively high zinc content of brass, brass fittings will often dezincify in a marine environment, leaving behind a spongelike mess. Be especially careful in buying plumbing fittings, which are often made in both brass and bronze. If the valve is being used for the kerosene line to the stove, brass is fine; if you are using a ball or gate valve on a through-hull or an engine fresh-water cooling line, you may end up in trouble from the dezincification of the brass fittings.

Aluminum   Aluminum is a splendid metal for marine use: light, strong, easily worked, and with the ability to develop an oxide coating which protects it from the ravages of weather. But aluminum is low on the galvanic scale, and it can react quickly and devastatingly in the presence of metals that are

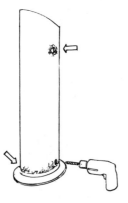

high on the scale. The copper in anti-fouling paint, the mercury from a broken thermometer, or the graphite in certain lubricants can wreak havoc with an aluminum hull, aluminum framing or floors in a boat, or aluminum spars. Even cleaning aluminum fittings with a steel wire brush will eventually cause pitting from the tiny bits of steel that become embedded in the aluminum, and a pencil mark on a raw aluminum spar will cause etching of the aluminum if the spar is wetted with salt water. Aluminum should also be watched when it is in contact with a wet wicklike material, for example when wet wood is in contact with aluminum in the bilges of a wood boat with aluminum floors or aluminum frames. The result is often poultice corrosion, a sticky white hydroxide that oozes out of the contact area in copious amounts. Aluminum fastenings are generally too weak for use on aluminum, so Monel or stainless steel fastenings have to be used, but to avoid surface corrosion and freezing of the threads of screws, the fastenings should be insulated from the aluminum by sleeves, washers, or a coating of zinc chromate paste.

ZINCS

When it is not possible to insulate dissimilar metals from one another—for example, when a bronze propeller is used on a stainless steel shaft—it is often necessary to provide protection to the less noble of the two metals. The most common method is by attaching a zinc, usually in the form of a sleeve on the shaft, so that the zinc becomes the least noble metal in the sandwich, and through its own decay protects the more noble metals.

Zincs work well, especially if they are correctly installed and of the proper size. Too much zinc can actually do damage to metal fittings and to the wood around fastenings in a wooden boat; too little zinc and the protection of the zinc is too short-lived or too local to accomplish its purposes. A zinc that is not in direct electrical contact with the metal it is supposed to protect will accomplish nothing. Thus fastening a large block of zinc to the exterior of a wooden hull without a direct electrical connection to the metal parts that are supposed to be protected will do nothing.* Hanging a zinc guppy from the shrouds of the boat into the water will also accomplish nothing, unless the shrouds are internally bonded to the metal parts that are supposed to be protected by the external guppy. Painting a zinc will pretty much negate its value.

Usually zincs are installed on the propeller shaft in the form of collars. The collars are of differing quality, with some having carefully seated fastenings and others so crudely cast and so cheaply made that as soon as the zinc begins to deteriorate —which, of course, it is supposed to do—the entire collar falls off the propeller shaft. If the zinc is impure it will deteriorate asymmetrically, leaving a large blob sticking off one side of the shaft and almost no zinc on the other side. The resulting imbalance of the shaft will quickly wear your cutlass bearing and shaft log, and transmit enough vibration to the boat to make certain that you don't fall asleep while motoring. And of course the vibration may be just enough to make the lopsided zinc fall off the shaft, which will leave the precious underwater metals unprotected.

There are two ways to calculate how much zinc you need:

(1) there are tables on which you enter the length of the boat and the configuration and type of underwater metal; the table then recommends how much zinc will be needed for a full year's protection of the underwater metal; or (2) you can measure the flow of current, which can be done with a sensitive millivolt or milliamp meter.† Either method can give good results, but for boat owners who do not have severe corrosion or stray-current problems, the usual way of determining how much zinc is needed is to examine the zinc periodically by diving. If the zinc deteriorates so quickly that it needs to be replaced more than once per season, it might be advisable to use two zincs or a larger zinc. And if you find that the zincs are deteriorating very rapidly, so that replacement is necessary after a month in the water, it is a fairly good indication that a stray current is reaching the bonding system of the boat.

STRAY CURRENTS

The tiny currents induced by galvanic action, if ignored, are capable of slow but steady destruction of underwater parts of a boat. When a stray current is introduced into the process, deterioration that might take months or years through galvanic corrosion takes place instead in weeks, days, or even hours. You can't ignore a stray-current problem in the hope that it will go away.

There are obvious stray-current problems that can spring

---

* Actually, the large block of zinc will probably cause some harm. Excessive protection is bad for a wooden boat, because wood in the way of the large electrical currents induced by the protection will eventually deteriorate through decalcification, turning gray and powdery and making you wonder if your boat has a rare form of rot.

† Nigel Warren, *Metal Corrosion in Boats* (Camden, ME, 1980), pages 128–129, provides tables. Warren also provides some good information and drawings of how to attach anodes to boats in cases where a shaft collar is insufficient for protection. Edgar J. Beyn, *The 12 Volt Doctor's Practical Handbook* (Annapolis, 1983), pages 106 ff, is a good guide to using a millivolt meter to measure the effectiveness of zinc protection on a boat.

up, such as live extension cords dropped into the water while you are working on the boat at dockside, or reversed polarity of connections to the AC shore power, but most stray-current corrosion occurs instead because of simple, scarcely noticeable wiring mistakes.

For example, you might install a new bilge pump and accidentally reverse the polarity of the connections, which is not difficult to do because the color coding of marine wiring is so confused that the brown wire of a brown/white pair may be the positive lead on the pump, and at the same time the brown wires in the boat distribution box might be the negative or ground leads. However it happens, you are headed for a potential disaster as the 12 volts flow from the casing of the bilge pump, through the bilge water, to whatever other "grounds" are present in the bilge. If the underwater fittings in the boat are all bonded together and any one of them is in the bilge, they will all be subjected to 12 volts of potential, which is enough to turn solid bronze sea cocks into pink gauze.

Or suppose the wiring that leads to the new bilge pump is marginal in size, and the pump operates under a 7 percent voltage drop caused by the small wires. And to save some wiring, the ground for the bilge pump goes directly to the engine block. The engine electrical systems will be at a full 13.0 volts or whatever your battery puts out; the pump will only get 12.1 volts, which is enough to operate the pump adequately. You hear the pump purring, you're sure everything is fine. Except that electrical currents abhor an imbalance, and with the bilge water as a conductor, current will flow to even out the imbalance between the potential at the pump and the potential at the engine. Less than 1 volt doesn't sound like much, but it is thousands of times the potential

that galvanic mismatches produce. The situation would produce quick havoc.

The only way to avoid stray current is to be extremely careful in wiring a boat. Check connections with a VOM before you make hookups permanent. The pump instruction manual or a wiring diagram on the case will tell you which wire is the positive lead. You can find out which of the wires coming out of the box is positive by putting the VOM leads on them. If you are using long leads and the wire sizes might be marginal, test the voltage under load.*

BONDING

One of the battles that marine electricians wage is over the virtues of bonding systems within boats. One side contends that all the metal in a boat, especially the underwater metal, should be bonded together and protected by a suitable anode (generally a zinc). The bonding, which would include the propeller and shaft, through-hulls, engine, rigging, and keel, provides protection against lightning (since the rigging will be grounded to the keel) and against stray-current corrosion, since any fitting that is likely to be affected by stray current will be protected by the zinc anode connected to the bonding network.

The other side argues that with rare exceptions a boat does not need bonding, and that in fact the bonding network in-

---

* It does no good to try to test the voltage drop when the device is not hooked up and running. Without a load, the voltage will read from 13.0 to 13.6 volts. It is only when the full load is on the wiring that you will get the voltage drop that causes troubles. If you ever feel a wire that is hot to the touch, you can suspect that there is enough resistance in the wire to produce a significant voltage drop, and that it should be replaced with a larger size.

duces corrosion problems by connecting dissimilar metals to one another. When a mass of stainless steel, copper, bronze, lead, and iron is connected up, it is almost impossible to determine what protection is needed, and since the protection afforded by a zinc is determined not only by the mass of the zinc but by the distance from the underwater metals that are to be protected, a zinc on the propeller shaft will do little to protect a through-hull fitting for the head in the bow of the boat. If the protection attached to the bonding network is inadequate, what you have accomplished by the network is to *induce* galvanic corrosion by connecting dissimilar metals through the bonding wires.

Should you have a bonding system? If a boat has no record of galvanic problems and if there are no potentially problematic uses of metals, such as aluminum floors, and if no shore power is wired onto the boat, a bonding network may indeed induce rather than cure problems. Some owners whose boats have severe galvanic corrosion problems discover that the simplest and most effective cure is to remove the bonding system and treat the underwater fittings one at a time for whatever galvanic problems they may have. A bronze through-hull bolted to the hull with bronze bolts, and with no other metal underwater fittings nearby, should have no galvanic corrosion problems. Indeed, the only protection that most boats need is for the shaft and propeller combination, and if a Monel shaft is used instead of stainless steel, or sometimes even with a stainless shaft and a bronze prop, it is possible to use no zinc at all and experience negligible galvanic corrosion. The exact composition of the underwater metal parts, the water temperature, the metallic content of the water, the proximity of nearby boats, even the speed of the current flowing by the boat, will all directly influence the level of galvanic activity, so that firm pronouncements that a boat needs or does not need a zinc or bonding are difficult to make.

If you determine that the boat does need a bonding system, or if a boat was built with a bonding system, it is important to maintain the system. Connections should be made with heavy-gauge wire (#8 or larger) or with solid copper straps. All electrical connections should be soldered, and the bonding system should never be used as a common ground for lorans, SSB radios, or other instruments or devices.* You will need an electrical brush to make a proper electrical contact with the shaft (you can make one from parts of an old electric motor, or buy the relevant parts from an appliance or vacuum cleaner dealer). And when a bonding system is installed, you will need to pay careful attention to providing corrosion protection to the underwater components of the system.

Any bonding system should be checked from time to time for stray currents by disconnecting the bonding system wires from the farthest forward or aft fitting and measuring the current, if any, between the bonding system wires and the fitting with a VOM set on the mA scale. If the bonding system is picking up stray currents, or if you attempt to protect all of the metal fittings on a bonded boat with a single zinc on the shaft, you will see current on the meter. As a monitoring system, the meter works best if periodic readings are taken, which will show changes caused by problems within the bonding system, the zinc, or with unanticipated stray currents.

---

* Jerry Kirschenbaum, "Electrolysis and Corrosion," *Wooden Boat* 24, September–October, 1978, has some excellent pointers on the installation of a sound bonding system.

SHORE POWER

The most likely source of stray currents is shore power. The ground wire in the shore power connector effectively connects your boat to every other boat on the dock, so that a zinc on any boat on the dock is in effect "protecting" all the other boats. Because the other boats are farther away, the protection afforded by the zinc is minimal, but it is possible for one boat with a galvanic or electrolytic problem to quickly dissipate the zincs—and then the rest of the underwater metals—of other boats connected to the same shore power ground.

You cannot disconnect the ground wire to isolate your boat from stray currents from other boats, because in case of a short anywhere in the AC wiring of the boat, the electrical box housing the AC circuits would become "hot." The alternative of using the boat's ground or bonding system as a third-wire ground is a worse solution, because in case of a short the current would flow through the bonding or ground system into the water, creating a fire or shock hazard. If the shore ground wire is causing corrosion problems on your boat because of other boats on the dock, the only safe alternatives are: (1) find the culprit boat and get it fixed; (2) use a ground fault circuit interrupter in the hot and neutral wires to the AC circuitry on your boat; (3) use an isolation transformer in the shore power wiring of the boat; or (4) wire silicon diodes in the ground wire to block stray currents. The threshold voltage for a silicon diode is 0.6 volts, so any voltage difference over 0.6 volts will cause a circuit breaker to trip, while smaller voltages will be blocked by the diodes.

If you elect to install a ground fault circuit interrupter or isolation transformer, make sure it is rated at the full capacity of the devices it will isolate. And if you are installing silicon diodes, make certain that they are rated for a current exceeding the circuit breaker tripping currents they are protecting.

LIGHTNING PROTECTION

One reason that is often given for bonding systems is protection against lightning. If you want to ground the rigging for protection from lightning, it can be done by connecting the chain plates, stem fitting, and backstay fitting to the keel. It is possible for lightning to strike any metal parts on a boat, including lifeline stanchions, genoa tracks, and winches, but the mast is so inviting that it is highly unlikely that lightning will choose a lesser target. The connections should be made with #8 or larger wire, with soldered terminal connections; the wires should not be used for any other purpose; and the wiring should be insulated from contact with other metal in the boat. One problem for many boats is that epoxy coatings or fiberglass over the keel lead effectively insulates the keel from the water. The propeller then becomes the largest conductor in the water, and lightning may follow an unpredictable path between the mast and the propeller. Hence it is a good idea to connect the mast base to the electrical ground point on the engine, again with heavy-gauge wire.

If lightning does strike your boat, the electronics will probably be fried. A VHF antenna that is electrically grounded (like many of the masthead metal whips) may help to prevent substantial damage to the electronics, but count on some damage to the electronics and electrical systems, and be prepared to spend time diagnosing exactly what damage the lightning has done, including burned or melted insulation, "cooked" electrical and electronics components, and "spiked" electronic components that may look healthy but have effectively been destroyed by the lightning or by induced voltages in other wiring within the boat.

CATHODIC PROTECTION

An alternative to using zincs to protect a boat from corrosion is the use of impressed current, which is nothing more than an induced current that counteracts the current generated by the galvanic reaction. Impressed current devices are complicated and expensive, depending on a platinum sensor in the water to read the required current, which is then drawn from the vessel's DC supply by a controller circuit. On steel ships, an impressed current system can protect bare steel from rusting if enough current is available. On pleasure boats, the impressed current systems are usually reserved for very large steel or aluminum yachts, although OMC and Mercury manufacture smaller impressed current systems that can be used to protect the aluminum drive legs and propellers of their I/O (inboard/outboard) units. The CAPAC units manufactured by Engelhard Industries in Newark, New Jersey, are available for vessels of all sizes. Naturally the systems have to be installed and monitored carefully. The boat should always have backup power available, since the protection system may exhaust a battery while the boat is on a mooring, and there should be an alarm to warn if the power or the cathodic protection system has failed.

PREVENTION

The most important measure you can take to prevent corrosion of the metal fittings on your boat is to conduct a periodic inspection of the fittings, their installation, and the wiring of the boat. In particular, watch out for contact between dissimilar metals, or for stainless steel or aluminum in contact with seawater. For example, the base of aluminum masts, if they are not properly drained, will corrode. Drill drainage holes as required, and make certain that existing drainage holes stay open. Centerboard pins or cables are often made of stainless steel; because they are wet some of the time and damp all of the time, they are subject to corrosion caused by oxygen deprivation, which makes some of the stainless steel "active" and some "passive." Stainless steel shafts, especially in areas where the metal is covered by barnacles, cutlass bearings, or the hub of the propeller, can go "active" and cause pitting to the shaft. Propellers are subject to galvanic corrosion and to cavitation and velocity corrosion. Whenever you see pitting on a propeller, it is time for reconditioning and for investigation of just what caused the problem. And the wiring on a boat should be examined periodically to make certain that there are no voltage drops, reversed polarities, or sloppy wiring practices that will lead, almost as fast as you can say it, to severe electrolytic corrosion.

22

SAFETY

Most new boats are sold with what the dealer or manufacturer variously calls a Coast Guard or "safety" package, consisting usually of one or more fire extinguishers; four, six, or eight orange life vests; an air horn; a flare kit; a plastic first-aid kit with Band-Aids, cola syrup, and a mouth-to-mouth resuscitator; and possibly a bell. Some dealers also put dock and ground tackle into the package. And if the new boat owner expresses an interest in safety gear, or an interest in racing, the dealer will probably sell him additional safety gear, such as a man-overboard horseshoe equipped with a floating strobe light, a man-overboard pole with a flag at the top, and an inflatable life raft. If you are relying on a list of safety gear like that on your boat, chances are that you have been either very lucky or very timid in your sailing experiences.

The accidents or disasters that most frequently occur on a sailboat are fire, collision with other boats, grounding, dismasting, someone falling overboard, and a variety of medical emergencies that can range from abrasions and seasickness to broken bones or appendicitis. And even when accidents don't happen, the fear of accidents, especially on a boat that is not equipped with comfortable and effective safety gear, can so lower crew efficiency that fatigue or anxiety can invite a different kind of disaster: if no one is willing to go to the foredeck to take down the #3 genoa and set a storm jib, the boat can end up a pile of rubble on a lee shore.

The most important safety precaution on any boat is careful, workmanlike installation of hardware and equipment. Inappropriate or inadequately sized fittings and fastenings, poorly swaged rigging terminals, badly spliced lines or Nicopressed wires, sloppy fitting of gear, improper bedding practices, and general lack of maintenance on materials and equipment in a marine environment can, and eventually will, lead to the unexpected. The dramatic accidents on a boat rarely have freak causes: masts don't fall down for no reason at all; turning blocks don't pop off decks without warning; stoves don't flare up because of poltergeists; and boats don't explode because of voodoo curses. The cause, almost every time, is careless workmanship, careless maintenance, or careless use. An improperly swaged rigging terminal, or a terminal that has been repeatedly filled with water and frozen, will eventually fatigue or fail, usually taking the mast with it. An inadequately sized turning block will eventually distort or explode, usually when the #3 genoa is up in 25 knots of true breeze and the boat is falling off seas and putting tremendous shock loads on the genoa sheet. If somebody is standing in the bight of the genoa sheet when the block explodes, they will be hurt, probably badly. If the shut-off valve for a stove is hard to reach, there will come a time when a minor flare-up will become an inferno that consumes the headliner, the galley, or the boat. And it doesn't have to happen.

FIRE

Stoves, engines, generators, and electrical systems pose a constant danger of fire on a boat. Whether the stove fuel is supposedly safe alcohol, kerosene, diesel, CNG or LPG, remember that if it is hot enough to cook with, it is hot enough to consume the boat. Gasoline engines are time bombs on a boat. On the highway, gasoline vapors can sink harmlessly to the highway. On a boat the fumes will accumulate in the bilge, where it takes a single spark—one loose or frayed wire

on the engine or the wiring network that powers the boat—and that teacup of gasoline vapor becomes enough to blow off decks or houses and to burn the boat to the waterline. Even diesel engines are dangerous. Diesel fuel has a high flash point, but once a fire starts, the fuel will burn; the surfaces of an overheated engine, or the exhaust system of an engine, are hot enough to burn lubricating oil, diesel fuel, and, eventually, the rubber hoses, plastic parts, wiring and sound insulation, and deck and joinery panels.

Although you are surrounded by water, when a fire starts on a boat, you rarely have time for the bucket brigade, or even to use the puny fire extinguishers that are supplied as part of a safety package. Hence fire safety should begin with prevention, which means absolutely sound installations. Plumbing should be properly installed and fastened in place against vibration and chafe. Shutoff valves should be accessible from far enough away from the stove or engine that the fuel can be shut off while a fire is raging. Surfaces that are likely to become fuel for the fire—such as the paneling of a stove compartment or cabinets over a stove—should be at a safe distance, or at least should be covered with materials that will prevent a minor flare-up from turning into a major conflagration.

The bilge of a boat should be kept clean and ventilated, not just for pride or to keep away the uninvited smells of oil, diesel fuel, rotted food, grunge, yuk, and the other unnamed substances that gather there, but because the bilge is primary fuel for a fire on board. Oil in the bilge is often the first fuel for an engine fire. Food in the bilge can turn to methane gas; a single spark from a loose bilge pump wire will eliminate the wretched smell of the methane along with the boat. Regular scrubbing and pumping, use of bilge cleaners to emulsify oils, or the use of oil-absorbent materials (made by 3M in the form of rags and by other companies in the form of "logs") will keep the bilge clean, sweet, and safe.

On a gasoline-powered boat, or a boat that uses heavier-than-air vapor fuels (LPG) for cooking, use a bilge blower to clear the bilges and a vapor detector or alarm to find out if there is a leak you don't know about. It isn't enough to install an alarm or a bilge blower. Install it so that it gets used. If you are not rigidly conscientious, use one of the engine and battery switches which forces you to run the blower before starting the engine.

Then install fire extinguishers which are large enough to put out a fire, easy to use, and benign enough in the damage they cause to the rest of the boat that you and your crew will be willing to use them on a small fire. The cheap fire extinguishers that are sold for use on boats will put out fires, but only if you aim the limited flow right at the base of the fire. Since boat owners know that the materials inside the fire extinguisher will make a mess of their joinery and cushions, they are often reluctant to use the extinguisher until the fire is so big that it is too late. The answer is to use Halon fire extinguishers, which are more expensive but do not leave damaging residues in the interior of the boat. The Coast Guard requirements represent a minimum for fire extinguishers. But just as the designation "suitable for a 30-foot boat" is nearly useless in picking rigging gear, the specification of overall length helps little in identifying the needs for fire extinguishers. What is more important is to have *accessible, usable* fire extinguishers available wherever there is a potential danger of fire. A large fire extinguisher is of no use if it cannot be reached, and relying on a single extinguisher installed midway between the galley and the engine compartment is foolish.

The most dangerous fires occur in the engine compartment. With a gasoline engine, the combustion of fuel vapors in the closed confines of the engine compartment is explosive. With a diesel engine or generator, a fire usually starts because of an oil leak, and by the time the fire is discovered, the temperature in the engine compartment is so high that opening an inspection port wide enough to insert a fire extinguisher would be difficult, if not impossible. The only really effective fire extinguisher for the engine compartment is an internally mounted extinguisher which either triggers itself or can be triggered from outside the compartment by a remote cable release. The Halon units that are sold for engine compartment use come in two types: the less expensive units will automatically trigger but lack the external trip wire; the more expensive units, with the external trip, are often Coast Guard–approved for commercial installations. If you are installing a Halon extinguisher, make sure it is large enough. The usual measure is by engine compartment size, because the volume of Halon will quickly disperse—without extinguishing the fire—if the engine compartment is too large for the extinguisher.

Remember too that every fire needs oxygen. Shutting the air intakes to a tightly sealed engine compartment or smothering a galley fire can be as effective as a fire extinguisher. Just make certain that in your panic you don't reach for a blanket made of Dacron or other synthetic materials. Buckets and water are effective on fires in wood and fabric, but for most boat fires water is not an effective answer. If you throw buckets of seawater on a alcohol stove flare-up, you will eventually put the fire out, but you will also slop enough water around to assure the rusting of the stove. And on electrical fires or chemical fires, water could convert a small fire to a major disaster.

MAN OVERBOARD

The thought of someone going overboard strikes fear into every sailor, and most boats carry gear that is designed to avoid a disaster. Even boats in coastal cruising areas are sometimes seen equipped with the full range of man-overboard gear: a 15-foot pole with a flag, a horseshoe ring, lights, drogues, dye for high visibility from the air, flashing strobes, and frequently special devices to hold the apparatus at the ready, so a single pull of a toggle or string will fire off the rescue equipment.

The horseshoe rings do float, the poles are ballasted so that the flag is visible from some distance, and on a very dark night the flasher can also be seen for some distance. But even if the devices have been released immediately after a person falls overboard, the procedures required to rescue a person are exacting, difficult in the best of circumstances, and require numbers of able crew members that are usually available only on racing boats:

1. In any weather, you need one person to do nothing but watch the person in the water. In bad weather—which is when the incident generally occurs—you need two or more people who do nothing except watch the person in the water.
2. You must turn the boat around and follow a reciprocal course. There are many theories about how best to come back and approach the person in the water, whether to take an exact reciprocal or to approach from upwind. You will find yourself hard pressed to remember or even think about theories when someone falls overboard. Depending upon your point of sail, certain sails may have to be dropped quickly, and depending upon wind conditions you may need to hoist other sails to get the boat to make decent progress on the opposite course.
3. If you are sailing, you have to make certain that the prop is clear of lines and that the engine can be started. The hurry to start the engine in a situation like this is a prime time for an explosion on a boat with a gasoline engine.
4. After sailing back, you have to find a way to bring the boat to a position close alongside the person in the water, and with no way on. In the magazine articles that tell you to come onto a beam reach or head to wind with the sails luffing, it sounds easy. Try it in a strong breeze with a sea running! And remember that you are going to be reluctant to use your engine with a weak person in the water next to the boat.
5. You have to find a way of getting the person on board the boat. In calm water, even if the person is strong enough to help, it is often difficult to get him or her up over the high freeboard of a modern racer-cruiser. Remember that the person in the water is tired, cold, and frightened, possibly close to panic. It is unlikely that they will be able to help themselves up a swim ladder. Again, the magazine articles describe marvelous techniques of lowering a fold of the mainsail or using a 4:1 "handy billy" tackle which is kept convenient for just such purposes. Try the technique before you put much faith in it.

In sum, unless you have a full crew aboard, have practiced the routine, and have additional equipment ready to help pull the person from the water, you may not be able to effect a rescue of a person who has fallen overboard. Even life jackets, which are rarely worn on any except small boats, are no answer. If the water is cold, hypothermia may set in before you can get a person back on board, and while the descriptions of snuggling up with a hypothermia victim to warm them with body heat may sound appealing, first you have to locate the person and get them aboard, and that is not an easy task.

The only answer is to make sure that people do not fall overboard. In mild weather, you keep people on the boat by providing decent non-skid decks, plenty of convenient handholds, and good lifelines—three features that are not always present on boats. In heavier weather, there is no substitute for good harnesses and secure attachment points for the harnesses.

Non-skid decks, especially in the areas where people are likely to be working on the boat or carrying heavy sails or equipment, should be *non-skid*. Raw teak, good molded gelcoat non-skid, painted finishes with the proper additives, and glued-on non-skid materials like Treadmaster all work. But if you find areas or places on your boat where people frequently seem to loose their footing, such as a foredeck hatch or the counter (where many crewmen spend at least part of a sail, with one hand on the backstay, "checking the depth of the water"), you can add additional material or supplement the non-skid with glued-on strips of special anti-skid material or Treadmaster. Boats with cambered decks, which when heeled present an almost vertical leeward deck, are the worst offenders.

Almost as dangerous as bad non-skid are deck fittings that seem placed to trip. Spinnaker pole chocks, cleats on side decks, and genoa cars are frequent offenders. There is little that can be done about the genoa cars, but if you find yourself or your crew frequently tripping on the spinnaker pole or deck cleats, a little time working on cleat or chock guards, or moving the pole, may prevent an accident.

Handholds are usually put on the top of the house, where they are useful for tying spare sheets or halyard tails. If you find that you are constantly grasping for a grip on the mast or boom while working at the mast or halyards, or that whoever works the foredeck frequently has feet or hands locked in positions worthy of a Houdini, it may be worth considering additional handholds, which are available ready-made in teak and mahogany, easy to add, attractive, and useful for more than a grip. The easiest way to add a handhold is to through-bolt with another handhold on the inside of the boat. In any case, make certain that they are through-bolted with large washers and locknuts, and that if they are installed on a cored deck, that the core material is epoxy-soaked. The loads on a handgrip can be substantial enough to crush core material.

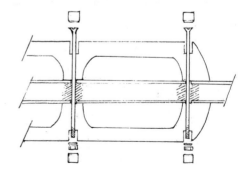

Lifelines keep a falling person on board and serve as a stronghold to grab when you need it. Unfortunately some lifelines are not built strong enough to withstand the load of a person thrown across the boat, or a person putting full weight on the upper lifeline or the top of a stanchion. In effect, the length of the stanchion and the size of the base form a lever; the taller the stanchion and the smaller the base, the greater the loads exerted on the deck and stanchion base. Improperly engineered or installed stanchions and stanchion bases will bend, distort, break, or crush and break loose from a deck under the weight of an adult thrown across the boat by an unexpected wave or a banana peel on the deck.

A good stanchion base is welded, not cast, and has a strong welded bail, which while useful for attachment of snatch blocks, barber haulers, and spring lines, should be placed so that it strengthens the base of the stanchion against the anticipated loads. The base should be large, fastened with four well-spaced bolts (which should be at least ¼ inch and preferably larger), should be bolted over solid deck or with epoxy or metal spacers, should have a large backing plate and lock washers or aircraft nuts. There are alternatives: some of the California ultra-lights are built with stanchion bases molded into the fiberglass. If it is done well, it can be strong, light, and clean. The stanchions themselves should be strong enough to not bend when a heavy adult falls against the top. In particular, watch for stress or deformation at the point where the stanchion leaves the base. Finally, the holes for the lifelines should be bushed to prevent chafe. If you see your stanchions bend when you approach a dock too fast and someone uses the stanchion to fend off the boat, imagine what will happen when someone is thrown against the stanchion during a broach.

Pulpits and pushpits (stern pulpits) should be of sturdy, welded construction, with bases large enough to spread the loads of a bowman standing on the pulpit to reach the end of the spinnaker pole, or of five crewmen, hunched together in the stern to keep the bow up on a wild downwind "sleigh ride," suddenly thrown against the pushpit when the boat comes off a wave. Make certain that the bases of pulpits and pushpits are welded or forged, not cast, that the feet of the bases are large enough to spread loads, and that the pushpit and pulpit are properly mounted with backing plates, spacers or epoxy plugs in the holes, and adequate bolts with locknuts.

Finally, the lifelines should run all the way around the boat. A gap between the forward lifeline and the pulpit, supposedly to allow the foot of the genoa to run smoothly between them, is a gap that a bowman or a sail will fall through. Lifelines that do not extend to a pushpit, or to strong, braced corner posts and lifelines across the stern, are an invitation to fall overboard. Remember that the most common cause of men overboard is not horrendous gales at sea; it is a crewman taking a leak off the stern at night who uses two hands to zip up his fly when he needs one hand for the boat. Without lifelines, there is nothing to keep him in the boat.

The lifelines themselves are traditionally vinyl-covered 7 x 7 stainless cable. The vinyl chafes and discolors, and the wire underneath is frequently rusty.* You can clean the vinyl with commercial cleaners, but eventually it will be scored by chafe with lines or worn away at the stanchion bushings. If you try strong solvents as a cleaner, the vinyl will turn sticky. When the time comes, replace it with 1 x 19 stainless cable, which is substantially stronger for the same diameter, has a smooth finish which will not corrode or need frequent cleaning if left exposed, and is cheaper. The additional flexibility of the 7 x 7 wire is not needed unless your lifelines are making bends that they shouldn't make in any case. You can use $\frac{3}{16}$-inch wire for upper lifelines in boats up to approximately 40 feet overall, and $\frac{7}{32}$- or $\frac{1}{4}$-inch wire for larger boats. Lower lifelines can be a size smaller ($\frac{5}{32}$ for smaller boats and $\frac{3}{16}$ for larger boats).

Lifeline terminals are another weak point. Pelican hooks and snap shackle hooks are convenient at a dock or mooring.

* See Chapter 21 for a discussion of why "stainless" cable rusts, and why a vinyl-covered lifeline is an almost certain invitation to rust.

But if the hook is convenient to open, it is too easy to open and an invitation to an accident. The so-called safety hooks, which have a provision for a cotter pin for offshore sailing, require that you remember to put the pin in. It is much safer to eliminate hooks from the lifelines. The lifelines should be toggled at the terminal ends, so that no leverage is put on the exit from the terminal, which is generally a weak point. Nicopress fittings are not a good idea for lifelines, and the terminal fittings which are applied at home with a Nicopress machine are a worse idea. They are called lifelines for a reason: use the safest possible terminal—a carefully swaged marine eye or forged lifeline eye.

Most lifelines are fitted with turnbuckles, but a lashing at one end is a better idea. The turnbuckles need to be pinned, which means a wad of tape to make a fitting that will not chafe sails or people. The complete circuit that is formed by lifelines, pushpit, and pulpit can interfere with radio reception and especially radio direction finding. And in emergency situations, such as trying to hoist a person from overboard onto the deck, trying to undo a turnbuckle or to pull the clevis pin from a terminal fitting can waste precious time. With a lashing, you take a knife and cut it! It takes only a few minutes afterward to restore the lifeline, or to retighten lifelines after they have stretched. If you do have turnbuckles, be sure to peel the wads of tape off each year and examine the screws and pins. Replace cruddy cotter pins or wingdings, and watch for bent turnbuckle screws, which are probably weak points. If they are locknut turnbuckles, replace them! Your favorite rigger can build a new mast to replace the one that falls down because the turnbuckle backed off; when the lifeline turnbuckle backs off at the wrong time you lose more than the mast.

HARNESSES

Lifelines and handgrips are fine in moderate weather. When the seas get rough, when the wind is piping, and especially at night, there is only one safe and sure way to prevent man-overboard accidents: harnesses. Without a harness, a crew member on deck needs at least one and sometimes both hands just to hold on to the boat. In cold, wet weather, or when fatigue makes even simple activities difficult, a crew member who is trying to hold on can accomplish little more than tentative stabs at getting work done. If a seasick person is on deck without a harness, trying to get a breath of air in rough weather, it will take two other people to hold the person on board. If a person goes forward to change a headsail when seas are breaking on the bow of the boat, a job that might take two minutes in good weather, or five minutes in rough weather with a harness, will take half an hour without a harness. If you have never experienced the inefficiency of working on deck in rough weather without a harness, try tying a bowline in the clew of a sail, on the leeward rail, with the boat heeling enough to put the rail under.

A life jacket, even the most comfortable design of life jacket, impedes your freedom of motion, leaving you less adept at holding on. For children, most life jackets are uncomfortable or unsafe. Indeed, for children on the deck of a sailboat, a harness is the only way to guarantee their safety. By the age of five or six, a child can learn how to clip on his or her own harness, and how to clip and unclip as he or she moves forward on the boat. If they are taught that harnesses just like theirs are routine on big racing and offshore cruising boats, that racers use the same kinds of clips and the same proce-dures for safety, children will enjoy the harness and be pleased with their own agility in moving around the boat. And when you and your children are confident about their safety, you will all enjoy sailing more, especially in the moderate or heavy weather that would otherwise confine a child to the cabin.

Two criteria define a good harness: (1) Is it safe, which means strong and reliable? And (2) is it comfortable enough that it gets worn? Safe means strong, wide webbing; welded D-rings; carefully sewn terminations of the straps; and very strong clips. Most of the best harnesses now use webbing rather than rope for the tether, and specialized large marine hooks rather than carabiner hooks. A carabiner may work fine in mountain climbing use, because mountain climbers inspect and oil their equipment before each use, and in climbing a steady tension is applied to the carabiner. On a boat, the harness and its hardware are subjected to salt spray and to long-term storage in a locker under the berth, and the hook is subjected to load only in an emergency; the rest of the time it is twisted and pressed against lifelines, stanchions, and deck hardware at angles that can easily open almost any kind of hook. And when loading is finally applied to the hook, it is the shock load of a person being thrown across the boat, over the lifelines and to the full length of the tether. If you are buying harnesses for safety—and you should!—don't scrimp on harnesses, hooks, or tethers.

The second criterion is comfort, which is a matter of fit and of preference. The Lirakis harnesses are comfortable but must be purchased in specific sizes. Other harnesses are not as comfortable but can be adjusted, so that a single adult harness will fit a range of sizes. There are also good harnesses that are built into foul-weather gear, floatcoats, or vests. It is tempting to buy all-in-one gear, but there are conditions when you want a harness and not a floatcoat, or when you need a slicker top and don't want to wear the heavy jacket with a built-in harness. Whatever harnesses you are buying, try them on. Some harnesses that work well on men are exceedingly uncomfortable for women. And remember, if a harness isn't comfortable, people won't wear it routinely in heavy weather, which means that their own safety and efficiency and the safety of everyone else on the boat will be at risk.

The best harnesses in the world won't do anything if a boat is not equipped with plenty of secure, strong pad eyes and other clip-on points. Lifelines and stanchion bases are often used, but they are not ideal. If you are going to be on one side of the boat for a long time, a stanchion base is strong and reliable, but remember that if the boat broaches, your clip-on point may be underwater.

It is possible to fasten a harness tether almost anywhere by looping it around a spar, stanchion, traveler bridge, and handhold and clipping it onto itself. If the clip-on point is the mast or another strong point, and the snap on the end of the tether is not twisted, and the tether does not chafe, it will work fine. Heavy seas at night are not the way to test for chafe or twist by experiment.

A well-rigged boat should have a number of strong throughbolted pad eyes or other strong points available close to the centerline. The stern side of the bridge deck, the underside of the traveler bridge, the aft edges of the companionway, and the middle of the foredeck are excellent positions for pad eyes. The companionway or bridge deck pad eyes enable a crewmember to "hook on" before coming on deck and to get partway belowdecks, to the safety of the companionway ladder,

before "unhooking." The middle of the foredeck gives a bowman enough tether to do the work he needs to do, but keeps his extension short enough that he doesn't end up in the water; often a staysail tack eye will be ideally placed. Finally, pad eyes in the center of the cockpit let crewmen move from side to side for tacking or other maneuvers without unclipping and reclipping.

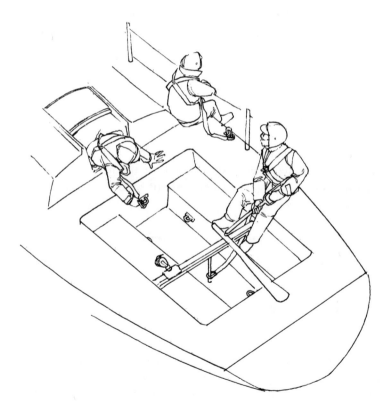

Boats that do extended offshore sailing go one step further and use either permanent or easily rigged jacklines, usually of ¼-inch stainless cable, which are rigged to strong points fore and aft on the boat. The advantage of a jackline is that it enables a person to go forward and aft without unhooking. The hardware should be strong, especially if more than one person will ever be hooked to a jackline. Use heavy-duty pad eyes, 7 x 7 cable, and strong screw shackles at the ends, with wiring holes and wires to secure the shackles. And if possible run the jacklines where they will not be a trip point for lines or feet. Close to the coaming or cabin is sometimes a good place for the lines, which need not run all the way to the bow and stern. Many boat owners think that if the need ever arises they can quickly rig temporary jacklines with lengths of line. If you've never tried it, you may discover that what sounds like a great idea is almost impossible in practice.

There are also devices manufactured which use clever engineering to allow a person to hook onto a device that rolls along a wire fastened to the inside of the stanchions. The devices I have seen always work flawlessly at the boat show demonstrations, but I would be wary of trusting any clever device offshore, at night, in inclement weather. Real safety comes from simple, strong equipment, not gadgets.

BOSUN'S CHAIR

Even if you hire a professional rigger for everything from taping your spreader tips to changing a light bulb for your masthead light, you need a safe, reliable bosun's chair on board. No matter how cautious and careful you are, no matter how thorough your preventive maintenance schedule is in the spring and fall, there will come a time when someone will let go of the end of a spinnaker halyard and hoist it all the way up the mast, or when a halyard will part, or a sail catch under a tang. And while it is possible to jury-rig a bosun's chair from knots such as a Portuguese sheet bend or a French bowline, the cost, bulk, and weight of a bosun's chair is so modest that it is wise to carry a comfortable and safe chair on the boat.

If you build a bosun's chair from a plank with drilled holes, cross the lines under the plank, watch out for chafe at the holes, and perhaps include a line or sail tie across the back to keep you from sliding backward when you are working in the chair. If you buy a chair, you have a choice between soft chairs that are safe but have a tendency to reduce the width of your hips after a half hour aloft; plank or board chairs, which are comfortable but less secure; and harness chairs, which can be very uncomfortable but which are so secure that you can hang upside down with no danger of falling out.

Although it is used only occasionally, a bosun's chair must be absolutely secure and reliable. Look for wide webbing, reinforcing patches, welded D-rings, and double- or triple-sewn seams. The most efficient chairs have the attachment points low, so that you can work on the masthead without having to reach over your own head, but that kind of short-ened hoist is safe only in a chair that holds you securely with harness straps on your legs and middle. Trying to hoist a plank chair on a short bridle is an invitation to fall out of the back of the chair.

For tools, some of the chairs have built-in pockets, but it is sometimes tricky to fish around in a pocket when you are 50 or more feet off the deck. The easiest way to carry tools aloft is in a canvas bucket, which can either be tied to the bosun's chair or hoisted on a separate halyard.

Whatever kind of chair you use, be cautious of the halyards that are used to hoist you or anyone else aloft. You may not weigh much more than a heavy genoa, but the repair rates charged by orthopedic surgeons are substantially higher than the rates charged by any sailmaker. If you aren't absolutely sure of the condition of the halyard, inspect it. It takes only a minute to attach a messenger to the shackle and pull the halyard far enough to see if there are any weak or chafed points. Avoid snap shackles in favor of a strong screw shackle placed directly into the Nicopress loop or through the welded or forged eye of the snap shackle. Or better yet, use a rope halyard and tie a bowline directly into the ring on your bosun's chair. If you do use a snap shackle, tape it closed, and tape the lanyard so that it cannot snag and accidentally pull the shackle open. If you go up in a seaway or a rough anchorage, consider a line from the bottom of the bosun's chair to the deck to steady the chair. Wear long pants if you aren't absolutely sure that there are no snags on the rigging or the spar.

Finally, be suspicious of every piece of gear that is used to hoist you. A self-tailing winch is a fine way to get aloft, but when you are at the top, make certain the line is cleated on a reliable horn cleat. Don't trust halyard stoppers, cam cleats, or clam cleats. The cautions you take may seem excessive, but you will find that you can work better and more efficiently if you aren't clinging to the mast with two legs and one hand, bracing yourself because a little voice inside tells you that you don't really trust the chair, the halyard, or the person operating the winch.

LIFE RAFTS AND EPIRBS

Life rafts are required equipment for racing in some areas, even on inshore overnight races or round-the-buoys races. There are also many coastal cruisers who include a life raft as regular equipment, sometimes with a full safety kit of emergency rations, a still for fresh water, signaling mirrors, flare kits, and an automatic EPIRB.*

There is rarely any harm in carrying a life raft or an EPIRB, but in coastal waters both are of limited usefulness. The life raft, in particular, can be in the way or dangerous if misused or improperly stored, and both pieces of gear will detract from the safety of a boat if they are used as a substitute for working safety gear, harnesses in particular.

Racing or cruising offshore, where there is a constant danger from unseen or unavoidable ship traffic, or perhaps from whales and other large objects, every boat needs a reliable life raft, positioned for quick access and stocked with the proper emergency gear. Many survivors of shipwrecks have chronicled the hazards of the sea, the need for immediate access to the life raft, the dangers of not having a painter attached to the raft and a knife to cut the painter, and the requirements for an adequate life raft and adequate supplies. And there are now many testimonials to the effectiveness of EPIRBs, including the newer satellite-monitored EPIRBs, in directing aid to a shipwreck victim within days or even hours of the wreck.

* EPIRBs (emergency position-indicating radio beacons) are compact, self-contained radio transmitters which transmit a distinctive emergency signal on two frequencies (121 MHz and 243 MHz) that are monitored by commercial and military aircraft. There are also VHF EPIRBs which transmit a short-range distress signal for boats not equipped with VHF radios.

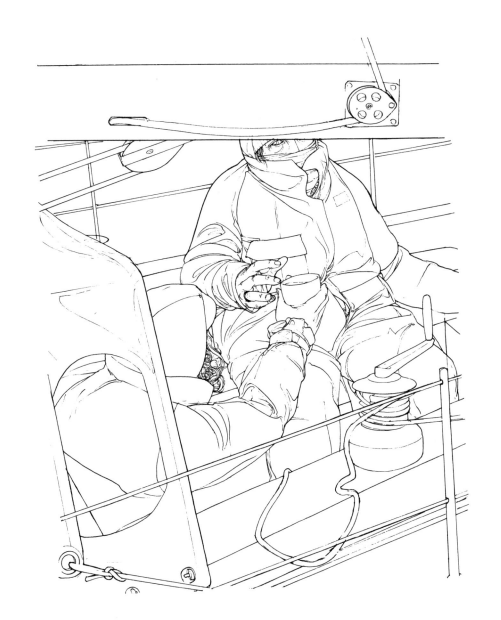

But the suitability of that gear for offshore racing or cruising, through shipping lanes and across intercontinental aircraft routes, does not mean that the same gear makes a comparable contribution to the safety of a boat used in coastal or inshore racing or cruising. Boats are wrecked inshore, and recently pleasure boats have collided with tugs and barges with tragic loss of life, but it is rare that a boat goes down suddenly and without warning. A grounding, whether gentle or violent, is more likely. And while there are aircraft overhead in Chesapeake Bay or Long Island Sound, an EPIRB will probably not contribute much to your safety in those waters, because aircraft on their approach to National or La Guardia are not likely to notice your beacon.

If you do carry a life raft, whether to meet safety requirements or because you feel that it is necessary safety gear, you will face the problem of where and how to store it. Cruisers often favor deck mountings, which require hard storage cases and lashings or quick-release snap shackles. The life raft presents windage and must be lashed so securely that it cannot break loose in heavy seas; at the same time it must be easy to deploy, which means strong, well-maintained snap shackles, or heavy lashings and the absolute availability of a sharp knife. If you haven't tried cutting a substantial lashing, try it under calm conditions; then imagine breaking seas, whistling wind, and perhaps the panic of a sinking boat. (You may discover that for rope larger than small twine, a bread knife is more effective than even a sharp "sailor's" knife.)

The alternative is a compartment with access from the cockpit, such as an under-seat locker or a special compartment in the cockpit sole. Racing yachts are often designed with compartments built in for life rafts. If you keep a life raft there for any reason other than a statutory compliance with the race regulations, make certain that it can be removed in the conditions when it is likely to be needed. Imagine if the rig were to topple: would the boom or other rigging make it nearly impossible to reach the life raft?

A life raft can also be stored belowdecks, but remember that it will be needed in a hurry, and usually in conditions that are not conducive to digging through piles of gear in the bottom of lockers. The most out-of-the-way locker is inviting, but if you are carrying a life raft with an idea toward ever using it, it should be accessible.

Finally, life rafts are of no use unless they work. The schedules recommended by the manufacturers and by various safety regulations may seem excessive, but a life raft that is ignored for too long often turns into a moldy mess, with rusty valves that may inflate the raft but that will not hold air or CO_2 long enough to qualify the raft as anything other than a brief spectacle. Try to resist the temptation to test the raft yourself, or at least to enjoy the spectacle of an inflation before you send it in for inspection and repacking. Most packers and inspectors add a surcharge if you have inflated the raft.

RUNNING LIGHTS

On a dark night, especially in foggy or murky weather, you can sometimes almost be on top of another sailboat before you see the hull or sails. The running lights that are installed on some boats don't help the situation much.

The regulations that have been specified for running lights are good guidelines, *if* the running lights on the boat are chosen for the actual use the boat will see. For example, masthead tricolor lights do meet the requirements for boats under approximately 40 feet, and for offshore sailing they offer both a simple installation and the advantage of maximum range and visibility over large seas. But the seas in Long Island Sound or the Chesapeake are rarely big enough to warrant a masthead running light, and in inshore waters an observer on another boat may be looking for lights close to the water and actually miss you because of your masthead lights.

Running lights installed on the deck or a flush installation in the topsides is also dangerous, because the light is so close to the water that it is obscured when the boat heels. And many of the older deck- or hull-mounted lights use bulbs and glasses which are not visible for anything approaching the ranges needed for safety. For most sailing, the pulpit and pushpit are better locations for the running lights. There are many units available which are relatively inexpensive, and which by using vertical filament bulbs are able to combine port and starboard lights in a single unit.

ANCHOR LIGHTS

In many anchorages, marked "special anchorages" on the charts, you do not need an anchor light. It is still a good idea. The last boat to show up in an anchorage is likely to be carrying weary sailors. They will have their eyes on the charts and the channels, and without a light they may not see you until your anchor rode is wrapped around their propeller. Again, while masthead lights are popular, they aren't always the safest light. They will protect you from low-flying airplanes, but the crew that is motoring in at 2 a.m., ready to drop a hook

and flop off to sleep, is likely to have their eyes glued to the water, not up in the air. It is simple and inexpensive to rig an anchor light that goes up between a halyard and a downhaul or that lashes onto the headstay.

SAFE GEAR

Safety gear and equipment can contribute to your safety on a boat, or at least help pick up the pieces when something goes wrong. No safety gear can really make up for shoddy, unsafe, or missing gear on a boat. A good first-aid kit will help patch up someone who has cut a hand on a meat hook on a halyard or been smashed in the face by a runaway winch handle in a reel winch. A good mallet and drift pin, or a hacksaw with plenty of blades, or a very large and strong cable cutter will help you cut away broken rigging. An emergency call on a good VHF may help locate medical assistance for someone who has had a skull split open by an exploding block. But there is no excuse for meat hooks, reel winches, exploding blocks, sharp corners and edges, poorly fastened fittings, stoves without crash bars, batteries that come loose during a knockdown, companionway washboards with no way to lock them in place, or the thousands of items that are mentioned on every checklist and then routinely overlooked. Elaborate safety gear seems more real than a latch for a locker or a barrel pin for a stove, but the primary dangers in a sailboat come from shoddy workmanship, lack of attention to detail, and accidents. And most often the accidents arise because rigs and hulls are subjected to fatigue, weather, shock loads, and the relentless beating of the sea and the wind—none of which should be any surprise to a sailor.

23

TACKLE

Anchors and anchoring—the words should convey a sense of peace, surcease, and calm, like the photographs of cruisers in serene harbors. The reality for many boat owners is that anchoring, or weathering a moderate blow in a crowded anchorage, is a cue for unrelieved anxiety.

Sometimes the anxiety is totally without foundation. One look at the tiny 12-pound anchor and the ⅜-inch anchor line, and then back at the massive 14,000-pound boat that the delicate tackle is supposed to anchor against the forces of wind and sea, is enough to keep otherwise complacent owners awake all night, or sleeping so lightly that a passing wake, a 10-degree wind shift, or the slightest increase in the welcome 3-knot breeze is enough to make the owner spring from his berth to the deck. Other owners have had an experience or two to fuel the anxiety—a night when a sudden thundershower or windshift caused the anchor to drag, resulting in a panic drill, a bump against a neighbor who no doubt hit the deck shouting, or an unwelcome encounter with a sandbar or rock pile. After spending a night on a rock because the anchor dragged, it takes most owners a long time before they are able to sleep soundly on an anchored boat.

Some boat owners become so anxious that they purchase new ground tackle, a rig designed to hold "no matter what." Instead of a 12- or 20-pound anchor, they may go to a 35-pound anchor, which is so heavy that it requires either a windlass or two very strong backs to raise and lower. A windlass may be a terrific addition to a large cruising boat which can afford the power, the weight, and the clutter on the foredeck; on a smaller boat, it is weight in the wrong place, heavy wiring and current demands, a relatively delicate gadget exposed to weather, and an obstacle positioned almost ideally to assault shins and ankles and to catch on a sail that is lowered to the foredeck. Without the windlass, the heavy anchor is so inconvenient to use that instead of anchoring, the boat owner will seek out an unused mooring, trusting his fate to the unknown rather than the backbreaking task of anchoring and raising the anchor.

ANCHORS

Modern lightweight anchors are effective. A 12- or 13-pound anchor, in certain designs, will hold a large boat in moderate to heavy winds, if the entire anchoring system is correctly matched and used. There are exceptions—certain anchors that work better in a grassy bottom or are particularly ineffective in a rocky bottom—but in general, problems in anchoring are not caused by the anchor being too small or the wrong type. Modern lightweight anchors are designed to hold the boat not by weight but by their gripping action on the bottom. If they are properly rigged, so that the loads of the anchor rode are applied in the right direction, the anchor actually buries itself deeper with increased pull. The exceptions (read: *problems*) occur when the boat owner cannot anchor with the recommended scope, so that the pull is more vertical than the anchor designer anticipated, or when the rode does not properly absorb surge loads and instead transmits them to the anchor.

Scope is almost always a problem. Anchoring guides seem to have been written for mysterious waters where each anchorage has one or perhaps two boats and there is plenty of room to ease out a true anchoring scope of 7:1 or more.* In

crowded anchorages it is difficult to achieve anything like the recommended scope without running the risk of fouling the ground tackle of other boats or getting into a bout of bumper boats if the wind or tide shifts. If the anchorage mixes power-boats and sailboats, or more precisely, boats of high windage and small underbodies with boats of relatively low windage and large underbodies, the chaos and shouting can be incredible as some boats swing to the current and others to the wind.

Because they often cannot achieve the recommended scope in anchoring, many boat owners decide to "upgrade" their ground tackle by getting heavier rodes. "Sure," the thought goes, "if I could let out plenty of scope, that light line would be fine. But I've got to anchor with short scope. I'd better spring for a good heavy rode that will hold in a blow. Right?"

Wrong! There are two reasons for the recommendations of scope. First, the true scope determines the angle of pull on the anchor. If the lead of the anchor line is too vertical, the pull will disengage the anchor instead of burying it. Most anchor manufacturers build their anchors for optimum holding power with a pull at an angle of approximately 8 degrees from the bottom, which in shallow water corresponds to a scope of 7:1.† The second reason for scope is stretch. Stretch

---

* The true anchoring scope is calculated as the length of rode (including any chain) divided by the height of the anchoring cleat, samson post, or windlass over the bottom. Failing to take into account the 3 to 5 or more feet between the deck and the surface of the water means that the actual scope of an anchoring system is often far less than the yachtsman has calculated. If 50 feet of line is eased out when the depth sounder reads 7 feet, and the anchoring cleat is 4 feet above the surface of the water, the actual scope is 4.5:1, which for many anchors would be marginal in a blow.

† In deeper water it is possible to use less scope, because the weight of the anchor rode will produce a catenary sag that reduces the angle of pull on the anchor.

in the anchor rode absorbs the surge loads that would otherwise be transmitted directly to the anchor and to the mooring cleat or samson post on the boat. Adequate stretch can be achieved through a chain rode, which will hang in a catenary sag, or by using a small enough and long enough nylon rode.

With chain, the heavier the rode the better, because the stretch in the system is achieved by the sag in the rode: a heavier chain sags more. If you have ever dived down in relatively clear water to examine your anchor on the bottom, you will often see that in light or moderate air there is no pull on the anchor at all. The sag in the rode absorbs all of the load, and a portion of the rode, or the chain that is used between the anchor and the rode, lies on the bottom.

With line, the priorities are reversed: you want the smallest line that is adequate for the load and chafe requirements. The anchor manufacturers generally recommend relatively small-diameter laid rodes for their anchors. Danforth, for example, recommends ⅜-inch twisted nylon as a rode for the 13S or 12H anchors which are used on many boats from 26 to 35 feet or even longer. Danforth even specifies that braided nylon should not be used for the anchor rode. What happens if instead of following their recommendations you step up the size to 7/16- or even ½-inch nylon, as many boat owners do, or if you substitute braided nylon for the recommended laid line?

A ½-inch line has almost double the cross-section area of ⅜-inch line. Stretch in a line under load is inversely proportional to the cross-sectional area (the more area, the more fibers to share the load), which means that for a given anchor load, the ½-inch line will stretch substantially less than the recommended ⅜-inch line. Braided nylon also has less stretch than laid nylon, so you have again reduced the stretch in the

line. The maximum surge loads on the anchor of a 35-foot boat might approach 1000 pounds, which is 27 percent of the typical breaking strength of ⅜-inch line and 15 percent of the typical breaking strength of ½-inch line. The safety margin with the smaller line is over three to one, which is more than adequate. The larger line has a safety margin of close to seven to one, which is more than necessary for most applications, and because the line is so lightly loaded and so resistant to stretch, the shock loads on the anchor and the boat will actually be greater than the original anchor recommendations anticipated, in some cases so much greater that the larger rode should only be used with a larger anchor.

There are advantages to a larger rode: the greater surface area means that abrasion and chafe are distributed. What might be a nick in the heavier line could cut most of the way through a strand of the smaller line. And braided line presents more surface to weather chafe for a given diameter, offers a softer hand, and gives a ready indication of excess chafe when the outer braid is worn through to expose the core. But remember that those advantages come at the sacrifice of stretch, which is what keeps your boat from pulling your anchor out of the mud. If you want to use a larger rode, you will need a larger anchor.

Failure in the anchoring system is almost never caused by the anchor line breaking. The usual problems are chafe at the boat end because of inadequate chocks or chafing gear; chafe at the anchor end if there isn't an adequate length of chain for protection against rocks or bottom debris; and failure at one of the connecting links, such as shackles that come unscrewed, splices that fail, or missing thimbles that allow the anchor stock or chain to chafe through the line. With decent

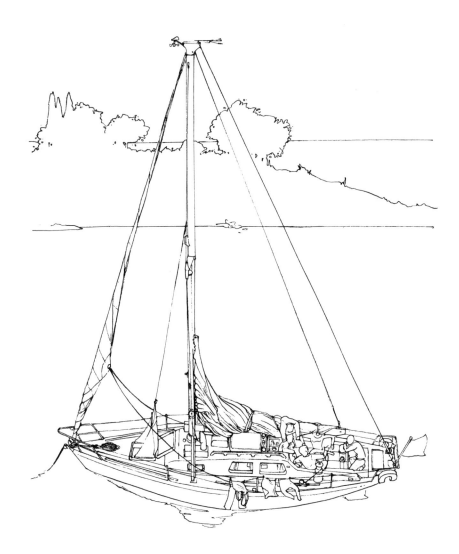

chocks, chafing gear on the anchor line in a blow, an adequate length of chain between the anchor line and the anchor, and periodic inspection of the line, the shackles, and the other links, the small anchor lines recommended by the manufacturers will give reliable service.

For mooring service, where the boat is on the mooring for months at a time and the rodes wear at the same point week after week, priorities have to be reversed. Chafe becomes the principal enemy, and mooring rodes are sized accordingly. But most boats used for coastal cruising are at anchor for periods measured in hours or perhaps days.

Sizing and Selecting

The composition of the bottom, the anticipated wind and sea conditions, and the room in the anchorages ought to determine the selection of anchor types and sizes, but there are inevitably other considerations, such as stowage, weight, and the fantasy elements that sometimes prompt the owners of 15-foot boats to buy "Navy" type anchors. In general, the lightweight burying-type anchors, such as the Danforth, and the plow-type anchors are reliable for coastal service and provide more anchoring power per pound than the older Herreschoff or other kedge designs. Boats with a fixed pulpit and rollers often prefer the plow designs because they can be latched in place on the pulpit. Boats that store the anchor below or on deck prefer the Danforth designs because they can be stowed flat. Both designs are adequate for most coastal cruising, but if you frequently anchor in an area with special problems such as exposed anchorages, heavy grass, rocks or coral, be certain that the "convenient" anchor is also effective for the antici-

pated conditions. Whatever design you buy, be cautious of look-alike copies of reliable and tried designs. A slight variation in the angles of the components can turn a burying-type anchor into a skidding-type anchor, and shoddy engineering or manufacturing practices can result in castings that snap under load.

In selecting an anchor and anchoring system, remember that manufacturers are basing their recommendations on supposedly typical boats of a given length. If your boat is heavy, or has substantial windage from high freeboard or a high house, roller-reefing gear, a dodger, or a dinghy on deck or in davits, you should probably pick an anchor at least one size larger than the manufacturers' recommendations. Very light boats and boats with substantially reduced windage can get by with anchors one size smaller than the manufacturer's recommendations, but the anchor sizes recommended by companies like Danforth are so modest that there is rarely a reason to skimp down to a smaller size.

In selecting line or chain, remember that larger chain won't hurt if your boat can carry the weight. Longer or larger chain at the end of the anchor rode is almost always a good idea, but substituting larger line will reduce the effectiveness of your anchor system. If you are worried about chafe, instead of a larger rode add a longer chain at the bottom of the rode, and spend some time inspecting, smoothing, and if necessary, realigning your bow chocks to prevent chafe to the anchor rode. And beware of gadgets that promise to compactly store your anchor line by substituting flat braid for nylon line. The braids have less chafe resistance than line and are usually made of polyester (Dacron), which has much less stretch than nylon. If you decide to use a flat braided anchor rode, you may need a larger anchor to compensate for the reduced stretch in the anchoring system.

The cleat or samson post on the boat should be strong, securely bolted, and smooth enough not to chafe line. Although most boats spend far more hours at a dock, mooring, or anchor than at sea, some builders do not build or install the mooring cleats to take the continual punishment of anchoring or mooring. A cleat should of course be backed up, and if installed in a cored deck, the mounting holes should be epoxy-saturated so that the continued sheet loads don't wear the holes and allow water seepage. Most cleats and chocks are large enough for anchor lines, but the leads are frequently designed for dock lines which lead horizontally from the chocks, rather than for an anchor line which leads down. Watch for chafe on the edge of the deck, the stem fitting, or in the case of boats with bowsprits, the dolphin striker.

More and more boats today are being fitted with bow rollers for the anchor line, and while the fittings are good for raising and lowering the anchor, the roller should be designed with a pin or other guard to keep the line from jumping off the sheave and onto a sharp edge that will chafe or cut through the line.

Stowing the anchor and anchor line is a perpetual problem on most boats. Anchor rodes are often stowed in the forepeak, and lead down through a ventilator or a special so-called chain pipe. For rodes other than chain, the disadvantages of stowing the rode in the bow would seem to outweigh the convenience. Weight that far forward degrades the performance of any boat, and while the rode is convenient to pay out, it is time-consuming to feed the rode back into the small fitting or ventilator. An alternative for boats that anchor infrequently is to stow the rode in a nylon ice bag, which can be taken up on deck whenever you are going to anchor. When the anchor is hauled up, the line is easily flaked down into the bag; if you don't lose the end, the line won't tangle. And whenever fresh water is available, it is easy to hose down the whole line, unlike an anchor line that is stowed in a chain locker.

For anchor stowage, the usual solutions are hooks or chocks on deck or on the housetop, an under-berth or lazarette locker, or a special anchor compartment that is built into many boats. The anchor compartments in the bow are convenient, but only if there is no sail on deck. And again, the weight of the anchor in the bow will have a noticeable effect on the boat's performance. An inviting alternative is a vertical anchor compartment in the middle of the boat, like the anchor lockers built into the decks of the J-30. Sailing Specialties makes a molded compartment that can be installed in other boats to provide the same convenience.

DOCKING GEAR

There are no special tricks to selecting docking gear, but there are some mistakes that can lead to abraded topsides, torn off or loosened cleats, rapid wear of dock lines, and broken fittings.

Using old genoa sheets instead of nylon dock lines is inviting problems. Chances are the old sheets were rejected because they were worn, and while the loads on dock lines are generally not great, the lines frequently chafe in unpredictable spots, usually just where the lifelines or a bad lead already has worn the old genoa sheet. And the Dacron and other low-stretch materials that are usually chosen for genoa sheets are uniquely unsuited for dock lines, which if they can stretch, will absorb the surges that would otherwise wear at deck fittings and slam your boat against the docks. Nylon line is cheap. You don't really need splices; in fact, a proper hitch is more secure and allows you to adjust the point of chafe.

Many boats are equipped with too few cleats, cleats that are too small, inadequate chocks, or a lack of chocks, so that whenever the boat is tied up to a dock, a system of snatch blocks, lashings to stanchions, and lines looped over winches is necessary to rig the needed spring, bow, and stern lines. The stanchions and winches are, or ought to be, strong enough for docking lines, but make certain that when tying to a stanchion you tie to the base so that you do not lever the stanchion off or through the deck. And if you dock often enough, either move the cleats to where they will lead fairly to the dock or install proper chocks for the lines. Snatch blocks used in mooring service are just waiting for a failure. The time when someone doesn't snap the block completely shut, or when the swivel snap shackle fouls and snaps, will be when the big unexpected blow comes through the anchorage. A chock is a lot cheaper than refinishing your topsides.

Even boats that do have chocks sometimes have them mounted or aligned so that dock lines are cut or abraded rather than protected. If a bow chock works for a mooring line or anchor, it might not provide adequate chafe protection for a dock line which leads horizontally and farther aft. Sometimes cross leading from a different cleat helps. Otherwise it may be necessary to change or move cleats to get the proper protection for your lines. Chafe gear, such as neoprene hose, fire hose, leather wrappings, or heavy layers of duct tape, is only temporary protection against the chafe of sharp edges.

24

WINTER

Unless you sail in an area that offers a twelve-month sailing season or are one of the fortunate few with the time and money to campaign or cruise on an extended schedule by moving the boat to warm-water areas for the winter months, sailing is a sport of four, six, or perhaps eight months of the year. For some boat owners, the off months are the time to ski or to concentrate on work to pay the boating bills; they would just as soon forget the boat for a while. Others spend the long winter months building gadgets, shopping through the catalogs to select new electronics and rigging gear, or counting the days until the cover comes off the boat, the ragged trousers and sweatshirt and tool boxes go into the car, and the spring cycle of "getting her ready" begins.

The one season that no one has time for is the fall, that interlude between the end of the sailing season and the beginning of the fireside days. The season usually ends with a late, cold sail and a hurried trip or two to get essential gear off the boat before she is entrusted to a boatyard for the winter or just put to bed quickly, with maintenance and new projects deferred until the first sunny day of spring.

As hard as it is to force the discipline, fall is the time when boats need attention, even if it is nothing more than a careful list of jobs for the boatyard, rigger, electrician, or sailmaker. Preventive maintenance is the way to avoid surprises, catastrophes, and the kinds of bills that can sour the rest of a sailing season; and getting repairs and projects for the next season underway in the fall means that you are less likely to end up a victim of the spring crunch that makes the Fourth of July the beginning of the sailing season for some boats.

WHERE TO KEEP HER

As the yard storage rates in or near urban areas have begun to approach the prices for commercial rentals in midtown Manhattan, many boat owners have become inventive about finding places to store boats. Backyards, rented lots, the parking lots of yacht clubs, and hideaway spots up isolated quiet creeks have become an answer to winter storage charges of over $20 per foot (which doesn't include bottom cleaning, mast removal and storage, framing, covering, or mechanical work). The question is convenience. If you are planning to do extensive work on the boat over the winter, it can be economical, safe, and efficient to seek a boatyard that is far enough away from the crowded urban areas to offer lower charges and a less hectic schedule in the spring and fall. The charges are sometimes as little as half the charges in a major yard close to a large city.

For smaller boats, the cost of a trailer can be recaptured in a season or two of storage in the backyard. Some boat owners have even discovered that if they live near the water there are riggers who will haul their boat and deliver to the backyard without a trailer. If you engage a rigger, remember that blocking and leveling the boat, or at least supervising the operation, may be your responsibility. And if the boat is too large to have an integral lifting eye, you may also have to supervise the positioning of slings, making sure that an inexperienced rigger does not put a sling under your shaft or prop. You may get an excellent price from Fly-by-Night riggers, but remember that someone will have to pick up the pieces if the boat is dropped, and that Fly-by-Night may have flown when it is time to launch the boat in the spring. If you choose an unorthodox storage scheme, check with your insurance agent to make certain that your insurance will cover any losses.

If, like most owners, you decide to keep your boat in a yard, make certain from the outset that you and the yard agree on the conditions and charges for winter storage. Some storage contracts are written so ambiguously that an owner is hard pressed to parse the conditions of storage. Frequently, in addition to the basic storage charges the yard will surcharge for bottom scrubbing, blocking, cradle storage, and rig work. Some yards charge by a complex formula that measures length, beam, or even displacement; some charge for unstepping and storing spars by a formula that not only measures length of the spar but counts the number of spreaders. Some yards require yard painting of the bottom as a condition of winter storage. If you are planning to do your own work on the boat or to bring in outside contractors for work, make certain that it is permitted. There are yards which require that they do all work below the waterline or below the deck, and others that might permit you to do the work, but only under impossible conditions, with your boat sandwiched close to other boats, in a sea of mud, and on a restrictive timetable that effectively makes it impossible for anyone except the yard to do the work.

You also need to make certain that you and the yard agree on the schedule for the work and the launch of the boat. If you know in the fall that you will need to be launched early for a cruise or a spring racing series, make certain that the yard understands exactly how important the launch date is. They may have to position your boat in the yard for easy access, and if you are doing some of the work on the boat yourself, they may be eager to blame (or even charge) you for any delays. Finally, most yards have clear policies about how long you may remain dockside after launching. Make certain that you and the yard agree on where the boat will be and for how long you may keep it there for work, provisioning, or just the wait until your regular dock or mooring is ready.

WET OR DRY?

Wet storage provides better support for the hull of a boat. Any cradle or combination of poppits leaves the weight of a boat supported on relatively few points, which can cause distortions in the shape of the boat or even structural weakening of the boat. Wet storage also offers steady control of humidity, which for wood boat owners can mean the difference between healthy storage and glued seams cracking, caulked seams opening, and planking and frames splitting. A wet-stored boat can often be stored with the rig in, which is cheaper and leaves the boat ready to sail late in the fall or early in the spring.

In the spring, the dry-stored boat can have a head start on bottom work and painting and may be ready for launching when the wet-stored boat is waiting to be hauled for bottom work. There is a hearty battle raging over the effects of continued immersion on gelcoat and bottom paint. Some argue that alternate absorption of water and drying out promotes or accentuates osmotic blistering ("boat pox"); others point out that without periodic drying out, the gelcoat and the underlying layers of fiberglass can absorb so much water that they add significantly to the weight of the boat. Finally, while it is impossible to work on the bottom of a wet-stored boat and difficult to work on the topsides or to perform routine maintenance tasks (such as checking sea cocks or winterizing a head), there is the advantage that for fall and spring work on winches, rigging, interiors, or deck you don't have to climb up a precarious ladder, dragging your tools and materials.

If you elect wet storage, make certain that the bubblers or other antifrost equipment are reliable and properly installed, so that both your boat and the docks to which you are tied are protected against freezing up. Most boatyards use either compressed air systems to bubble warm water up around the boats or electric propeller devices under the boats. The placement of the air hoses or propeller devices should be adequate to keep the boat and the adjacent docks free-floating (some yards place the hoses to protect the docks, which in a hard freeze can leave boats frozen in, their waterlines victim to scoring or crushing as the ice breaks up and moves with the tides). Check also that the bubbling equipment is adequately protected against catastrophic power failures, which invariably occur around the time of heavy freezes. Some boatyards rely on chain saws to cut away the ice in prolonged hard freezes. A freeze probably won't hurt your boat as much as the shifting of blocks of ice by tides or icebreaking efforts. Also make certain that your dock lines are doubled as protection against accidents, ice loading, chafe, and failure of the cleats on docks. Remember that a boat tied up for six months puts incredible chafe loads on the lines, which are weakened by icing on the surface and inside the line. The protection afforded by chocks might be adequate for ordinary mooring or docking but is generally inadequate for long-term storage. Also, make it a habit to check the lines of boats near you. Most boat owners won't consider it trespassing if you check their chafe gear and lines, or supplement their lines with one or two of your own. The extra precautions you take will be rewarded in nights of calm sleep while a winter storm rages.

The important precautions for dry storage are that the boat be adequately supported and level. The weight of a keel boat should be taken primarily on the keel, with cradle supports or poppits positioned to hold the boat upright and level. Beware of cradles that have been modified for bottom painting by sawing away diagonal supports or a keel shoe. If the keel is not supported underneath with blocks, the weight of the keel will stress the hull. On a boat without strong floors, the keel attachment points could be permanently distorted or weakened. Make certain that any poppits have adequately large surfaces, with soft wood or other padding on the bearing points, and that poppits are properly chained or otherwise braced. Finally, make certain that the yard has put your boat on your own cradle, or at least one identical to your own cradle. In the hurry to haul and block boats, more than one yard has discovered that some cradles have mysteriously grown or shrunk over the summer and thus need a little adjustment with a chainsaw, hammer, and blocks to fit properly again. It is a month later that you or the yard discovers that the cradle is not yours.

After the first good rain, check that the boat drains properly through deck and cockpit scuppers. Even if you cover the boat thoroughly, there will always be some water under the cover, and without proper drainage the standing water can cause havoc by freezing, or can leave stains on the deck and cockpit. If the ground under the boat is unpaved, make certain that the poppits or cradle don't settle or shift after a heavy rain, leaving the weight of the boat unevenly supported.

SPARS

Except with overuse of hydraulics, underengineered rigging, and wild sailing, such as repeated death rolls that put a spinnaker pole in the water, it is rare that standing rigging fails from overload. It generally fails either from careless maintenance—a missing cotter pin, a bolt that should have been secured with Loctite and wasn't, a corroded and cracked fitting that should have been replaced and wasn't—or from the wear and tear that results from the rig being too slack. A slack rig left to slat on the mooring will gradually wear the tolerances around clevis pins until the bearing surfaces are out of round. The rigging loads are then taken unevenly, the clevis pin distorts, and the rig fails. The only way to be safe is to undertake a regular maintenance program on your spars. You can make an occasional trip aloft during the sailing season to look around for chafe and wear and to lubricate sheaves, but the bulk of the maintenance is usually left to the winter. All too often it never quite gets done.

The spars of a boat create enough drag to enable you to sail under bare poles. The same drag is enough to topple a boat in winter storage if the spars are left in, especially when the weight and drag of the spars is increased by ice loading. In general, it is not a good idea to leave the spars standing in a boat that is dry-stored for the winter. And even in a wet-stored boat, leaving the spars in for the winter will require special efforts for inspection and routine maintenance. The lower terminals of the wiring are exposed to rain and snow, even under a cover. When water enters the terminal through the tiniest check in a swedge, it can freeze and weaken or break the terminal. The inspection for cracked, stripped, or weakened fittings, which is simple when a mast is tied up for winter storage or laid out on sawhorses in the spring, requires a long trip aloft in a bosun's chair for a spar that is left standing.

Removing spars and wrapping them for winter storage requires caution if the boat and spars are not to be damaged. Sometimes yards use part-time or inexperienced help to cope with the fall rush of removing masts and storing them, so it is a good idea to check and make certain that cables or rod rigging are not bent or stressed when the mast is tied up, that twine or line is used to wrap up the rigging instead of tape that can trap moisture and lead to corrosion, and that the spar is adequately supported along its length. The spar should be washed in the fall to get off caked salt and the grunge from airborne pollution. If an unpainted spar is going to be stored outside, fall is a good time for a coat of wax.

Wherever the spar is stored—standing on the boat, in a shed, on an outside rack under a tarpaulin, or in the case of a boom or spinnaker pole, inside the boat—the standing rigging should be thoroughly washed and inspected. Unless you know that a competent rigger is actually inspecting the spar when it is put away for the winter, either arrange for an inspection or do it yourself. At a minimum, examine all terminals on the ends of shrouds and stays. Use a magnifying glass to look for hairline cracks or signs of corrosion, or if you want to be extra cautious, use a stain that shows up cracks. X-ray inspection is rarely necessary. If you're in doubt about a fitting, replace it or ask a rigger whether the terminal needs replacement. Run your fingers down the full length of wire or rod standing rigging. If there are nicks in rods or broken strands in 1 x 19 cable, or kinks or bends in either, the rigging may require replacement. The tangs should all be properly aligned with the pull of the shroud. External tangs are sometimes misaligned from the beginning, and the slow wear of the clevis pins or the distortion to the rigging terminal is hidden under the mass of tape that covers the tang. With internal tangs, look for creep of the tang fitting and a bunching of aluminum under the tang—a signal that the section should be reinforced with an external or internal plate. Some internal tangs for rod rigging are designed to allow the rod head fitting to pivot as the mast bends; if the head isn't free the rod will fatigue. Runners on larger boats and standing rigging on smaller boats are frequently attached with T-ball terminals, which are simple and strong. Make sure the T-terminals for runners and babystays have rubber plugs inserted to keep the terminal from jumping out when the runner or stay is slack.

Inspect the clevis pins in chain plates, tangs, and turnbuckles for wear. Clevis pins should turn freely; if they do not, there will usually be signs of excess wear of the pin or elongation of the clevis hole, which may require repair to the tang or chain plate. When you remove cotter pins, don't plan on reusing them in the spring. If you pull the spar every winter and your fingers are tiring of opening and removing stainless cotter pins (or bronze pins in the case of bronze turnbuckles or bronze chain plates), you can use brass cotter pins to make the work easier. Just remember that if you are planning any extensive offshore sailing, or if the spar is left in the boat for more than a single season, the brass cotters should be replaced with stainless or bronze to match the turnbuckle, tang, chainplate, and clevis material.

Although they are not moving parts in the traditional sense, turnbuckles require regular cleaning and lubrication. Specks of dirt on the screws can act as cutting tools and destroy the threads, and while it is possible to adjust an unlubricated turn-buckle under load, the overheating, which you can feel with your fingers on the threads, is buying an early ticket to rig failure. The safest procedure is to use WD-40 or another moisture-displacing lubricant in the fall, then clean the turnbuckles with kerosene in the spring and lubricate them with a dry molybdenum disulfide (MoS_2) lubricant such as Moly Coat 321R or McLube 108. In a pinch use a Teflon grease; any waterproof lubricant such as winch grease or Lubriplate will work, but it will pick up dirt and grit and may stain your sails.

Look at tangs, spreader support brackets, spreader tips, headstay and forestay attachment points, the gooseneck fitting (both the boom and mast), spinnaker pole ends, the spinnaker pole carriage or rings on the mast, and the mast base. Any sign of distortion or hairline cracks may mean a fitting that is on the verge of failure. The welds on the aft edge of stream-lined spreaders often fail because of the loads imposed by mast bending, and from chafe from runners or flapping halyards. Many spars have compression tubes in the way of the spreader brackets. If there is any distortion to the section near the brackets, it is a good indication of a failure of the compression tube. If your halyards have been jamming or moving only with difficulty, disassemble any internal tangs or compression tubes that might be the cause of chafe. Once chafe starts, the compression tube and the halyard will quickly destroy each other. It is also a good idea to look for telltale signs of abrasion and chafe to the electrical wiring, such as fine black powder from a worn coaxial cable shield. Once it starts, usually from a loose wire that has wrapped around a halyard, it is only a matter of time before the wire is pulled apart or the halyard is totally jammed. Corrosion of a mast base is usually caused by inadequate drainage. All mast fittings will profit from a spray with

WD-40 or a comparable moisture-displacing lubricant after the inspection.

The running rigging too needs inspection, and a look in the fall means that new or repaired halyards and reef lines can be ready in the spring. If the spar is stored off the boat, the halyards can be left in, but try to run them far enough both ways to inspect the full length of wire, the wire/rope splice, and the length of tail. The usual points of chafe are the section of wire that bears on the masthead sheave when a sail is up, Nicopress fittings that jam against masthead sheaves when headsails are fully hoisted, the wire/rope splice, the point on the tail or wire of the halyard that rests on the masthead sheave when the halyard is tied away at the mooring or dock, and the section of halyard that ends up in a halyard stopper when the sail is hoisted. If strands in a tail splice are broken, in either the core splice or the cover splice, if there is excessive chafe on the halyard tail or broken strands (meat hooks) on the wire, you probably need a new halyard. It is possible to resplice wire and rope, but if the wire or the rope has had more than minimal use, the splice is so much more difficult that it is wise to replace both. If the wear in a halyard is close to the shackle end, you can shorten the halyard and prolong its life. Just make sure before you snip off the shackle that shortening will not cause more problems by putting the tail splice around a small sheave or at a mast exit hole.

Halyards should be thoroughly washed. They can be left in the mast, but if the mast is left standing, it is a good idea either to messenger the halyards out for the winter or to tie all the shackles together on a length of line and hoist them fully so that the wire sections of the halyards are protected inside the mast. The rope tails can then be coiled under the winter cover.

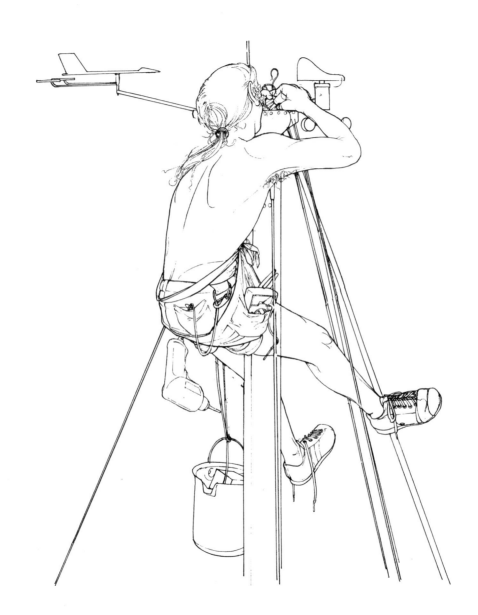

Inspect mast sheaves for wear and chafe. Once chafe of the sheaves or the guides and other anti-chafe fittings begins, it rapidly accelerates as the rough edges and the wire halyards work on one another. If there is a problem, a misled line or inadequate chafing protection (which is common on triple-halyard rigs), spend a while playing with the lines, crossing spinnaker halyards over as if you had jibed the spinnaker. Sometimes the problem can be fixed with a small weldment on a removable sheave cage or guard, which means that the welder doesn't have to come to the boat. Sheaves get chafed at the edges and cracked by excessive loads in a fixed position, and the bearings can be worn out of shape or frozen. Worn sheaves should be replaced; always take the time to search out or insist on an exact match or fit for the replacements. Trying to get by with a sheave that is slightly smaller will usually result in halyards jumping sheave or wedging between the side of the sheave and the sheave box, which will leave you with a halyard that looks like spiral pasta.

Headstay systems take abuse from heavy loading, the sideways pull of the genoa, and slams of the spinnaker pole. Look for bends, nicks from the spinnaker pole or wrapped halyards, and gaps between sections. If the headstay has bearings (like the Stearns stays or any of the roller-furling stays), they may need disassembly and or replacement, especially the lower bearing, which is subject to constant salt spray. It's an easy job, but be sure to use an exact replacement bearing, to replace all bushings in the exact order, and to use plenty of waterproof grease. Many of these bearings are not stainless and require substantial regular lubrication if they are to keep working.

When the rig is stepped in the spring, make certain that the spreaders are at the same angle as they were the previous season. Marking the shrouds before the rig is taken down in the fall is the best insurance. If the spreaders are too far off, the rig will be weakened, and you will discover that spreader patches on your sails are in the "wrong" place, that old settings of rig tension marked on the turnbuckles no longer work, and even that bending the mast produces a different curve. Check also, before you tune the rig, that all of the turnbuckles have been hooked on to the correct chain plates, that all the cotter pins are in place, of the right size, and correctly bent back. Although most riggers are conscientious, the spring rush and the use of temporary help can lead to omissions. It is a good idea to tune the rig yourself, not only because the rigger cannot be expected to know *exactly* how you carry the rig on your boat, but also because tuning the rig allows you to tape the turnbuckles and chain plates yourself and to make sure that everything has been put together correctly.

DECK FITTINGS

Whatever can be removed from the boat, such as blocks and shackles, should be removed. On deck they are a temptation to casual gear thieves, and the alternating cycle of freezing and thawing certainly won't do them any good. A good wash and a dose of WD-40 is usually sufficient for the winter. Fall is the time to check for damage to blocks and other gear. In particular, look for distorted sheaves, missing rolled pins or setscrews, chafe from unfair leads, distortion in swivels or shackles, and wear on parts such as the spring or screw pins that hold genoa lead cars in place on a track. You may also notice wear or rough spots on perforated toe rails or genoa tracks. Sometimes a little work with a file can fix the damage. If the holes in genoa tracks are so worn that there is the possibility of the cars slipping, it probably means that the track and cars are slightly undersized for the genoa loads on the boat. It may not require upgrading, but you may want to remove and reverse or replace a section of track, which is a good opportunity to inspect the integrity of the bedding of your deck fittings. Even with miracle sealants, water eventually works its way under bedded fittings. If it freezes, the expansion will cause trouble, perhaps only a minor leak that takes a long time to rot the core of the deck, but trouble nonetheless. A periodic inspection and rebedding of fittings that are potential trouble spots, especially heavily loaded fittings that are likely to work loose, will go a long way toward preserving the boat.

The winches should be stripped and cleaned in the fall if possible, and certainly in the spring. A large disposable paint bucket, some kerosene, and a toothbrush are the only tools you will need for most winches. A small screwdriver, a drive punch, and a plastic mallet can be useful; if you find that you need the mallet more than occasionally, you have probably neglected maintenance too long. If you have never dismantled the winch before, it is a good idea to make a sketch as you begin dismantling the unit. Reversed pawls and inverted bearings rarely add to the efficiency of a winch.

The steering mechanism of a boat also needs annual maintenance. Tiller-steered boats are generally trouble free, at least until the rudder bearings begin to wear. Once a wobble starts, it will usually deteriorate quickly. There are some simple solutions using epoxy and graphite fillers to create a new bearing surface,* but the best solution is usually a replace-ment bearing, either in hard Delrin or one of the ball-and-roller bearings for rudder shafts that are now available. The bearing manufacturers can help select a bearing that is strong enough and that will not require too much surgery on the boat. They also will recommend installation procedures.

A more common problem for a tiller-steered boat is weakness or damage to the tiller. Laminated tillers frequently delaminate, usually near the mounting bolts in the tiller head. The beginnings of the cracks or checks are usually concealed by the tiller head, so that your first awareness comes on a hard reach when you pull hard on the tiller to forestall a broach and the tiller totally delaminates. If you discover checks or cracks around the mounting bolts, the best solution is usually a dowel, pin, or bolts through the tiller vertically. If the holes are carefully bunged, the reinforcements will not mar the beauty of the tiller, and they will prevent the disaster of losing steering. A dab of glue in the checks and a clamp generally won't work (good glue on bad is only as strong as the bad), and if one glue seam fails, it is likely that another will follow.

Checking the pulleys, quadrant, gears, chain, pins, and rudder shaft attachment point on a pedestal steering unit is rarely fun. The access is usually terrible, the grease invariably drips into your face, and the weather in late fall is cold enough to make working with the metal fittings unpleasant. If you don't think you can bear to give the system a proper inspection and lubrication, just think of trying to repair it on a wet and windy night, with a flashlight in your teeth and the boat

---

* The Gougeon Brothers' publications detail the use of epoxy and graphite to make new rudder bearings. The process is appealing, but undoubtedly more difficult to execute than their drawings and description make it seem.

broaching through seas as you try to fit a replacement pin into one of the linkages, or try to restring a steering cable that has jumped off its sheave because the turnbuckles weren't kept tight enough.

COVERING

There are good reasons to cover a boat for winter: pollution, the ravages of the cycle of snow and rain on deck alternately freezing and thawing, the damage that the weight of heavy snow can cause, and ventilation. Unless you live in a fairly remote area, four to six months of continuous exposure to airborne pollution without frequent wash-downs will leave a boat grimy. A good scrub, polish, and wax can usually restore the shine, but the filth on an uncovered boat means many extra hours of scrubbing in the spring. Snow or rain won't necessarily cause damage to a boat, but the continuous thawing and refreezing of snow and ice on and around deck fittings, rigging terminals, and other gear most certainly will cause damage, usually the hidden damage of tiny leaks into the core of the deck. In areas of heavy snow, the weight of a blanket of snow can add thousands of pounds to the load on the deck and hull, and in turn to the cradle, poppits, and keel. If the cockpit fills with snow and the scuppers freeze—which they almost certainly will do—the melting and refreezing of the snow will often cause damage to the structure of the cockpit, and the runoff of the melt may go belowdecks through a low companionway slider, a vent in the cockpit, or even such unlikely access holes as the engine controls. Finally, an effective cover lets you keep hatches and vents open on the boat, which will prevent mildew and keep the interior sweet smell-ing. You can leave a boat uncovered without damage if you are willing to visit and sweep off the snow, and if your winters do not involve repeated freeze and thaw cycles, but most boat owners prefer the security of a cover.

Although it isn't difficult or expensive to frame and cover a boat, the invitingly simple techniques of using the boom and spinnaker pole, or even some of the techniques that are used in many boatyards and then copied by many boat owners when they build their own frames, can cause a great deal of damage to a boat after heavy rain or snow. Most boatyards attach a long stringer to the upper lifelines, either by tying it to the lifeline or by using strapping tape. They then nail ridge supports from the stringer to a ridgepole built on two or three supports, add a few carpet patches on the rough edges, throw

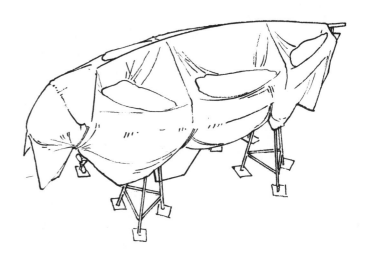

a cover over the top and lash it on, and they're finished. The problem is that the stanchions are bearing the weight of the accumulated snow and rain, and if the cover does not drain properly, because the ridge supports are too far apart or sloped too gently, the weight of the accumulated rain or snow bears upon the stanchion. And since the stanchion functions as an efficient lever,* the result is to crush or rip out the deck of the boat around the stanchion bases.

There are two ways to avoid the problem. One is to make certain that the cover is steeply pitched and that the supports are close enough to one another that no part of the cover will sag and fill with rainwater. The steeper the angle at the top, the less problem you will have with accumulation between the supports. The second is not to use the lifelines for support of the cover at all. Either remove the stanchions from their bases and build a cover that avoids them, or build the frame and cover to rest on the deck inside the lifelines. The latter solution works very well for a partial cover over the cockpit and house, which is adequate in many sailing areas.

The most common material for framing a boat is wood, which is easy to work with, cheap, relatively light, and strong. The problem with wood is that the dismantling each spring requires endless removal of nails and staples, and the construction each year is almost as time-consuming as the first year. You don't have to cut each piece to fit, but you do have to nail the joints and then pad the rough edges with carpet.

For boats that are owned for more than a season, it is worth exploring the alternatives, such as aluminum, steel, or PVC pipe. Aluminum and steel tubing can be used either with the various clamp systems that are sold specifically for boat covers, or with simple U-bolts or even lashings or strapping tape. The first year you will need a good tubing bender and a tubing cutter, and the hoops of tubing are somewhat awkward to store, but dismantling and rebuilding the system is quick and simple, the smooth hoops and tubing do not snag on covers, and it is possible to integrate the system with the lifelines and stanchions, either by using the stanchion bases to hold the hoops of tubing, or by clamping or taping the hoops to the stanchions.

Finally, the lightest and simplest frame of all can be built from PVC tubing. The tubing should be at least 1½ inches, and preferably 2 inches, in diameter. It is a good idea to standardize the whole frame in one size of tubing so you can take advantage of the variety of T and elbow fittings that are available. You can cut the tubing with any saw, or borrow a PVC tubing cutter. Unless the loading on the joint is straight compression, the joints should be cemented with PVC cement, which takes about one minute to cure. For crossovers, such as the joint between the rafters and the ridgepole, you can use strapping tape. Ninety-degree elbows or a combination of two 45-degree elbows work well for the peak of the rafters.

The best boat covers are canvas, because when it is dry, canvas breathes, and fresh air is what keeps wood boats healthy and fiberglass boats smelling more like boats than like musty basements. Canvas is also expensive, heavy, hard to keep clean, and difficult to rig with ties. Most boat owners today use plastic covers, usually the lightweight, strong polyethylene covers that are either made with grommets on the

* With a 24-inch-tall stanchion and the mounting holes on the base offset 1½ inches from the center of the stanchion, the leverage is 16:1, which is twice as powerful as the high gear of a typical primary winch. And of course the lever is more efficient than a winch, wasting little of that power.

edge or are used with plastic fittings that can be put anywhere that a tieline is needed. If you leave adequate openings for ventilation, you can literally wrap the boat up, tying the cover underneath the hull. Many owners prefer instead to cut the cover to fit at the hull-deck joint, fastening to the toe rail or to genoa cars and stanchion bases, or to a stringer that is run around the bases of the stanchions on the outside. If you are covering inside the lifelines, or with the lifelines removed from the boat, you can also tuck the cover under the edge of the frame and do all the fastening from inside. Heavy twine or light line works fine for fastening a cover. It should be tied taut so that the cover will not sag too much under the weight of rainwater or snow. If the cover is not canvas, leave breathing holes at the ends.

If the yard is secure and the temptations like electronics have been removed from the boat, you can leave hatches or the companionway open during the winter. Some boat owners build special boards for the companionway for winter storage, with large holes cut in them to allow circulation of air through the boat. It is a good idea to leave the vents on the deck of the boat open as well.

ELECTRONICS

Even if you keep the boat tightly locked up for the winter, the electronics should be removed and taken to a dry place. Aside from keeping the connectors clean, there is generally little maintenance work for electronics over the winter, but it is a good idea to use either a regulated power supply or just a 12-volt battery to turn on the electronics from time to time. The heat from the components will dry any moisture out of the unit. Antennas and wind instruments should also be removed from the mast, to protect them from damage when the mast is stored and later stepped. It is a good idea to make sure that the terminals at the ends of the coaxial cable and the electronics cables are clean and bright (a few swipes with fine emery-cloth paper will remove any corrosion, and a shot of WD-40 will hold off corrosion during storage).

PLUMBING

The first and easiest step in winterizing plumbing is to drain as much of the water system and head systems as you can. You can pump water out, or you can disconnect plumbing at a low point, drain the balance of the water into the bilge, and use the bilge pumps to clear it out. When the water is out, you have two choices for antifreeze. The commercial antifreezes are cheap and effective, but even after two or three rinses of the water system in the spring, the faint taste and pink tint will remain in your water. The alternative is to buy a half gallon of the cheapest vodka you can get, pour it into the water tank, and pump it through the system until vodka comes out of the sink, shower, and other taps. In the spring you can pump the vodka out of the system. You don't have to.

Heads should be drained as completely as possible. Then disconnect the intake hose from its seacock, put it into a bottle of antifreeze, and pump until antifreeze goes through the bowl of the toilet. If you just pour antifreeze into the bowl of the toilet, you miss half of the pump system.

Sea cocks are easy to winterize if the boat is hauled. Just open them and use the drain screws to make sure that no water is trapped inside. If the boat is hauled, fall is a good time to dismantle the sea cock, gently clean the interior parts, and lubricate with water-pump grease. If there is severe galvanic corrosion, you may be able to save the valve by lapping the plug and valve surfaces with valve grinding compound. Just smear a small amount of the compound on the faying surfaces and turn gently. Don't overdo it. You're trying to polish the two surfaces against each other, not to grind them away. If the corrosion problem is allowed to go on uncured, you will eventually need a new sea cock. Corrosion severe enough to destroy a sea cock should be enough to get you worrying about fastenings in a wooden boat, and the general integrity of underwater fittings in any boat.

For boats in wet storage, sea cocks are a little trickier. The optimum solution is to plug the valves from the outside, but that requires a haul or a diver. One alternative is to pump antifreeze through the sea cock and close the valves when the sea cock is full of antifreeze. If you have access to a compressor, you can hook an air hose to the sea cock and blow the water out. With either technique, you should then drain the body of the sea cock through the tiny drain screws that are provided. If your boat is equipped with gate valves or ball valves instead of sea cocks, you will not be able to drain the valve, but you can usually disconnect the hose and pour antifreeze solution through from a high enough hose to get it well into the valve.

ENGINES

Winterization of an engine is not difficult, but by the time you combine an oil change, oil filter change, and fuel filter change for diesels with the basic winterization schedule, it is a good couple of hours of messy work. Most engine manuals contain fairly detailed procedures; few let on how many hands and arms you need to juggle the engine controls; to hold the intake hose in the bucket, first of fresh water to flush the system, then of antifreeze mixture; then to drain the oil from the hot engine without converting your bilge into a waste oil reservoir. It's a good job to do with a friend or to entrust to a mechanic.

Engine servicing should also include periodic inspections of the engine control cables (especially the ball joints at the end, which are subject to failure from vibration), the water pump, alternator and water pump belts, internal zincs, and in the case of gasoline engines, the ignition wiring and components. Before the bilge is cleaned up is a good time to look for oil leaks. Finally, the bilge should be left spotless.

If the boat is being wet-stored and it leaks enough to require periodic bilge pumping, you will have to give some thought to setting up a reliable bilge pump. Most boats will leak less in the winter than in the summer sailing season, but unless the regular bilge pumps have no sections of horizontal piping and no water traps of any kind, the water in the bilge pump lines will freeze. All sorts of schemes have been tried, from salt and chemicals in the bilge to on-board heaters for the piping. Whatever you plan, remember that the dockside power may fail or may be less than diligently attended. If a storm shorts a line and blows the fuse, it may be a while before anyone discovers the fault.

If your bilge pumps will not be used during the winter, they should be drained or at least pumped dry. It is a good idea to flush the salt out of the bilge pumping systems by washing the bilges with fresh water and pumping it out. You may have to disconnect some of the plumbing from the pumps to get them to drain properly.

Batteries can be left aboard a boat if they are kept charged, but if there is no need for the batteries, it is better to take them ashore. They should be stored charged, and if necessary recharged periodically. They should not be kept on a charger all winter, and should not be stored on a cold concrete floor.

FALL SURVEY

The final and most important step in the fall is an abbreviated survey of your boat. Outfit yourself with a clipboard and go over the boat from stem to stern, making notes on what should be done for the next season. There will be lots of little things that should be done and that you know won't be done. Write them down anyway. If you've been thinking about certain improvements or remember that certain items of the rigging bothered you, or that certain sails looked tired, or that parts of the hull, deck, cockpit, or interior were in need of attention, make a note. Then in the leisure of winter you can order work to be done before the spring rush, decide what work you will do or have done in the spring, or choose winter projects. With a little conscientious attention in the fall, you won't face a spring of surprises, many of which nag at you with a reminder that they didn't need to be surprises.

25

SAINTS
and SINNERS

Every boat owner has stories to tell about his experiences with boatyards, riggers, and sailmakers. And every boatyard, rigger, and sailmaker has stories to tell about boat owners. Listening to the two sides is like hearing differing versions of a criminal trial from the prosecutor and the defense counsel.

The complaints from the boat owners have a persistent ring:

- The work is never done on time. When you go to the yard, no one is working on your boat, yet there are thirteen workmen crawling all over a gold-plated 75-footer that isn't even a regular customer.
- The labor charges are excessive, both in hourly rates and in man-hours. The billing is for two men when one could have done it, and in intervals of round hours. There are charges for travel time, wait time, cleanup time, all sorts of "times" that seem to belong in the category of overhead.
- Equipment and supplies are billed at list price when they are available everywhere at discount. The use of expendable supplies seems profligate: "Why do they always need six new wipes, or another quart of acetone? Can't they reuse anything?"
- Unexpected and unordered work. A boat owner asked that his prop be "checked" and he gets a bill for reconditioning the prop. He arranged for winter storage and gets bills for framing and covering the boat. He asks for a "coat of paint" on the bottom of the boat and gets billed for ten man-hours of sanding time, forty sheets of sandpaper, twenty sanding disks, seven wipe-off rags, a quart of acetone, and a whole tube of the special cement that is used to attach sanding

disks to the sander, on top of the anticipated charges for a gallon of bottom paint, a quart of thinner, brushes, disposable paint buckets, roller covers, disposable gloves, and masking tape.

- The bill for estimated work is much higher than the boat owner expected, usually by a factor of anywhere from 50 to 200 percent. "You said it would be around $400," the owner complains. "Right here, I heard you say it: 'Ballpark around $400.'" The bill is for $1000.
- Unexplained and unanticipated charges: storage charges for the cradle, an extra charge for restepping the mast in the spring. "Tell me," the boat owner wants to say, "how many people have you upstep and store and then don't go ahead with the restep in the spring?"
- Obvious work that never gets done. "You launched it without waxing the topsides? Did you really think I wanted to sail a pigsty all season?" "You didn't lubricate the forestay? What do I have to do—detail every single item?" "There was a tear in the upper leech that didn't get sewn. I assume that at least you look at a sail when you've got it on the loft floor . . ."
- The work is rarely done the way you want it. You ask them to install a bilge pump, and instead of a $20 pump with a length of 50-cents-per-foot hose, you end up with a $175 pump, check valves, $2-per-foot hose, a $100 sea cock, and a huge bill. "All I wanted was a lousy bilge pump . . ."
- The service that was promised with an order is never delivered. When you ordered the new racing inventory, the sailmaker told you that your boat was so important to the loft that they wanted to make sure that hot-shot trimmers from the loft were aboard in all of your major races. Come racing season and the hot-shot trimmer is suddenly hard to

locate—and ultimately available for only two races in the entire season.

And while boat owners recount these tales of woe to one another, boatyards, riggers, and sailmakers have their own complaints:

- Customer procrastination: waiting until the spring rush or a total breakdown before they order the work that the boat needs. When they do finally order work, they put an unrealistic timetable on it, ordering a new spar in April and insisting that they need it for the spring series in May.
- Customers never appreciate the cash-flow crunch of a seasonal service business. They demand materials and gear at discount prices without realizing that one way or another the yard or rigger has to make a profit to stay in business. They insist that travel and wait time be absorbed as overhead, then complain when the labor charges are $35 or $40 per hour to cover overhead.
- Advice is solicited and not paid for. Customers ask a rigger what winches to use, then buy them at heavy discount from a mail-order house. Customers "shop" the field of sailmakers, asking each one what the inventory should be, picking up free advice and tips on what works for the particular design, then order from the sailmaker they have used all along and from whom they were going to buy no matter what. Or customers come to a boatyard with equipment they have bought from a discount house, asking that the yard install it. When the pump or stove or winch or loran later proves inadequate, the customer blames the yard and wants them to take care of warranty or other problems.

- Customers meddle while work is going on in the yard or rigging shop, watching every step of the work, asking questions, trying to get a free education, offering free advice that is worth exactly what it costs. Customers insist on doing their own work on the boat in the midst of yard work, or ask for the use of tools, even help by riggers, sailmakers, carpenters, painters, and others—as if the business were some kind of cooperative.
- Customers demand cut-rate or "quick and dirty" work from a craftsman whose future livelihood depends on his reputation. A customer says that he read in a magazine that you can apply the Awlgrip without a primer and save half the cost, and insists that his own Awlgrip job be done that way.
- Customers request work that the yard or loft is ill equipped to handle—such as racing sails from a cruising sail loft, or wooden planking repairs from a yard that specializes in fiberglass work—then complain when the work does not match the quality of work done by yards that specialize in wood boats or lofts that specialize in racing sails.
- Cavalier treatment of employees. Customers intervene as bosses ("That's my boat you're working on, BE CAREFUL with that sander!"), request special treatment or services, tip or make side payments to employees.
- Vague orders and work requests ("You know what I mean") followed by an explosion because ESP and mind-reading are not among the skills of the yard and the work (and bill) aren't what the owner anticipated.
- Customer "specifications"—precise, detailed specifications for every step of the work, from the grades of sandpaper or the exact lot of sailcloth to use to the details of preparations and spraying for paint jobs. Then when the halyard is too short or the antenna doesn't work properly—after being fabricated or installed to "customer spec"—the yard is blamed.
- Customers who care about how much it costs but are too shy to ask, probably because they think the yard or loft won't do its best work for anyone except the big spenders. And for every customer who is shy there is a "shopper," who begins haggling about the price and scheming how to get it done cheaper even before the job has been agreed upon.
- Arbitrary demands at critical times. "I need that genoa this weekend," when the need isn't real. Insistence on service —a sail check or an on-board inspection of the rig—when the customer's need is psychological rather than real.
- Fuzzy agreements cited as firm prices. Ballpark figures that are treated as guaranteed estimates. Threats of litigation when the yard or loft tries to point out that they are in the boat repair or sailmaking business rather than the credit business.
- Customers who use a flimsy excuse "The area under the poppits wasn't painted properly") to take a boat and "stiff" the boatyard, delaying payment or even refusing to pay the entire bill for a job or a whole season of work.

The differences between boat owners and marine professionals generally arise for one reason: what is business to the marine professional is pleasure to the boat owner. At the same time, the inescapable gap between the wealth of many boat owners and the wage scale of yards, lofts, and rigging shops leaves lots of room for resentment by marine professionals, especially toward cavalier and demanding owners who are ever ready with demands and complaints and rarely ready with the check or the often deserved praise.

There are some terrible boatyards, riggers, and sail lofts, but in a competitive market they rarely survive. Most marine professionals are dependent upon their reputations and the word-of-mouth advertising of contented customers, and they are eager to do good work and to have satisfied customers.*

AVOIDING MIX-UPS

Whether it is a one-time-only job with a rigger, a major order at a sail loft, or the beginning of a long-term relationship with a boatyard, the best way to avoid mix-ups is to make sure that the yard, rigger, or sailmaker understands exactly how you expect the dealings and the relationship to function. If you really don't want to be bothered with details and don't mind surprises in how the job or jobs are done, or with the bill or timetable, go ahead and give them carte blanche. They will love you for it. But remember that in granting that carte blanche you have surrendered your right to complain about what they did, how they did it, and the bill.

If you have precise ideas about every detail of the work on your boat, if you are the kind of boat owner who reads through manufacturers' catalogs, cross-correlates winches and blocks and comes up with exact specifications of what you want, where you want it, and how you want it installed, then you should make that clear to the yard or rigger from the

---

* There are some famous exceptions, of course. A few yards are run by characters who are famous for their growls, tantrums, and routine abuse and overcharging of customers. In some instances the quality of the work or the availability of services that are otherwise unavailable may justify the whole pattern of outrageous behavior. But just as often, I suspect, the pattern is fed by boat owners who take a perverse delight in telling stories of the outrages that have been committed upon them. Boat owning, like other forms of pleasure, attracts a few with kinky tastes.

beginning. You may find that some yards cannot work well with "owner's specs" and that some will not appreciate constant oversight of projects. There is a sign hanging in one rigger's shop that sums it up:

LABOR CHARGES
Regular labor —$35 per hour
Owner watches —$60 per hour
Owner makes suggestions —$100 per hour
Owner helps —$200 per hour

Without realizing it, many boat owners do give carte blanche orders. "I think I need an electric bilge pump," the owner says. The yard manager looks over the boat, a well-maintained and well-equipped 40-foot cruiser, then has his workmen put in a first-class pump installation, including a heavy-duty pump, commercial-duty-rated reinforced hose, a new sea cock for the pump discharge, a check valve to keep the water in the hose from rolling back into the bilge. The bill is just shy of $1000. The owner, who pictured the photographs in the discount catalog ("High capacity bilge pump, $19.88") and who just wanted a simple pump to get out the little dribble of rainwater that leaks down the mast, cannot believe his eyes.

If you are not sure of what you want and you solicit the advice of the yard in a discussion, make certain that you listen and that you and the yard or rigger finally agree on what is to be done. All too often the discussion goes like this:

Boat owner (pointing to a corroded prop that is covered with barnacles): "What do you think of that prop? I haven't been getting full speed out of the boat under power. Could that be it?"

Yard Manager: "Could be. I'll have Ray check it out."

Two months later the bill arrives:

Martec prop (18 x 13, rh)	$653.75
Monel cotter pins (4)	4.90
R/R prop (6 hours)	240.00
Take old prop to reconditioner for exam and estimate	n/c
TOTAL	$898.65

The boat owner, expecting a bill for an hour of work to clean off the old prop, screams bloody murder. And the yard, which graciously didn't charge for the trip to the prop conditioner who said that the old prop was corroded beyond repair, considers the owner an ingrate for not appreciating that the charges were in fact less than they might have been.

The moral is simple: ASK! Some yards will call you at each step of a complex job to get approval for more extensive work. There are other yards where the manager is more comfortable with a pneumatic sander than a telephone in his hand, or where the limited number of employees and the complexity of scheduling employees and jobs mean that there are genuine delays and inconveniences if the yard has to put a man on the prop job, let him do a part of it, start another job, do part of that, and then have to come back to do more of the prop job. If you know or sense that the yard works that way, try to explore the options at the beginning with estimates or ballpark figures. *If you don't ask or specify, the yard or rigger will probably assume you don't care about money.*

Estimates and ballpark figures are another area of constant misunderstandings. In most states, an estimate—whether written or verbal—is a contract to effect the repair for the price of the estimate. Obviously, if a dispute later arises, you are on firmer ground if you have a written estimate. The yard or rigger may want to hedge a written estimate with conditions, such as "Estimate does not include repair or replacement of rotted timbers" or "All estimates are within 10 percent of final price" or "Adjustments in the cost of materials or for work from outside contractors will be added to the estimate." There are many kinds of jobs for which a boatyard or rigger cannot be expected to give a firm estimate. Rot work on wooden boats, repairs to heavily crazed or pocked gelcoat, and tracking down of electrolysis problems are among the jobs that are difficult to estimate in advance. Some work is too small for an estimate. It is unreasonable to expect a yard manager to do the research in catalogs and on the phone, and the critical surveying work, to give you a firm estimate for a small job. If you insist on an estimate he will probably throw you a high ball, a guess that is deliberately high enough to cover himself.

Prices are sometimes quoted as "ballpark" figures. You ask what it will cost to refinish the topsides and the reply is "Around $80 per foot." To avoid trouble, find out what a ballpark figure means. Does it mean that $80 per foot is the price unless there are special problems? What constitutes "special problems"? Is the crazing that you can see on the topsides a special problem? Or are special problems remote possibilities that really cannot be anticipated, like chemical incompatibilities between the gelcoat on your topsides and the usual primer that is used for painting? If you and your yard or rigger spell out beforehand just what the ballpark figure means, you will avoid misunderstandings in the spring, when your anxiety to get sailing and the yard's anxiety to get paid can meet in a head-on collision.

Try to think ahead and take advantage of the slack months in marine professional schedules. Rigging work that is ordered in the fall for delivery in the spring can probably be done cheaper and at a leisurely pace that allows for better work and for periodic inspections and discussions with you. Ordering sails off season gives you a price break and will usually get the sails done before the great crush of recutting and special orders in the spring. Some sailmakers have special price breaks for off-season orders. If your sailmaker doesn't, ask for one. Many riggers will inspect your rigging for an inviting price in the fall, usually as a "loss leader" so they can find problems and invite you to order the work over the winter. It is usually a wise investment.

If you don't want to pay huge bills, look for ways to save. For example, if you need a new halyard, messenger out the old one yourself and take it in. If you need lubrication or a light bulb changed at the masthead, do it yourself with a couple of crew members or friends. A light bulb change at the masthead, with a quick inspection and lubrication of the sheaves up there, will take you less than thirty minutes if you've got one or two crew members to help grind you up. By the time two riggers (it almost always takes two, especially for any work aloft) drive out to your boat, wait for the launch, get up the mast, do the work, get down, wait for the launch again, and drive back to the loft, they have used up a minimum of two or three hours, which can quickly total up to a nifty $200 or more.

If you need work done on your boom, take if off the boat and bring it in to the loft. Or at least remove the sail and any other extraneous gear, and leave the boat at a service dock rather than out on a mooring. You will pay for the riggers'

time while they wait for the launch, while they remove your mainsail and fold it, and while they fumble to get your boat unlocked. If you are having a marine electrician install a radar or an SSB unit, try mounting the units yourself, making the cutouts for the wiring and securing the wiring. Then instead of paying the electrician for carpentry that you could probably do as well yourself, pay him or her for the electronics work that you cannot do. Some boatyards will let you prep a bottom yourself before they spray it. It will take you longer than it takes them to fair and prep the bottom, but your rates are probably cheaper.

If you are ordering a lot of gear from a rigger, chandlery, or boatyard, and you know pretty much what you want, try looking up the specs and part numbers that need to be ordered from manufacturers' catalogs. You will be saving them the labor costs of researching the hardware, and they may be able to offer you a better price on the gear.

Finally, with any work, make a realistic appraisal of how you will use the boat and how long you will own the boat. Ordering work you don't need, or to specifications that are inappropriate for the kind of sailing you do, will only cost you money and time. And asking any marine professional to do work in unfamiliar areas is inviting trouble. If the rigger you go to specializes in high-tech grand prix racing hardware and rigging, he may not be the right person to rig your boat for single-handed cruising. If you have special needs—a wooden boat, a gelcoat pox problem, topsides refinishing, sails for a cat ketch, a sonar installation—choose a yard, rigger, sailmaker, or electronics expert with some experience in the work. If you don't know whether the loft has ever built sails for a cat ketch, ask. And then call up the boat owner they made them for and ask if he's satisfied. If possible, go take a look at examples of the work. A good yard or rigger will be proud of their work and eager for you to see it.

RELATIONSHIPS

Because of the seasonal nature of marine work, yards, riggers, and lofts treasure steady customers. If you make every purchase and every work order seem as though it is the final decision in a process of competitive bidding, you are probably doing yourself a disservice. If you like the work that a rigger or yard has done, it is wise to discuss long-term programs for the boat with them. The new cabin sole might be a project for one year, stripping and varnishing the exterior teak a project for another year. With a wood boat a steady maintenance plan is almost a necessity, but most fiberglass boats can also stand a program of constant preventive maintenance. Rigging and sail inventories also can stand constant attention. Halyards and sheets wear out, standing rigging eventually fatigues, sails lose first their racing effectiveness and then, depending upon the material and construction, either begin to break down or blow so out of shape that their occasional resemblance to their former selves is pure coincidence. A program to replace the #1 genoa this year and the main next year means predictable cash flow to a sailmaker, and the importance of cash flow in a seasonal business will endear you as a regular customer.

PRIORITIES

There is a basic conflict of priorities between boat owners and professionals in the marine business. The owner weighs decisions and priorities against the pleasure they provide, tempering his choices with considerations of the ultimate resale value of the boat and the cost of his plans. The marine professional is in business to make money, and while long-term considerations of keeping customers happy and maintaining friendships and reputation are important, in what is essentially a small business the marine professional sometimes has to make choices that are incomprehensible to a boat owner. After you have been a customer of the yard for five years, a new 70-footer can show up in the yard, needing work on a mashed keel, and everyone drops their work on your bottom to rush over to work on the 70-footer. The same thing happens in sail lofts, rigging shops, and marine electricians' shops.

If your own schedule is truly being jeopardized because work on your boat is allowed to slide while the work goes forward on the big boat, tell the yard. "I have to leave for that cruise next Monday. We discussed that when I brought the boat in. And I expect you to adhere to the schedule." If you are a long-term customer, and if your demand is legitimate— if you really do have to leave on Monday—most yards will probably try to accommodate you. But if your deadline is arbitrary, if what you are really complaining about is that your pride is hurt because Mr. Goldpockets and his 70-footer are getting the attention instead of you and your Plodalong 27, you may find that your complaints will fall on deaf ears. The yard or sail loft cannot take a holier-than-thou attitude toward a big order, even if they know that they run the risk of offending customers who have been loyal. If you cannot stand the fact that big orders or big boats are pushed ahead in priority, you would probably be wise to take your business to a yard where the appearance of a Megabucks 80 is unlikely.

WARRANTIES

Most manufacturers in the marine industry are honest, interested in the quality of their products and their own reputations, and are willing to stand behind their products and their warranties. Some are exemplary. Harken, for example, for years has had a policy of replacing any Harken block that breaks in use, asking only that the owner describe the use to which the block was put when it broke. In general, if you are within the terms of a warranty and if the hardware or other item was used in normal service, most manufacturers are eager to honor their warranties, especially if your initial phone call or letter has the tone of "My _____ broke. Here's how it happened . . ." instead of "If you _____s don't replace my _____, I'll . . ."

If you suspect that you have a major warranty problem, something that cannot be fixed by having the company send you a new part which you can easily install, begin by collecting as much information about the problem as you can get together, including dates, photographs, and exact descriptions of what failed or appears to be failing. If your rudder wobbles or the deck tin-cans, notify the builder as soon as possible and with descriptions as precise as you can make them. Invite them to inspect the boat at the earliest possible date, and suggest that if they are reasonable, you will be too. Often your phone call may be the second or third call about the same problem, and the builder will ask fairly precise questions: "Under what conditions do you feel the wobble in the rudder?" or "How much does the deck deflect, and exactly where?" After you have called, no matter what the response, follow up your call with a letter confirming your understanding of what was said in the conversation. If a dispute does develop, it is effective to be able to refer to letters stating that "you agreed that at the end of the season, when the boat was hauled, you would pay to . . ."

Usually you will be able to work out some arrangement for warranty replacements or repairs. If the problem is serious enough that the boat cannot be used, you can and should insist on immediate attention to the problem. If the problem is a minor inconvenience or preventive maintenance, you will generally do better by agreeing to a reasonable schedule for repair or replacement. The real trick is to apportion and negotiate the true cost of the work. If your transmission fails and the company offers to replace the engine, admitting that the old engine was faulty, who pays the labor costs of replacing the engine, which in some boats can be as much as the price of the engine itself?

In many instances, even after a warranty has expired, if the product, installation, materials, or construction is faulty, companies will still agree to repair or replace the failed or failing gear, either at their own expense or at some prorated charge. If they refuse and you are convinced that your problem is caused by negligence or fault on their part, you may have recourse under an implied warranty or other cause of action. Before you press claims make certain that you are chasing after the right party. If the claim is for mast problems on your Hoodwink 28, you may discover that the warranty for the Hoodwink boats disavows any responsibility for work done by others, and that your only claim is against Crumbum Riggers, who built the spar. Before you rail against the Hoodwink company, it is worth trying to engage their help and advice in pursuing a claim against Crumbum & Co.

In those rare instances where serious problems emerge, be prepared for disputes that resemble the classic lawyer's protestations on behalf of his client:

"He didn't do it . . . "

"If he did, so did everyone else . . . "

"It isn't really illegal . . . "

"If it is illegal, it is only a technical violation . . . "

"In paying the fine, my client is not admitting any guilt or liability . . . "

Keep complete records of your dispute, not only of the status of the problem but of the companies' responses to your inquiries as well, and remember too that the ultimate goal is to get your boat fixed at minimum cost and inconvenience to you, not to score "points" by forcing a public confession or humiliation of a company.

DISAGREEMENTS

Usually, with open communication, up-front questions, and estimates or agreements on the price of major work, disagreements can be avoided. If a genuine disagreement does develop, think twice before you blow up. Yards, riggers, sailmakers, and manufacturers in the marine industry can be as touchy as anyone else. They resent being called crooks, bandits, or butchers. Unless they're truly fly-by-night phonies, they take pride in their work and they care about their reputations and about pleasing their customers. So try to go easy. Be firm if need be, but be careful—explore first, raise the question of how the disagreement came about, just what happened. Suggest that there may be an element of mutual screwup (a better term than "fault" every time) and that you're willing to work it out. And until it is absolutely clear that you cannot settle your grievances, don't threaten or take other drastic steps.

If the disagreement is over the quality of a job, you may find that by proposing a reasonable timetable for a redo or repair of the job, you can get the yard or rigger or loft to make good on the work. If you insist that the loft build you a brand new mainsail immediately, or that the yard interrupt a busy spring schedule to repaint your bottom, they may conclude that they cannot make you happy without jeopardizing an entire schedule of commitments. And once they are willing to lose their relationship with you, you will have no leverage at all to get the work you wanted done right. By making it clear that you want the work redone, that you expect that in the future there will not be another slipup, and that you are willing to be postponed until the slow season, you may end up with work that is properly done and a productive long-term relationship. And in cases where there is some ambiguity over the liability, an offer to split the cost of redoing the work or to pay the cost of materials often makes more sense than a prolonged dispute.

Disputes over bills are frequently more acrimonious than disputes over quality of work. Marine professionals are wary of getting "stiffed," they are often in a cash-flow crunch, and there are genuine resentments of what is seen as cheapness on the part of boat owners who can afford to pay. Owners, from the other side, underestimate the costs of running a marine business and the cost of skilled handwork done in a seasonal business.

WHEN ALL ELSE FAILS . . .

Usually the blowups come in the spring. The yard has finished the work—installing the new diesel engine—you are anxious to get sailing, and the only thing that is stopping you is the difference of $5000 between what the yard manager told you the installation would cost and the final bill. You point out the difference and the yard says that (1) working on your Hellbat 39 is a royal pain, (2) the original estimate didn't include repairs to the shaft that you somehow managed to bend, and (3) the price of the engine went up by $1000 since they quoted that figure. You answer that (1) if you had known the work was going to cost $5000 more you wouldn't have started it, (2) the shaft was already bent when they gave the estimate, and (3) why didn't they warn you that the engine had gone up in price so you could have canceled the order? The yard answers your letter with a simple ultimatum: they won't launch your boat until you pay the bill in full, by cash or certified check.*

Once the dispute has reached ultimatums, chances are that you are not going to settle your differences by haggling at the last minute. The yard knows you really want the boat. They also know that feelings are so strong, both ways, that it is unlikely that you will come knocking in mid-season to settle up the differences. What can you do?

---

* At one well-known East Coast boatyard, where the owner is famed for his temper and the extraordinary volume achieved by his vocal cords, a boat owner who had stopped payment on a check when he discovered incomplete work on his boat came back to pick up the boat when the work was redone and found it suspended some 40 feet over the water in the slings of a crane. In a voice loud enough to be heard over much of Long Island Sound, he was told, "When I have the cash or certified check, it goes in the water!"

1. You can steal the boat. Sometimes the yard will have launched your boat and not put the rig in. You could show up with a gang of your crew, tie the rig on top, and motor away. In general, trying to steal the boat is not a good idea. In most states the yard has an implied or stated lien on the boat, and if the sum is large enough to merit the legal fees and court costs, they can get a court order that will impound the boat until you pay. And even if the sum is small enough that they are unwilling to take you to court, chances are that they will relate their experience with you to other marine professionals. In short order you may find it hard to get work done on your boat. In some states you could find yourself arrested for stealing your own boat, or if tempers rise high enough, you could find that your own action is answered in kind or worse.

2. You can propose an escrow scheme. Offer to give the disputed amount to a neutral party pending resolution of your disagreement. Unless you know that the yard uses a corrupt brother-in-law as lawyer, offer to let the yard's lawyer serve as escrow. Then specify in writing that it is a formal escrow arrangement, that the lawyer is to hold the funds until there is a resolution of the disagreement between you. Some yards will refuse, but it is enough of a step of good will that the yard might agree in the hope of a successful and peaceful resolution of the dispute. Be warned: it will take a bit of negotiation to come to terms. The yard will want some term that says that within a reasonable period they get the escrow money if you fail to agree; you obviously want a requirement that they submit to a means of arbitration—whether a third party that you both agree to, a formal arbitration, or a simple agree-

ment that you will each make good efforts to come to an agreement.

3. You can threaten to publicize your dispute and the practices of the yard. If you are sure you're right and that you have been badly mistreated, make it clear that you wish it weren't so, but you're willing to make a real squabble. And tell them where and how: local yachtsmen (if everyone at your club uses the yard and you are respected at your club, it carries weight), the local yachting newspapers, the national magazines, the Better Business Bureau. It sounds frail, but it isn't. No small-businessman is so well established that he can ignore this kind of pressure. Obviously you don't want to do this unless you're really up against the wall and a considerable sum is involved. If they overcharged you for bottom paint and they won't come down to what you think is a reasonable figure, just don't buy your bottom paint there anymore. But if they demand payment for a bill that is double the written estimate and there is no clause in the estimate that gives them the right to go over by that margin, you may have a legitimate cause. Explain that you're sure the misunderstanding can be cleared up and that you don't want to broadcast it, but that you will. . . . Then remember that once you have played that card you are an implacable enemy and resolution becomes acrimonious and possibly impossible.

4. You can go to a lawyer, who at least initially can write a strong letter for you and, in effect, threaten litigation. Most boatyards, riggers, and sailmakers are small businesses. The threat of legal expenses and the fear that a prolonged lawsuit may cause trouble with their creditors may persuade them to reconsider their position on the dispute. A lawyer may also see the dispute in a different light and might persuade you or your adversary of either the righteousness or foolishness of your position. A lawyer might point out that what really happened is a clear violation of a statute (in many cases the auto repair statutes cover work with boatyards and other marine professionals, and they frequently provide strong penalties and recourses for a consumer). A lawyer may also come up with a scheme to pressure or embarrass your adversary into settling the dispute.*

5. Finally, what you really don't want: litigation. In general, litigation is so expensive and so time-consuming that it is warranted only if there are very large sums involved or if you have a major point to make. For small sums in dispute, and the limit varies from state to state, you can resort to Small Claims court, where you can file claims without a lawyer. Be warned that the filing and follow-up of a claim is time-consuming and tedious, and that frequently the case that sounded so persuasive as you prepared it will sound less persuasive to a judge who may be more sympathetic to a small-businessman than to a "yacht owner."

If the sum in question is too large for Small Claims court, you have to face the fact that the minimum legal and filing costs for litigation may prove larger than the

---

* One lawyer and boat owner in Connecticut, after suffering a package of outrageous delivery charges from a boat dealer in Long Island, waited until the next large boat show in Connecticut, where the Long Island dealer had a booth. The lawyer marched into the show with his friend the sheriff, and shouting "Thief!" and "Crook!" loud enough for a crowd of thousands to hear, they served the boatyard owner with a complaint on the spot. He settled that afternoon.

amount of money in question. You may have some early visions of treble damages and "pain and suffering" compensation paid to you because you missed the Spring Series, but in general, litigation will be a long, slow, and costly process, and since you will probably have already paid the boatyard in order to get the use of your boat, it is you who will suffer under the continuous delays that the other side can introduce into the proceedings. Unless you have cheap or free legal help, or the sum is so large that legal assistance is warranted, you may discover that the pressure, anxiety, and time consumed by a pending lawsuit can ruin your sailing season.

Fortunately, knock-down, drag-out disputes are rare. Most professionals in the marine business are just that—professionals who are eager to do good work and are proud of the work they do. If you pick your yard, rigger, sailmaker, and other professionals carefully, keep your relationships and communications open, and try to understand the pressures of their businesses, you can go through years of boat ownership without surprises or disputes.

26

GUNKS, GOOPS, AND PAINTS

Every chandlery sells tubes of miracle gunks and goops that promise to "seal hatches, bed fittings, fill teak decks, cure leaks, fix bathtub seams," and no doubt perform half a dozen other on-board chores not thought of in time by the advertising agency. Among paints and varnishes, too, there are constant claims that finally the "ultimate" finish is here—a finish that will survive six years of tropical sun, requires no sanding between coats, and not only preserves the underlying surface but "breathes new life" into tired wood and fiberglass. It's only a matter of time before some advertising agency plagiarizes *Saturday Night Live* and proclaims that their miracle hull cleaner doubles as a salad dressing or dessert topping.

The virtues of the new products of the chemistry labs seem endless: a deck soap that truly gets off all stains, a teak sealer that requires no work at all to use, a polish that needs no rubbing, a bilge cleaner that needs no scrubbing, a paint that is self-leveling, a wax that protects "season after season." And boat owners flock to buy the new products, grabbing any bottle with the word "marine" on the label, sometimes paying exaggerated prices for ordinary products with exaggerated claims, all in the hope that maybe they have finally found a product that will solve the problems of cleaning and protecting a yacht against the ravages of water, sunlight, and salt air.

There are a few exceptions, but in general there are no miracle chemicals, and the "marine" label will not make ordinary cleanser any more efficient or make a long-oil varnish last any longer under the ravages of sun and sea. What will save time and money is to select sealants, paints, and other marine chemicals carefully, matching properties to actual needs instead of expecting miracles.

SEALANTS

Every time a fitting is fastened to a boat, you need to bed the faying surfaces with a sealant to keep water out of the joint. If the fitting is on deck, rainwater that leaks into the joint will eventually find its way to the fastenings, run down their shafts, and ultimately either leak into the interior of the boat or penetrate the core of the deck and cause delamination, rot, blistering of gelcoat, and a host of other problems, at least some of which do not show up until the damage is considerable. Underwater, an improperly bedded fitting can cause the same damage to the core of the hull, although salt water will rarely cause rot; the real problem underwater is that without adequate and effective bedding the hull fails at its primary purpose of keeping the water out.

Many boat owners grab the nearest tube of all-purpose goop and use it for bedding, or go into a hardware store for a "silicone seal" that is touted as being as good for a boat as for a bathtub. Depending upon where a fitting is, the kinds of surfaces and materials being mated, and the needs for flexibility, easy cleanup, future painting, or adhesion as well as bedding, it makes sense to spend a few minutes reading labels and choosing sealants that are right for the purpose.

Oil-based Oil-based bedding compounds, also called natural bedding compounds or boatyard bedding compounds, are compatible with oil-based paints, easy to apply, easy to clean up with turpentine or paint thinner, remain somewhat flexible for a long time, and are easily painted. They are not recommended for underwater use, have no adhesive qualities, and will eventually dry out and require replacement. Some natural bedding compounds are available with a fungicide component, which helps to prevent dry rot in wood surfaces. Oil-based bedding compounds are recommended for use on wood surfaces (which should be painted before they are bedded) and are preferred by many boat owners, riggers, and painters for general use because they are easy to clean and predictable in their performance.

Butyl rubber Butyl rubber–based sealants have very little flexibility and are not recommended for underwater use. They also require strong solvents for cleanup. They are easily paintable and do not shrink when they dry.

Acrylic latex Acrylic latex sealants have poor flexibility and are not recommended for underwater use. Their advantages are that they can be cleaned up with water, they cure quickly, and they are readily paintable.

Silicone Silicone-based sealants are made with either acid or ammonia as blocking agent. The sealants with ammonia blockers are supposed to be less corrosive to metals. (You can tell by the smell: the acid blockers smell like vinegar.) Silicone-based sealants retain some flexibility when cured, they are difficult to clean up, they cannot be painted, and they must have air to cure properly. They are not suitable for underwater use.

Silicone-acrylic Silicone-acrylic sealants are easier to apply and clean up than silicone sealants, they can be cleaned up with water, and they are paintable. They are not suitable for underwater use.

Polysulfide Polysulfide-based sealants are adhesive, flexible, sandable, and do not shrink in curing. They are fuel resistant, they can be used underwater, and they have a long life. They are not easy to clean up, and they will violently attack certain plastics, including those used in some instrument cases.

Polyurethane Polyurethane-based sealants are moisture cured, are extremely strong adhesives, cure very slowly, are moderately difficult to clean up, and are suitable for underwater use. Once they have cured, the parts bonded by the sealant are difficult to separate. Polyurethane sealants react with some teak cleaners.

PAINTS

The paint finishes available for boats range all the way from traditional oil-based finishes that have changed little in the past forty years to complex linear polyurethane coatings developed for use on aircraft. There are plenty of paint maker brochures and magazine articles that will tell you how you can use one of the new miracle coatings to convert your tired hull into better-than-new condition, but boat owners who have tried to spray or brush these coatings know how intolerant they are of inadequate surface preparation or sloppy application. The thin coatings of LPU paints reveal the tiniest imperfections of the underlying surface, and the paints are extremely sensitive to temperature, humidity, and chemical incompatibilities with underlying paints and primers, gases in gelcoat, or the slightest traces of wax, grease, or other surface contaminants. It is possible for an amateur to apply a satisfactory finish with the do-it-yourself kits, but it is not an easy

procedure. Before you set out to refinish your topsides with a two-part linear polyurethane finish, ask whether you feel confident enough to paint your own car. If the answer is no, you may be disappointed in the results you get on the boat.

On wood boats, in particular, the results with modern synthetic coatings can often be disappointing. Coatings like Awlgrip were developed for use on airplanes: the finishes are not flexible enough to work with the inevitable shrinking and expansion of the planking of a wood boat of traditional construction. Traditional oil-based paints are more forgiving and are generally more suitable for planked construction and for the interiors of fiberglass or wood boats.

With any painting you elect to do, make certain that every step of the work is compatible with the subsequent steps. If you are going to use a linear polyurethane finish, make certain that the primers, fillers, surfacers, and even the sandpaper that you use is compatible with the finish. Some finishes that seem almost identical in composition show sharp incompatibilities across brands or manufacturers, and occasionally you will discover that a finish will react with traces of stearates left behind by some sandpapers, or even with a thinner or solvent that seems chemically identical but contains a trace of some agent. If you have a reason to mix brands, you can often find out about incompatibilities with a phone call to the maker of the paint.

BRIGHTWORK

The decline of brightwork can probably be attributed directly to income taxes. Yachting books of an earlier era are filled with marvelous prescriptions for sparkling brightwork:

wipe it down with dew each morning, sand it lightly once a month before applying an additional coat of varnish, apply three or four coats in the fall (sanding between each coat with 220-grade paper), and finish off with five or six coats in the spring. The regimen would work today too, but most boat owners today can't quite get to the boat in time to wipe the dew off on weekday mornings, because they're busily running off to earn enough money to pay for the boat.

Despite all the advertisements and claims about new miracle coatings and paints, sparkling varnished brightwork still requires constant attention and care. It may not be necessary to wipe off the morning dew with a chamois, but a scrape that goes untended quickly turns into a black streak, and there are few finishes that can take more than a season of exposure to the sun without needing a sanding and another coat of varnish or two.

Some boatyards and owners have experimented with clear polyurethane finishes used alone, over epoxy, or over varnish. Sometimes they provide a hard, shiny finish that will survive years of use, even in the tropics. Just as often, sunlight or a slight movement in a joint in the brightwork will accentuate some unpredictable reaction between the miracle coating and an underlying coating, and before a full season is out, sheets of the finish are peeling off the boat.

There are no easy answers to brightwork. If you want a hard, shiny finish, it means hours of preparation and constant upkeep. If the finish is never allowed to deteriorate to the point where it is time for the scraper or the paint remover, it isn't unpleasant work, and there are no special health hazards in varnish or sandpaper. But caring for the brightwork takes time, and if it is neglected for even a single season the repair

is time-consuming. With teak it is sometimes possible to sand a worn or abraded spot, apply a few spot coats, then perhaps a coat or two over the whole piece, and let the sun complete the blending. With other woods, an abrasion or scratch that is not repaired immediately will develop into a black spot that can only be repaired by scraping, bleaching, and filling. And while household bleach may be enough to take out the stain (instead of the stronger bleaches that are usually recommended), it will generally be impossible to blend the bleached area with the rest of the wood, which means that you have to bleach and refinish whole areas of the brightwork.

There are no shortcuts that will produce a satisfactory job, and with the exception of using a "speedbloc"-type sander on large open areas, there are few time savers that can be substituted for the exacting work with sandpaper on either a block or a hard foam pad.

There are finishes that supposedly give the appearance of varnish without the work, but many boat owners have discovered that applying ten or twelve coats of an oily coating, followed by five or six coats of a second type of coating, isn't really much easier than varnishing. And while some finishes promise no sanding, the resulting plastic-coated appearance never really equals the richness or shine of varnish.

Increasingly today, the exterior woodwork of boats is being made of teak, which, though spectacular varnished, is oily enough to survive on the deck of a yacht with an oil finish or even with no finish at all. The yachting magazines are filled with articles recommending and comparing the different finishes for exterior teak, and if you listen on the docks or in the chandleries you will hear stories of good and bad experiences with the same substance. There are many brands that work, but all of them must be applied to a clean surface, and there are enough differences in chemical composition between the different finishes that a boat owner may invite trouble if he uses one finish one year and another finish the next. If the first finish, for example, contains stearates, it will be difficult to get other finishes to stick to the wood, and it may prove impossible later to get varnish to stay on the wood.

For any of the oil finishes, the teak must be cleaned beforehand, which can involve anything from a strong cleanser or TSP solution used with scrub pads, bronze wool, a coarse brush, and lots of elbow grease to single and two-part acid cleaners, which do a miracle job of cleaning the teak but may also dissolve the bedding compounds that are often used on the teak trim.*

The acid solutions do clean the teak. They also raise the grain, which will generally require some sanding, usually with 120- or if necessary 80-grade paper, followed by 150-grade paper. Sanding before the teak has been cleaned is usually a waste of time, or worse, since the sanding may only drive surface dirt into the grain of the wood.

The best applicator for teak oil is a foam brush or a rag. The thin, almost invisible solution generally leaves stains on fiberglass surfaces, so if you elect not to take the time to mask off the fiberglass, be careful in applying the finish and go back over the areas with a soft rag to catch the oil that flows onto the fiberglass surfaces.

---

* 3M 5200 adhesive bedding compound, in particular, is susceptible to damage by teak cleaners. It is wise to ask the manufacturer or builder what kind of bedding compounds and caulks were used, or perhaps to test around a single strip of teak, before coating all of the teak on a boat with strong acid cleaners.

INTERIOR BRIGHTWORK

Acres of hand-rubbed, varnished surfaces inside a boat invariably inspire oohs and aahs. No other finish comes close to the gloss or classiness of varnish, and for traditional mahogany or butternut joinery, or for the ash and other light woods that some builders are again starting to use instead of the much overused teak, varnish is essential to preserve the wood against the ravages of moisture. Varnish holds up well inside a boat, where it is protected from the sun and from constant wetting by salt water.

If you aren't lucky enough to have a varnished interior, be warned that applying a varnish finish to a boat interior is not a simple job. To begin, the wood must be absolutely clean of all grime, grease, and oils, and sanded with the grain until there are no scratch marks or surface imperfections. Even tiny scratches from sanding across the grain in a corner with very fine sandpaper will show up through varnish, and any trace of oil in the wood, or stearates from some grades of sandpaper, or surface oil from teak that has not been wiped down with acetone, can ruin the adhesion of varnish.

It is possible to use a "speedbloc" sander, such as a Rockwell or Makita, for the preliminary sanding with 150 or 220 paper, but for best results the sanding between coats should be done by hand with 220 paper on a foam pad. The gray "clear-cut" paper will last longer than regular garnet paper. There are then two choices of varnish: the semi-gloss varnishes, in either long-oil or polyurethane formulations, or regular high-gloss varnish, which is hand rubbed after you have a good base of four or five coats and a nearly perfect final coat.

The semi-gloss ("rubbed effect") varnishes should be shaken

before use, and the first coat should be thinned 25 percent with mineral spirits or turpentine before applying. If you are using a polyurethane varnish, such as Valspar, you can apply two coats, four to twelve hours apart, with no sanding in between. Either a very fine badger-hair brush or a foam brush works; anything in between will probably streak. You will quickly discover the mysteries of "flowing" varnish, the difference between a too heavy coat, which leads to curtains and runs, and a too thin coat, which leaves holidays (bare spots), a stringy finish, or a coating so thin that the next sanding leaves you back where you started. Let the built-up finish dry very hard, at least twenty-four and preferably forty-eight hours, then sand with 220 paper on a foam pad until there is a fine white haze everywhere and all the uneven spots are perfectly smooth again. Then two more coats, a good dry, another sanding, and you are ready for the final coat, which should be applied as a single coat. With long-oil varnishes, the two-coats-before-sanding technique may not work as well: you will need to sand after each coat. The trade-off is that long-oil varnishes have a deeper finish, unlike the "plastic-coated" look of some of the polyurethanes.

If you choose to use a glossy spar varnish instead, do not shake the varnish. Otherwise the sequence is the same. When the final coat is very dry and so glossy that you are tempted to wear dark glasses below, it is time to rub it down, either with very fine bronze wool and Duffy's Elbow Grease or with the more traditional treatment of powdered pumice applied with rubbing felt and water, followed by rottenstone, crude oil, and soft cotton cloth. Hand rubbing an interior is not an easy job. If you are tempted, try a small area or single accessory before you take on the whole job. Varnished surfaces can be waxed for protection, but you will have to get every speck of the wax off before another coat can go on.

If it sounds like a lot of work, it is! The vertical surfaces—like bulkheads, cabinet fronts, doors, and panels—are extremely difficult to varnish without leaving curtains and runs. The confined working space of the interior, the difficulty of vacuuming out the sanding residue, the difficulty of seeing the surfaces under enough light to varnish well, and the demanding schedule of the numerous coats may take up much of a spring to get the job done. One alternative is to varnish selected areas, like trim pieces, and either paint or oil the large surfaces like bulkheads. Trim work is actually easy to varnish, compared to the broad vertical surfaces, and while many boat owners may recoil at the thought of painting the teak bulkheads, it is really plywood that you are painting. A traditional "white and bright" interior will considerably brighten the average boat interior. Interior enamels are easy to apply with a roller followed by a foam brush; one or more prime coats followed by a good sanding (a "speedbloc"-type sander is ideal), followed by two coats of paint, should leave a superb finish that is easy to maintain and will look spectacular against the bright trim work.

The usual alternatives to varnish are oils, ranging from special "marine" finishes to Scott's Liquid Gold, Watco Oil, or the Minwax finishes that are used in homes. Scott's or Minwax will give a relatively durable oiled finish, but like any oil finish, it will darken the wood over time, and the surface of the wood will pick up dirt, grit, and oils. If you like the oiled finish, apply it with a rag, wiping off the excess. Less, rather than more, oil should be the rule, with a reapplication whenever the finish shows wear.

For those who not satisfied with the appearance of an oiled interior and cannot afford the time or expense of a varnished interior, there is another alternative. I have had excellent luck with ValOil, a soy-oil–based product designed to seal flagstone and other masonry floors and walls. It has the consistency of thinned varnish, goes on easily with either a brush or a rag, and then cures to a relatively hard finish in either semigloss or gloss. It is easy to clean up, it doesn't curtain or run on a vertical surface, it doesn't have to be sanded between coats, and after two or three coats the resulting finish is handsome, durable, easy to repair and maintain, and light in color, lighter even than varnish. I have had the most success applying a fairly heavy first coat with a foam brush to seal the wood. If there are any runs or other imperfections, they can be sanded or rubbed down with a fine Scotchbrite pad. Then one or two more light coats will fill in the surface and leave an excellent finish that is attractive and easy to maintain. The Valoil finish isn't as smooth or glossy or durable as varnish, but the ease of application may make it a good trade-off, especially in a yacht that takes hard abuse down below from a racing crew or children. To repair a nick or abrasion in the Valoil finish you need no more than a quick sanding or rubbing with a Scotchbrite pad, a local coat to seal the exposed wood, then a light coat over the whole area.

Teak cabin soles will deteriorate rapidly if they are left bare or oiled. A good varnish or Valoil finish will protect them, and if the finish is not high-gloss and there are sufficient handholds, your crew may even survive a quick tack while standing on the cabin sole.

BILGES

Most boat owners might not be eager to include the bilge as part of the interior, but there is generally little more than a layer of plywood separating you from the secrets that have accumulated in the bilge. Engine oils, hydraulic fluids from transmissions and hydraulics drives, seawater, fresh water from rain or leaks, spilled soup, children's toys, pencils from the navigation station, cooking and rigging tools, race instructions, cassettes from the stereo, and a variety of unclassifiable crud all tend to accumulate in the bilge. The commercial bilge cleaners, or dishwashing soap, can help to emulsify oils and greases which can then be pumped out through the bilge pump. You will still be left with mysterious crud that gravitates toward the limber holes and the bilge intakes.

Distasteful as it may be, the bilge has to be cleaned, and the more often it is done, the better the boat will smell. Once it is clean, the easiest way to keep a bilge clean is to paint it, preferably white. It is an easy job which requires no special painting skills, but remember that paint will not stick until every last speck of oil and grease is removed with successive washings with bilge cleaners, and with a trisodium phosphate cleaner like TSP or Spic and Span. There are frequently hoses and electrical wires in the bilge, all of which should be removed or at least loosened before you paint. The usual fastenings are cable clamps, which can be removed easily.

For paint, a good grade of interior marine enamel is the best choice, although some owners have reported good experience using exterior house paint on the insides of their boats. For a bilge, you will want a paint that is oil and grease resistant. And if you are ever painting any surfaces close to a stove or heater, there are special enamels that are fire-resistant. They won't put out a flare-up, but at least they won't add fuel to the fire.

MISCELLANEOUS CHEMISTRY

If you have doubts about any terminals or fittings on the rigging, you can use Ardrox 996 or Probe to detect cracks in swaged fittings or other hardware.

To remove wax before painting a bottom, use toluene. To clean up surfaces that are to be glued with epoxy, use acetone or, preferably, MEK (methyl ethyl ketone).

The patent metal cleaners and polishes do work. If bronze or brass finishes ever get too corroded for cleaning with the usual finishes, try a weak hydrochloric acid solution (toilet bowl cleaner). An alternative for badly corroded brass is to soak the fixture in ammonia.

Some deck soaps and other specialty cleansers do work well, but the label "marine" is often only an excuse for a higher price for very ordinary soaps, cleansers, and solvents. Dishwashing detergent works as a bilge cleaner and on the deck of a boat. Bon Ami will clean fiberglass decks. Fantastik and similar products work on boat stains. And some automobile cleaners, polishes, and waxes work well on boats. The one place to be cautious is with linear polyurethane finishes. The paint manufacturers and most boat refinishers will tell you how to care for polyurethane and other modern finishes and it is generally unwise to think you can improve on their advice, even if you think that polish and wax will do more good than the soap and water or solvent that they recommend.

27

BOTTOMS

Boat bottoms are the curse of spring. After a long winter of looking forward to the sailing season, anticipating the warm sun and fair breezes, the tasks of spring present themselves, and the bottom—with its flaking paint, corrugated surface, pockmarks, cracks between the keel and hull, and dings on the keel the size of golf balls—seems to stand between you and the pleasures of sailing.

The bottom of any sailing boat should be a high priority: few improvements can add more to the performance of a boat than a really good bottom. Cruisers who think of a super-smooth and fair bottom as the special problem of racers owe it to themselves to calculate the effect of a 10 or 15 percent increase in speed on the amount of time it takes them to sail almost any distance. And boat owners who think that any old paint is good enough for a boat bottom should wonder why shipping companies are willing to spend thousands of dollars on the development of new paints for the bottom of their ships.

The steps necessary to produce a good bottom are few, and they sound simple. You can read the same listing of procedures on almost any can of bottom paint: (1) clean the old surface, (2) fair and prepare the bottom, (3) apply good paint. Wet sanding or burnishing the dry paint is an optional final step that many racers will follow. The problem with most bottom jobs is that while the steps sound easy, they are not, especially if they are attempted with the kinds of tools that most boat owners use. And in their eagerness to get the job done, far too many owners pay far too little attention to the health hazards of working with bottom paints and bottom fairing materials.

BOTTOM PAINTS

Bottom paints range—in cost, hardness, toxicants, vehicle, color, and ease of use—all the way from the familiar and inexpensive utility paints that are used on workboats to the expensive and temperamental copolymer paints. Binders include rosins, acrylics with rosin or copolymer, fluorocarbon (Teflon), chlorinated rubber, epoxy-rosin, and vinyl-rosin. Toxicants (poisons) include Cu_2O (cuprous oxide), organic tins (tributyltin fluoride, tributyltin oxide, and other tin compounds), and metallic copper in suspension. The miracle coatings usually bring mixed blessings. A copolymer coating may stay totally free of fouling on an oceangoing ship, which is constantly moving at 20 knots; on your boat, which spends most of its time standing still at a mooring and only some of its time sailing at 6 knots, the miracle coating will still need a diver from time to time to keep it clean. And some of the copolymers are soft, so that an encounter with an anchor line or lobster pot will remove valuable bottom paint that was supposed to last for three seasons. Most of the "miracle" coatings require special application techniques, either extremely thin coats or extremely even coating applications, which are difficult for professionals to achieve and nearly impossible for amateurs.

On the whole, you get what you pay for in bottom paint: the more expensive paints have higher percentages of toxicants, are configured so that the paint will last more than a single season, or are hard enough to be burnished or sanded into a super-slick finish. But cost is no guaranty of compatibility or suitability. Applying expensive paint to a poorly prepared bottom is a guaranty of long-term troubles rather than long-term protection. In choosing a bottom paint, pay attention to your own needs and budget, your intended use of the boat, and the findings of an informal survey of what paints seem to work well in your sailing area. A paint that is effective in a cold climate may not work well at all in southern waters. And there are frequently special problems that only local boatyards and boat owners will recognize. For example, the cold water of New England retards fouling, but if you moor near a sewage treatment plant or the warm-water outlet of a utility plant, you will need anti-fouling paint comparable to what is used in the worst tropical fouling area.

Paint won't stick to wax, grease, oil, flaky undercoats, or prior incompatible coats. With a new fiberglass boat, every trace of the mold-release wax has to be wiped off the surface, which can be done only with strong solvents and continual replacement of the wipe rags. The mistake that is usually made is to reuse the rag after a few wipes on the surface, with the result that the wax is actually rubbed into the surface. If you are preparing a new boat for paint, buy a large sack of rags and plenty of solvent, and change rags after a single wipe on each surface of the rag.

If you are painting over a previously painted surface, all loose paint has to come off. And if you are changing paints, make sure that the new paint is compatible with the coats underneath. Some incompatibilities will show up immediately: if you paint vinyl-based paint over a non-vinyl-based paint, it will bubble. Other incompatibilities won't show up until long after you have paid the $1500 price for the paint job (including 6 gallons of paint at $160 per gallon). Non-graphite-based paint might not bubble off an earlier coat of graphite-based paint, but after a few weeks, if you try to clean the bottom of the boat with a towel, you may come back up to the surface with much of the new bottom paint on the towel. In some cases the manufacturer of the paint can advise you of compatibility problems. When in doubt, the surest solution is to sand off the old finish. As with any painting, the ultimate adhesion is only as good as the adhesion of the worst layer of the paint sandwich.

PREPARATION

Surface preparation, for most boat owners, means hours of sanding, often with small orbital sanders. It's possible to prepare a boat bottom with an orbital sander, but to do it right requires so many hours that most owners end up slacking off to a "once over lightly" standard midway through the sanding job. The solution if you really want to do the bottom yourself is to use the right tool: a foam-backed disk sander, either pneumatic or electric, and for fairing of keels or other sections, a jitterbug sander, which is a long orbital-motion sander, usually air driven. The reason for the foam pad is that a foam pad sander can be laid "full disk" onto a curved surface without the scoring and edge cuts that result when a hard disk is used. An electric drill with a sanding disk generally won't work, because most electric drills do not have the power needed to swing a 6-inch disk in continuous contact with the surface. You need a real disk sander, which if it is electric, can be heavy. Some brands, such as Makita, are available with foam disks and self-sticking sanding disks. If you plan to do more than occasional work, it is far more economical to buy conventional disk paper and use 3M sanding disk adhesive. As long as you change disks while the paper is still warm, you can use a single application of adhesive for several disks.

A disk sander is a formidable tool, which if misused can cause considerable damage. If you decide to get one and try it on your boat bottom, practice first on another surface, even an old piece of plywood, until you have a sense of how quickly the sander will cut. And if you have access to a jitterbug sander, be sure to practice using the sander before you try fairing your keel or rudder. For your first tries with powerful sanders, it may be wise to use 150-grade sandpaper instead of coarser and faster-cutting paper.

An alternative to a disk sander is hand sanding, either with sheet sandpaper fastened to long sanding boards (use old plane or trowel handles to make the sanding board comfortable to hold), or with Foamglas, a coarse abrasive material which is used as insulation in building. The Foamglas comes in sheets or bricks, and if used with heavy gloves (it is just as abrasive to your hands as it is to the boat bottom), it will do a good job of removing old finish and fairing a bottom. You can do the job by hand, and in the final fairing of keels, rudders, or sections of the bottom, the long sanding board will give you the best finish. It will also leave you with strong upper arms and shoulders for the sailing season.

Whether you sand by hand or with machines, you need more protection from the paint residue than a cheap throwaway mask for your nose and mouth. The sanding residue from some highly toxic paints (especially the copolymer coatings) is enough of an irritant to leave you with a rash on any skin exposed during sanding. Imagine what it does to the mucous membranes of your lungs and nose! Disposable suits to cover your clothes and a hood for your head are hot and bulky, and a proper respirator mask is expensive and uncomfortable. But remember that bottom paints are brewed to be toxic. The better the paint, the more toxic it is. And instead of the minute doses that leach out to kill barnicles, you are breathing the toxins straight.

There are two goals to keep in mind when you are sanding a bottom or keel. You want the surface to be as smooth and as fair as you are willing to make it. Smoothness you can feel with your hand. If the surface has any surface imperfections —valleys, peaks, bumps, ripples, cracks, craters—before you paint it, it isn't smooth enough. The only answer is more sanding, or in the case of substantial imperfections, filling and sanding. Paint will not hide imperfections. If anything, it accentuates the roughness of the surface because it is impossible to get an even coat on a rough surface.

FAIRING

The other goal is a fair surface, which generally cannot be determined with the touch of the fingers. The real measure of a fair surface is that if a long flexible batten is held along the surface, it will not reveal depressions or elevations. Fairing a keel and rudder can make a tremendous difference in the performance of a racing boat, especially in upwind performance. The lead castings that emerge from the foundry are invariably rough, and depending upon the quality of the mold and the temperature and conditions of the cast, the keel will vary widely from the section specified by the designer. Most production boats are then finished with anything from a quick sanding of the lead to a coating of epoxy. The keels are rarely true to the designer's sections or fair. Changing that is not an easy job. You need a trained eye, a careful touch, a lot of sandpaper, long sanding blocks for the final faring, and either battens, templates, or a shadow frame.*

For templates, you can usually get the offsets of the keel sections from the designer of the boat.† Loft the section measurements onto thin plywood or Mylar, cut them out, measure the position of each station, and you can exactly reproduce the section that the designer intended. Even without fairing the keel to templates, by using battens or a shadow frame you can get a surface that is true and fair, and which will make a substantial difference in the upwind performance of the boat. Whatever method you use, it takes a great deal of time and patience to achieve a truly fair surface. An experienced professional will charge over $1000 to fair the keel and rudder of a 25-foot boat. You are paying not only for the hours of labor but also for the skill and experience that knows when to build up and when to grind down to achieve a fair surface.

FILLING

When you are smoothing or fairing a hull, there will be imperfections and depressions that require filling, ranging from surface imperfections of improper painting or a gelcoat "ding" from an encounter with a lobster pot, to cracks that

---

* A shadow frame is a wooden frame laced with a grid of wires. To determine the fairness of a surface, you line up the shadow frame in front of the surface and shine a bright light onto the frame so that it casts a grid of fine shadows onto the surface. Bumps or depressions in the surface will show up as "squiggles" in the shadows, and they can be marked for further fairing.

† If you are eager to fair your keel and/or rudder to templates and you cannot get the section information from the designer, *The North U Fast Course*, by Robert Hopkins, Jr. (published by North Sails), contains a chapter on how to make a template from the NACA sections in *The Theory of Wing Sections*, by Abbott and Von Doenhoff (Dover Publications).

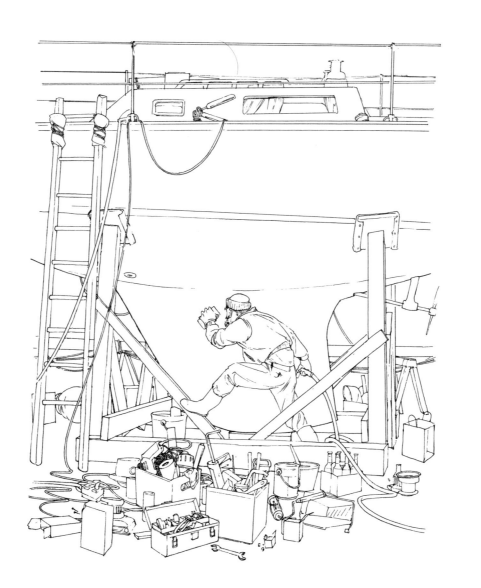

perniciously appear between the stub of the fin keel and the hull no matter how many times the joint is faired and filled, to the scars of the inevitably losing encounters between the keel and uncharted rocks.

The surface dings are easily patched with a two-part polyester or epoxy filler, which can be sanded and faired after curing. The easiest filler to use is one of the auto body putties, like Bondo, which can be mixed casually (the ratio of hardener to putty is not critical), will set up quickly, and can be easily shaped afterward. Unfortunately, the auto-body putties are not strong and many of them contain talc or other fillers which absorb water, so they eventually fail in underwater use. There are other polyester-based fillers, such as MarGlas, which mix fiberglass strands into a polyester base. They are not quite as quick or easy to use as the auto-body putties, but they are stronger and in many cases more suitable for underwater use. The epoxy-based compounds, such as Marine-Tex, are extremely strong, critical in mixing proportions, and hard to work when they have finally set up. Unless structural strength is required in the repair, the epoxy compounds are unnecessary. Finally, for fairing work that requries substantial bumping or filling, you can use microballoons, which feel like flour and when mixed with epoxy resin will make a lightweight but still strong filler compound. The microballoon mix can be purchased ready-made in two parts, or can be mixed up from bags of the microballoons and epoxy resin. It takes a little experimentation to get it right, but usually adding colloidal silica or microfibers to the microballoon and epoxy mix will give you a paste thick enough not to run, but thin enough to spread easily.*

* The Gougeon Brothers, makers of the West epoxies, produce a number of excellent pamphlets, brochures and books with epoxy "recipes."

Whichever filler compound you use, try to stick with just one, so that you don't end up putting epoxy compounds on top of polyester. The various compounds are best applied with broad knives—either a flexible putty knife or a plastic spatula will work. For filling large areas, a serrated trowel (available in a masonry supply) works well, leaving a ridged surface that is easier to grind down. If you use a cardboard palette for mixing the compound and plastic spatulas for spreading, the cleanup is minimized. Remember when you are spreading the filler that "what goes on must be ground off," and that depending upon the particular filler and its shrinkage rate, you may have to fill so that the filler stands proud of the surface. The bigger the knife and the better your application technique, the less grinding and refilling you will have to do.

On many boats the joint between the fin keel and the hull or the molded keel stub on the hull will open during winter storage. It is tempting to fill the gap and fair the surface completely, but since the crack is usually caused by movement in the hull under the weight of the keel, it is unlikely that any filler, even the strongest of epoxy fillers, will hold as the hull flexes.† The only real cure is stronger floors inside the boat to spread the load of the keel, and possibly taping the joint with fiberglass tape. Sometimes tightening the keel bolts can help. Otherwise, go easy on the filling at the crack, because if the joint has been overfilled, the new filler will squeeze out under the flexing.

Major dings in a lead keel are not hard to fix. Begin by cleaning away paint and traces of old filler from the damaged

† Sometimes the problem is loose keel bolts, although keel bolts tend to waste and corrode rather than loosen. If your keel bolts seem perpetually "loose," it may be time for either X-ray examination (on stainless or mild steel bolts) or removal of one or more bolts for inspection.

area with a hand or power wire brush. If the lead has been displaced into bulges to the sides of the ding, use a ball peen hammer to forge the lead back in place. Then use Vaseline as a lubricant and a coarse file or very sharp plane to fair the remaining bulges. Clean the surface with acetone, and use an epoxy/microballoon mixture to fill in the missing area. For the best possible adhesion, all filling on the lead keel should be done on a shiny clean surface, with a coat of epoxy applied to the surface before the filler.

PAINTING

When you have filled, sanded, filled, and sanded until the hull, keel, and rudder are smooth and as fair as you want to make them, wash the surface before painting to remove the traces of dust. If you have sanded adequately, it is usually not necessary to wipe down with solvent, although some paint manufacturers may recommend a wipe-down with thinner. Use fineline tape for any masking, and don't mask until you are ready to paint. Masking tape left on for a few days, especially in damp weather, is difficult to remove.

In general, paint can be applied to fiberglass or wood without any special priming, but check carefully that the paint you have chosen does not require special preparations. Lead keels, bronze underwater fittings, and other underwater metals present special problems. For a steel or aluminum hull, you must follow the special isolation schemes that are detailed in manufacturer's publications. Lead keels need either a coating of epoxy or one or more coats of a primer suitable for lead. And to get the best adhesion between the primer and the lead, the lead should be shiny clean, which generally means sanding it immediately before applying the primer or the first of several coats of epoxy. Bronze underwater fittings are difficult to paint with many modern paints. Either a primer or several coats of epoxy may work. Make certain that the zincs on the shaft or elsewhere on the bottom of your boat are masked off before painting.

The application of bottom paint is straightforward, as long as you follow exactly the recommendations of the manufacturer. Because of the angles of spraying, it is not an easy job to spray a boat bottom. To do the job right requires spray equipment with a remote gun that can be used upside down, and unless you have very good (and expensive) safety equipment, spraying bottom paint can be extremely hazardous to your health. But spraying—if it is done well—will generally provide the smoothest surface, which will require the least amount of sanding or burnishing afterward. The alternative is to use a roller followed by a foam brush. Generally bottom paint does not need to be sanded between coats, but depending upon the kind of paint you may have to let the previous coat dry overnight or longer between coats. Remove the masking tape as soon as possible after painting.

If you plan to burnish or wet-sand after painting, you will need an additional coat which is, in effect, sanded off. With a well-applied sprayed finish, it is sometimes sufficient to use fine bronze wool to take off the high spots, or to wait until the boat is launched and then burnish the paint underwater with burlap, bronze wool, or wet-sanding. Remember that the more paint you remove in the process of polishing the finish, the less paint is left to serve the primary purpose of antifouling protection.

Poppits and cradles are a special problem, and often the finest of bottom finishes are spoiled because there was no method planned for the fairing, preparation, and painting of the surfaces that rested on the cradle or poppits. If you have an adjustable cradle and plenty of time, you can lower the cradle supports one or two at time, prepare the surfaces underneath, paint them and let them cure completely, then restore the cradle and fair the edges of the paint so that the subsequent painting of the rest of the bottom doesn't leave ridges. Without an adjustable cradle, the painting of the surfaces that rest on the cradle or poppits, and the bottom of the keel, must be done while the boat is in the Travelift or crane slings. It would require several days in the slings to apply two or three coats, letting the paint dry thoroughly after each coat, and then wet-sand to fair the overlaps with the rest of the painted surface—time unavailable at most yards during the crowded schedule of spring launchings. In many yards, the policy is to have a number of cans of the most popular bottom paints and colors available and to do a modified "sand and slap" job on the poppit areas. Come the fall and the inspection of how the bottom fared, the area of the boat that is most likely to develop peeling or blistering is often the area under the cradle supports, which is hidden from inspection and proper repair by the poppits or the cradle.

One possibility, if you are concerned about getting a good finish for the bottom, is to arrange for the yard to suspend the boat for preparation and painting of the area under poppits and the bottom of the keel *before* the rest of the bottom is painted. With some bottom paints, those areas could even be painted in the fall. Even if you are not concerned about getting the perfect racing finish to your bottom, it is wise to ask how the yard paints those areas, or what the yard policy is about letting you have a little extra time in the slings to make sure that those areas are fair and that they get enough paint.

PROBLEMS

On some bottoms, despite the care and time that are put into preparation and fairing, and scrupulous adherence to the specifications and instructions of the paint manufacturer, the paint just doesn't stick. Some boat owners have actually seen flakes or sheets of bottom paint come off. Or have gotten the bad news from a diver that the six coats of expensive paint that were applied in the spring have all mysteriously disappeared from the keel. Or you haul the boat after one season and discover that the bottom is covered with pockmarks, like a case of severe acne.

When you have a real problem with a bottom, slapping on more paint or changing paints rarely helps. If the paint is peeling off in sheets, the most likely cause is inadequate cleaning and preparation of the surface underneath, and the only way to cure the problem is to sand off the remaining paint and thoroughly clean the surface with plenty of solvents and clean rags. The work sounds formidable, and it is, although a powerful rotary grinder/sander with a foam pad and plenty of fresh sandpaper will cut away bad bottom finishes remarkably quickly.

A more severe problem is pocking or blistering of the gelcoat under the paint. Some kinds of gelcoat are more prone to blistering then others, and some kinds of bottom paint, especially the hard nonporous polymer coatings like Micron 22 or 33, seem to accentuate the problem. It can appear as nothing more than a few tiny blisters that you are tempted to fill and ignore; or entire areas of the bottom can be covered with pits and craters as large as quarters. If the underlying problem of osmosis through the gelcoat layer is not cured, the problem becomes chronic, with more and larger blisters each year.

The most reliable cure is first to dry the hull thoroughly, either indoors or with heat lamps under a temporary tent of plastic sheeting. Then sandblast or grind off the old finish, including cleaning out the blisters and craters with a burr or a wire brush. Clean the bottom with acetone before coating the entire bottom, including the inside of the blister craters, with epoxy, using a foam roller. Before the epoxy has fully cured, fill the insides of the blister/craters with an epoxy/microballoon filler. When the filler has cured, it should be faired and the entire bottom sanded with 80-grit paper. Then the surface should be wiped with solvent and coated with two or three more coats of epoxy. If subsequent coats are applied to a surface that has not fully cured, it is not necessary to sand between coats. When the final coat of epoxy has fully cured, sand thoroughly and clean before applying the bottom paint. If you manage to go through the epoxy in some places during the sanding, don't cheat: go back and clean and recoat those areas with the full three coats of epoxy.

An epoxy coating is sometimes used on new boats to prevent blistering. It works, but only if the hull is sanded thoroughly before the first layer of epoxy is applied, if three coats of epoxy are applied, and if the temperature and humidity are within the guidelines specified by the manufacturer. The epoxy should be mixed in exact proportions and should not be thinned. And be careful not to put epoxy over masking tape, unless you want masking tape to be a part of your hull decor. As a preventive measure, the full epoxy treatment is expensive, time-consuming, and often unnecessary. But epoxy does provide the absolute waterproof barrier that will prevent osmotic blistering of gelcoat.

Boat owners are tempted to curse the manufacturer or to blame demons when paint that was supposed to last three years falls off in three weeks, or when a bottom that was flawlessly fair and smooth blisters until it looks like the surface of the moon. There have been some bad paints on the market, but most of the time the problem is in preparation of the bottom. It is one area where shortcuts—whether taken by a tired boat owner or by a yard trying to save money—will invariably lead to grief.

No one else will see the bottom of your boat, but the blessings of a job done well can be felt every time you take the helm. Racers joke that just *knowing* that the bottom is fair and clean makes them sail faster and point higher. It is no less true for the cruiser who wants to make harbor before sunset, or before the last mooring or slip is gone.

28

SAYING
GOODBYE

O ver half the marriages in the United States end in divorce, often after about seven years. The statistics are similar for boat ownership, except that the intervals are closer to three and a half or four years. For some owners, each boat is the final boat, the perfect boat, just big enough, not too big, with everything they have always dreamed of—the right rig, the right accommodations, the right equipment, and of course, the right size. And then after about two and a half years the bug bites, and the galley that seemed just right is suddenly inadequate, the rig that was perfect for two seems small, the deck layout that seemed ideal . . .

Whatever the reasons, most boat owners follow a consistent pattern, with the boats getting bigger and bigger until finally one boat seems too big. Each new boat means beginning anew the excitement and anticipation and anxiety of the thousands of decisions that go into the well-found boat. And the contemplation of each new boat is tied up with the choice of how to get rid of the old boat, the one that was going to be the final boat, and which is now a burden standing between you and the new dream boat. Even if you are not getting a new boat, almost every change to a boat means leftover gear, old sails, electronics, winches, and rigging that accumulate in the lazarette, the garage, the basement, or the yacht club locker. With boats or gear, you have the same choices: you can sell it, trade it, or give it away.

With boats, there are often strong tax arguments in favor of trading instead of selling, even if the prices of used boats in the BUC book or in newspaper advertisements suggest that the trade-in value is not as high as the cash value that you might realize in a sale. Some states charge sales tax only on the cash difference between the new boat price and the value of the trade-in, and in states where the sales tax is as high as 7½ percent, the difference in tax, together with the money and time that are *not* spent advertising the boat and the value of the money that is *not* tied up in the unsold boat, makes for a considerable saving.

Selling a boat is not an easy task. The used boat market fluctuates up and down in cycles that depend on some bizarre correlation between interest rates, the level of the stock market, the patterns of the local weather, and that mysterious factor that always makes prices low when you are selling and high when you are buying. Unless your boat is an inexpensive "starter" boat, a one-design that is raced in your area, or a stock design with a local following, it is not easy to attract a buyer for a boat through owner advertisements. Many boat buyers are reluctant to buy anything larger than a starter boat directly from another owner because they fear that they have nowhere to turn if a problem develops with the boat. And there are many boats which are sufficiently different that although everyone notices them and comments on them, it can take a long time to find a suitable buyer. Your flawlessly varnished bright hull may attract compliments wherever it goes, but many buyers will be wary of assuming the burden of maintaining the boat.

If you choose to sell through a broker, make sure you and the broker come to a precise agreement about commissions, about what is included on the boat and what is not, and about the negotiable range for prices. The broker will ask for a listing, which he will transfer onto his own form; make sure that there are no ambiguities that get translated into features that are described incorrectly or misleadingly. If your cold-water foot-pump shower gets put down on the listing as "hot pressure shower," a prospective buyer may be disappointed.

One area where disagreements often develop is when a prospective buyer makes an offer that is lower than the seller anticipated, but which the broker thinks is the best they are likely to get for the boat. Sometimes the seller will ask that the broker forfeit part of his commission, which if the broker has worked long and hard to find the buyer is an unwelcome suggestion.

Whether you choose to sell a boat yourself or through a broker, prepare the boat for sale and showing. You may think that the glass-doored liquor cabinet you built in the main salon or the double-ended multiple-purchase cunningham tackle you rigged is the best feature of the yacht, but almost every prospective boat buyer looks first at cosmetics. Shiny topsides, a spotless bilge, well-cared-for brightwork, and a general appearance of careful maintenance usually count for more in the eyes of a buyer than gear, gadgets, and equipment. If there are problems with the boat—an oil leak that you never got to, a frozen sheave in the masthead, a leak that has the bilge pump cycling enough to keep you awake at night —trying to hide them will probably get you in more trouble than candor. Unless the buyer elects not to have a survey, or the surveyor is so incompetent that he doesn't notice that the foredeck has the resiliency of a slice of Wonder Bread, the flaws with your boat will be found, and you will have to renegotiate the price and the conditions of sale. It is far better to advertise and present the boat as she really is. Let the listing say "interior woodwork in excellent condition, settee upholstery slightly worn," so that when a prospective buyer sees the boat he or she doesn't catch a discrepancy between promise and reality that will encourage skepticism. If you can offer solid evidence of your claims, such as a mechanic's notes from the last inspection of the engine ("compression check OK, adjusted injectors"), you will impress a buyer not only with the condition of the boat but with your own maintenance and care as well.

In general, making improvements for the purpose of a sale is not a good idea. If the topsides are scuffed, pay for a good polish and wax job and admit on the description and inventory of the boat that there is "minor" scuffing, or even that the buyer might elect to refinish the topsides, which at your asking price he can afford to do. A quick Awlgrip job might make the boat look like new, but it will also set you back by an amount that you probably won't recover in the resale price. Many prospective owners are not looking for a "sailaway" special, but prefer to have a boat that they can make their own with the addition of gadgets, new sails, equipment, or a paint job.

CHARITABLE DONATIONS

For some boats, donating them to an appropriate charitable recipient may prove easier and ultimately more profitable than selling them. The boats that are suitable for charitable donations are generally custom or one-off boats for which prices are not readily available from the BUC book, and for which the appraisable fair market value is high. An older wooden boat or a custom racing boat, which may have a high appraisable value but be difficult to sell in the marketplace, is often suitable for donation to a qualified recipient. Your beautiful wooden boat might ultimately bring a price of $60,000, but the process of finding the one buyer who will fall madly in love with it may take months or even years. If the appraised

value of the boat is high enough, you can realize much of what you hoped to realize from a sale by donating the boat and deducting the appraised value from your income tax. If your boat is listed in a reference like the BUC book, you will generally not be able to persuade the IRS that the value of the boat is substantially different from the ranges listed there, which include provisions for specific features and the condition of the boat.

Obviously you need to be in a high income-tax bracket for the scheme to work; the higher the bracket (including state income taxes), the more you will realize for a given appraised value.* The process is simple and straightforward, but to avoid complications it is important that the transaction and the appraisals follow the IRS guidelines precisely.

If you have a boat which you believe is suitable for donation, the first step is to find a broker who is familiar with the process. The broker will normally be paid by the recipient institution. You and the broker should then choose a suitable institution and explore whether they would be interested in receiving the yacht as a donation. In most cases, they will want to examine the boat, and you will want to examine the documentation of their IRS status to make certain that they are eligible as a recipient institution and that their program is in keeping with your own ideas and values. Beware of organizations which accept or advertise for boats but have no relationship with marine activities in their charitable or educational programs. You may believe that the work of a hospital or church in Kansas is a worthy cause, but you will probably face problems when you try to explain to the IRS why you chose them as the recipient of your 55-foot ocean

* Unless the income-tax laws are changed to disallow deduction of the appreciated value of donated items.

racer. A donation to one of the maritime academies, to a university or school with a marine science program, or to an organization that uses boats for research or educational programs is less likely to be questioned by the IRS.

You or your broker will have to arrange for appraisals of the fair market value of the boat. It is wise to have more than one appraiser, and for at least one of the appraisers to be a qualified marine surveyor who can attest to the condition of the boat at the time of appraisal, which should be as close as possible to the time of donation. The other appraisers could be yacht brokers, custom boat builders, or other individuals who can be expected to know the current market value of a boat like yours. Choose the surveyors carefully. The IRS will not be impressed by your brother-in-law's opinions, even if you consider him the best possible judge of the value of a boat. Try to find people who are especially qualified to appraise your boat: if it is a wood boat, choose a surveyor who is experienced with wood boats and whose appraisal can certify his qualifications; if it is a racing boat, choose a yacht broker who is experienced with racing boats and can attest to the yacht's value as a racing boat; if it is a world-cruiser type with special equipment, or built to demanding specifications, find an appraiser who understands and can address the value of those special features. If your appraisers are not familiar with the format of appraisals done for tax purposes, give them a sheet specifying what should be included in the appraisal.* An

---

* The details are specified in IRS Publication #561, "Determining the Value of Donated Property." Essentially, the appraisal should include a statement of the appraiser's qualifications, a statement of the estimated value (fair market and replacement) and the reasons that support the estimate, a full description of the boat, the basis on which the appraisal was made (such as restrictions or agreements limiting the use of the boat), the date of the valuation, and the signature of the appraiser.

appraiser will probably charge you between $150 and $300 for his services, and these fees are deductible as miscellaneous deductions.

The recipient organization will normally prepare any documents required by the transfer, and you will probably want to have them examined by a lawyer. If the documents do not state that the organization is accepting the boat for use in the programs of marine science, education, research, or other related area, make certain that your letters to the organization state clearly that it is your understanding that they are accepting the boat for use in the program. This is to protect yourself if they immediately charter or sell your boat instead of actually using it. The deduction of appreciated value is reduced substantially if the contributed item is not put to a use related to the charitable function of the organization. Many organizations receive more boats than they can use, but if you can document that in donating the boat you believed that it would be used for charitable purposes, you should be protected.

When the transfer is actually made, make certain that you obtain a signed receipt from the transfer agent, specifying the date and time that delivery was accepted, so that if an incident occurs in the course of delivery you have a charitable donation rather than an insurance claim.

The specifics of deducting the value of the boat are something to work out with your accountant or your computer tax program. For most taxpayers, the boat will qualify as a 30 percent charitable donation, which means that you can deduct up to 30 percent of your adjusted gross income in each year, carrying forward if necessary until the full value of the boat has been deducted. The trick is to decide what value to claim. The appraisals will probably span a range of values, and no matter what value you choose in that range, the IRS will be inclined to want to discuss it all with you.

You will probably be audited and the IRS may act tough, but if you have obtained honest appraisals from qualified appraisers, you will have the upper hand, since by the time they get around to auditing your return, generally at least a year after the donation has been made, the only valid appraisals of the condition and value of the boat at the time of donation are the appraisals you ordered. Be cautious if there are other indications or evidence of the value of the boat. If you once listed the boat with a broker who advertised it at $100,000 and you then try to deduct a value of $200,000 for the donation, you may find that you will need some tricky arguments to support your claims to an IRS auditor or appraiser. If you had your boat insured for $45,000 and suddenly claim that the value is $100,000, you had better be prepared to indicate how shocked you were when you realized from the appraisals how truly valuable the boat was! An IRS auditor may consult with appraisers or surveyors, but the real discussion will be of your appraisals, and how to reconcile the different values that your appraisers may have assigned to the boat. If you can point to the qualifications of your appraisers as appraisers, the arm's-length nature of your relationship to the appraisers, and can offer the additional evidence of photographs or other documents to validate the value assigned to the boat, you should survive the audit.

In sum, a charitable donation is an excellent "good-bye" procedure for a boat which can be convincingly argued to have an appreciated market value. It is not a useful alternative for a dog that has been on the market for months without an offer.

GEAR

After a few seasons and a few boats, it is rare not to have accumulated boxes of miscellaneous hardware and bags of sails that seem too good to be used as boat covers and yet are not really needed anymore on any boat you own. It is unlikely that you will be able to fund an Admiral's Cup campaign or a circumnavigation through the sale of the excess equipment, but used marine gear is valuable.

Local advertisements will work for items that are easily recognized and applicable to other boats, such as a VHF radio or a man-overboard pole. Items with specialized value, such as a pole end fitting for a 4-inch-diameter spinnaker pole, are hard to sell through general advertisements. The best bet is to try one of the specialized brokers who deal in marine gear, and who advertise in the back of the sailing magazines. A few will actually buy your gear, though generally at a substantial discount. Others serve as brokers, listing your gear or accepting it on consignment for sale in their shop. There are several sail brokers who perform the same service.

If you elect to use a broker for your marine gear, be cautious. Some are scrupulously honest. Others are, shall we say, creative and enterprising. Make certain that the broker is reliable and that the agreement for consignment or sale, including the minimum net price you are willing to accept, is spelled out before you send off expensive sails, winches, and other gear. Some of these brokers will inform you immediately if a sale is made. Others don't really say much until you ask, and may be a little hazy about just how much they realized when they sold your gear. If you don't have an agreement specifying the minimum net, you may find that your gear was sold for less than you expected, or at least that the broker claims it was sold for less than you expected.

The alternative to selling gear is to donate it to an eligible recipient. Some of the big boat shows, like the Stamford show, feature flea markets where consignments and donations are accepted. You set the price for consignments, and the sponsoring institution (in Stamford, the Red Cross) takes a modest consignment commission. You also have the option of donating the equipment and taking a charitable deduction on your income-tax return.

Finally, for substantial items, some of the schools or organizations that accept donations of yachts will also accept donations of gear. Schools that use racing yachts in their programs will often welcome sails and winches as charitable contributions. As long as the value is under $5000 you do not need an appraiser, although you should be cautious in assigning inflated values to used equipment. If you do elect to donate equipment, make certain that the recipient institution is a legitimate charity for tax purposes. The IRS will probably not look kindly on your donation of used sails to your brother for use on his Familyway 33.

29

BUYING

I t's easy to buy a boat, easier in some ways than buying a car. You don't even need a license. Walk into a showroom, meander around a boat show, kick a few cradle supports during the winter, and a broker will show up, ask you a few questions, and offer you the boat of your dreams. Most brokers will take care of all the details for you: insurance, financing, survey, sails, equipment, options, accessories. In less than an hour, you can work out every detail of what may prove to be the second largest or even the largest purchase you will ever make.

As an alternative, you can decide to go it alone, studying brochures and magazine reviews, crawling into cramped lazarettes, sniffing behind bilge stringers and sheer clamps, thumping on planking and ribs, pulling up bilge boards, feeling for deck-to-hull joints, inspecting core sections taken from a through-hull installation, questioning the specifications of keel bolts, deck hardware, mechanical and electrical equipment, and spar details, asking to see maintenance schedules, or even visiting factories to watch the layup of hulls and the fabrication of joinery. There are buyers who spend two or three years narrowing the choices for the elusive dream boat, or searching out the perfect specimen after they have concluded that only the Hasitall 32 will really fit their needs.

Whichever option a prospective owner follows—carefree abandon or infinite care—it is rare that there aren't surprises waiting after the first sail or the first season or the first visit to the boatyard to fix problems that were overlooked or discounted amidst the enthusiasm of the purchase. Slowly the owner discovers that the magazine reviews missed or overlooked a noisy engine installation, that his own inspection uncovered everything except the impossible weather helm, that the speed the manufacturer promised for the new Glory 41 is somehow an elusive promise, that the financing arrangement leaves a balloon payment to pay after five years, or that if the boat is sold after two years the owner will have accumulated, through the inexplicable mathematics of the Rule of 78s, an unanticipated debt called negative equity.

There are two goals in buying a boat: finding the right boat and avoiding surprises. Telling someone how to find the right boat is a little like telling someone how to find the right spouse, a thankless challenge that can only lead to an eventual breakdown in the friendship between the person giving the advice and the person receiving it. Magazines, brokers, friends, books, advisors, competitors, and conscience all nag at you with advice, tips, criticisms, and questions. Ultimately, after all the studying and analyzing, the calculation of predicted performance, predicted range on a tank of fuel, and predicted resale value, after studying and comparing the specifications, the final choice is influenced if not decided by an infatuation as elusive as the attraction between men and women. Once the bug bites, the infatuation of owner for boat is so strong that only rarely can a smitten buyer be dissuaded from the wrong boat. But it is possible to spare yourself surprises by making use of qualified professionals, free advice, and a little time and energy before you commit yourself to a purchase.

BROKERS

Choosing a broker is a little like choosing a psychiatrist: what you really want is someone who knows how to ask the right questions. If you're sure exactly what you want in the next boat, if you have read and poked and analyzed and concluded that only a pre-1978 Nifty 35 will really make you happy, you are in the position of shopping for a boat rather than a broker. The only choice is where to find the boat, and how to find a broker who is honest and helpful to you. If, like most boat shoppers, you aren't completely sure what you want, selecting the right broker is almost as important as selecting the right boat. The right broker will help you avoid mistakes, will sort through what may be a conflicting list of priorities, will point out why some criteria you have in mind may not be appropriate for the use you propose or the area where the boat will be moored or sailed. And the right broker can steer you in the direction of the many services you need as you outfit, commission, upgrade, and use your boat.

How do you choose? Aside from a recommendation you can trust, the only reliable guides are an inspection of the yard where the broker works and a talk with the broker. Is the yard clean and orderly? Try to catch a glimpse of the mechanics' workbench or the carpenters' or riggers' work areas, and their tools. Mechanics who take pride in their work generally take care of their tools. Are the boats in the yard well maintained? It is possible that a well-cared-for boat will end up in a yard that specializes in cheap and dirty care, but you have to wonder why. Or ask.

The initial questions and attitude of a broker can also tell you a lot. Some come on with the enthusiasm and pitch of a desperate used-car salesman. Be wary: it is rare that a once-in-a-lifetime, decide-now-or-lose-it opportunity comes along on the boat market. Other brokers listen, trying to discern what you really want in a boat, trying to find out enough about you and your sailing plans and experience to help you find the elusive right boat. Once you find the right broker, honesty, patience, a willingness to listen to advice, and an effort to distinguish between fantasy and reality in your sailing plans will lead you in the right direction and eventually to the right boat. The very best brokers won't tell you what to buy but will listen between the lines of what you tell them, and by studying your reaction to boats that they show you, will help you refine your own criteria and standards.

SURVEYS

The best way to save grief on the purchase of any used boat more complicated than a Sunfish or a Windsurfer is through a survey by a qualified and impartial surveyor. The bigger the boat, the more complex the systems aboard the boat, the more sophisticated the construction practices, and the older the boat, the more you will learn about the boat from the survey and the more important it is that the survey be done by an individual who is specifically qualified to survey that kind of craft, and who is hired by and reporting to you and you alone. The purchase of any substantial boat will probably be agreed to "subject to survey." The contract will specify what constitutes "passing" the survey and under what conditions you can cancel the purchase on the basis of the findings of the survey. But a survey should constitute more than a pass/fail examination of the boat. It should be a chance for you to get to know exactly what you are buying, and what surprises may await you in the ownership of the boat.

There is no such thing as a licensed surveyor. There are professional organizations of marine surveyors, but the profession is not regulated or even self-regulated. Hence bro-kers, boat builders, sailmakers, naval architects, and marine carpenters offer their services as surveyors, along with a few individuals who have no discernible qualifications as survey-ors. And even surveyors who are highly qualified sometimes find themselves in the position of representing several interests at once. There is a boatyard owner in the Northeast, well known for his work on wooden boats, who has from time to time served in a single transaction as both broker to the seller and surveyor for the buyer of a wooden boat. It is possible that he or other individuals are capable of completely separating their interests as broker for the seller from their obligations as surveyor for the buyer, but it takes an extraordinary individual to do so.

If you are buying a used boat from a broker and you don't know where to find an appropriate surveyor, you might begin your search by asking the broker. If the individual or individuals he suggests are connected with the brokerage or the yard that is selling the boat, you would be wise to look elsewhere. You want a surveyor whose sole interest in the transaction is to represent you. Whatever individual you find, make certain that he or she is qualified to survey the particular boat you are buying. If it is a wooden or metal boat, a boat of specialized construction, engineering, design, or purpose, make certain that the surveyor is experienced with the construction mate-rials or design. If you are buying the boat for a specialized purpose, make certain that the surveyor understands your intended use of the boat, and that he or she is familiar with the needs of a boat used for world cruising or grand prix racing or whatever you have in mind. A good surveyor will have no qualms about showing you credentials or sample surveys that he has done.

Finally, make certain before the survey that you and the surveyor agree on the purpose of the survey, how thorough the examination of the boat will be, what will be covered and what will not be examined, the form of his report and recommendations, and his fee. If the boat is afloat, you will also have to arrange to have it hauled, and should schedule the haul with some consideration of the surveyor's convenience. Some surveyors will welcome your presence during the examination of the boat and may give you a running commentary on what they find as they go along. Others will much prefer to be left alone to do their job and will present you with their findings in a proper written report.

What to Expect

A surveyor will probably spend at least half a day with a boat, and much more for a large, complex, or problem-laden boat. Much of the inspection is routine, a checklist of points —such as the inclusion and condition of fire extinguishers or dock lines—that the surveyor may even have written out in a checklist format. The rest of the time, and in most cases the most important portion of the survey, is the actual assessment of the condition of the boat. And for this part of the task the surveyor relies on his ears, nose, and sense of touch as much as his eyes. A good surveyor will use his mallet to sound a hull and deck, looking for the dull thump of rot, delamination, or "bubbles." He will sniff in suspect areas for the faint fermenting-leaf odor of rot. He will feel with his fingertips for unfairness in a hull or loose taping of a bulkhead or signs of an unreported repair from collision damage. He will sight along the sheer line and the spar sections to look for hogging that

may reflect poor storage, structural weakness, or misuse. He will look under ice chests or in the bilge for signs of dampness or oil leaks or fresh paint that may conceal sins rather than reflect care. He will also look for telltale signs of future problems, such as dried or missing bedding under fittings or in joints, blackened brightwork, wobbles in steering or cutlass bearings, hints of creeping in stressed deck fittings or chain plates. Finally, he will try to assess the general level of care that has been given to a boat, looking for indications of cleaning, oil, grease, varnish, paint, and wax—each in the appropriate place.

The surveyor's written report should give you an assessment of the quality and condition of the hull, deck, interior, mechanical and electrical systems, rig, and sails. It should point out any potential or actual problems, such as leaks, rot, delamination or distortion of hull, deck, or interior structures; galvanic or stray-current corrosion; weaknesses of design or maintenance in the rig, steering system, engine, plumbing, or electrical system. The survey should specify areas where repairs definitely are required, or will be required, and any statement or appraisal of seaworthiness should specify the sailing conditions for which the boat is suitable. Depending upon the format of the report, the complexity of the boat, and how much detail the buyer requests, the report could run anywhere from three to ten typed pages.

A surveyor's report will probably suggest what repairs are necessary to bring a boat to a seaworthy condition, and may suggest what additional repairs would be required for cosmetic conditions, to reach a higher level of seaworthiness (for example, to make a coastal cruiser suitable for offshore passage-making), or for conditions that do not yet require repair.

Some surveyors will include ballpark estimates of the cost of repairs.

You should not expect a surveyor to give you an exact estimate of the cost of repairs, or to serve as a bargaining agent in your negotiation for a reduction of the price of the boat. You also should not expect a surveyor to serve as an unpaid advisor or consultant in planning the improvement and repair of the boat. If there are parts of the survey that are unclear or ambiguous, ask what is meant. If the survey says that the deck shows signs of delamination and may require major repairs, go ahead and ask whether "major repairs" means a new deck or something less drastic. But unless you are willing to hire the surveyor as a consultant, don't expect a list of the pros and cons of the various procedures that can be followed to repair a delaminated deck or a detailed budget for the repairs. And while you will learn a great deal about a boat from a survey, and most surveyors will welcome questions about what they saw in a survey, you should not expect a free education from the surveyor unless you are willing to hire him or her as a consultant, advisor, or boat guru.

Specialized Surveys

Although you can expect that any qualified surveyor will spot egregious weaknesses or flaws in a boat, you may want to call on other experts to examine certain systems in the boat. And even on a new boat, which unless it is very expensive, complex, or perhaps built overseas, will frequently be purchased without a survey, there are probably parts of the boat that you should have inspected by individuals you can trust. Your sailmaker can give you a good rundown on the sails, especially if he can see them hoisted. If sails are packaged with the boat, your sailmaker can tell you how suitable they are for the sailing you have planned, and help you plan any additions to your sail inventory with those sails in mind. A mechanic can examine the engine installation and listen to the engine and probably tell you whether there are any special problems that you may have to watch for. (Most mechanics will quickly comment on what for them is perhaps the most important criterion in surveying an engine installation: how easy or difficult it is to get to the engine.) If a boat has extensive electronics, in addition to testing them you may want to have a marine electronics expert look at the installation to see if it is sound. Some of these people will charge nothing for a quick inspection, especially if you have dealt with them in the past and if one reason for your request for the inspection is to consider future orders of work or equipment. If the mechanic or electrician is not someone with whom you have dealt, you might investigate beforehand to find out his or her reputation and also negotiate an appropriate fee for the inspection.

If there are major problems with the boat, you may wish to reconsider or renegotiate the purchase. If the surveyor finds only minor problems, or potential problems, such as a mast base fitting that, in typical surveyor language, "shows signs of" corrosion, you would be wise to initiate a program of preventive maintenance. Problems don't go away. It is rare that a *sign of* corrosion (or delamination or rot or whatever) does not bloom into a full-scale case of whatever the signs portended, and if you are like most boat owners, it is far easier to budget for a repair in the heady days when you are buying the boat than it will be a few years down the road. The hard evidence of a survey is also a good jumping-off point for an honest evaluation of your plans for the boat. Are you really going to take the offshore cruise for which the surveyor questions the suitability of the boat? If the answer is an honest yes, you probably want a different boat. But it may be that the boat is perfectly suited for the real use that she will actually see.

If major repairs are required, you will of course want firm estimates, or at least ballpark estimates, of how long the work will take, how much it will cost, and how successful the repair will be, before you buy the boat. If there are a number of minor repairs suggested by the surveyor, you might want to look for a boatyard where you can arrange a long-term program of repair and improvements to the boat. The boatyard will probably welcome an organized program of repairs and the assurance of future work that it implies, and you may in the end profit from having all of the work done by a single yard that is aware of the condition of the boat and the variety of work that needs to be done.

The Other Survey

Whether you are buying a new boat or a used boat, and even if you have hired the most reputable and expert surveyor in all the land to examine the boat, you should make your own survey, clipboard in hand, to make certain that the boat is all you expected. A surveyor can tell you the condition of the interior joinery and cushions; he cannot tell you whether the interior layout will work for you, your family, or your sailing companions, and the way you will probably use the boat. The same is true of deck configuration and rigging layout. A surveyor will probably inventory the numbers and condition of the deck gear, but it is rare that a surveyor will comment on the functionality of the rigging and gear.

Before purchase is a good time to take the kind of imaginary or real sail suggested in Chapter 3. If you can take the boat for a sail, try to take your usual crew along, or at least stand-ins, so that you can approximate what it will be like to sail the boat. Try hoisting the mainsail yourself. Try tacking the jib. Try steering, looking at the instruments and compass, easing and trimming the mainsheet in response to a puff, folding or furling the sails. Go below and reach into the ice chest as if you were getting something out, pretend you are cooking in the galley, or taking a shower, or getting gear out of a locker under a berth. Try climbing into and out of berths, *all* of the berths. Bring a sail on deck, and then stow the sail below. Try the navigation station—not at the dock, but with the boat heeled.

If you cannot take the boat out for a sail, it is a little harder to make your personal survey, but it can still be done. Fill the cockpit with people, the way the boat will be sailed, and try to imagine the boat going to weather or sailing under spinnaker. Figure out where the lines will lead, or rig temporary lines to get a sense of what simple and complex maneuvers will require from you and your crew. If the boat is not rigged, ask exactly how gear like the vang, halyards, and sail controls are rigged. If you find flaws in the rigging, or styles of rigging that do not seem appropriate or adequate for your anticipated use of the boat, make firm notes of what has to be changed and either price and plan the changes, or consult with a rigger to find out when the work can be done and what it will cost.

Your own survey should assess the hardware and rigging on the boat for quality and size. Catalog what rigging you will need to replace and which hardware and gear you will want to upgrade. Are the winches big enough? If not, will it be possible to swap winches so the too-small primaries can be used as secondaries or halyard winches? What condition are the sails in? The surveyor will tell you if the sails are rotting, completely blown out, moth-eaten, or mildewed. But it is up to you to determine, usually after a consultation with your sailmaker, whether the sails are suitable for racing, or for the kind of cruising you anticipate. If you are buying a boat that has been used for racing, the racing sails may no longer be competitive, and you may need a new light #1 genoa, spinnaker, or other sails to race the boat. If you were planning occasional racing and "performance cruising," you may discover that the tired racing sails are also unsuitable for cruising because of cut or material.

The engine, plumbing, electronics, electrical wiring, and galley systems should be given the same inspection. The surveyor will tell you whether there is a loran or VHF and whether they work or "appear to be in working condition." You are the one to decide if the equipment on the boat is really suitable for your use, and installed adequately and conveniently for your use. If it isn't, if the loran is a unit that is inconvenient for the way you sail, make plans early on to trade the unit for a loran that is more appropriate for your use of the boat.

Finally, before purchase is the time to assess the performance potential of the boat. Assemble the relevant measurements and numbers and calculate the important ratios for the boat and for other comparable boats; or purchase a yacht analysis that will calculate the ratios and estimate the performance characteristics of the boat. Remember that the performance of prototype racing boats is rarely the same as the performance of the production models, and make allowances in your calculations for the difference in weight and crew skills between the semiprofessional campaign of the prototype and the boat you are buying. If you are buying a boat for club racing and are unfamiliar with the performance of similar boats against the fleets in your area, use your calculator, a computer yacht analysis, or the tables and formulas in Chapter 2 to assess your performance potential against your probable competitors. And even if you have no interest in racing at all, make certain that the boat you are buying is suitable for your sailing area, that with the anticipated weight aboard and the rig you are buying the boat will perform as you expect. The numbers rarely lie. If the disp/LWL ratio is high, the boat will do more motoring than sailing; if the SA/disp ratio is low, the boat will have trouble accelerating, sailing off the wind, or in light air. Despite the claims of builders and designers, breakthroughs are rare, and most boats will sail pretty close to what the numbers predict.

FINANCE

Years ago, when loan rates were fairly steady, the only choice a buyer faced in financing a boat was whether to get a simple interest loan or a Rule of 78s loan. If you were planning to own the boat for only a short time, the simple interest loan made more sense, because under a simple interest loan you accumulate equity in the boat even in the first year of payments. If you were planning to own the boat for a long time, the Rule of 78s loan made sense, because in the long run you were charged less interest and the loan offered certain tax advantages.

Today Rule of 78s loans are rare. In their place is a cornucopia of loans and financing arrangements, from flexible rates to zero-principal loans to balloon payments to manufacturer "buy-down" programs. The creative financing of boats has begun to approach the financing of homes in complexity and multiplicity of choices, and the boat owner is left with the task of working out the true cost of each alternative with a calculator, computer, or a large stack of scratch paper.

To select the right package you will need to balance the tax advantages of different plans and schemes, your own anticipated finances, and the length of time you plan to own the boat. Most owners do well on the tax and cash-flow parts of the equation, then negate the wisdom of their choices by making gross mis-estimates on the timetable. Unless you are certain that you really will own the boat for a long time, that it really is your final dream boat, you would probably be wise to arrange your financing so that you do not suffer a substantial penalty if you sell the boat after the three or fours years that is the typical duration of an owners' affair with his boat.

Most of the loans offered on boats today are calculated on a simple interest basis, like a home mortgage, and offer a combination of fixed and variable rates. If you're fairly certain that you will own the boat for only three years, it would be wise to seek an option like a fixed rate for the first three years of the loan, with a variable rate afterward. Or some loaning institutions will give you a balloon payment option, a loan that is calculated on a fifteen- or twenty-year basis, but which is payable in full after five years; the payments will be low, and if the boat holds its value you can use the proceeds from the sale to pay off the loan. A few lenders go a step further to offer zero-principal loans, in which you pay interest only with the entire principal due at the end; it sounds like loan-sharking, but calculate how much equity you have in the boat after three years of payments on a fifteen-year loan, and zero-principal may not seem a bad idea. Another option is to use the collateral in a home or a portfolio, rather than the boat itself, to finance the purchase. Although some lenders favor boats as collateral, because boat owners are traditionally a good risk, it is possible that you can obtain better terms with a second mortgage on a home or a loan against a portfolio of bonds and securities. Homes and portfolios have the advantage, to a lender, of not being prone to sinking at the mooring.

Finally, make sure that your rough calculations take into account the actual cost of the funds to you for the period of the loan. Loans that charge "points" up front are "front-loaded," and even if the rate is less the points may make the actual cost of the money more if the boat is owned for only a few years. A manufacturer's "buy-down," which is a subsidy to lower the actual interest you are paying, may sound like a very generous offer if you calculate how much you will save over a fifteen-year loan. But a straight concession on the price may be a better deal if there is a possibility that this boat (the one you were sure would be the last one) turns out, like the others, to be a step up the ladder.

Many buyers rationalize the amount they spend on a boat, even to themselves, with the explanation: "Sure it's a lot of interest, but after all, it is deductible. . . ." True, the interest is deductible, but even if you are in the highest tax bracket in the most heavily taxed state, the deductibility of up to 60 percent of the interest still leaves you paying a considerable sum. And the tax changes which are currently under discussion would not only lower the overall tax rates, making any deduction worth less, but would also curtail or eliminate deductions of interest paid for yachts.

In calculating the budget for a new boat, most owners try to avoid checkbook surprises by adding a figure, labeled "Miscellaneous" or "Unanticipated," to cover those expenses which are not included elsewhere in the budget but which seem as inevitable as July thunderstorms and August doldrums. The goal in buying a boat is to avoid all the surprises that can turn a dream boat into a burden or a dog.

With a little honesty about your own sailing, and a hard look at the next dream boat *before* you buy her, even before you fall in love with her, you can avoid surprises. You can also know in advance what it will take to transform the promise inherent in the boat into all that she can be, a boat that will repay the time and thought that you put into the kinds of changes suggested in these chapters—modifications to the layout, rigging, gear, and equipment—with hours, days, and years of sailing pleasure.

Happy sailing.

INDEX

Tackle. *See also* Lines; Rigging;
    anchor, 304–10
    compound, 105–6
Tape decks, 249
Teak, exterior, 340–41
Tillers, 30–31
    converting, 81
    extensions for, 81–83
    helmsman and, 81
    length of, 81
    locks for, 248–49
    maintaining, 319–20
Toilets, 208
Tracking ability, 20
Tracks, 125
Transverse metacentric height, 21
Travelers, 113–16
    control lines for, 115–16
    location of, 114–15
    midboom, 4
    modifying, 115
Treatment systems, 209–10
Trim angles, 125–26
True wind
    angle of, 253
    calculating, 260–62
    direction of, 253
    speed of, 253
Turnbuckles, 296
Turtles, 99
Twist, 124

Ultra-light-displacement boats
    (ULDB), 15, 16

Vangs, 108–13
    big boat, 111–12
    compound, 110–11
    lever, 113

placement of, 34
power required for, 109–10
purposes for, 108
simple, 110
sizing gear for, 113
solid, 112
Varnishing brightwork, 340–41
Velocity made good (VMG), 253,
    262–64
    indicator for, 262
    polar speed curve and, 262
Ventilation, 185–89
    of berths, 186–87
    of bilge, 187
    deck layout and, 185
    of engine compartment, 187
    of head, 187
Vents, installing, 188–89
VHF radios, 6, 217–25
    antennas for, 223
    auto-revert to channel 16,
        218
    autoscan, 217
    channels needed, 220
    dual watch, 218
    for emergencies, 303
    hailer, 218
    installation of, 222–25
    international channels, 218
    keyboard station entry, 218
    maintenance of, 225
    performance of, 219
    reliability of, 219–20
VMG. *See* Velocity made good
Voltage regulator, 277–78
Voltmeters, 276–77

Warranties, 332–33
Waterline beam, 10

Waterline length (LWL), 9–10
    beam and, 22
    displacement and, 11, 14–16
Weatherfax, 244
Weight
    calculating, 11–12
    distribution of, 12, 23
    motion and, 23
    performance and, 24
    sail-carrying ability and, 18
    sailing style and, 15–16
Wetted surface, 17–18
Wheel locks, 248–49
Wheels, 31–32
    converting, 81–82
    footholds and, 84
    helmsman and, 81
    pedestal of, 81–82
    placement of, 31
    size of, 81
Winches, 5, 47–53
    construction of, 50–52
    deck layout and, 85–86
    efficiency of, 47–48
    gear and power ratios of, 47–49
    halyard, 49–50
    handle load of, 48
    lifelines and, 86
    lines and, 58
    lubricants for, 52
    materials used in, 50–52
    power and, 47–48
    primary, 49
    reel, 37–38
    removing, 87
    secondary, 143–44
    selecting, 47, 49
    self-tailing, 50
    servicing, 52–53

size of, 48–49
speed and, 47–48
stoppers and, 61
Winch mainsheets, 104–5
Wind
    angle of, 253
    apparent, 253
    direction of, 253
    speed of, 253
    true, 253, 260–62
Wind instruments, 259–64
    apparent wind, 260
    installing, 264
    selecting, 264
    true wind, 260
Windlass, 304–5
Wind vanes, 248
Winterization, 311–24
    covers, 322
    of deck fittings, 318
    of electronics, 322
    of engine, 323–24
    of plumbing, 322–23
    of rigging, 316
    of sheaves, 318
    of spars, 314–15
    of steering mechanism, 319–20
    storage, 312–14
Wire, Nicopress fittings for,
    77–79
Wiring, 270–80
    butt connections for, 273–74
    control panels of, 274–76
    corrosion of, 271–72
    soldering connections of, 272
    troubleshooting, 278–80
    type of wire used, 273

Zincs, 284–85